Policing Black Athletes

GLOBAL
INTERSECTIONALITY
OF EDUCATION, SPORTS,
RACE, AND GENDER

Billy Hawkins
General Editor

Vol. 2

The Global Intersectionality of Education, Sports, Race, and Gender series
is part of the Peter Lang Education list.
Every volume is peer reviewed and meets
the highest quality standards for content and production.

PETER LANG
New York • Bern • Berlin
Brussels • Vienna • Oxford • Warsaw

Vernon L. Andrews

Policing Black Athletes

Racial Disconnect in Sports

PETER LANG
New York • Bern • Berlin
Brussels • Vienna • Oxford • Warsaw

Library of Congress Cataloging-in-Publication Data

Names: Andrews, Vernon L., author.
Title: Policing black athletes: racial disconnect in sports / Vernon L. Andrews.
Description: New York: Peter Lang, 2020.
Series: Global intersectionality of education, sports, race, and gender; Vol. 2
ISSN 2578-7713 (print) | ISSN 2578-7721 (online)
Includes bibliographical references and index.
Identifiers: LCCN 2020024898 (print) | LCCN 2020024899 (ebook)
ISBN 978-1-4331-6787-4 (paperback) | ISBN 978-1-4331-8107-8 (ebook pdf)
ISBN 978-1-4331-8108-5 (epub) | ISBN 978-1-4331-8109-2 (mobi)
Subjects: LCSH: Racism in sports—United States. | Discrimination in sports—United States. | African American athletes—Social conditions. | Hispanic American athletes—Social conditions.
Classification: LCC GV706.32 .A56 2020 (print) | LCC GV706.32 (ebook) | DDC 796.089/96073—dc23
LC record available at https://lccn.loc.gov/2020024898
LC ebook record available at https://lccn.loc.gov/2020024899
DOI 10.3726/b17123

Bibliographic information published by **Die Deutsche Nationalbibliothek**. **Die Deutsche Nationalbibliothek** lists this publication in the "Deutsche Nationalbibliografie"; detailed bibliographic data are available on the Internet at http://dnb.d-nb.de/.

The paper in this book meets the guidelines for permanence and durability of the Committee on Production Guidelines for Book Longevity of the Council of Library Resources.

80 Broad Street, 5th floor, New York, NY 10004
www.peterlang.com

Contents

Foreword

The Ripple Effect of Colin Kaepernick—Within and Beyond the NFL

Colin Kaepernick sat down during the national anthem. In modern patriotic America, Kaepernick did the social equivalent of sitting on the front of the bus in Alabama in 1955. And you know what happened after Rosa Parks got bold and refused to "stay in her place." After the social activist decision to sit down during the Star-Spangled Banner on the sidelines during the San Francisco Forty-Niners third preseason game in August of 2016, he stated very clearly after the game the intent of his actions:

> I am not going to stand up to show pride in a flag for a country that oppresses black people and people of color. To me, this is bigger than football and it would be selfish on my part to look the other way. There are bodies in the street and people getting paid leave and getting away with murder.[1]

Kaepernick made the decision to *kneel* during the anthem in the final preseason game—and for the remainder of the 2016 season. He switched to kneeling on the advice of a former NFL player and U.S. military veteran, Nate Boyer. Kap's decision to kneel was to honor and respect former and current military members

Figure F.1. Where it all began. Colin Kaepernick (on the right) and Eric Reid, brothers in arms. Source: Michael Zagaris/San Francisco 49ers/Getty Images

who fought and died for that flag ... while still protesting police brutality.[2] As the familiar African American saying goes, he was "sick and tired of being sick and tired."

The first ripple of activism, like the toss of a pebble into a lake, hit teammate Eric Reid, who decided he would kneel with Kaepernick during that last preseason game and for the remainder of the season. Reid's reasoning was that:

> Things have happened in Louisiana and the injustices that are happening could have happened to one of my family members. It touched close to home [Reid is from Baton Rouge, the site the 2016 unarmed shooting by cops of Alton Sterling, and the subsequent shooting of six police officers], and I just wanted to show my support to him [Kaepernick] and let him know that he is not the only person who feels the way he feels. There are a lot of people out there that feel that way.[3]

Reid might also agree with Kaepernick's follow-up statement, intended to preempt any confusion as to what he was *not* doing:

> Once again, I'm not anti-American. I love America. I love people. That's why I'm doing this. I want to help make America better. I think having these

> conversations helps everybody have a better understanding of where everybody is coming from.[4]

Part of the "everybody" he was referring to is the *Black Lives Matter* (BLM) movement, started by three African American women who were tired of police brutality and unwarranted shooting deaths. More on BLM, later.

I give quizzes to my students on occasion. Right about here is where I'd quiz them. Here is your quiz, instead:

> (1) Why did Colin Kaepernick sit during the national anthem? (2) Why did Kaepernick switch to kneel during the playing of the anthem? (3) Why did Eric Reid join Kaepernick in protest? (4) Did Colin Kaepernick hate America? (5) Was Colin Kaepernick's *intent* to disrespect police, American war veterans, current deployed military, or first-responders?

The answers would seem to be straightforward. But this is America, and we are so divided at times over social issues that we, on occasion, choose to frame incidents in ways that sometimes contradict the facts. We see and hear what best suits our view. I do it all the time when I hear of O.J. Simpson or Michael Jackson; I don't want to believe either of those two people did anything wrong. My feelings are not rational. My feelings are emotional. I want those two to represent athletic and musical talent and good Black men. To say ill of those two is to speak ill of *all* Black men.

So, I put my hands on my ears and hum a song to myself, so I don't hear any of the bad. I am self-aware enough to know that what I am doing is silly and flawed. But many Americans did that same silly and flawed act when Kaepernick kneeled and said, "America is not perfect."

Our Stars and Stripes Are Sacred to Flag Patriots

For well over two years (2016–2018) debate raged in the USA about the *intent* of Colin Kaepernick's social protest and the *unintended consequences* of kneeling in front of our sacred symbolism in the United States—the flag. I understand how those steeped in patriotism worship the flag in the USA. Further, I understand how much "flag patriots" want *everyone* to worship that flag, too. I distinguish those who love our country with our "reservations" about its imperfections as "American Patriots" vs. those who are blind to every flaw and only see her as perfect as "Flag Patriots." Whether you are Black, Brown, naturalized citizen, Native American, LGBTQi+, or "fresh off the boat,"—100% compliance to the flag and our anthem shows the world we are a unified nation; indivisible.

This is the goal of the Flag Patriot—100% compliance—regardless of how you are treated. As a matter of fact, to the Flag Patriot, if you are treated badly, it was probably your own fault. The flag comes to symbolize everything right and good. One should covet the flag, love the flag, protect the flag and fight for the flag. Flag Patriots in America are the closest we get to the swastika flag-worshipping that befell Germany. When the symbol becomes more important than the lives of people … not good.

Kaepernick is an American Patriot, proud as anybody to live in America, but aware that at key times, dissent is a necessary element of any good democracy. Robert T. Martin (2015) speaks to our collective history in his book: *Government by Dissent: Protest, Resistance, and Radical Democratic Thought in the Early American Republic*, by reminding Flag Patriots that "American was born of dissent … from the framers to the farmers … the new nation made an unprecedented effort to theorize the place of dissent in democracy."[5]

I remember dissent happened with a challenge to that flag in the fourth grade at Horace Mann elementary school by a little White boy in my class named Jeff. Heck, I guess we were all little. So little our parents had to tell us what to do. Jeff's parents told him not to stand for the "Pledge of Allegiance" with the rest of us every morning. Jeff was a Jehovah's Witness. His parents protested, noting their religion says they "Should not worship false idols."

There was one key line that had Jeff sit: "One nation, under *God* …" Take God out of the anthem, and everything would have been fine for Jehovah Witnesses. Otherwise, pledging allegiance to the flag (as symbolic of God) was crossing a religious line. His parents petitioned. And won. Jeff sat down every day while we stared at him—wondering why *we* had to stand.

So, while most Whites back then in the 1960s saw the flag as a sign of national pride, others saw it as sacrilegious. Such is the nature of the signification of national symbols. Colin Kaepernick likely saw saluting the flag in a time of great social dissent as hypocritical. Our nation didn't show respect for him or the many people of his skin color.

Kaepernick would be showing implicit agreement with everything the flag stood for if he continued to stand, and sing, and salute. Many would tell him that he should "hold whatever beliefs you have inside … keep your protests to yourself … this is not the time nor the place for social activism. This is a sacred moment." And I completely understand that perspective. Those people screaming loudly about staying in line and obeying the rules—even if they don't benefit you—are akin to what it must have felt like to be German in Germany in the late 1930s ... and of Jewish heritage. Do you "go with the flow" and look the other way, or do you stand up—or kneel—and say, "WTF!"

Yet another crowd—those Black and Brown people Kaepernick spoke of—would think,

> Athletes are the most visible and 'sacred' public African Americans in the USA. Why would you continue to bury your head in the sand when the police are having target practice with Black and Brown bodies out here in the real world? Has your million-dollar salary bought your silence? Are you just like Michael Jordan in the 1980s and 1990s—only concerned about your paycheck and your "brand?"[6]

Hey White People: What's the Best Way to Protest Police Murder?

Harsh criticism. Many would say athletes' silence for decades was just that—condoning the violence around them. Others say that every Black, Brown and White person is just as guilty for not protesting loudly the targeted shooting of Black men and boys and the continued rape and abuse of Black women and girls by a small percentage of law enforcement officials that taint the entire police force.

You'd be forgiven if you were at a loss as to what to do. Many of us have been at a loss since the Civil War as to what to do in the face of social injustice. Do we appeal to our local congressman or woman? Do we fight each battle in court? Do we sit with the Sherriff and ask for instructions on how to act around White officers? Yes we do. Yes we have. Many would say it has gotten us nowhere.

That might be wrong. Many more Black and Brown men and women may have been killed had it not been for the struggle for civil rights—and continual battles with local police forces, letters and pleas to Congress, and Attorneys General reviews and law changes. But "*surviving in terror*" is no longer good enough. Mothers and fathers who bury their sons far too young and console their raped daughters can no longer live with, "Well, aren't you glad your sister's son isn't dead, too?"

It does us little good to know that 100, *not 500*, defenseless Black and Brown people were shot dead. Colin Kaepernick decided that nobody was listening. That nobody watching their sports event really cared about the lives of victims outside the stadium.

He made a bet: "I'm betting more people in America care about the perfect symbolism of the anthem and the flag than they actually care about the murdered people. I bet they will pay attention when *something they care about* is disrespected. I'm betting they love their flag and their worship and their 'rockets red glare' more than they actually care about the lives that flag is supposed to represent."

He was right.

Many U.S. citizens—especially football fans—were infuriated with Colin's apparent disgrace of patriotism, his disrespect of American troops, veterans, and anything remotely related to America and her high ideals. People even said Kaepernick was disrespecting our "first responders." Everyone who had ever served America was now rolling in his or her grave at this "high-paid, pampered athlete" showing ingratitude. "How dare he—after all America has given him!"

Before I completely slap those people and their comments to the curb, I want to say again—I understand. I understand because I've lived overseas for 14 years in New Zealand and know what it is to call America home. I now have two homes as I am also a New Zealand citizen. I know our red, white and blue are sacred colors, and our stars and stripes are beautiful symbolism that veterans of foreign wars marched behind and died holding onto. The same holds true for New Zealand veterans marching, defending, and dying for their flag.

True, I am both a "Kiwi and a Yankee" as they would say. That doesn't mean that when American professors and students overseas get together, we don't long for our country. We do. We barbeque, make American food, joke about our slang and favorite TV shows or our love for our childhood sports teams. Living abroad makes you appreciate the homeland just that little bit more.

So, I know how you feel when you say people should not disrespect that flag. But you should also realize that that flag represents me—my flesh and blood. My family. People. Lives. While the boundaries of the USA is the territory we share, *humans* within our country boundary are what that flag represents. With no people inhabiting the USA, the symbolism is useless. You put that flag on an island in the Pacific with no people, and the flag blows meaninglessly. The stars and stripes have been politically disembodied from the beautiful and conflicted people it is supposed to represent.

When we get to the moment when the flag does not represent people—but an idea disembodied from people—a symbol, then it is worthless … no more valuable than a rusty military tank sitting face down in a ditch.

And when our flag becomes a symbol—more than the representation of people and a cause—then the worship we give it is meaningless. We will then love the flag simply because we love the flag. Because we are told to love the flag. And we make believe what it represents, like children looking at a Christmas tree—and thinking of a perfect baby Jesus. The tree is just a big piece of wood from the forest. But we can make it mean so much more in our minds. Like the flag means to so many Flag Patriots.

And woe unto the man or woman or child who disrespects what the flag represents—perfection and unity of a nation. It matters little if we really ARE a perfect union. What matters is that we *make believe* that we are unified. Like a wife standing with her abusive husband at church holds his hand and snuggles up next to him hoping that her affection will stop his oppressive behavior. This time.

As congregants in that church we really don't care if that unity—that tormented marriage—is imperfect. We just want you to *pretend* that your marriage is perfect. So we don't have to think about it.

Colin said no. "This marriage of the police and the people they are sworn to protect is not a perfect union. This marriage is flawed. And I want to let everybody who is pretending know that I no longer want to pretend." And so he decided on a very, very simple form of protest: Kneeling during the national anthem before football games.

Standing in the Face of Our Horrific History in the USA

Kaepernick, like most Americans who know our U.S. history, is well aware that the problems between police and Black and Brown bodies is nothing new. This terrorizing has gone on for decades. Dating back to the post-Civil War period, Black bodies have been brutalized by both the criminal justice system—and everyday Americans. Thousands of African Americans were shot, hung or burned after the Civil War "for the sheer love of killing."[7] Victor Kappeler discusses the targeting of African Americans for abuse, especially in the South:

> In no small part because of the tradition of slavery, Blacks have long been targets of abuse. The use of patrols to capture runaway slaves was one of the precursors of formal police forces, especially in the South. This disastrous legacy persisted as an element of the police role even after the passage of the Civil Rights Act of 1964. In some cases, police harassment simply meant people of African descent were more likely to be stopped and questioned by the police, while at the other extreme, they have suffered beatings, and even murder, at the hands of White police. Questions still arise today about the disproportionately high numbers of people of African descent killed, beaten, and arrested by police in major urban cities of America.[8]

For decades after the Civil War, Black Americans were open fodder for all sorts of abuse in public by Whites during Jim Crow segregation, during the Civil Rights Movement, and thereafter by police in every corner of this country. Slavery has left a long legacy of trauma—for Whites, who still feel aggrieved that they lost their free labor, free sexual exploitation of Black women, and the perpetual feeling of superiority that stems from treating Black people as 3/5th human. K.B Turner, David Giacopassi and Margaret Vandiver note,

> The literature clearly establishes that a legally sanctioned law enforcement system existed in America before the Civil War for the express purpose of controlling the slave population and protecting the interests of slave owners. The similarities between the slave patrols and modern American policing are too salient to dismiss or ignore … the slave patrol should be considered a forerunner of modern American law enforcement.[9]

If we skip ahead past all of the injustices of the late nineteenth century—on through the multiple wrongful deaths at the hands of police in all the decades of the twentieth century, there was a moment when we could have righted the ship. When we could have made a statement as a country that, indeed, wrong was being done and we needed to stop it.

What Rodney King Represented to Black People

When Los Angeles police beat Rodney King after a speeding stop, we watched the videotape in horror—but with a sense of hope. Odd, I know. Hope—because that videotape finally vindicated all that we had been saying for over a century: That Black people get an ass-whuppin by cops as if we were animals. We saw with our own eyes a gang of cops taking turns beating down a defenseless man on the ground as if he was target practice for their batons. Every bit of frustration in their cop lives was let loose on Rodney. Mr. King took the physical abuse for the rest of us. King was written off by most Whites because he was running from the law and high at the time. But what if we substitute Martin Luther King? What if it was him on the ground being beaten? We would have lost our minds.

Nonetheless, the beat-down was caught on film and our nation would finally think, "Hey, maybe Black people have a point here. Maybe they weren't always guilty of aggression or wrongdoing. Maybe we should look into more cases of brutality we often hear about." Hallelujah! We collectively thought we had the cops cold: They would finally be guilty of excessive force.

When a predominantly White jury from a community dense with police residents in Simi Valley, California, decided that there was no abuse, and that the officers in question had every reason to beat on Mr. King's Black body (because he represented a "threat"), that was a clear-as-day sign to Black people that something unknowable besides the obvious—Black hatred—was at work. The law was not on our side. Never has been. Is not to this day. (Please see Bob Manafort's 2019 jail sentence of 4 years from a judge who said, "He's otherwise led a good life"—though he sold our country out to Russia. Getting caught with marijuana in many places of America gets you more time than that.)

What Kaepernick and Activist Friends Are Protesting

The recent spate of Black shootings since 2015 is further evidence that justice is elusive. The ongoing *Washington Post Project* has found that police "Have shot and killed 3,309 people since 2015, or more than twice as many fatal shootings per year as the average reported by the FBI. Seven percent of those killed, or 231, were not armed with guns, knives or other objects ..."[10] In more detail, in 2015 police shot and killed 94 unarmed individuals, but that number fell to 51 in 2016 before rising to 68 in 2017. Turning to African Americans specifically, 36 unarmed Black men were killed in 2015, 18 in 2016, 19 in 2017 and up to May of 2018, 7 had been shot and killed. That is a low number compared to other years at the same time. Good.

I should note I am also concerned with "Hispanic" (41 since 2015) and White (85 since 2015) wrongful shootings, too, even though the number of Black men (80 since 2015) represents a larger number of per capita deaths.[11] I feel for ANY family that has to go through this trauma, Black, Brown or White.

Even with officer body cameras, pleadings by Black victims not to shoot, with no weapons in sight and no apparent threat, and onlookers crying foul, people get shot in cold blood with little to no repercussions. If this were brown-skinned police officers killing unruly White teenage girls, we'd have a national crisis.

There would be no need for bending knees during football games. White people would shut the country down. I think if Black and Brown officers were shooting White people's *dogs*—there would be more outrage than what Flag Patriots show for Black people suffering at the hands of officers. Something would be done. There would be a national outcry. People would be fired. Cops would be thrown in jail. Laws would shift.

Black people don't have that kind of power. Nor do Native Americans or Latinos. Rich and empowered Whites (and for that matter, many poor Whites) are so tired of powerless people of color complaining that they simply tune us out, like kids fighting over toys yet again in the den eventually gets parents to turn the stereo up louder to drown out the noise.

Dear America: We Don't Know What Else to Do to Get Your Attention

This is the true severity of the problem: Many White people don't even pull their heads up from the TV to ask *why* Colin Kaepernick is protesting. All Flag Patriots see is "flag disrespect!" It is akin to the sports-addicted boyfriend who doesn't listen to his spouse. She could complain and cry and walk through the house with a newly-broken arm—without notice. But the moment she crosses in front of the TV to get his undivided attention, he yells—"Hey—I'm watching the game here!" He notices, but his attention is on what he sees as *her disrespect*: He has a right to watch his game free from politics or females. In truth, every NFL football game is infused with politics—from flags to anthems to military marching to bomber jet flyovers. That's as political as it gets.

That's where we are in America. America has tuned us out to the point where many White Americans no longer care what we are complaining about. Whites have heard Blacks complaining since abolitionist rants before the Civil War. So, you've labeled us with the derogatory, powerless term, "victims." And then tell us to "stop acting like victims." Thereafter inventing a term called, "Victimhood." (I notice how you slipped "hood" in there. Gives victimization a *color*.) Then you get "victim fatigue." Then you don't listen.

What are Black and Brown folks supposed to do to get your attention? Riot? Strike? March on Washington? Arm ourselves? Get a new Black Panther Party? Start as many Black militias as there are White nationalist militias? "No. I'll just show my outrage by kneeling quietly during the national anthem, thank you very much." You might be looking at the most passive form of retaliatory protest in the face of criminal state-sanctioned injustice—in the history of Planet Earth. Strike that—Jews in Germany during the Holocaust showed even more restraint in the face of terror. And that didn't work out too well, either.

Others around the world revolt. Frustrated citizens in some countries overthrow the King or kill the "Strongman." Still others bomb buildings and assassinate random government officials. Here in the USA, athletes from 2016–2020 kneel during the national anthem.

As a reward for their respectful restraint, athletes who join the silent protest of kneeling in the face of years of terror in Black and Brown communities are told by the (then occupant of the) White House that they should be fired. What are we to do? In his own words, "Wouldn't you love to see one of these NFL owners, when somebody disrespects our flag, to say, 'Get that son of a bitch off the field right now. Out! He's fired! He's fired!'" I mean, really. When the highest government official—and biggest Flag Patriot—in America spits on every protesting athlete, what are we to do? One thing athletes did was stop going to the White House for photo opportunities with said government official.

We love this country. We love her people. We love and admire our veterans and war heroes. We appreciate our firefighters and first responders of every kind. My mother taught me to respect police because they are sworn to protect us. And most do. We are veterans and firefighters and police and first responders ourselves.

What we are wondering is this: When will America love us back?

We will know you truly love Black and Brown Americans as much as you love the flag … when you grant us the *special favor* we are asking of America in return …

Stop killing us.

The Kaepernick Ripple Effect

Many of us fell in love with Colin Kaepernick because he put his career on the line for a cause that is bigger than he is. He isn't under threat every day by the possibility of a violent death by someone sworn to uphold his rights. *We are.*

He did what politicians and Spike Lee Hollywood movies and civil marches and voting and Black Lives Matter protests could not do—got your defiant Whiteness angry enough to sit up and take notice. Just long enough to scream at us and call us "son of a bitches."

Kaepernick's bet was likely that he'd start a wave of people who would also see the injustice he felt inside his bones and protest in some small, defiant way. His cause was our cause, and his hope was that we would follow suit—that he'd start the stadium "wave" as it were, and that we would follow—until the roar was so loud you could not drown it out with cursing at the TV.

And that you'd start *convicting* the few cowardly bad cops that "shoot and ask questions later." And you'd further retrain police to see Black and Brown folks as human, too. You would have officers meet Black and Brown families during their training. Have them hear presentations of families who have lost members due to "death by police." You would have officer training that emphasizes that cops need to follow the law *also*, and that submitting false reports will end with them in jail. And look officer candidates in the eyes and tell them that if they conspire to cover-up brutality by another officer, that they will go to jail also, just as co-conspirators do in a robbery.

Like politicians, ministers, professors and our military, the bar is higher for officers—because their primary job is to protect us. But as the rapper KRS-One said of the police, "Who protects us from You?" Apparently Kaepernick is not the only one tired of decades of ill treatment and bad officers. People of all shades are tired. Kaepernick has indeed started a wave of teams, cheerleaders, bands and those affiliated with sports and that national anthem—protesting by kneeling in the face of injustice.

Kaepernick Is Not the Only One "Sick and Tired"

Movements need support. Movements need momentum. When someone makes a bold stand for a just cause, people often follow. Sometimes hesitantly; sometimes with a stampede. While it remains to be seen how far the "taking a knee" protest will go towards social change regarding people of color being mistreated by police (including beatings, shootings, racial profiling stops, and the rape and abuse of Black females), there has been a clear signal that something must be done—or tensions and protests will heighten. We might have reached a moment when "enough is enough." Police have bullied Black people for decades, and now those pushed around are demanding a stop to the bully tactics.

There are two fronts for protest—the sporting world, and the non-sporting world. In the sporting world, other NFL athletes responded to Kaepernick's protest by joining—first Eric Reid, co-Forty-Niner. Then other teammates, then other teams, then a baseball player, then cheerleaders, then women in the WNBA, then high school teams (my high school, Castlemont, in Oakland—which Kaepernick later visited), then pee wee league football teams, then high school bands, then USA soccer players, then a Major League Baseball player (Bruce Maxwell, then a catcher on the Oakland A's baseball team), and then athletes and teams overseas. The wave went through teams and leagues—all in solidarity with Kaepernick and his goal to end police bullying.

Figure F.2. Bruce Maxwell, Oakland Athletics: First baseball player in the conservative sport to kneel for the anthem. Source: Michael Zagaris/Oakland Athletics/Getty Images

These acts were intended to raise consciousness and draw attention to death and harassment over a long period of time. The video evidence of these killings is what has people standing—and kneeling—together.

Academic Research on Social Activism in Sport

One major consequence of Colin Kaepernick's kneeling throughout the 2016 season is that he sparked and reinvigorated the conversation about social justice among academics. Not that we forgot about social justice; but the platform of a successful professional athlete in the USA who chooses to stand for a cause is immense. We forgot just how much controversy one athlete standing up—by kneeling for justice—could cause. We forgot how much attention you get when you say, "America—you are not living up to your high ideals—your potential greatness."

Peter Benson has written on corporate social responsibility, and highlights the issue of assimilation and redeployment of Black masculinity into palatable forms:

> Black players in the NFL, universities, and high schools now commonly take a knee, lock arms, or raise a fist during the pregame national anthem to signal support for Black Lives Matter and racial justice issues. Backlash among White

> fans and pundits is evidence of a reigning corporate and cultural ethos that presupposes that the player's value rightly belongs to an apolitical system of corporeal deployment and application, demands acquiescence to a dutiful post—a soldier—and embraces only certain acceptable and assimilable forms of Black Masculinity.[12]

A few corporations are slowly choosing to evolve from this model of authoritarian demands on the Black body. Professional sports institutions in the USA are rethinking their responses to protest by Black athletes, by women who are demanding more egalitarian pay and benefits, and by lesbian and transgender/transsexual athletes (and eventually, gay athletes).

Cole Armstrong, Ted Butryn, Vernon Andrews and Matthew Masucci left the cozy confines of San Jose State to visit the ESPY awards to discuss how professional sports teams can rethink responses to protest and athlete dissention.[13] ESPN is the media focal point for many sports viewers who process athlete activist issues, so athletes with answers—and teams with questions—flocked to the annual awards event in Los Angeles. We represented San Jose State's Institute for the Study of Sport, Society and Social Change, a Harry Edwards-led endeavor to highlight past and present social activism by women and men in sport.

Joseph Cooper, Charles Macaulay and Saturnino Rodriguez note that race and resistance in sport is now in a "fourth wave" where "… African American activism in the 21st century has been connected to strategic uses of … technology and social media as tools for disruption, information dissemination, organization and empowerment."[14] Indeed, Colin Kaepernick himself trolls Twitter and gives dap to many people who voice or show solidarity.

And if you do go online to view commentary about athlete social activism, just know there are multiple positive and negative comments that get quite heated. Montez de Oca and Cho Suh frame the various categories of dissent and thematically code protest debates. What stands out for me in debates is the irony of calling oneself "patriotic" while at the same time relying on an absolutist framework for critiquing behavior that seeks to improve America through protest.[15]

When uncritical Flag Patriotism yells at any challenges to upgrade our democracy with a "Love it or leave it" rant, then we smell the whiff of privilege and the killing of dissent. Montez de Oca and Cho Suh frame this as "patriarchal patriotism" which has as its children such phrases as "get the hell out" and otherwise anger at someone who refuses to show blind obedience.[16]

The irony is that the arc of American equality and the inclusion of non-Whites has been (slowly) bending in the direction of the acceptance of multicultural citizens, multi-religious affiliation, LGBTQIA+ friendly workforces, female empowerment and equal space for the differently abled. Given this slow but steady movement toward America's highest ideals, where everyone is recognized as "valid," the operative "love it or leave it" phrase might very well be turned on those who are repressive, hypocritical and un-democratic: You might want to get with the program or go to another country that better suits your kind. America is no longer the place that tolerates intolerance towards diversity. We will not go quietly back into submissiveness.

But herein the NFL has a dilemma to resolve—Black players represent the largest group of athletes in the NFL (hovering around 70%)—and White Flag Patriots represent a large percentage of NFL fans. What to do? Theresa Walton-Fisette points out this dilemma and points to an ideological collision course that could have been predicted:

> The NFL is currently in a tough place with the protests. On the one hand, they have millionaire and billionaire owners who benefit from the economic, gender, and racial status quo ... On the other hand, they have 60% of their profit coming from ... a population very similar to Trump's voters. As Pesca (2017) of *Slate* notes, "In many ways, the Trump voter is the NFL viewer ... Seventy-seven percent of NFL fans are Caucasian; 87% of Trump voters are Caucasian[17] (para. 6)..." At the same time, a majority of NFL players are black.[18]

One chilling review of Black football players' strength and tenacity in the face of injury serves as the backdrop for why it was "okay" for Darren Wilson to shoot Michael Brown. Wilson asserted that the 18-year-old Michael Brown was "bulking up to run through the shots" he was about to be riddled with fed directly into the narrative of the myth of Black animal-like strength.[19] These narratives have been pervasive in American society since the end of slavery (please see Ethnic Notions, by Marlon Riggs) and are also pervasive in sport, transferred into social discourse by announcers, and believed by White juries who acquit police officers.

These "positive stereotypes" of Black strength and resilience "... may lead to Black people being unreasonably considered a lethal threat and jailed or killed for it. Police officers' 'fear' is a viable legal defense for murdering Black people."[20] Which, of course, it isn't. And this is the very reason why Colin Kaepernick kneeled in protest. We are not animals, not 3/5th human. As a Seattle member of the Red Neck Brigade (a gun-toting, pro-Black militia) surmised in 2019, the thing White people fear the most is, "A Black man with a gun."[21] Which might explain why some cops shoot Black suspects when wallets or cellphones appear near Black hands.

Athletes around the country have followed Colin Kaepernick's social activist lead by protesting during the national anthem. Here is a sampling of athletes, teams, and others who have protested—and their stated reasons. Kaepernick has started a ripple of protest that has continued into the (Covid-19-interrupted) 2020 season.

1. *Seth DeValve, Cleveland Browns*: "The issue is that it doesn't provide opportunity to everybody, and I want to support my African-American teammates today who wanted to take a knee. We wanted to draw attention to the fact that there's things in this country that still need to change."[22]
2. *Michael Bennett, Seattle Seahawks*: "We have nothing against the military flag. We love the military and America. But we don't love oppression, we don't love discrimination, we don't love racism. For us, that's what it was about."[23]
3. *Titans and Seahawks joint protest:* Before the anthem, the *Seattle Seahawks* released a statement: "As a team, we have decided we will not participate in the national anthem. We will not stand for injustice that has plagued people of color in this country. Out of love for our country and in honor of the basic sacrifices made on our behalf, we unite to oppose those that would deny our most basic freedoms. We remain committed in continuing to work towards equality and justice for all."
4. *The Tennessee Titans* followed with their own statement: "As a team, we wanted to be unified in our actions today. The players jointly decided this was the best course of action. Our commitment to the military and our community is resolute and the absence of our team for the national anthem shouldn't be misconstrued as unpatriotic."[24]
5. *Eric Reid, San Francisco Forty-Niners*: "I believe what I'm doing is bigger than my career, and quite frankly we need more people to take that position. The system will only change via public pressure."[25]
6. *New Orleans Saints:* Although players could not all agree on a form of protest, many sat—some with hands over their heart. Cam Jordan stated, "It only gives us more pride to say, hey, this is the day and age where I can show and demonstrate something and what's on my mind and what's on my heart and prove this to the world that this is an important topic to pay attention to while in the meanwhile trying to unify a single mind." P.S. Restaurants refused to air the Saints games in their businesses and a legislator wants to cut off funding for the team.[26]
7. *Malcolm Jenkins and Chris Long, Philadelphia Eagles*: Chris Long puts his arm on teammate Malcom Jenkins, fist raised. "I think it's a good

time for people that look like me to be there for people that are fighting for equality," Long (white) told reporters.[27]

8. *A San Francisco Forty-Niner Cheerleader:* Though I don't have her name, nor have a quote from her, she needs to be acknowledged as the first NFL cheerleader who kneeled in protest. She took her social action during a home game vs. the Oakland Raiders. (Which is my way to also insert in this book the name Oakland Raiders. Because, Vegas.)
9. *Meghan Linsey, Singing the National Anthem at Tennessee* **Titans** game: Meghan Linsey sang the national anthem. On one knee. In Nashville, Tennessee. Linsey wanted to use her privilege and do the right thing. She stated, "I am a white, blonde, privileged woman in the music industry, and I knew the weight it would carry, and I knew I had to do it … I wanted to take a stand for people of color facing police brutality. Yesterday was not a demonstration against anyone, it was purely in support and solidarity with the NFL players." P.S. She received a lot of backlash from fans and harsh comments were made via FOX news. Meghan Linsey gets the "Badass Ally" award for being outrageously wonderful and showing the way for other White people who haven't realized how powerful their voices are.[28]

Figure F.3. 49er Cheerleaders don't make much money and don't have job security. But they speak up. Source: Thearon W. Henderson/Getty Images Sport/Getty Images

10. *Howard University (Washington D.C.) Cheerleaders* for the Howard college football team. The cheerleaders were inspired by a University of Pennsylvania cheerleader who had knelt at a previous game. All were inspired by Kap's message to stand against injustices.[29]
11. *Marcus Peters and Kansas City Chiefs* football team. Peters raised a power fist as his teammates locked arms. He stated, "I salute Colin for what he's doing for a great cause. I'm 100 per cent behind him. What's going on in law enforcement, it does need to change and it does need to change for everybody, not just us as black Americans."[30] (Full disclosure: Marcus Peters is from Oakland and is a relative through marriage.)
12. *Marshawn Lynch, Oakland Raiders* football player. Lynch says he will continue to kneel and that this is nothing new. He supports Kaepernick, "I'd rather see him take a knee than stand up, put his hands up, and get murdered … I just hope people open up their eyes to see there's really a problem going on, and something needs to be done for it to stop. And I mean, if you're really not racist, then you're going to see what he's done, what he's doing, [not] as a threat to America, but just addressing a problem that we have."[31] (full disclosure, I met Marshawn's Uncle, former NFL linebacker with the Chicago Bears, in the Carolina Panther's hotel in San Jose during Super Bowl week. We hopped in his car and drove to see the "Concussion Doctor" speak in San Francisco. So, basically, Marshawn and I are first cousins).
13. *Arian Foster, Kenny Stills, Michael Thomas, Miami Dolphins.* "They say it's not the time to do this," Foster said last week. "When is the time? It's never the time in somebody else's eye, because they'll always feel like it's good enough. And some people don't. That's the beautiful thing about this country. If somebody feels it's not good enough, they have that right. That's all we're doing, exercising that right." P.S. The union for Broward County sheriff's office wants police to no longer escort players to their games and stop their protection for Dolphins players.[32]
14. *Megan Rapinoe, USA Soccer Player.* Rapinoe stated she wanted to stand in solidarity with Colin Kaepernick. She believes, "… We should always value the use of our voice and platform to fight for equality of every kind." P.S. A US Soccer Federation policy was created stating players "shall stand respectfully" during national anthems. They also played anthem *before* the teams took the field during a match in Washington.[33]
15. *Southern Methodist University (Dallas, Texas) Band* members along with students in the stands. One student stated "I'm not against all police officers, I'm not saying all cops are bad, I'm not saying all Caucasian people are bad, because they're not," Boyce said. "I just believe that the

injustice being shown in the past couple of years has been too much to handle. And I'm a little tired of it."[34]

16. *Indiana Fever WNBA Team* (whole team). Protesting recent police shootings. Coach Stephanie White stated, "It's bigger than basketball."[35]
17. *Brandon Marshal, Denver Broncos* football player. Marshall stands with Kaepernick and against social injustice. He realizes that he has the platform to be heard and he needs to use that to societies advantage. P.S. Marshall lost his sponsor, CenturyLink. Shame on you, CenturyLink.[36]
18. *Baltimore Ravens and Jacksonville Jaguars* (27 players in total). While playing a game in London, England, Jaguars owner Shad Khan locked arms with players in protest, stating, "… to express my support for them, all NFL players and the league following the divisive and contentious remarks made by President Trump, and was honored to be arm and arm with them … Our team and the National Football League reflects our nation, with diversity coming in many forms—race, faith, our views and our goals."[37]
19. *Castlemont High School football players, Oakland, California.* Players, and some coaches, laid down with their hands up as Kaepernick knelt among them. Kaepernick came to the Oakland school and delivered an inspirational speech to the team, "You are important. You make a difference, this matters. Everything you do matters. Look out for one another, lift each other up. That's what this is all about." (P.S. This is the author's alma mater, as you will find out later in this manuscript.)[38]

Of Course, There Are Always Haters: A Review of Twitter Commentary

There are many venues where people in America voice dissent about anything and everything: Facebook, newspaper letters-to-the-editor, talk radio, and Twitter, among many others. I've assembled commentary from the past three years on Twitter that are strongly against athlete protests. While I don't agree with these citizens, nor their logic, it is instructive to know how dissenters view athlete activism, patriotism and love of country, and issues of police brutality being debated.

Rarely does any dissenter comment on the social issue at hand—the multiple wrongful death shootings of civilians by police officers. There seems to be a conspiracy to avoid an honest discussion of profiling and brutality. This is in keeping with historical protests of African Americans that mostly have been met with, "this is not the place and this is not the time." I am conscious that though I might not agree with the below commentary, I don't want to invalidate their concerns for country.

I do understand their emotions, their concerns, their fears and their devout patriotism. Which is why I feel it is important to voice their views. I just don't agree with their conclusions, nor do I think they grasp the issue Kaepernick and other players are protesting about. I have edited their commentary for clarity and ease of reading, not a usual custom in quoting individuals. But in this case, I want to privilege the central thought without evaluating any errors in communication. I don't want you to judge them—I want you to hear them. I'd want the same courtesy (to read opposing views) in an extended *negative* commentary about athlete activism.

The first Civil War, if we can expand on the use of the word "Civil," was "civil" because it was between people who knew each other. The South was not a foreign enemy. The *New Civil War* is grounded in race and ideology and supremacy. We also know each other—very well. There are no borders between us. The primary fighting ground is in the media. The platform for the New Civil War, as above with the anti-protest commentary, is primarily the internet.

The anti-athlete/anti-free speech commentary by fans fall under five general categories: (1) Anti-American, (2) Anti-Veteran, (3) Anti-Police, (4) Politics don't belong in sport, and (5) America—Love it or leave it. All bullet points are quotes.

Athlete Protests Are Anti-American

- Kneeling for the National Anthem and disrespecting the Flag is not courage it is the exact opposite of courage and slaps those in the face that the flag and anthem is meant to honor. Those such as George Washington, Abraham Lincoln, Martin Luther King, Rosa Parks, JFK.
- I wonder if you or they realize the flag they were taking a stand against was the same one that defeated the confederacy?
- I stand for boycotting the NFL and its cry babies and will see by season's-end who is still kneeling and disrespecting the USA.
- Disrespecting this country is not OK. Those that do will continue to lose their fan base and your revenues will continue to go down.

Athlete Protests Are Anti-Veteran

- Kneeling during and anthem is not courage ... Get that shit outta here. Go watch some WW II documentary to see real courage ... jokers!

- You and they are cowards. You think this is a way to make a point? Powerless actions that disrespect real heroes and unity. Dumb to follow a guy who grew up in a white family, privileged in sports & made mega money OFF this issue at the expense of our fallen and injured. Colin sucked.
- Your defiance is at the sake of disrespecting those who are sworn to keep you safe. Stereotyping individuals of a profession or service is no different than stereotyping an entire race. It leads to hate, divisiveness, destruction of a peaceful society and above all bigotry.
- Taking a knee disrespects blacks who fight and died, but you know, "activism."
- I watched from 1971 to last year. No More. I'm an Army brat, and your players are disrespectful to the flag on soldiers' coffins.

Athlete Protests Are Anti-Police

- Stand up, apologize to fans, owners, your country and all police world-wide and maybe The League will show you love.
- The police and military make it possible for the *National Felon League* players to get wealthy playing a boy's game.
- Coward! Respect and support our brave military and police who protect, serve and sacrifice—and do very much for all of us! I'm shutting off the NFL.
- Saying you are proud of players that disrespect our country & police while being good role models is what's wrong with the NFL and you!

Politics Don't Belong in Sports

- Trump is right. Sport is not a platform for political messages. It is an event for human unity—not for opinions and agenda.
- There is a time and a place for everything. I don't feel the football field is the proper forum for protesting. It should be done on your own time and not at your place of work. Most people would be fired if they protested at their jobs. Why do you feel you deserve special treatment?
- Your first amendment rights should not apply while you're on the clock at your job. The NFL players are being paid to do a JOB. You want protest? Do it on your own damn time! Normal people in society that have everyday jobs would NEVER be allowed to protest during business hours!!
- You should resign. No one wants sports served with politics. The NFL is going down along with other sports that allow taking a knee.

- Trump has already done more good for the black man than their so called brother (OBUMA) did in eight years. Play ball and leave the politics to people who know what they are doing.

Protesting Athletes Should Love America—or Leave It!

- I am ashamed. It's the NATIONAL ANTHEM and if you can't stand for it LEAVE THE COUNTRY!
- Laughed my ass off. Dude, you're so oppressed you get paid large stacks of cash to suck at football. Move to Russia and see what kind of life you can live there if this country sucks.
- I've lost respect for you. The NBA [and NFL?] is boring anyhow. Move to another country. Military veteran from 2002–2006.
- Get out of our country! Bet we wouldn't see you on the [military] front line. Take a knee in China.
- You are a football player, not a politician. The only time you get a say is on Election Day.

Celebrities Weigh in on Activism and the New Civil War

This is America. Which means we are opinionated. And just like the fans above venting their frustration at everything BUT police brutality, there are those that link arms with athletes because they agree with the underlying issue of protesting unfair and often brutal treatment by *some* law enforcement officials. Many in Hollywood and the entertainment industry have joined the *New Civil War*, with movie stars and popular singers and performers weighing in on the controversy in society. Here is a smattering of pro-activist comments by some you'll easily know, and others you might not know.

Ava DuVernay: I will not be a spectator, viewer or supporter of the #SuperBowl today in protest of the @NFL's racist treatment of @Kaepernick7 and its ongoing disregard for the health + well-being of all of its players. To watch the game is to compromise my beliefs. It's not worth it. #ImWithKap.

Cardi B: Colin Kaepernick, as long as you kneel with us, we're gonna be standing for you, baby. That's right, I said it [at the 2017 *MTV Video Music Awards*].

Jay-Z: "I said no to the Super Bowl/You need me, I don't need you/Every night we in the end zone/Tell the NFL we in stadiums too."

Amy Shumer: Friday thought: I wonder why more White players aren't kneeling. Once you witness the truly deep inequality and endless racism people of color face in our country, not to mention police brutality and murders. Why not kneel next to your brothers? Otherwise, how are you not complicit? I think it would be cool if @maroon5 backed out of Super Bowl like @badgalriri did. I personally told my reps I wouldn't do a Super Bowl commercial this year. I know it must sound like a privilege ass sacrifice but it's all I got. Hitting the NFL with the advertisers is the only way to really hurt them. I know opposing the NFL is like opposing the NRA. Very tough, but don't you want to be proud of how you're living? Stand up for your brothers and sisters of color. And the hottest thing a guy can do is to get down on one knee. Not to propose but to reject the treatment of his teammates by this country. Anyone who says it's disrespectful to our military please read up on the fact that a lot of veterans are proud of what @kaepernick7 is doing and fully support him.

Angela Davis: We are never assured of justice without a fight. I'm no longer accepting the things I cannot change. I'm changing the things I cannot accept. You have to act as if it were possible to radically transform the world. And you have to do it all the time. #ImWithKap.

Colin Kaepernick: I can't explain how much it means to have the support of the Icon Angela Davis! She has laid the foundation for me and many others to fight against anti-Blackness and has never wavered! We love and appreciate you!

Amber Tamblyn: Hi there. While you're enjoying this mediocre Maroon 5 halftime please remember a football legend was blacklisted from this entire sport for merely putting his knee on the ground in protest of Black people being murdered. Enjoy your pop music!

Goapele: Super what? Nah! I'm with @kaepernick7 #ImWithKap

Common: "If you stick a knife in my back 9 inches and pull it out 6 inches, there's no progress. If you pull it all the way out, that's not progress. The progress is healing the wound that the blow made. They won't even admit the knife is there." Malcolm X.

Piper Perabo: I am in solidarity with @Kaepernick and the struggle for racial justice #ImWithKap.

Nick Cannon: Forever "Standing" with my brother! @kaepernick7.

Eddie Vedder: Vedder took a knee during his headlining set at the Tennessee Pilgrimage Festival. Earlier that day, his band Pearl Jam, tweeted their support for protesters: "We support …@Kaepernick7, and everyone's constitutional right to stand up, sit down or #takeaknee for equality."

Stevie Wonder: Tonight, I'm taking a knee for America. Not just one knee, but I'm taking both knees. Both knees in prayer for our planet, our future, leaders of our world and our globe. Amen.

Other supporters who wear the #ImWithKap jersey or who have kneeled to show support for the cause: Jalen Brown, Boston Celtics; Steph Curry, Golden State Warriors, Michael Bennet, Seattle Seahawks, and Stevie Wonder *with* Dave Matthews. This is just a few of the many.

Figure F.4. The truth is out there. X-Files "Scully and Mulder" kneel in support of one social activist truth. Fair Use Photo From //GillianAnderson/Twitter

Conclusion: The 2018 Celebration Rule Change Is No Coincidence

This book focuses on the ways African Americans express themselves in sport and society, often in conflict with White normative and institutional values, which center on control of the body for utilitarian (or violent sports) purposes. African Americans, I contend, dance and otherwise express joy in the end-zone for a variety of personal and social reasons. NFL and NCAA rules have severely constricted Black expression since 1984 (NFL) and 1991 (NCAA). I have closely observed the contested terrain of league rules and player self-expression and celebration in spite of the rules.

Truth be known, I've spent far too much of my life obsessing over the matter of Black people having to constantly adjust to White rules of behavior in every institution—and suffering the consequences for rule-breaking. Black and

Brown, male and female skin is constantly interrogated for behavioral conformity in places of employment as varied as sport, the military, and academia. I observed Colin Kaepernick, NFL and fan tussles over social activism vs. patriotism, I'm also watching another subterranean issue.

Imagine being chained in a basement for 35 years. Your idea of physical expression would be limited by how far your chains were apart from each other. And suddenly, without warning or reason, your chains are unlocked, the door to the ground floor was flung open, and you were allowed to go free. This is akin (apologies to any victims I might have triggered) to the NFL saying at the beginning of the 2018 season, "You are free to dance in the end zone—or anywhere else."

This is not logical. This makes no sense. My evidence is the continued level of intense scrutiny the Black body has received in the NFL since 1984. I submit this book as hard-core, historical evidence that over the past 30 years since I've been cataloging this phenomenon, and there has been a deep, irrational need to control Black behavior. Their obsession with our bodies ... has been my obsession. Not because sport is more fascinating than any other social institution. Far from it. But sport as an arena of study gives us the opportunity to observe the microcosm of power at work.

If we observe social ills like racism, sexism, homophobia or ableism in a society, we should see these ills show up in sport. The rhetorical question on my radar was this: Since Black bodies are under constant surveillance and norming in society, how does this phenomenon show up in sport? And since it appeared that touchdown dances and celebrations were a targeted area I could microscopically observe, I'd focus on this act as a solid representation in football of social oppression of the Black body.

And here we are. A rule changed on Black expression. But why? Why would owners change a rule they've said follows "tradition?" Did social conscience suddenly perk up in owners that had them collectively stand and say, "By George, we've been wrong all these years—Black men must be allowed their own definitions of what it is to work and play and achieve and celebrate that success, even though they were not raised by my parents in the proper way of how to comport oneself in public."

Really? No. This is not an accident. This is by design.

The NFL changed its rules on celebration in a direct response to Colin Kaepernick, who's kneeling and social activism was embarrassing and was compromising the League and was pushing young Black male expression in a defiant direction. The entire affair was taxing for the League, what with both Black fans and White fans gathering signatures for boycotts of the NFL in 2017.

Imagine the brains and craftiness of a group of White men meeting to dream up a solution that would eliminate most athlete protests. And then somebody said the words, and everyone agreed: "Let them dance. Let them shimmy. That will take their minds off of protests. We give them celebrations, maybe they give us peace. Sure, White fans will object to the preening; but they'll sit easier with celebrations as the lesser of the expressive evils. That flag represents the embodiment of everything America loves about itself." And so, it was done.

Given what you are about to read in the next 10 chapters, you'd think I'd be happier. I was for a while. Until I had a shot of "Writers Tears" Irish Whiskey late one Sunday afternoon. I shut down the analytical side of my brain long enough to say, "Wait a minute!"

I was so thrilled that players had been having fun and enjoying their bodies in motion, that I'd put my critical lens on the back shelf of my analytical closet. It had been exhausting cataloging data, both social and academic, on the Black body in public over the past 30 years. I shared the joy of walking out into the sunlight myself. I simply enjoyed players enjoying themselves.

The NFL stopped warring in the media. They paid $89 million to Malcolm Jenkins and a couple of foundations; Jenkins called off his protests, and the movement lost steam. Maybe this is why Eric Reid and Malcolm Jenkins had fiery words with each other on the field in 2018 when they met. Then the league jumped in to cement the deal by allowing celebrations.

Colin Kaepernick no longer kneels on the sidelines of Football games. He has been blacklisted out of the NFL for good. He also settled a lawsuit with the NFL, and I suspect he was paid for their apparent "collusion" to keep him out of the league. He asked a question in 2016 that still resonates: "Do these various United States documents and symbols that you cherish so much still not apply to African Americans? Because if they do, you should act like it. If they don't—which is what it appears like, given the random (nearly) legalized killing of Black people by police officers—then I am asking for a change. I can no longer, with a clear conscience, accept the status quo."

Thank you, Colin Kaepernick. I like how you started the wave. Social activism is not a spectator sport. The rest of us have to step up and keep the ripple effect of your wave going. We are still in the middle of the New Civil War.

Notes

1. Wyche, S. 2016. "Colin Kaepernick explains why he sat during national anthem." *NFL.com*, August 27.

2. Witz, B. 2016. "This time, Colin Kaepernick takes a stand by Kneeling." *New York Times*, September 1.
3. Ibid.
4. Ibid.
5. Martin, R. W. T. 2013. *Government by Dissent: Protest, Resistance, and Radical Democratic Thought in the Early American Republic*. New York: New York University Press.
6. Brown, C. 2017. "Michael Jordan isn't sitting out anymore, says protesting athletes 'shouldn't be demonized.'" *Washington Post*, September 26.
7. Hine, D., Hine, W., and Harrold, S. 2018. *The African American Odyssey*. New York: Pearson.
8. Kappeler, V. 2014. "A brief history of slavery and the origins of American policing." *Eastern Kentucky University Police Studies Online*. January, para 4.
9. Turner, K. B., Giacopassi, D., and Vandiver, M. 2006. "Ignoring the past: Coverage of slavery and slave patrols in criminal justice texts." *Journal of Criminal Justice Education*, vol. 17, issue 1, p. 181–195 (p. 186).
10. Sullivan, J., Tate, J., and Jenkins, J. 2018. "Fatal police shootings of unarmed people have significantly declined, experts say." *Washington Post*, May 7, para 8.
11. Ibid. Para 14–16.
12. Benson, P. 2017. "Big football: Corporate social responsibility and the culture and color of injury in America's most popular sport." *Journal of Sport and Social Issues*, vol. 41, issue 4, p. 307–334.
13. Armstrong, C. G., Butryn, T. M., Andrews, V. L., and Masucci, M. 2018. "Athlete activism and corporate social responsibility: Critical lessons from sports industry professionals." *Sport Management Education Journal*, vol. 12, issue 2, p. 110–113.
14. Cooper, J., Macaulay, C., and S. Rodriguez. 2019. "Race and resistance: A typology of African American sport activism." *International Review for the Sociology of Sport*, vol. 54, issue 2, p. 151–181.
15. Montez do Oca, J., and Cho Suh, S. 2019. "Ethics of patriotism: NFL players' protests against police violence." *International Review for the Sociology of Sport*, vol. 54, issue 1, p. 1–25.
16. Montez do Oca, J., and Cho Suh, S. 2019. "Ethics of patriotism: NFL players' protests against police violence." *International Review for the Sociology of Sport*, vol. 54, issue 1, p. 1–25.
17. Pesca, M. 2017. "Trump and the truth about NFL ratings." WFAE (90.7), Charlotte's *NPR* news source. October 4. Retrieved from http://wfae.org/post/trump-and-truth-about-nfl-ratings.
18. Walton-Fisette, T. 2018. "Metaphorically 'taking a knee': Pausing, reflecting, acting." *Sociology of Sport Journal*, vol. 35, p. 293–300.

19. Haslerig, S., Vue, R., and Grummert, S. 2018. "Invincible bodies: American sport media's racialization of Black and white college football players." *International Review for the Sociology of Sport*, vol. 53, issue 1, p. 1–19.
20. Please see Light, C. 2017. *Stand Your Ground: A History of America's Love Affair with Lethal Self-Defense*. Boston, MA: Beacon Press, and Marcus, N. C. 2016. "From Edward to Eric Garner and Beyond: The importance of constitutional limitations on lethal use of force in police reform." *Duke Journal of Constitution Law and Public Policy*, vol. 12, issue 1, p. 53–106.
21. Bell, K. 2018. "Not all White People." United Shades of America. *CNN*. Season 4, episode 2. May 5.
22. Baccelllieri, E. 2017. *Deadspin*. "Seth DeValve is the first White player to kneel for the anthem." Deadspin. (https://deadspin.com/seth-devalve-is-the-first-white-player-to-kneel-for-the-1798295618).
23. Barron, D. 2017. "Michael Bennett aims to 'change the culture' with anthem protests." *My San Antonio*. (https://www.mysanantonio.com/sports/texans/article/Michael-Bennett-wants-to-change-the-culture-12244967.php).
24. Condotta, B. 2017. "Both the Seahawks and the Titans decided to remain in their locker rooms and not participate in the national anthem prior to their game in Tennessee." *The Seattle Times*. (https://www.seattletimes.com/sports/seahawks/seahawks-stay-in-locker-room-during-national-anthem-prior-to-sundays-game-in-nashville/).
25. Jan, T. 2017. "Despite risk of being 'Kaepernicked,' 49ers safety Eric Reid will keep kneeling." *The Washington Post*. (https://www.washingtonpost.com/news/wonk/wp/2017/10/29/despite-risk-of-being-kaepernicked-49er-safety-eric-reid-will-keep-kneeling/?noredirect=on&utm_term=.0180466dba2d).
26. Katzenstein, J. 2017. "Saints players discussing future protest options aimed at promoting unity." *The Times-Picayune*. (https://www.nola.com/saints/2017/09/saints_protest_drew_brees.html).
27. Mather, V. 2017. "Eagles' Chris Long joins Malcolm Jenkins as N.F.L. anthem protests continue." *The New York Times*. (https://www.nytimes.com/2017/08/18/sports/football/malcolm-jenkins-chris-long-eagles-anthem-protest.html).
28. Sanders, L. 2017. "'Voice' star Meghan Linsey defends her national anthem knee despite backlash from country fans." *Newsweek*. (https://www.newsweek.com/meghan-linsey-national-anthem-protest-take-knee-nfl-670441).
29. Sanders, L. 2016. "Cheerleaders at Howard University kneel during national anthem." *Teen Vogue*. (https://www.teenvogue.com/story/cheerleaders-howard-university-kneel-during-national-anthem).
30. Sims, A. 2016. "NFL Kansas City Chiefs player Marcus Peters protests during anthem on 9/11 anniversary." *Independent*. (https://www.independent.co.uk/news/world/americas/nfl-kansas-city-chiefs-player-marcus-peters-protests-during-anthem-on-911-anniversary-a7237561.html).

31. Stites, A. 2017. "Marshawn Lynch sat during the national anthem in his first game out of retirement." *SB Nation.* (https://www.sbnation.com/2017/8/13/16139872/marshawn-lynch-national-anthem-protest-colin-kaepernick).
32. Armen, B., and Carpenter, L. 2016. "Dolphins sit out anthem as police union says they have forfeited free speech." *The Guardian.* (https://www.theguardian.com/sport/2016/sep/18/miami-dolphins-players-protest-police-union-nfl).
33. Associated Press. 2017. "Megan Rapinoe says she will respect US Soccer policy for national anthem." *The Guardian.* (https://www.theguardian.com/football/2017/mar/06/megan-rapinoe-us-soccer-national-anthem-policy).
34. Tsuji, A. 2016. "SMU band members kneel while playing national anthem." *USA Today Sports.* (https://ftw.usatoday.com/2016/09/smu-band-members-kneel-national-anthem-protest).
35. Vasilogambros, M. 2016. "A WNBA team's protest against police violence." *The Atlantic.* (https://www.theatlantic.com/news/archive/2016/09/wnba-protest-police-violence/501098/).
36. Villanueva, R. 2016. "Broncos' Brandon Marshall loses another sponsor, will continue to kneel during anthem." *USA Today.* (https://www.usatoday.com/story/sports/nfl/broncos/2016/09/12/brandon-marshall-centurylink-sponsor-national-anthem-kneeling/90277042/).
37. Weinstein, A. 2017. "Ravens and Jaguars players kneel, lock arms together for anthem at London game." *Sporting News.* (http://www.sportingnews.com/us/nfl/news/ravens-jaguars-national-anthem-protest-london-game-donald-trump-tweets/1mh474zytu84q1t7ew3x4mc2ek).
38. Curtis, C. 2016. "High school football team does haunting national anthem protest with Colin Kaepernick on sidelines." *USA Today Sports.* (https://ftw.usatoday.com/2016/09/colin-kaepernick-49ers-castlemont-oakland-protest-national-anthem-video).

Acknowledgments

First, thank you to the many academic scholars who read my many versions of this manuscript over the years and offered sage advice. Thanks, also, to Billy Hawkins and Patricia Mulrane at Peter Lang Publishers for showing faith in the project. In no specific order, these professors aided whatever is right in this manuscript. Special thanks, first, to my mentors, John Fiske and Jane Piliavin, who stuck with me for many years on this project. Also, the late Irv Piliavin, Gerald Marwell, Jane Collins, Franklin Wilson, Julie D'Acci, Nina Eliasoph, and Bert Adams (all from the University of Wisconsin).

Also, Harry Edwards, Michael Eric Dyson and Cornell West, Earl Smith, John Loy, Douglas Hartmann, Herb Simons, Mitch Duneier, Herb Foster, Herman Blake, Joe Feagin, Gerda Lerner, Yevonne Smith, Gary Sailes, Eldon Snyder, Elmer Spreitzer, and Walter Allen. With all this hands-on and conversational help, you'd think I would have finished faster.

A special thanks to professors who served as friends and soldiers in writing, who discussed my project or otherwise gave support—too many to include by name—but I need to start with Robert Burton, who read draft after draft and offered great encouragement over the years. Others aided the cause, including Jennifer Frost and Paul Taillon in New Zealand, my good friend and scholar Andrew Flescher, whose East Coast teeth bit into the manuscript more than once. Others provided advice, including Compton's own Mario Sims, Darrell Motley

Newton, Kevin Glynn, Fritz Polite, Keith Harrison, Herman Gray, Rick Rigsby, Richard Majors, Ben Carrington, Sarah Pike, and Laird Easton.

Others served as readers or people willing to have extensive conversations, including Derek Greenfield and Bob Speer, my first editor. Tim Wise, Dave Zirin and Joe Feagin provided inspiration, while Stephen Colbert, David Letterman, Chris Rock and Dave Chappelle provided a backdrop of insightful humor.

Wanda Benson, and the rest of my Benson, Andrews, Clifton, Smith, Thrower and Pettis family (yes you, Stacey and Gary) helped push me through graduate school, and have waited patiently for the finish line, including my biggest supporter and reader of every draft—Myron Clifton, my nephew. My big brother and constant supporter, Bill Andrews, is always there … and a warm shout-out to my late mother and father, who could not make trip into the end-zone with me. The same for my three beautiful, inspirational sisters, Betty, Floy and Kathy, resting in peace. Much love.

My original editor, Susan Malone, gave wisdom and writing help and the kind of general enthusiasm and support I thought didn't exist anymore. She's a Cowboy fan, but I'm okay with that. To fans everywhere who live and die with their teams each week, we are the true owners of sports franchises. They are OUR teams. If we truly knew our commercial potential, we'd start a Fan's Union and institute our fair share of power at the bargaining table.

Special thanks to the University of Wisconsin and Barry Alvarez for allowing access to his players, Canterbury University (and my many readers and friends) in New Zealand, and both California State University, Chico, and San Jose State University for supporting my work over the years. My students in my classes have been big critics of racial intolerance and big supporters of equality. My White students have come around to seeing the benefit of acknowledging White privilege as I see my male privilege in ways I didn't before women made me self-aware. My seminar students reviewed my Kaepernick chapter and gave solid advice, especially Tyra Burks, Kimani Davis II, Thomas Gastelum, Robin Miki, Shaina Olmedo, Camelia Rahmati, and our French import, Arlyne Vermilas. A special thanks to Ruby Ferguson for her tireless efforts as my genius research assistant.

And lastly, my partner (and now wife) Erin Hannigan—thank you for your support and for being right by my side as I crossed the finish line. It is my sincere hope that the racial strife we see in the USA and around the world can somehow be lessened by dedicated public servants like you, Erin. And also by the solutions to racial strife and coachable lessons herein centered on the freedom of expression.

Vernon L. Andrews

2020

Introduction

Meet Your New Neighbor, Richard Sherman

Sport is a microcosm of society. What we see played out in society will likely be played out in a nation's sport, and what transgressions and restrictions we see played out in sport will likely be transpiring within society. This book explores how conflicts over diversity, culture, inclusion, exclusion and control have been played out over the twentieth century in various sports and institutions, and what lessons we can learn from our overlapping—though at times, separate—cultural histories of Black and White. This book is about how we learn to act when out in public … and when playing sport. Infused in this discussion is the ever-present policing of Black bodies in sport and society, and the disconnect we have as citizens living in the same country perpetually divided by race.

Everybody is just a little bit different from each other. We see evidence of this as we interrogate every social interaction, every day. Those differences are not the problem—it's what we *make* of those differences. By way of example, what if Richard Sherman moved into your White neighborhood?[1] He'd start unloading a large rented van with the aid of a couple of friends while blasting *Public Enemy's* "Welcome to the Terrordome" social activist hip-hop music. They would be loud-talking and laughing. Maybe with the aid of a beer or two—before the pepperoni, mushroom and pineapple pizza arrives. As you peeked from across the street behind your cultural curtains, your thoughts, if you lived in an all-White community, might be, "What the hell do we have here? Honey, should I call the cops?"

Sure, Sherman is from the heart of Los Angeles. He would know better than to wear a "Straight Outta Compton" tee shirt on moving day. He wouldn't want to cause his new neighbors alarm. Too late. He's Black, with long braids, which signifies Sherman visually as a "threat" to the peace. But wait. Sherman is also a Stanford graduate and is, as the media would say, "articulate." You call the cops, of course. But they reply that "Mr. Sherman already notified us that in the case of a neighbor calling, we should notify all parties that he has purchased the home and is not robbing the residence. Stay calm and carry on with your day."

After Sherman kindly introduces himself to your family (with a fresh peach cobbler delivered to your door) and you caught a glimpse of his Stanford logo tee-shirt, you might chuckle in relief and say, "Whew! Mr. Sherman, I thought for a minute you were that guy on TV yelling into the camera all that thug stuff after the Seahawks beat the Forty Niners in the playoffs in 2014! You had me scared there for a minute. Because that guy is from Compton!"

Sherman might sense your racial disconnect—and then reconnect with you with a bit of genius that all Black folks of any status have to engage in. He'd laugh with you and say, "Yeah, that was me. I was a bit fired up." Sherman would own every side of himself.

In that moment you would be allowed your natural White-American Eleven O'clock news-induced fears. These fears were magnified back in 2014 with the continual headlines of Black athletes, most notably football players Ray Rice and Adrian Peterson, in trouble for spousal abuse and child abuse. *Bad Boys,* the name of a long-forgotten cop show, highlighted Black men chased, captured, and then put into handcuffs. This theme—and this fear of Black men—has a long history in the USA. Throw in a Black man who claims a city/area like Compton or South-Central L.A., Oakland, Detroit, Houston or Baltimore, and your TV fears, and you'd be forgiven if your blood-pressure rose a bit. Unless you had many Black friends, co-workers and acquaintances. Unless you were awake to the many shades and social flavors of Blackness. Or as the kids say, unless you were "woke."

You might also walk away shaking your head and asking, "Will the real Richard Sherman please stand up?" Is he the "thug" fans and some media labeled him? Is he the taunting, chest-thumping, overly expressive Black athlete many in America loved to hate? Or is he the sharp-witted, well-spoken, educated man who serves as a role model to both Black and White youth? Is he the embodiment of the rags-to-riches, ghetto-to-superstar, Compton-to-Stanford-to-the-NFL "bootstraps" story America loves to point to as a sign of U.S. equality of opportunity? He might be a little of both. He might be *a lot* of both.

Whatever Richard Sherman might be in his private life, in his public life he represents an America enigma, embodying both what is most loved ("he made it out of the ghetto and he is a model for his people") and what is most hated ("if he would just learn to behave and act like a gentleman on the field, then I would respect his people more. Until then, he's a thug"). He hits at the core of the love/hate relationship America has always had with African American culture since the Civil Rights Act and taps into the love/hate relationship and disconnect Black people have with American White culture forever. To be sure, not *all* White people.

While White people, concerned with social decorum, are perpetually asking, "Why can't they behave," Black people are asking, as Whites did after 9/11, "Why do they hate us?" The study of sports culture serves here as a microcosm of the conflicts between Blacks and Whites in other institutional settings in America. "Policing" is an overarching term I use to exemplify the ever-present ways American society sharply, daily, works to keep Black people in check for "inappropriate" behavior.

Every day people "police" our behavior. Sometimes the real police get involved when peering eyes sense we are "out of place" when walking, talking, asking for coffee, sitting in a dormitory lounge, barbequing, moving into the neighborhood, or otherwise "breathing while black." This policing happens annually in sports, too, as you will see in this manuscript. And while rules governing Black behavior in sport are not quite the overseer's cracking whip during slavery, the intended effect is the same: Stay in line.

Black individuality and expression in sport and society challenge traditional White behavioral rules centered on humble respectability. Yet there is a growing diversity of fans that love the insertion of *American individuality* in the context of team sports. Some corporations love unique Black expression, which is why advertisers use Black expressive gestures and language in television commercials, as do networks when they promote upcoming sporting events.

Where humility and mild-mannered celebration are the White norm, Black—and some White athletes—have chosen to cross the social boundaries and express joy, elation, style, and individuality after successful plays. This book peeks behind the curtain of Blackness and Whiteness in America to expose how we think about our bodies and behavior in sport and society. And while points of connectivity between Black and White are becoming more present every day, there is still a racial disconnect with many people who want America to be like it was in the 1950s: "Traditional."

Expression and Resistance Over Time

Across sports and down through history, African American athletes have expressed individuality, political resistance, culture, and improvised sportsmanship—and quite often in very different ways from White athletes. Resistance to racism existed long before Clippers owner Donald Sterling decided he didn't want Magic Johnson—and other Black people—to be visible at his team's games at the Staples Center in Los Angeles.

Athletes in the four national playoff games on April 29, 2014, decided to boycott all games if a stern edict was not handed down by the (then) freshly minted new commissioner of the NBA, Adam Silver. Fortunately for everyone involved (except Mr. Sterling), the boycott was avoided by giving the racist team owner the equivalent of the Basketball Death Penalty—a hefty fine, a lifetime ban from basketball, and a resolve to force the sale of the team to new ownership. When roughly eighty percent of the NBA is African American, resistance to the *policing of Black fans* in Los Angeles can be swift.

The athletes did not have to bring the "boycott" hammer down, but they could have. In the previous Clippers game, players chose to show their resistance with uniforms turned inside out so as to hide the team logo—logos they now saw as shameful. Tommy Smith, John Carlos, Lee Evans, and others from the 1968 Mexico Olympics would have been proud that their legacy of activism and expressive protest lives on. This was all a lead-up to Colin Kaepernick's protest in 2016.

The most significant expressive figure of protest and expression and model for contemporary athletes is the 1960s radical Muhammad Ali—who many called a "loudmouth" during his time for disturbing the implicit physical and verbal expressive "peace" between Black athletes and American society. Ali was policed right out of boxing for a few years.

Today, with our *year 2020 vision*, we have a clearer understanding of the historical context of Ali's forcefulness and verbal dexterity and can better see the social, racial, political, commercial, and religious reasons for his brash behavior. This book strives to reframe contemporary "unsportsmanlike" behavior by African American professional and college football players in a more historic, individualist, and sometimes activist, framework. At the same time and of equal importance is to interrogate our ideas of "normal" behavior and White power in framing contemporary arguments and constructing rules about correct and incorrect ("illegal") sport and social behavior.

The book centers on an analysis of Black and White cultural norms and behavioral values in the context of collegiate and professional football. Both the NFL and NCAA have instituted "conduct" rules against many forms of physical expression, most especially centered on touchdown celebrations. Considered "excessive celebration" and illegal in collegiate football, these acts are penalized fifteen yards. These same acts are often penalized and even fined in the NFL—until very recently, as noted in the forward to this book. The NFL has the right to enforce or relax rules in any given season at its discretion. Author's prediction: Those rules will change again. Bet on it. Because those celebration rules are still in the rule books. They have been "relaxed." Power dances to its own self-serving beat.

Both the NFL and NCAA cite that "all" athletes who break expression rules are penalized. This is only fair, of course, and keeping with the American ideal of equal treatment before the law. However, while rules appear overarching and equal in their intent, the effect of sanctions is primarily on those athletes who traditionally have exhibited those targeted behaviors—most often, African Americans.

While the focus of the book is on celebration and celebration rules, what is born out through intensive interviews with athletes, fan surveys, media scrutiny, and historical research is that codes of social and sporting conduct vary by neighborhood, gender, sexuality, class, city, state, region of the country, and especially racial/cultural groups. What is acceptable by one demographic group or individual may be beyond the boundary for another. This expressive dissonance—the trouble with accepting the expressive behavioral codes of other groups despite realizing we all have the right to exercise our "freedom of expression"—works both ways.

We all have trouble at times accepting the behaviors of others outside of—or even within—our social group. I've found that many White people are far more woke than some Black folks. We need to check ourselves, too. I check myself every time I see a young man with sagging pants. Just because I don't understand it doesn't mean it is altogether bad or should be illegal. I simply choose not to do it myself. My 1970s bell-bottoms and platform shoes and nine-inch afro might look odd to him today. We were expressing our potential growth and newfound "bigness" in society after Civil Rights—our hair was bigger, our bodies were taller and our pants legs wider. Norms about clothing and hairstyles are not static—they change as eras change. Which is to imply that back then many people, Black and White, didn't like our "bigness" at all. Aware of this, I work to diffuse my negative attitude towards behaviors I don't employ or agree with.

One finding from interviews and fan surveys is that *attitudes* about expressive athletes vary between Black and White players. Imagine that. Black athletes—even those who were not as expressive as others, like former All-Pro Al Toon—showed a high level of tolerance of the individuality and celebration styles of both Black *and* White athletes. Quite often, the more outrageous the act, the more both groups didn't concur with the behavior. But for on-field behaviors that would otherwise warrant policing and a penalty, Black athletes were showed sympathy with the individual and did not demonize the act or player.

White players would often side with the game rules and the implied "equal" application by referees. "We all have to follow the same rules," was the general thought, "And if you break the rules, you should be penalized." This finding points to how some Whites, but not most, believe in the implied fairness of social rules and that powerful committees serve a vital function by constructing "universal rules" based on the most acceptable norms of social behavior—that *anyone* would agree on. Other White athletes thought some celebration rules, well, "sucked."

A Study in Black Male Expression in Sport Over Time

This is a study over time, over the decades. My study looks at one topic, Black male expression, through various lenses in society over five decades. The story began in 1972 on a track field in Oakland. I saw a race that changed the way I look at sport and everyday life. In the 1980s I decided to pursue a doctorate degree in sociology, and specifically sport after I heard a player on Wisconsin's team described as "retarded" and "street" by his basketball coach primarily because of the student-athletes post-game celebrations.

In the 1990s I interviewed numerous athletes in an attempt to understand the racial disconnect. How were people raised to express themselves socially? What do Black and White athletes think about celebratory expression in football? You will hear White twenty-year-old athletes speak about race in 1994—knowing that in 2020 they will be over forty-five years old and, possibly, view their own policing of athletes quite differently.

In the 2000s, I conducted research with a UC Berkeley professor as we surveyed students and student-athletes trying to figure out how Whites processed the love of hockey fights compared to the hatred of the touchdown dance, in addition to what they thought about race as a factor in the making of celebration rules. And in the same decade, I interviewed an Olympic swimmer about her homeland, New Zealand, in an effort to figure out why New Zealanders were so humble—and why they thought U.S. White athletes were "over the top" and arrogant.

In the decade of the 2010s, since back in the USA, I've attended professional football and baseball games, viewed thousands of hours of televised sport, presented and debated papers at conferences, and recorded U.S. media commentary on rules and norms on race and athlete "arrogance." The book thus serves as a time capsule of the critique of African American cultural expression—especially as it relates to males in sport—over the past fifty years.

Over the years, I've travelled to Madison Wisconsin, Christchurch New Zealand, Australia, Scotland, Wales, England and Eton College with a huge question mark above my head as I tried to crack the code of behavioral choice and attitudes, to fit together the pieces of a cultural jigsaw puzzle about parents and norms they instill, and to make sense of unwritten rules and social codes of behavior that worked against my upbringing.

I frame my background as Black working-class, Oakland public school-raised, and later as college-educated, and public relations manager at a high-technology firm in Silicon Valley, where I occasionally defaulted to my own cultural style that clashed with corporate style. We all look to our own backgrounds, neighborhoods, parents, and education when we interrogate the correctness or incorrectness of sports behavior—which complicates how we label those from different backgrounds. I include intensive interviews with White athletes in this study because we, as African Americans, make mistakes in labeling Whites who don't share our background and history. I thoroughly enjoyed my deep dive into White family culture, rural America, and White interrogation of rules and Black behavior.

Limitations of the Study and Frame of This Book

This book is neither exhaustive nor definitive. That is, there are many issues that intersect with the book and could enhance my arguments but are not included, primarily due to the sheer volume of space needed and time dedication: (1) a thorough analysis of the protestant work ethic in relation to White and Black norms of behavior, (2) a complete review of Black women in sport down through history and how African American women are similar yet uniquely different in their socio-cultural histories and expressive styles from Black men, (3) a review of Historically Black Colleges and Universities (HBCUs) and their teams and expressive bands, which privilege unique styles and break down the fourth wall between athlete, bands, and fans, (4) high school sports in various regions of the country, and how coaches in Texas differ from football coaches in northern California or Florida or West Virginia, (5) a complete analysis of the NCAA and NFL rules and committees and administration over the years and in-depth analysis of rules changes, (6) a more in-depth analysis of sport in England, including soccer and rugby, and especially the "wall game" as I observed it in Eton on my trip to their archives, (7) other groups, such as Latinos in sport, and how their experiences and sports styles and culture intersect with African American culture, and (8) a review and critique of issues of machismo and spousal abuse by athletes and child-rearing practices and conflicts between African Americans and Whites in America. These aspects I would hope my colleagues would take up and run with and expand upon in future scholarly work.

This book is by no means definitive. Rather, it is designed to be a review of the field and a continuation of the ongoing discussion of sport and issues involving sportsmanship, athlete celebration styles and cultural expression. This book is but a small example of the many conversations that go on daily throughout the world on appropriate social behavior by athletes in and around sport. As such, the many topics I am approached about and which I feel are vital in any broader discussion of sport and politics, are not discussed in great detail herein.[2]

I lived my early years in predominantly Black enclaves in a very political and policed Oakland, California, which gave me unfettered access to all things Black, including African American west coast ways of expressing and behaving in sport and society. I come from a large Bay Area family of roughly eighty Black cousins, aunts, uncles, nephews, nieces, and siblings that has shown me by example the complexity of every day Black life. My high school—Castlemont—at my graduation in 1976 had roughly 2,000 students, and only 12 or so who were White, Asian, and Mexican American. Blackness was the water I swam in for years until arriving in nearly all-White Chico, California, right next door to the (now) *Camp Fire* demolished town of Paradise.

While in Chico, then later Palo Alto and Madison, Wisconsin, I became intimately familiar with White culture on a daily basis. Thus, there is a Black/White frame to this book, partly to do with my own background but mostly to do with what I see as the epicenter of cultural disconnect over appropriate behavior in sport between the two dominant cultural groups in American sport, White Americans and African Americans. These two groups are the last to fully integrate in America outside of the sporting arena. We could have anticipated post-Civil Rights Movement racial clashes and battles over the freedom of cultural expression in sport—as in every other U.S. institutional framework.

The focused viewing of the issue of sports conduct centered on nationality and race might help us in pushing the "reset" button on *sportsmanlike* and *sportswomanlike* conduct. With hope, we can work toward conceptualizing cultural adaptation for everyone. What would a culturally adaptable code of sports conduct look like? I don't have the answer, but I think an idealized concept of "sportsmanship" comes closer to existence by discussing how various cultures view sport.

Another cultural framework is important to this work, and that is the frame of social class and the growing divergence among the Black middle-class from otherwise urban and "lower-class" ideas of sporting behavior and appropriate social behavior in general. That micro-level social-change arena is where we will later discuss norms and customs about good and bad behavior.

True inclusion into the rule-making process—and cultural flexibility by organizations such as the NFL and NCAA—would be a step in the right direction. This book might not change your view of Richard Sherman, but it might aid in your understanding that he represents no threat. The greater threat still resides with people like Donald Sterling who refused to let time, integration, and cultural knowledge change his cemented and disconnected views on why Black people at sporting arenas need to be policed.

Figure I.1. Richard Sherman can now celebrate an interception with his new team, the Forty Niners, thanks to Kaepernick and other brave citizens who kneeled during the national anthem. Let's hope progress with policing keeps us safe outside of those white lines. Source: Cody Glenn/Icon Sportswire/Getty Images

Notes

1. I capitalize both the word Black and White in this essay. John Fiske notes that "Black" has earned the capital over the years with 'blood, sweat and tears' (personal conversation, 1994). I capitalize White in this essay as I no longer want Whites to be hidden. That lower-case white allows for visual normality, for a blending in will most other words in a sentence. White stands out, stands up, is noticed, is out in the open—in your face. I see you. My White students feel uncomfortable with White so tall and visible. But I tell them that White isn't about them as individuals, it's social, it can be oppressive, it can control. Whites can also help. But insisting that everyone else is "a culture" and "a group" while denying your own part in the process is, well, very White. Criminal suspects are noted in the evening news if they are Black, Latino, or Asian. If no race of the subject is mentioned, we should all presume as viewers that they are "normal" and need not be mentioned. They are White. Just say it. With a capital W.
2. That said, there are two bits of "Dancing with White politics" that do warrant addressing. I do believe that the ever-expressive "N" word should be banned on the NFL field of play, primarily because of the "workplace" argument and the message it sends to Whites about the acceptable use of the word. No qualifications, such as "Well, we tell whites they can't use it but we can; that should be enough." It isn't enough. See Jonathan Martin verses Richie Incognito as exhibit A. We have plenty of other places to use the word. And I see how we use it in a very different way than Whites can. I have no issue with the use of the word in all-Black company, though I do understand that even this concession can be problematic for our collective self-esteem. Despite the great argument put forth by Michael Wilbon of ESPN, that Whites should have "no say" in the process, I disagree. Yes, Whites should have a say in the process. My reasoning? They invented the word. They have a right to say, "enough," if to nobody but White players like Riley "I will fight every nigger here" Cooper, who in July 2014 used this phrasing at a Kenny Chesney concert. When the N-word is used in a context like this, it hurts. Actually, it cuts to the bone. So for me, it is personal. Others can understand and accept this type of usage by Whites, but I can't. And I am for doing something to prevent it. Sorry for being the N-word police.

   Policing Team Names: The Washington Football Team. Choosing a name for your child is a form of expression. Actually, it is a celebration of life and hope for the future yet to come. Teams chooses names for similar reasons. To celebrate their local heritage or customs or nearby animals. Like Bears, and Pelicans and Dolphins and Teams can choose racist names, also. Awful names that mock Native American life and culture. Even names that are derogatory and offensive and hurtful. We should consider the past when we choose names. The NFL football team from Washington chose a name that offended a huge section of our native population in the USA. And ownership—and many fans—were non-apologetic. In fact, they are doubled down on the name and dug trenches of resistance rather than stepping up, like Stanford University and the University of Miami-Ohio (see below) and others have done, by saying: "Well, if this is in anyway offensive to millions of people, we now are smart enough—and socially conscious enough—to change." Instead, the team—via its owner—seemed to be saying, "This is our history—our tradition—and you simply don't understand. This is Washington Business. Stay out of it." Well, I do understand. I see such behavior all the time. I live in California, and I've noticed a trend here. Cut almond trees down—rename the strip mall "Almond Orchard Strip Mall." I see walnut trees chopping to the ground and the new apartment complex in its place named the "Walnut Tree Apartments." Sacramento Airport's new B Terminal has a giant jackrabbit as its central art piece. Guess who was likely displaced to make room for the new wing? I live near Coyote Valley Golf Course in Morgan Hill, California. Not too many coyotes running along Highway 101 these days. Atlanta has a whole lot of "Peachtree" this and that, and I'm guessing most have been eliminated to make room for progress in the "Peach State." This pattern of killing animals, trees and other fauna and mockingly renaming the locale after the displaced is an ironic blind-spot we Americans rarely notice. We buy into the belief that our nostalgia is saintly. We "honor" those whose ass we've kicked to claim the land—by renaming the place after the kicked. This "honorable naming," of course, is ONLY meant to show respect to the vanished. Of course it is. The important issue of Native Americans and sports team names is vital to our cultural health as a nation. Other teams need to check themselves, namely Cleveland and Atlanta (baseball), the team in our nation's capital should be ashamed of themselves for using that name as long as it did. As Dave Zirin notes in his book, *What's my name, fool?*, "In the old days, trappers would kill a Native American, slice some bloody skin off the top of his head, then put a 'redskin' in their pouch with the deerskin, bearskin, and other nonhuman skins." (Zirin, 2005, p. 158)

But team ownership, and their fans who buried their hog heads in the sand, had no shame. And they have zero respect for Native American culture. Yes, I said it, zero. We laughed in the face of years of stolen land and culture and dignity. We are all guilty of looking the other way at that crime, truth be told. And we are all the beneficiaries of those crimes. Black folks, included. There is no way to justify the use of that football team's name that does not include a hard slap in the face of Native Americans, along with a scream that: "We don't care what you think about our use of this obviously racist name—we don't respect you anyway. You are dead to us!" I further didn't know what to think about African Americans who played for Washington and looked the other way, as if the only issue they need to be concerned with is their paychecks. I know, "Don't hate the player, hate the game." I am guilty, too. I worked in Corporate PR when Hewlett-Packard Company did business in South Africa, Apartheid South Africa. We had good justifications for being there, we chimed. May South African Blacks loved us being there. Well, at least those Blacks who worked in our sales office. Easier to agree with a behavior when you benefit directly. I got a nice check in Palo Alto, every two weeks. I kept my head down with most others saying, "it is not our problem.' So, I'm putting myself on blast as guilty of doing exactly what you are doing, those Black and White, who look the other way. It IS our problem. But I do recall the position African American athletes took when Arizona refused to institute a holiday for Martin Luther King. You took a stance. And the NFL listened. They cancelled the Super Bowl in Arizona. And Arizona, suddenly, decided an MLK day was – surprise! – a good idea. And the Superbowl came back to Phoenix. The Washington Wizards used to be the Washington Bullets. Someone saw the irony of having a warhead of death as the main symbol of a city riddled by murder. Change can help remove some of the pain—and all of the irony. There are two African American beacons of light, Hall of Fame receiver Art Monk and Hall of Fame cornerback Darrell Green (see below). "[If] Native Americans feel like R******s or the Chiefs or [another] name is offensive to them, then who are we to say to them 'No, it's not'?" said Monk. Darrell Green ads: "It deserves and warrants conversation because somebody is saying, 'Hey, this offends me.'" Monk and Green, you were both right. Once, while living in New Zealand, I met a White guy from Los Angeles while waiting in line at the latest hip club. He kept saying, "Nigga" this and "Nigga" that. I said, "I feel very uncomfortable with you using that word so comfortably around me." He said, "Ain't no thang. I got a bunch of black friends in L.A. and we use Nigga all the time with each other. I respect black people." I told him, "If you respected black people, then he would listen to the black person standing in front of you in line and not use that word. Else, your 'respect' is just lip service." I wasn't mad or angry or in fight-mode. I was reasonable. He stopped talking. Listened. Then said, "You are right. I'm sorry." We were cool after that. This racist and disrespectful symbol changed because the NFL listened. To Black people. And finally, to Native American voices. So expect a great PR campaign when the team finally chooses a new mascot name, something to the tune of: "This change was a long time coming. We know our previous name wounded many people. We are doing our part to be a positive symbol in our nation's capital. We welcome a chance to embrace the new era of the 'Washington Redtails' (or whatever). Now get out there and buy our new jersey!" http://espn.go.com/.../art-monk-darrell-green-washington-reds... http://nacc.stanford.edu/mascot.html http://miamioh.edu/.../miami-tribe-re.../mascot-story/index.html

1

"Act Like You've Been There Before!"

The Age-Old White Taunt of Privilege

There is no more powerful position than that of being "just" human. The claim to power is the claim to speak for the commonality of humanity … The point of seeing the racing of Whites is to dislodge them/us from the position of power, with all of the inequalities, oppression, privileges, and sufferings in its train, dislodging them/us by undercutting the authority with which they/we speak and act in and on the world.[1]

On Being Human—and Humble

Picture this: Two people sitting on a park bench. A man dressed in red has a large cartoonish *exclamation* mark over his head. He is on the left. The other person, a woman dressed in green on the right, has a large cartoonish *question mark* hovering above her head. They talk. Well, the guy on the left *talks* as the woman on the right *listens*. More and more, louder and louder, the guy in red on the left talks. His exclamation mark gets bolder and larger. The woman in green on the right shrugs in despair and her question mark remains. In fact, it gets smaller.

This goes on for minutes, hours, days, years, decades, and centuries until something crazy happens. The woman in green on the right—question mark-woman—gets up, yells many things, points at the guy in red, says a few more heated words, and then stomps off. As she walks off dressed in green, an exclamation mark suddenly appears above her head where the question mark once resided. She turns around and notices that the man in red now has a large question mark above his head. They go their separate ways.

This is pretty much a history of White and Black interaction in America.[2] That woman on the right in green—question-mark woman—she's Black. For decades she listened to the hypocritical rhetoric of equality until she had enough. She morphed into an emboldened Rosa Parks, got up, told the man in red man where to go, and then rode her imaginary bus toward freedom. On her way out of the park and in clear eyeshot of exclamation-mark man in red, she did an end-zone dance. She was happy.

She had remained quiet in mind and body far too long. She now inhaled the "freedom to express" that the exclamation-mark man in red had enjoyed all these many years on the park bench. She took small comfort in seeing the man in red's new question mark above his head grow larger with each liberating step away from him she took in her newfound freedom.

Oh, there was one instant—maybe a second or so—that the man in red got his exclamation mark back. In that instant the woman in green halted, turned to look over her shoulder, and noticed it also. She also noticed the question mark above her own head was back. But after that instant, they both returned to the previous state—the man in red with a growing question mark and the woman in green—leaving the park, with her ever-growing new exclamation mark. What did the man on the left in red scream in that millisecond? *"Act like you've been there before! Act like you've had an exclamation mark before!"*

In point of fact, the woman leaving the park in green had not. She had always been the quiet, acquiescing, humble, question mark. She would, after a time, enjoy being an exclamation mark, and even come to revel in it. Being an exclamation mark felt great to the woman in green because she had always been a question mark. The man in red on the left felt little comfort in being a question mark and indeed showed his discomfort every chance he got. Where once he was arrogant and unforgiving, he now stewed in humility. He was used to expressing—and now this continual questioning truly rocked his world. Had he thought about it, and not been so arrogant, he could have asked the woman in green, "How do you live the life of a humble question mark? Teach me!

Acting verses Being

A common saying is uttered hundreds of times on sofas every weekend across America whenever a Black athlete gets exuberant after scoring a touchdown. The phrase is primarily directed at African American football players in collegiate or professional sport. Announcers will say it, ex-athletes will say it, coaches will say it, and fans will say it. Even righteous African Americans will say it on occasion. The phrase, almost always uttered by White viewers of sport is, "Act like you've been there before." In short:

> Don't get so excited if you score a touchdown or sack the quarterback or make a good tackle. Act like this is not the first time you have achieved in life. Be professional and maintain some dignity, and act like this is par for the course for you and your family. Be a bit more humble and less arrogant about your success.

The Phrase (as "Act like you've been there before" will be referred to) is interpreted on a humble/arrogance scale and has become part of the anti-celebratory-expression lingo by sports announcers, fans, players, and coaches. The most honorable thing for an athlete to do, if we obey the "been there before" narrative, is to hand the ball to the referee after a touchdown and non-emotively shuffle off to the sidelines.

But while "acting like you have been there before" might be a valid way of behaving after success in sport, it is but *one* way of behaving. Other interpretations of appropriate behavior in sporting contexts are equally as valid. Black athletes and everyday citizens have historically *not* had access or experience of the high level of success in social institutions that Whites have experienced, and as such social and sporting success might mean more in the greater context of our lives. Given our interconnected history in America, you'd think White citizens would expect that success means more to Black people than it means, historically speaking, to White people. There is a severe disconnect from American history when you tell us to behave like you behave, because "success is normal in everyday life."

What is interpreted as arrogance by Black athletes (by not acting like they've been there) is often the reverse—a flourish of happiness in the face of humble origins. Likewise, what is interpreted as humility by White athletes speaks to the reverse scenario—a show of ordinariness in the face of a past complete with success and power and, some would say, social arrogance.

After the Civil War ended and four million freed Black people celebrated, their former masters were likely upset, yelling that the slaves were "showing them up." And there was at least one owner who said, "Act like you've had freedom before!"

In 1954, when the U.S. Supreme Court overthrew the 1896 Plessey vs. Ferguson "separate but equal" lie, Black people celebrated again, likely to Whites in the Jim Crow south who taunted them with, "Act like you've had equal schooling before!" Of course they would say that.

Yet again, in 1964, once the United States decided to actually enforce the 1954 verdict with signed law and military enforcement of desegregation, Blacks once again danced in the streets, praising America for finally ending its hypocrisy and thereby becoming "the land of the free." No doubt there were thousands of Whites wondering why on earth Black people danced and cried and celebrated being able to use the best bathrooms, water faucets, swank hotels, and eat at ordinary restaurants alongside Whites. I can hear it as if it was yesterday, "Act like you've eaten a cheeseburger on a counter at Woolworths before!"

"Yes, I guess I could pretend. It is, after all, just a cheeseburger at Woolworths," would have been my answer. Followed by, "It tastes so good because it's awesome to feel this kind of freedom."

And so it has been with this taunt of The Phrase down through history, and even today in sport. White people—and even Black people who have jumped on the bandwagon—utter this phrase every weekend while watching sports in America.

The Phrase is attributed to the former National Football League (NFL) coach Paul Brown. This chapter is not intended to question Paul Brown's original intent or his views on celebration. That intent may never be known, though we can reason to guess that Paul Brown preferred his athletes to move as quickly and quietly as they could to the sidelines after scoring. Paul Brown's utterance has taken on a life of its own in the policing narratives of announcers, coaches, athletes, and fans.

But my specific reading of The Phrase from an African American male perspective is a reading from *below* of a White middle-class way of life (*of having been there*) only imagined.

Let's re-read The Phrase and its possible meanings as we look at "White ways" as a set of behaviors in sport and society. Blacks in sports, in contrast, are read in the text as *not* having been there (the greater end zone of social success) before and *not* enjoying the same historical privileges of bodily movement.

The Phrase represents a White taunt. We typically think of taunting as a specific Black activity in sport. In a Black context, the intent of taunting is to frustrate, embarrass, shame, or make fun of an athlete so as to negatively shift his/her behavior. Taunting can be considered psychological warfare in sport.

"Act like you've been there before" is a taunt of privilege, and its intent is also to embarrass, shame, or make fun of an athlete. The Phrase is psychological warfare against the "wrong element" (read, urban expressive Black male) creeping into sport. In this sense, The Phrase is intended to "instruct." The Phrase would point to Black taunting as negative and destructive. And therein you have the beauty of the power to define: Black people taunt—White people instruct. Black people "loot" after Hurricane Katrina and White people "find food."[3] Social power can marginalize one norm and privilege another.

To "reclaim" a phrase, a traditionally marginalized social group redefines a negative characterization into a positive one. "Bitch," "fag," and "coconut" are terms that come to mind that have been reclaimed by women, gays, and Pacific Islanders, respectively. But I don't want to reframe the negative association with Black taunting as a "positive." I'd like to suggest a different reading of *The Phrase* from a White definition of "social instruction" to a "taunt." Let's call a spade a spade.

We need to rebrand "Act Like You've Been There Before" to be exactly what it is—a nasty taunt intended to verbally punish Blacks by those who feel all people should act the same way they do ... as their parents did ... and their parents before them did.

There is no intent to suggest we should all *like* end-zone dancing, crazy slam-dunks, or slow home-run trots. It is fine to dislike celebration, showboating, and such. Like you, I don't like many of the expressive acts in I see in sports. I even think it is fine to shout at the TV or the athlete about whatever might cross your mind. But just know that when you shout, "Act like you've been there before," you're just ripping a mad fart because not everybody was raised by *your* parents and *your* grandparents. And that smell left behind? That's the smell of un-American ethnocentrism.[4]

That's the same smell most first-wave (Northern, Western European) and second wave (Southern and Eastern) immigrants had to get used to as they were stripped of their culture upon arrival in America. This is often the American reaction when confronted with cultural and racial difference—and most recently, religious (Muslim) difference. You also saw it with the responses to Kaepernick's kneeling for the anthem.

For privileged Whites (most Whites are not wealthy, but I am speaking of social privilege) and others (including Blacks) to instruct Black athletes via The Phrase *with malice* from a position of social power and privilege—as if everyone enjoyed those same powers and privileges—is to not only taunt, but to also position Whiteness as a "truth" and "authentic" and to *once again marginalize the Black experience of life, liberty, and the freedom to socially express* in all our varied (often policed) forms as un-American. The implied all-American and middle/upper-class consciousness in *The Phrase* pretends Black and White histories are the same. If not in society, then at least in sport.

As a matter of fact, the implication is that there is no history; there is only this moment in the end-zone, and whatever cultural history you might have as an athlete should be left on the sidelines, or in the parking lot, or outside the city. White history is everywhere at all times and is neutral and is only intended to instruct those who have not received proper instruction in how things should be done. Or rather, "I'm trying to help you out here!"

In truth, our histories were so divergent as to be considered two nations, as Thomas Hacker put in the title of his book, *Two Nations: Black and White, Separate, Hostile, Unequal.* This suggests that different social histories have led to distinctly different cultural discussions of the body. Acting like you have been there before verses *rarely having been there* are two competing narratives based on two differing historical dialogues with sport. The Black historical past informs present ways Black people articulate with the body in sport. So too does the White historical past inform how Whites articulate—and how *Whites taunt*—about "proper" ways to behave.

The phrase "act like you've been there before," though stated without historical context, is embedded within an invisible implied matrix: White Anglo Saxon Protestant (WASP) ways of knowing the body in sport that speak to downplaying individualized joyous emotion and physical enthusiasm at otherwise (well, to many) celebratory and expressive moments.

This knowledge of continuity—of "being there before"—comes from a social history that is unfamiliar or rare to the African American experience. That is, *we haven't been here before*, or at least not that long. We are experiencing—in the form of outward social expression—very new and unfamiliar territory, both in interracial sport and interracial society. By contrast, Black athletes and entertainers have enjoyed a long history of expression on Black-only teams and in predominantly Black social spaces such as churches, universities, and musical venues.[5]

Black people express themselves in life and in sports in ways that both converge and diverge with White behavioral patterns.[6] Black folks have a different knowledge of sport and sportsmanship than do mainstream Whites. Most African Americans have an unspoken understanding of the complex forms of Black expression. It appears more and more young Whites are starting to understand Black expression and agree that cultural difference is actually cool.

For many White Americas unfamiliar with Black knowledge of the body and performance, the complexity of gestures and movements and verbal rhythms represents a foreign language, a strange visual discussion unfamiliar to White eyes. It's as if Black expression is so foreign as to be criminal. Joel Dinerstein ironically terms the way Whites view Black end-zone expression as the "illegal use of Black culture."[7] More specific to this study, I'd say what we have is the illegal use of *Black expression*. And policing Black expression is a legacy of slavery and Jim Crow segregated America.

Black expression is legal—as long as we keep it "in house." Beyond the ghetto or Black church is a no-fly zone for Black expression. But more and more, Black actors, comedians, and singers are allowed more freedom to freely (and *Blackly*) express in public and in television shows.[8] And even athletes in pro sports.

The primary focus of my critique has been football's expression rules and the Black male body in sport and society, but Black females share in their knowledge of Black expression and participate. "Loudness" in public may be the Black female's way of counteracting the invisibility of her social standing in relation to Black and White men—and White women—specifically.[9] That said, looking closely at Black female track stars—(the late) Florence Griffith Joyner and Jackie Joyner Kersey specifically, we notice a similar flamboyance, if not in the end-zone, then certainly as expressed on the track field via clothing and hair styles.

Venus and Serena Williams certainly express themselves on and off the tennis court. They began their rise to fame with beads in their long hair (which once spilled onto the tennis court), constantly challenged the norms with their clothing (Venus has her own clothing line). The family even celebrates on the

Figure 1.1. Two sisters, Venus & Serena Williams, celebrating another victory. Source: Gary M Prior/Allsport/Getty Images Sport

court—father Richard Williams once danced courtside, to the chagrin of tennis purists, while Serena once did the "Crip Walk" on Centre Court after a victory at Wimbledon in the 2012 Olympics.

As more women become involved in big-time sport—post Title IX's leveling of the collegiate playing field by allocating equal amounts to men's and women's sports—the more we will see women (of all persuasions) challenging what is the male normative code of *appropriate behavior* in and around sport. I would especially expect to see more women in the WNBA show flamboyance and individuality in style and celebratory expression. Women's college hoops teams, such as Louisville in 2013, began using the "ringed circle" hype-chant before games.

Listen closely to how Black women express their individuality when allowed to sing the national anthem before a major sporting event. Different. Unique. Expressive. African American.

The expressive codes, historical knowledges, and bodily behavior of Black folks have proven difficult for Whites to understand, much less incorporate into sport or their own lives, though the high-five and fist-bump are now at home in White culture. When Terrell Owens scored a touchdown and signed the ball with a Sharpie pen in the end-zone or stands on the Dallas Cowboy Star with arms spread wide, we all laugh and tease the humorous and emotional Terrell. When Chad Johnson (formerly known as Ocho Cinco) did the Irish "Riverdance" after a TD or did the Lambeau Leap in an *away* game in Green Bay—we chuckle, laugh, taunt Johnson with jokes, and throw nachos at our flat screen televisions. It is okay to hate Black or White overly expressive athletes or coaches and mimic their often-awkward behavior.

But beware: The more we mock, the more likely it is that Black or White player will show up on an advertisement doing the same bit of expression. Many Whites, to be sure, love much about Black expression, as we all do to some degree; anything different from the plainness of everyday life.

But we also heard the jibes about Johnson and Owens from the high priests of behavior, White (and Black) sports announcers, and talk-show hosts. They certainly have a right to their own opinions, however narrow the bandwidth.

To be fair, many sportscasters such as Deion Sanders, Michael Irvin, Chris Carter, and many on the crew of SportsCenter love athletes who add spice to the game and give us a reason to laugh or joke at athlete antics and celebration signatures. Chris Berman, Stuart Scott (who almost single-handedly brought urban swagger to sports casting … rest in peace), Michael Wilbon, Tony Kornheiser, Toni Reali, Stephen A. Smith, Dan Le Batard (and especially his father), John Buccigross, Linda Cohn, Neil Everett, Steve Levy, Scott Van Pelt, Rece Davis,

Rich Eisen, Craig Kilborn, and Dan Patrick (some of the above formerly of ESPN) poke playful fun at expressive athletes, never demeaning the athlete or their culture.

I don't mean to act like a yard-monitor in elementary school saying every bit of roughhousing is bad, or the parent who feels every single team should get trophies for putting on a uniform. Rather, I'm the parent who doesn't like to see kids bully other kids nor taunt kids for not having the expensive clothes they "should be" able to afford.

ESPN is sports entertainment. The staff is well aware that their viewers are extremely knowledgeable about sport. Why not make "the news" livelier, fun, interesting? Simply reading the scores would have us in tears of boredom. We want a bit of spice in our eggnog. ESPN moves beyond the action and statistics to break down the fourth wall that separates the twenty-four-hour newscaster from fans. ESPN is to sports what Black expressive athletes are to football, basketball, and baseball. I'll bet that even one or two anchors have a tattoo. Their expression makes the mundane very watchable. See how that works? We don't simply want the scores. We want commentary. Black athletes express with Black bodily commentary.

Expression by athletes in any sport makes a sometimes-mundane event much more fun to report on. Announcers can then add their own individuality to commentary on the event. Each SportsCenter announcer has his or her own unique signature call for a home run or touchdown or three-point play or slam-dunk. How refreshing. I turn on ESPN for the sporting updates. I stay for sportscaster's individuality and flair and humor.

Other, less-humorous sportscasters often use the TD moment to reflect on Paul Brown, *The Phrase*, and "time-honored" ideas of sportsmanship and sportsmanlike conduct that are tied to traditions dating back to English boys' schools and rugby codes, as noted later in Chapter 6. These *Olde English* codes still influence American assessments of on-field behavior, and even extend to the Olympic-games "fair play" norms.[10] These conduct codes extend throughout college and professional football and into other major sports and society in general.[11]

We speak of "poor sportsmanship" or "showing a pitcher up" if an athlete (usually Black) does a home-run trot around the bases. Technical fouls in basketball are given for "trash talking" or hanging on the rim after a slam-dunk. A fancy pass—especially if missed—is called "hot-dogging" or "show-boating." Fair enough. But in these cases, the team penalties are not harsh—maybe a couple of points in basketball or a concussion in baseball after being hit by a pitch on your next time at bat. In football the penalty until 2018 was yardage and often a $1,000 fine. Which is about the time an announcer utters, "He should heed the words of the famous coach Paul Brown and 'act like he's been there before.'" Rules are rules.

The rules about "appropriate behavior" in sport—football specifically—give us a sporting landscape to explore the racial and cultural issues surrounding acceptable social behavior and the genesis of group norms. Though African Americans have been allowed to rub elbows with Whites at lunch counters and shopping malls, and allowed into desegregated classrooms and other social institutions, we still find that we live in two expressive nations. Black Americans, rich, poor, or middle-class, still compete with Whiteness as the norm and are constantly confronted with the challenge of proving our "normality" in order to win access to everyday institutions.[12]

In the most integrated work environment in the United States—collegiate and professional sport—there are still struggles to gain full acceptance. Constant Black awareness of behaviors and White racial stigma can lead to an ever-present stressful double-consciousness in both sport and society.[13] Yes, it is stressful to be a part of "the American freedom to express" and always have your persona vetted by White elites who run the show. We always ask: "Is this *bland enough* for you?"

I laughed aloud when watching an episode of the TV show *Mixology* in 2014 when the White friend says to his Black friend, "I see you in every TV commercial!" The Black guy responds, "Oh. Are you trying to call me the 'non-threatening' Black guy?"

"That's it!" I said through my chuckles. Black men, if we have moved up the ladder in any institution, have to learn the fine art of appearing humble and non-threatening. Unless you are Sean P-Ditty Combs, Ice-T, Dr. Dre, Ice Cube or Snoop Dogg. And even THEY have to play the non-threatening game, to a degree.

Though it is beyond the scope of this essay, many other non-White groups, females, and LGBTQIA+ (hereafter Q+) folks still struggle for both access and equal treatment in American society.[14] And by equal treatment, I not only mean getting in the institutional door—but having your cultural/gendered behavior receive equal respect. Gays and Lesbians, and to a lesser degree transgendered people, are slowly gaining support for their equality in U.S. institutions.

The oppressive historical disconnect between African Americans and Whites remains my primary focus. If the problem of Black-White relations cannot be solved here, as James Jones notes in 1993, it cannot be solved anywhere. With respect to Dr. Jones, I would rather think that if we *can* solve this long-standing problem here, racial conflict can be solved *anywhere.*

Until the signing of the Civil Rights Act in 1965, Black Americans could face severe hardship if they otherwise "stood up" to or "celebrated" in or around Whites. For someone under the age of forty, 1965 is a long time ago. But in the context of American history, this represents one generation of celebratory expression and/or unimpeded social freedom. In a broader historical sense, African Americans have *not* "been there" and "done that" before.

Think about that. Freedom for White males in 1776, and freedom for White women to vote in 1920, and freedom *and* legalized voting rights for the rest of us in 1965. Most White minds are not able to comprehend an America where they would have experienced so little access to freedom. But if you are White and reading this, I want you to imagine that.

Now I would like you to spend one day acting like you have not had freedom since 1776, but, rather, since 1965. Better yet, pretend this is pre-1965 America. Look no White person in the eye. Open doors and show uncommon respect for even the most unworthy of White people. Pretend White people are your God-given masters and you are not worthy of the ground they walk on. Act like you've been *there* before. That smell? That's the smell of Mr. Jim Crow.

What to Make of Black Expression

Black expressions of outward joy in the face of success in football can be read many different ways. One reading might suggest that African Americans do not know how to handle success. Another reading of Black athlete expression is that African Americans are young and immature in the face of social freedoms, fame, or wealth. Both of these assessments might hold a grain of truth. More importantly, these two readings are in contrast to a way of knowing America and success that is part of the framework for how America works historically for Whites—like clockwork over time, consistent and predictable. What's to dance about? Why the preening?

This implicit predictability of anticipated success in life is a privilege not shared by African Americans historically or contemporarily. *Act like you've been there before* might be a phrase applied to many other life situations where one feels "ownership" as a White American, rather than feeling owned, regulated, profiled, shackled, or followed for being Black and wearing a hoodie in a residential neighborhood. "So what, I succeeded. Big deal. This is how things work" is another implicit reading of why one should "act like you've been there before." The brilliant White social commentator Tim Wise, in an article titled "Whites Swim in

Racial Preference," summarized the effect of living in so much privilege that it is not even recognizable:

> Ask a fish what water is and you'll get no answer. Even if fish were capable of speech, they would likely have no explanation for the element they swim in every minute of every day of their lives. Water simply is. Fish take it for granted.[15]

I would love to take freedom for granted. Success for granted. Walking unfettered through a downtown department store for granted. But I know better. I don't assume success is something normal to Black people. Someone summed up the privilege many get at birth in America with a sports analogy about George W. Bush getting into Yale University, dodging Vietnam, becoming part-owner of the Texas Rangers baseball team, becoming Texas Governor, and eventually becoming a two-term president: George W. Bush was *born* on third base—but he wakes up every morning thinking he hit a triple.

Of course it is easier for George W. Bush to score. We *all* want to wake up having hit a triple at birth, so we don't hate *W* for that. We want *that* too.

Enough with the myth of meritocracy—that we all have an equal historical chance at any and everything. We want *W* to realize the privilege and benefit of his birth. He was *born* with connections. I always ask my students about America's high ideals of equality and meritocracy ... to finish this sentence for me: "It's not *what* you know, it's ____ ____ ____." The last three words of that sentence sum it up. It's *who you know* that can get your foot in the door, get you that job, or if need be, get you out of trouble.

American Whites take for granted imbedded social privileges so much so that many cannot conceive that others are not born into such "water." But for many Black, Brown, Asian, Q+, women, differently abled, and poor/conscious Whites, social meritocracy and physical freedom are as alien to us as a fish would feel walking through Oakland. Black Americans are finally experiencing (since 1965) the emotion of group success.

Some will argue that there is a long line of successful athletes and entertainers in Black American history. I agree. Yet only a fraction of African American individuals with success narratives were ever allowed to eat, drink, or sleep in the White hotels and clubs they played in (pre-1965) across the country. So, they've only "kinda" been there before, like people inhaling second-hand smoke. So close.

Yes, even while succeeding, that "question mark" of inequality hovered over our heads. Indeed, one jazz drummer, Panama Francis, summed up his experience of being a Black performer in the face of White privilege in chilling detail. This interaction points to *the public display of emotion* as a White privilege while *the control of emotion* meant survival . . . and the social theft of Black expression:

> Hiding one's feelings under the grinning black mask was a survival skill of great importance to all black males up though World War II; a black man could get lynched for pretending to be on equal terms with a white man under almost any circumstances. Drummer Panama Francis remembered a man who used to come see his band every week in his Florida hometown and every week put a hole in his bass drum. The man always gave him five dollars to fix it, but the drummer hated the ritual humiliation. "I used to get so mad, but I had to smile because back in those days, you had better smile, so I smiled; but I didn't like it too well." At the time, black sociologist Charles S. Johnson called emotional masking "accommodation" to white expectations; in the vernacular it was known as "Tomming."[16]

I've "Tommed" before, and it can hurt. Not always. But small acts of behavioral compliance can steal a tiny bit of your soul. I did what I had to do to get by. This way of going about life in America is the equivalent of eternally pledging a fraternity or sorority—and never being allowed to join. The "act" of having to enjoy your own ritual humiliation was part and parcel of the African American experience in the face of Whiteness and White privilege, whether your profession was jazz or your name was Jackie Robinson, former Black baseball great for the Brooklyn Dodgers. "Freedom and equality," while bandied about in White circles as the American creed and high-minded ideology, was merely a "taunt" in the face of African Americans who could not see freedom of expression in their own lives, feel equality with their own hands, or taste individuality and identity in their social consciousness.

A White researcher from Sweden, Gunner Myrdal, was fascinated by the contradiction between White privilege and American ideals and what he saw as the blatant, racist treatment of Black Americans—from athletes and entertainers, to common everyday Black folk in everyday places and spaces. He edited an award-winning (and history-changing) book entitled *An American Dilemma*, which sought to identify ruptures in the American Creed across the USA in Black institutions and lives.[17]

Though *An American Dilemma* was used to help defeat racial segregation in the 1954 Supreme Court case of Brown vs. Board of Education, Blacks saw the book itself as telling them something they already knew—they had few social rights compared to Whites. African Americans could *not* enjoy those rights and privileges accorded to Whites; even the ability to verbally contest your own subjugation was denied. Verbal defiance in the face of ill treatment in America — or *freedom of speech*, as it has been called—was not a privilege enjoyed throughout the Black community.

Indeed, many Whites looked at Black protest—even in its nonviolent form—as the *cause* of the problem of civic violence aimed at Blacks. Ain't that something? Case in point, the many Black athletes who locked arms, or kneeled, or raised a Black fist in silent protest during national anthems all across American from 2016–2020. This is akin to how sports commentators and coaches often view Black celebratory expression as the problem, rather than the physical aggression that sometimes happens as a result of Black expression. White sports aggression is implicitly condoned ("he had it coming"), while celebration is in many cases penalized and vilified.[18] Nineteen-sixties radical Stokely Charmichael commented on Black social expression/aggression and *The American Dilemma* in the context of discussing the behavior of American Whites with institutionalized racist values:

> What we have discovered, in short, is that all of the United States is racist to the extent and the degree that we have refused to admit ... much less face the tragedy of race in the United States ... The tragedy ... that in the United States there is no American Dilemma. White Americans are not torn and tortured by the conflict between their devotion to the American Creed and their actual behavior. They are upset ... to be sure. But what troubles them is not that justice is denied but that the peace is being shattered ...[19]

Hidden Transcripts in the End-Zone

To be sure, most African Americans are instructed to always respect White authority and power. Public defiance, if employed, has its negative consequences. So, while our parents often instructed on "proper" behavior, there has been a post-Ali and post Black-Panther undercurrent of resistance at work in sport and society. Black resistance shows up in various forms, and celebratory expression—in the face of constricting rules—is one form of Black defiance. Sport is a significant aspect of Black male culture.

Sports provide a great landscape for analysis of Black male achievement on a national platform where physical expression has an enormous impact on American culture. While White grandparents are obsessing over "unruly" behavior, White grandkids are adapting to Black cultural norms and learning the verbal and physical codes.

Young Black male ambition is often intertwined with Black identity in sport. For better or worse, sporting excellence has been key to Black male masculinity. In Chapter 4, Johnny Otis, a White musician, describes how Black jazz musicians formed texture and added character to their craft as part and parcel of the African American experience. Otis believed these facets of life were connected, and he framed this connection as the African American way of life.

Further to this, James Scott in 1990 described many aspects of local culture and resistance by groups as struggles for power and communication via hidden transcripts. Hidden transcripts are often expressed openly, but often disguised. Scott suggests we interpret rumor, gossip, folktales, and other vehicles that critique power and power relationships as hidden transcripts. I would classify end-zone expression and other sports expression such as defiant clothing, side-ways caps, do-rags, and brash and unapologetic athlete-to-media commentary as a sporting vehicle for challenging/destabilizing power and forging a resistant community. Gena Caponi speaks to the connectivity between the Black community and sporting expression:

> What was once derisively called "hot-dogging" becomes community building, whether the "hot-dogger" does it for anyone else or not. And when a performer does excel in a moment of brash and unexpected virtuosity, ordinary time and gravity disappear ... In these moments all, including observers, are participants. The individual who is the catalyst for such a moment is the ultimate team player ... and "showiness" has always been a part of African American expressive style.[20]

Trisha Rose, in her 1994 book, *Black Noise: Rap Music and Black Culture in Contemporary America*, suggests that rap music is a "... Contemporary stage for the theater of the powerless."[21] If rap signifies a transcript of resistance in musical form, athletes signify a physical transcript of resistance on football fields and basketball courts with their bodies. This public resistance by primarily young Black males is played out every week in various sporting codes in the United States. This high level of public resistance/public success is not what our grandparents expressed growing up. We have raised the bar ... even while lowering the knee.

Our grandparents cannot tell us to *act like we've been there before* because most of them have never *been there*. That "there" extends beyond the end-zone into work, job promotions, educational opportunities, and successes in various social spaces where Whites have a feeling of God-given rights to certain options. Many Whites *have been there before*, if not yet in real life, then in the stories of parents, grandparents, and others. Our Black collective consciousness has few memories of "being there," and so each time we *get there* it is a new experience, one to be told and retold to friends, often to inspire rather than to gloat.

"Let your little light shine" is a hymn African Americans hear in church that implicitly promotes and couples expression with success. In 1903, in *The Souls of Black Folks*, Dubois spoke of a "talented tenth" of African Americans that would someday escape their social chains and would be responsible for educating others. Blacks moderated that lofty goal in the 1960s to "each one teach one." The goal was to display one's success so that others might also be motivated to achieve by example. Hiding one's talents and success, on the other hand, was viewed as selfish and not "down" with the cause of "uplifting" the race.

When Black expression was combined with Black Power via the Nation of Islam, Malcolm X, The Black Panther Party, Muhammad Ali, and various Black athlete protests at the 1968 Mexico City Olympics, the result was a new self/social pride that screamed for recognition, as loud as James Brown in the historic song, "Say it Loud—I'm Black and I'm proud." Contemporary male and female athletes are feeling this rush of social pride and Blackness as they defiantly speak out against social police abuse and social injustice all up and down the criminal justice food chain.

"I Wish I Was White—Like Him"

> But what on earth is whiteness that one should so desire it? Then always, somehow, some way, silent but clearly, I am given to understand that whiteness is the ownership of the earth forever and ever, Amen! (W.E.B. Dubois, The Souls of White Folks).[22]

Okay, so now we have some idea of what it is to be Black in America. We need to, for the moment at least, leave *that* horse and go ride anew. This time, we ride a White horse—truly a horse of a different color. Wherein we ask the age-old question mumbled since 1619 when the first Black person arrived in the USA, "What is it like—I mean what is it *really like*—to be a White person?" Every Black person of age has given it thought, but try as we might in our own way, there is no psychological Avatar to help us walk in those White moccasins; no Jedi-mind-tricks or Vulcan mind-melds that allow us to see what life on that fantasy island would be like; no shape-shifting that allows us to morph into Whiteness and strut around wearing a Technicolor Dreamcoat of social power.

I am talking about *walking while White*. Applying for a job *while White*. Being successful *while White*. Celebrating my joy in sport *while White*. "Sporting success to me is no big deal," kinda *White*.

I had no idea of the depth of White acceptance of the God-given privilege of free bodily movement in society and sport until an incident in New Zealand shook me into a stupor. This is a story of arrogance and humility. Humility is what White athletes and coaches pride themselves on perpetuating, quite often through the veil of the Protestant work ethic. Arrogance is the label for Black athletes who exhibit expressive social/sporting behavior, quite often attributed to the stigma of poor cultural habits. Sometimes those labels just don't fit. This was one time.

Incident at Operation Deep Freeze

Access to the Super Bowl in New Zealand in 1997 required a visit to a U.S. military base in Christchurch. The base was connected to work at the South Pole called "Operation Deep Freeze," and a safe haven to view the Armed Forces television station. After an American breakfast of bacon, sausage, eggs, and pancakes (I love America) and the Super Bowl on satellite TV, the four of us began our cholesterol-laden walk through the military base back to our steering-wheel-on-the-right car. Our group consisted of one other American Studies professor, the husband of an American Studies professor, and a laid-off Flint Michigan auto-industry worker, John.

John had been visiting for the past week and spent most of his mornings micro-managing his horde of stocks purchased with his huge Ford Motors severance package. He was making money hand-over-fist as the U.S. economy grew under Bill Clinton and the "new" Internet technology. We envied him. I envied him for what he did next on that sunny Christchurch day for it showed me how different some Blacks and some Whites were from each other in mind and body. John taught me much about privileges I never experienced as a Black American.

As we strolled about the grounds, loaded down with comfort food, we noticed the military barracks and barbed-wired fencing that kept soldiers in and civilians, out.

John felt offended. John felt that this restriction of his access was un-American. He said, "I want to see the barracks."

I figured he was being whimsical. When he began walking in the direction of the entry gate I noted aloud that the sign said, "Private Property: Military Access by Authorized Personnel Only."

He said, "So what—I paid for these barracks."

"What?" I said, stopping literally in my tracks.

He replied matter-of-factly and never skipping a beat, "I pay my taxes, and since this is American property, I paid for this, and I should be able to see the barracks if I want to."

I noted aloud the "barbed wire" and the "private property" signs—*again* —and joked that he might be *shot* on sight.

He replied, "*Yeah, right*," and just marched right through the gate and down the rows and around corners until he was out of sight.

I was paralyzed and befuddled by his actions. How could he be so brazen and act so arrogantly in the face of supreme authority? How could he stare down sure reprimand? How could he brush aside barbed wire and an obvious sign restricting his access? Didn't he know military folks carried guns and were inclined to use them, given the opportunity? What was *wrong* with him?

And it hit me, right then and there, loud and clear, as bright as the Southern hemisphere sun that pierced the ozone layer on that day: *He was acting like he'd been there before.*

John was acting like he owned the place. John was not acting out of fear. John was acting within his God-given White American right to stand up and take—or at least view—what was his. True, the other two White guys in our group were far more petrified than John and sort of tiptoed in after him, as I did. None of us felt that strong about our flag-waving rights nor as bold as John. "How dare he go in there!" was my initial thought as I walked in, like a pigeon among cats. "Who the hell does he think he is?"

Why didn't John show more humility in front of the mighty force of the all-powerful, all-knowing U. S. government? Everything trained into my central nervous system by parents, friends, families, and the countless stories I heard told me that I, as a Black man, had no right to go beyond that gate with my body. My mind had been programmed to respond to certain marked social signs of bodily movement such that I had no choice on this bright day.

Black people joke about these kinds of situations, akin to how Richard Pryor joked about going beyond the "No Trespassing" signs on "Mr. Gilmore's property." If you are shot or otherwise harmed, while recovering on your hospital bed, Black people will ask, "Negro! Didn't you see the sign?"

If I respond to my Black family from the hospital bed in the vein of, "Well, I am an American, and I should have the right, since I pay taxes, blah, blah, blah . . ." The entire room of Black folks would fall out in laughter. They'd point at me, laugh again, and accidentally fart, tears rolling from their eyes. I'd finally have to start laughing just to stave off more embarrassment.

Once they caught their breath, the overriding response would be, "Boy—you think you're *White*? Just because the *White man* does something, you think *you* have a right to do it? What *books* have you been reading? Whose *pipe* have you been smoking? You have lost your mind." And once the morphine wore off,

I would understand what they were talking about. And they would be right. I should have known better. I am Black.[23]

Black Survival Means Being the Fittest

Survival mechanisms for people in the "non-White" status category are such that to be the "fittest," one must forever be vigilant about one's surroundings and the policed boundaries of the body. Black minds have been programmed to respect social spaces over centuries in America by millions of Black parents. These parents and elders trained our bodies about *where* to move, *how* to move, and how to *escape notice*, whether on the Underground Railroad or on a Montgomery, Alabama, bus. This training of Black bodies goes beyond what we traditionally call "socialization" about situated behavior into anticipatory modeling about social movement that is far more primal and mythological ... what Abraham Maslow might call "survival."[24]

For us to have physiological reactions to police officers, aversions to being followed down store isles, mild depression when women guard their bags on elevators, and to be physically paralyzed and brain-locked when attempting to walk on government property speaks of more than anticipatory socialization by parents and elders. It speaks to a subjugation of the body and mind that is at the core of Black *un-freedom* itself.

Truth be told, most Black Americans have never felt as free as the *poorest* White Americans. We know that *they* hold the trump card—White skin. Henry Giroux noted that working-class White youth are taught that Black youth are criminals, and that "Blacks and immigrants are responsible for the poverty, despair, and violence" that are a part of everyday life.[25] This vilification of Black youth is often translated into racial violence and counter-violence by Black youth. But this violence is not confined to Black youth, for right up the age groups Black American bodies are constricted in public spaces.

As bell hooks has noted, "All black people in the United States, irrespective of their class status or politics, live with the possibility that they will be terrorized by whiteness."[26] So the idea that one can simply walk about, willy-nilly, and be protected by a legal and constitutional framework verses oppressed into bodily and mental submission by the same framework is, well, *very* White.

Whites can act like they have been there before because *Whites, as a social class, have* been there before. Many Whites, as I envision the late Coach Paul Brown, are so unaware of the privilege of free movement that the assumption is everyone has it, has had it for centuries, and that it comes as part of the mental packaging at birth. Therefore, when Black people do freely move and *act like we've never been there* in our collective history, it seems strange and somehow out of place to many Whites.

Hence, the question mark above the man on the left in red on the bench as the newly freed-up woman on the right has had her say and done her dance. This freedom to express feels new to many African Americans—which seems odd to many White Americans who've always had it.

I can recall the exact moment I stopped watching the once popular television show, *24*. A White man (I can't recall if it was the show's lead actor, Kiefer Sutherland) was stopped by a police officer as he drove across a bridge. The White man was very upset about being stopped on his way to solve very important matters of global importance (diffusing a nuclear bomb or some such nonsense). He jumped out of his car, walked menacingly toward the cop who had gotten out of his car, and began yelling at the officer and pointing in his face. The angry White man yelled about his "people" inside the police force, badge numbers, reporting him, and that in the end the cop better let him go or there would be consequences. The arrogant White man then marched back to his car, got in, and sped off.

I turned the TV off. I couldn't believe what I had just seen. Was this a benefit of being White? No Black person in the history of America could get away with such an act. No Black screenwriter would ever write that scene—and no Black actor would walk through his/her lines in that scene with a straight face—unless this was a comedy. Okay, it was a fantasy show. But that's not a fantasy I'm familiar with—nor would ever try. I've never been there before. And the Black people who have been there before aren't alive to reminisce about it. I am very familiar with the phrase, "shoot first—and ask questions later."

White minds see the world in an entirely different way, and White bodies move to entirely different wavelengths that are congruent with those ways of seeing and knowing. When sports celebration and expression by Black athletes diminishes under its own momentum, then we might find that together we have gradually produced a society where we *have all been there before*.

To expect African Americans to graph White thoughts and histories onto Black bodies is as foreign a concept for us as it might be for Whites to graph Black thoughts and histories onto White bodies and successfully move and react in "Black" ways. Few succeed at taking the place of the racial other and successfully dancing in their cleats.

I am not suggesting Whites should adapt Black forms of expression and bodily movement. That would be extremely difficult and not diverse or multicultural.

What many African Americans have desired pre—and post-Civil Rights Movement, though, is that Whites view expression and African American cultural styles of life as part and parcel of the larger framework of race and ethnicity in America and as part of this cultural "salad bowl" that makes us unique in the world.

Whites should also realize that they, too, express in ways that could be considered "outrageous" and not the "norm" by many. At those times where White athletes are just as expressive as some of their most expressive Black counterparts—please see Aaron Rodgers, Clay Matthews, Mark Gastineau, Pistol Pete Maravich, Mark "The Bird" Fidrych, and the wrestler who inspired Muhammad Ali, "Gorgeous George"—they are labeled "quirky" or "individualistic" or "fiercely independent" or a "character" or "good for the game." Again, the power to define is a privilege.

Power and privilege can reformulate in-group actions by Whites—which could be deemed "inappropriate" and outside of White middle-class norms of expression—as well within the re-defined boundaries of acceptability. Privilege can define Whites as "individual and idiosyncratic" when it comes to expression and Black behaviors as "street", "urban," "unsportsmanlike," and "unacceptable." And for the record, I loved watching the White athletes mentioned above. They added flavor to the game.

Conclusion

Across sports and down through history, African American athletes have expressed spontaneity and improvisation, individuality, political resistance, culture, and sportsmanship in very different ways from White athletes. These different forms of physical expression and celebratory behavior have often been the source of conflict in both Black and White communities. Black and White alike called Muhammad Ali a "loudmouth" during his time (though few would confess to it now). Today, we have a clearer understanding of the historical context of Ali's talk and can better see the social, racial, political, and religious reasons for his brash behavior. A similar historical perspective by Whites might someday view "unsportsmanlike" behavior by African American professional and college football players today in a more positive framework.

No doubt many other athletes will be penalized for expressing their joy and freedom in football and other sports arenas and fields. When we have committees and rule-makers who are more representative of the variety of social histories, or at least knowledgeable of the different ways people see the world, then we will have a diminishing of the notion that we must "act like we've been there before." When White observers "act like they've seen Blacks express before," then we'll know White fans are making the mental shifts necessary to include Black expression.

If Black expression does indeed seem strange in sport, then we both have something in common—the view of the others' movements in society as strange.

There is a myth perpetuated in the United States that we all enjoy social and expressive freedoms. That mythology extends to sport. We need to stop the taunts that demand White conformity and *act like* we are equal in these various sporting and social institutions. We'll all be much better for it. Then all those exclamation marks and question marks will fade.

Notes

1. Dyer, 1997, p. 2.
2. When I say "Black" I often include women. In some cases, I even say "Black" when I am speaking about Black male behaviors. This is for convenience and not meant to generalize all Black behavior as male-based, or to exclude women. Black men and women share many norms for behavior but also have gender differences. (And some day I hope to contribute to a book about the expressive behaviors of AA women). I also use the term "Black" interchangeably with African American throughout the text. I believe Black Americans have earned the distinction of the upper-case B, for the same reasons Fiske cites in Media Matters: "[I] follow the practice of capitalizing the word Black to distinguish its enhanced value (the result of hard struggle) from the denigratory 'black'. The word white is not capitalized, for it has never needed a struggle to enhance it, though one may now be taking place to devalue it" (Fiske 1996: 277). I part from my mentor on the word "White" in an effort to reframe our perspective of the background, silent, invisible "normal" which is really Whiteness as hegemony. No more.
3. Yahoo.com's news page provided one of the most blatant examples of this kind of bias. The website featured a photo of two White residents, wading through the water with food. The caption read: "Two residents wade through chest-deep water after finding bread and soda from a local grocery store after Hurricane Katrina came through the area in New Orleans, Louisiana. (AFP/Getty Images/Chris Graythen)" Then there is a photo of a Black youth, wading through water with food. The caption reads: "A young man walks through chest deep flood water after looting a grocery store in New Orleans on Tuesday, Aug. 30, 2005. Flood waters continue to rise in New Orleans after Hurricane Katrina did extensive damage when it made landfall on Monday. (AP Photo/Dave Martin)" From an article by Van Jones, September 1,

2005, Huffington Post.Com: http://www.huffingtonpost.com/van-jones/black-people-loot-food-wh_b_6614.html.

4. Here is an extended citation from a great sportswriter, Joan Ryan. She says we need to think about the larger context of the USA when we critique athletes. She notes, in this extensive four-paragraph note quote, her opinion:

   The message is clear: Nastiness is not only tolerated but desired: "If investment banking firms and law offices needed as many customers as professional sports teams, they would be marketing themselves the same way. We might not like cold-blooded vultures, but we respect them, especially when they're on our side. We admire the person making the most sales, scoring the highest grade, winning the most cases. There is little admiration, or use, for the graceful loser. Chicago Bears linebacker Bryan Cox, who has paid out $140,000 in fines in his seven-year NFL career, talked on the ESPN show about the benefits of trash talking. He said there were few boundaries in attacking an opponent. He would tear apart the opponent, his mother, his wife and even his kids--w*h*atever it takes to get under the guy's skin and give Cox an edge. Unseemly and crude? Unsportsmanlike? Yes. But how is that different from what politicians do to each other during campaigns? Or what lawyers do to rape victims on the witness stand? We notice the crudeness in sports because it's often expressed physically and because we can't turn on the TV without seeing highlights of the worst behavior of the day. ESPN itself is a significant perpetuator of this. Its shows are packed with brutality—Roberto Alomar spitting, Dennis Rodman head-butting, Mike Tyson biting, Jeff Tarango throwing a fit at Wimbledon. The decent guys don't get the slow-motion replays. I'm not defending the behavior of boorish athletes. But I think we ought to keep it in perspective. Yes, their antics influence kids. Yes, they ought to be better role models. But so should we all. We live in a society in which vulgarity passes for wit, fame for respectability, and winning for success. What I find encouraging about sports—compared to other, equally screwed-up institutions—is that we care so deeply about its problems. We openly worry about our skewed priorities. Just the fact that ESPN held a town meeting suggests the decline in sportsmanship bothers us. Which means there is hope. In sports, anyway."
5. For more on Black expression in sport please see Ashe, 1988; Frey, 1994; George, 1994; Kochman, 1981; Majors and Billson, 1992; Andrews and Majors, 2004; Greenfield, 1975; Wideman, 1990; Dyson, 1994. For more on Black expression in churches please see Holt, 1972. For more on Black expression in universities and musical venues please see Dinerstein, 1998.
6. For more on expressive differences between African Americans and Whites, please see Andrews, 1996; Majors and Billson, 1992; Jones, 1986; Kochman, 1981; Greenfield, 1975.
7. In Caponi, 1999, p. 4.
8. For the record, "Blackly" is not a word. But it is now.
9. See also Fordham, 1993.

10. For more, see Cameron, 1993, and Abe, 1988.
11. See also Rigueur, 1981.
12. For more on this topic please see Feagin and Sikes, 1994; Feagin, 2001; Duneier, 1992.
13. Double consciousness is the phrase coined by W.E.B. Dubois over one hundred years ago to describe the dissonance all African Americans have to tackle when they enter White institutions. Double consciousness is the experience of having to appease (in voice and body) the White "out group" while maintaining a sense of Black self-respect and esteem.
14. When I wrote my first draft of this manuscript, the acronym was LGBT. As we have come to understand more and more about gender and sexuality and stigma, it became LGBTQ, then LGBTQA, then LGBTQAi, then LGBTQAi+ (that is, Lesbian, Gay, Bisexual, Transgender/Transsexual, Asexual, Intersex plus). I suspect there might be more initials added on as we come to understand more and more about identity and oppression. It is my hope that all disenfranchised groups will find a home in this historically marginalized grouping. As you read this off into the future, I want to be mindful that you, too, are represented, even if your initial is not yet included in the LGBTQAi+ community framing as of 2020. I therefore, herein, will use Q+ as a signifier of those groups who we look to respect and include today, and those groups yet to follow. This is a nod to the future. "Q" is used as it is a unique letter and the "+" signifies those marginalized today and into the future. You are valued and included here.
15. Wise, 2003, p. 1.
16. Dinerstein, 1998, p. 245. [In a personal memo from Helen Gibson, she points up the pervasiveness of whiteness even to Black Americans. She notes that: "Drummer Panama Francis remembered *a man* who used . . ."] A common critique is made about the invisibility of Whiteness in Whites' language that is, the common practice that "Whiteness" is never claimed/named by those who identify as White but taken as the *universal man*. [This] example highlights that this is also common in the discourse of those who identify as African American and can be argued as an indication of the relentless power of Whiteness to remain unnamed.
17. Myrdal, 1944.
18. Many womanists and feminists will note the similarities to another justification of physical aggression—rape. If you dress or act a certain way, somehow it justifies acts of aggression towards you. Similarly, when Black athletes express and are subsequently attacked, the idea is "He had it coming."
19. Charmichael and Hamilton, 1967, p. 5.
20. Caponi, 1999, p. 5.
21. Rose, T., 1994, p. 101.
22. Dubois, 1920.
23. As of last check in 2002, the report was that John had indeed played the high-technology stock market for too long and had lost all of the hundreds of thousands of

dollars he had negotiated and invested. He was last known to be living in his mother's basement. Many African Americans *have been there* before.

24. Maslow, A. "A theory of human motivation." *Psychological Review*, vol. 50, issue 4, 370–396.
25. Giroux, 1998, p. 124.
26. bell hooks, 1992, p. 49.

2

Exploring Sports Conduct and Cultural Identity

Everybody is just a little bit different. The woman sitting next to me was definitely different. I sat in Cowles Stadium in Christchurch, New Zealand, cheering on the Canterbury Rams basketball team. But what was up with the behavior of the woman sitting to my right? I was having a cultural moment, as we visitors overseas often experience. This "cultural moment" occurs when we come face-to-face with people who don't agree with how we see "appropriate behavior" in social settings such as sport. We have strong reactions to what we know to be wrong—and the "right way" to do it.

The Rams were part of the New Zealand Basketball League (NBL) and each of the twelve teams were allowed two "import" players, most of whom were journeymen hoopsters nation-hopping as seasons ended somewhere and started up somewhere else in the world. Many imports were African Americans. Meeting Black athletes on various teams was one of the attractions in a country where I was the lone African American professor. Yet, it was odd to be at a basketball game and hear Fiona, sitting next to me, say "no" when I nudged her to "Get into it—cheer for the team!"

She looked at me sideways and said, "They are losing—why should I cheer for them! I'll cheer when they start winning again. I am not going to encourage their bad play!"

For Fiona, cheering was a "reward for good play"—verses my concept of "encouragement to do better." Without any thought of irony in my cultural moment, I mumbled, "This woman is foreign."

The Rams had lost a twelve-point lead and were down by five points with three minutes remaining. They eventually won. But not before more back-to-back cultural moments with Fiona.

"Look at those rude boys over there—they're behaving just like Americans!" She was pointing to the five rowdy male fans situated in the stands right behind the visiting backboard. They were waving placards as the opposing point-guard attempted two free throws.

I felt compelled to explain to her the finer points of fandom in America: "Well, the fans *should be* trying to put the shooter off his game. That's what the home team fans are supposed to do!"

She was not amused, impressed, or convinced. "Maybe you do that over there, but over here we are better behaved and better sportsmen and women. Everybody deserves an equal chance to win, especially our guests."

"Guests?" Not where I'm from, Fiona. Not even the visiting fans are considered guests.

I have attended many tailgate parties before Oakland Raider games, and opposing fans (in their team jerseys) would walk through the parking lot drawing good-natured jeers.[1] After the game—if it was a Raider win—opposing fans might even be asked to join in eating tri-tip sandwiches and drinking beer at the back of someone's car as the evening wound down. But there was little such civility during the game: We were at war, and any premature celebration by visiting fans after touchdowns would get local blood boiling. When this blood boiling was fused with beer, heavy-metal rock and rap music blaring, a general East Bay "chip on the shoulder," and losing the game, things could—and often did—get ugly at the Oakland Alameda County Coliseum.

Just like the opposing fans who attend those Raider games, in America we rarely think of the opposing team as "guests." Maybe guests *before* the game and guests *after* the game (if the home team wins), but never guests *during* the game. If anything, we think of the opposition during the contest as "the enemy." The main goal is for the enemy to be defeated—by any and all means necessary, including intimidation of the players, coaches, and referees. But the more time I spent in New Zealand, the more I became convinced that there might be another way. I was conditioned to think that only one way existed to express my fandom: Cheer for the home team, boo the opposition, and boo the referees or umpires for calls I don't like.

I attended an All Blacks rugby international Test Match in Dunedin against South Africa a few weeks after the Rams basketball game and heard a fellow All Black fan chastise another for booing the referee: "Hey, he's doing the best job he can out there—some calls have gone our way—give the referee a break!" This was truly a different world … one where referees were thought of as human … and fair. (Which, of course, they aren't.)

What I thought was *the way* to behave as a fan was challenged by what I observed in New Zealand. The concept I knew as "sportsmanlike conduct" was exercised quite differently "down under." It seems passé to say that a concept like "sportsmanship" might be strongly related to where one lives, and local culture and norms influence "appropriate" social behavior. Why wouldn't norms and customs about sports behavior be localized?

This "relative to the environment you grew up in" aspect of sports conduct was especially evident when watching Black and White urban and suburban athletes in the USA and their slightly differing views of appropriate sports conduct. But never mind those differences. We all agree in the USA that the visiting team and coach and referees are all to be hated and heckled. I took it for granted that USA norms on fandom were the norms of sport globally—especially as applied to an American sport like basketball.

Baseball and football evolved from cricket and rugby, but basketball is "American," and it seemed that if we invented the sport, we should be able to set the global norms about behavior in and around the court. Except Fiona didn't think so nor did she care what Americans thought about appropriate behavior. This was her country, her city, her team, and her behavioral norms.

Some might simply have written Fiona off and said, "Oh, those quirky Kiwis are just a bit weird and prudish." Well, they are to a degree. Weird to Americans because they call the hood of a car the "bonnet" and the trunk a "boot" and call cookies "biscuits" and potato chips "crisps" and French fries "chips." But certainly not prudish. They show United States "Mature Audience" television programs during prime time with little concern for foul language or sexual imagery. Shows like *Six Feet Under*, *The Sopranos*, and *Nip/Tuck* appeared on network television during prime time without a hint of prudishness from the public. The legal drinking age in New Zealand (and the United Kingdom) is eighteen years old. Marijuana is decriminalized. Prostitution is legal in Christchurch. It is not so easy to write-off New Zealand as an uptight country.

We can simply dismiss New Zealand's norms as "not our own" and "not normal," thereby marginalizing their cultural choices, habits, and differences. The phrase "inferior" can easily become a convenient replacement for "difference." Yet study into the differences in cultural norms between our nations might yield some fascinating insights into our own behaviors and cultural customs. And that might be the very point: We are all a bit different from one another, but those differences do not necessarily make us better or worse. Sometimes a "tailgate party" at a football game can be called a "boot party" without any harm done to society. And maybe instead of the tailgate with chicken wings and drumsticks, the boot party has lamb chops and mutton stew. No fowl—no harm.

Difference? Let Me Count the Ways

We are *all* different from one another. You did not grow up where I grew up, and if you did, your family is different from mine. And you don't live where I live now. Add in a dose of sexuality, gender, race and ethnicity, religiosity or spiritual affiliation, atheism or agnosticism, political-party affiliation, birth order in one's family and—alas—my zodiac sign, Pisces, and you could be forgiven if you thought that we are a *lot* different from one another. Our differences and our individuality go hand-in-hand with how we frame the world and our attitudes about individuals and groups in society. Just ask Fiona.

We frame sport and social behavior in very different ways from one another, and these frames are often contingent upon the region of the country we live in, whether we have a prosthetic leg or participate in wheelchair rugby, whether we are lesbian and play in a San Francisco softball league or are a Black woman with braids playing hoops for Rutgers University. All of these demographics—and people—will shape how we see sport and the way it should be played, in addition to thousands of other opinions we make and re-make about right and wrong. Throw in our quirky parents and it seems a minor sporting miracle how people in the USA have (generally) agreed on league and team conduct without complete chaos.

But disruptions occur almost every week in one of the various sporting codes in America and tuning into sport on television or radio with a keen ear will bear this out. Broadcasters will note athletes who are "showing the opposition up," or engaging in "unruly" behavior, or "showboating." Football players who might exhibit some form of post-touchdown celebration are asked to "act like they've been there before." Fans boo the home quarterback or a starting pitcher or become unruly after their team loses (or wins) the Super Bowl. The media remains perplexed about many behaviors and yearns in post-mortem columns for "The good old days." Players fight, take steroids, cheat during games, cheat on their wives, bet on games, and beat their spouses. Athlete dysfunctional behavior is nothing new, though. Neither is the critique of the on-field behavior of athletes.

Every day, everywhere announcers, writers, fans, former fans, athletes and former athletes, coaches and former coaches critique the unsportsmanlike behavior of fans, coaches and athletes. They also praise athletes who exhibit good sports conduct. What is the genesis of these varying opinions about sports behavior? How do athletes formulate their codes of conduct and attitudes about the behavior of others? What do fans and players think about racial differences in sports conduct?

These are variations on some of the questions I have been asking since 1989 as I attended sporting contests primarily in the USA, but also in New Zealand, Australia, England, Scotland, and Wales. What I have found has surprised me, has influenced my views of sports conduct, and has given me a newfound respect for both Black codes and White codes of conduct.

Expressive Confrontations

Many New Zealanders are anxious to hear details about American culture. Many U.S. TV shows, as noted above, screen locally in New Zealand (also known as "Aotearoa," in Maori). Most Kiwis grow up on British and American television shows, but most have never met an American—let alone an exotic Black American. I was often asked to speak at schools, Rotary Clubs, and other civic functions on U.S. culture, the Civil Rights Movement, or American Sport. I represented not only Black America—but also all things American. This led to confrontations.

People assumed I worked for the American Embassy and that I was naturally a mouthpiece for the U.S. government and an apologist for anything "American." People would give me an earful (after a couple of beers) of how they "hate George Bush" or "hate American arrogance" or despise our "war mongering" and "nuclear weapons" and a culture that "fills kids heads with pop music" and kids' "stomachs with McDonalds, KFC, and Burger King." I let their full-frontal-attack anger run its course and would usually have the same, jarring response: "I agree." I usually did agree with them. Even when they hated "gangster rap as a bad influence on Kiwi youth." (Which might seem to contradict the fact that I taught the first hip-hop course in New Zealand.)

At this point they relaxed, took a deep breath, and then said what they really wanted to talk about: Sport. Kiwis love their sport. Rugby and cricket, especially. So, citizen-athletes would come up to me after my talks and mostly chat about their sporting lives. A few fought back tears as they told their personal stories of having people look down on them for their behaviors, or friends on the team who were ridiculed for expressing joy or individuality. Other athletes or audience members would go the opposite direction and rage about their hatred of cocky Black athletes—or any athlete who drew attention to him or herself. I completely understood—New Zealand worships the humble athlete (more on this in Chapter 9). Anything else is sacrilegious. But even that cultural institution called humility is changing.

I got an All Black jersey as a gift upon arrival in New Zealand in 1996 and wore it at a beer festival (there might be a theme here). An older gentleman came up to me and said, "Did you ever play for the All Blacks?"

I said, "No sir."

He replied, "Then why are you wearing that jersey!" He snarled and walked off.

He was a man from a different time. If you played for the All Black rugby team in the 1970s and 1980s when the sport was still "amateur," and you scored, you weren't even supposed to smile. You were a man. This was a job. You gave the ball to the referee and "didn't make an emotional fuss."

I was told in no uncertain terms that the only people in New Zealand allowed to don the silver fern were All Blacks and former All Blacks. Now that Adidas is a part of the marketing team, though, entire stadiums are told to "Black Out" the game by dressing in All Black jerseys. This type of change likely hurts those Kiwis who know the sport in a very different (amateur) way that emphasizes playing for the love of the game and not for money. You play to wear the silver fern. Traditions everywhere are being met head-on by new traditions. I understand the traditions and understand the reasons for change.

I agreed with New Zealanders (NZ) when they told me Black athletes were way over the top. Not because I shared their sentiment (which I sometimes did), but because I could understand the NZ cultural frame and how anything appearing "individual and egotistical" went against Kiwi DNA coding. Many Americans felt the same way, I would often tell them. Indeed, the academic beginnings of this line of research began my first semester at the University of Wisconsin with a coach who was strongly against non-traditional behavior.

An article in the *Capitol Times* highlighted star Badger student-athlete Willie Sims saying his head coach had called him "retarded" and "street" for jumping on the scorer's table and waving a towel to cheering fans (after home victories).[2] There is nothing wrong with disliking Sims' behavior. Name-calling and belittling and making fun of one's cultural background, though, cross the line. Contrary to this negative view of Sims, others in the USA would tell me warm stories about Black expression.

A man in Redwood City, California, spoke to me about the graciousness of San Francisco Giants first-baseman Willie McCovey in the early 1970s. McCovey, a tall easy-going African American athlete who had a ferocious home-run swing, signed an infinite number of autographs after a game and gave this White man's son a baseball and took a photo with him. The man was almost in tears as he retold the story (though that might have been the beer weeping. Yes, this was in a bar). A few audience members after my talks have said how they despise fighting in hockey—that they hated this form of White expression. An academic at a conference, though, noted some of his White friends are now following hockey—and golf and NASCAR—because they want to cheer for White heroes or winners.

With all this disagreement, you'd be forgiven if you thought hope didn't exist for agreement about sport and social conduct moving forward. But there is hope that the evolution of sports conduct is moving in the right direction, though on a day-to-day basis it appears we take one step forward and two backward. Much of the negative has to do with competitive media outlets wanting to report bad behavior that will "make a story."

But you'd be surprised to know many African Americans do not like "over the top" Black expressive behavior in either society or sport—especially in sport. The reasons are historical and greatly differ from why Whites (and many Kiwis) dislike Black expressive culture.

The Ethnic Ripple Effect

African Americans, often quietly and to ourselves, negotiate the sensitive territory of class and behavioral style on a daily basis. Dating back to slavery, African Americans were told (and told themselves) how to "act in order to get ahead." This often meant subservient behavioral codes such as not looking "Massa" in the eyes, agreeing with everything White authority figures said, and at times even telling those same authority figures that other slaves were plotting to leave the "cozy confines" of the plantation. For many traitors who told of impending escapes, it was a chance to "get mine" as the kids say. But for every person who "got theirs" the easy way, others would suffer the lash. What I do (tell the master) can affect how you (caught in the act of escaping) are treated.

Granted, we are not so intertwined in our behaviors and lives in America today such that what I do at my job in California affects your livelihood in, say, Minnesota, but a ripple effect of actions and consequences certainly can occur.

The ethnic ripple effect is when your behavior—good or bad—causes someone to reflect positively or negatively upon your group affiliation—be it Irish, Catholic, Jewish, or German. Just like Chaos theory predicts that a butterfly flapping its wings in Japan will (or at least theoretically could) affect the weather patterns in the USA, so, too, one working theory of Black behavior is that one act of social altruism or brilliance by one African American in the presence of Whites positively affects the whole image of the African American community.

Likewise, an asocial or negative behavior by a Black person toward—or in the presence of—Whites will negatively affect the whole of the Black community. Thus, bad behavior by one person could ultimately lead to a rejected housing loan for another Black person, or a job or promotion denied, or a grant for a new urban library in Oakland withdrawn from consideration. With every public ethnic/cultural transgression, there is one White person for whom that Black behavior might be "The last straw! I'm done with Black people!"

Our middle-class survival guide on Black behavior says that individual *and* group-level punishment is doled-out as a few people "spoiled it for everyone." This irrational thought is the cumulative negative effect of Black social behaviors Whites deem destructive in "our culture" and ultimately, in me. Because, try as we might, us good-acting, "civilized middle-class Blacks" are *really* "Black like them"—Blacks who are negatively stigmatized. We all suffer a blow—we all go down.

The ethnic and racial ripple-effect theory of behavior guides many social actions by non-normative groups as they attempt to fit in. "This makes all Black people look good," we think after we nail the corporate presentation. At the same time, there is chastisement of rule-breakers in non-normative groups who break away from social constraints and normative behaviors and otherwise "embarrass" themselves in the eyes of both those wishing to assimilate into the mainstream and the gatekeepers who would turn ethnic groups away. Indeed, there are times when even those who color within the numbers and walk the fine line say, "I don't give a shit! I'm tired of hiding my culture in the closet!" Those that adhere to the ethnic ripple-effect theory to its fullest would protest loudly.

The notion is that when people act as lone wolves and throw behavioral norms to the wind on a football field or at a lunch counter in Peoria, Illinois, they inadvertently take others in the group down, too. While I do think this unspoken "effect" has its basis in some bit of truth in our collective past—and for many Whites today with little or no exposure to African Americans—I think the effect has lessened its grip on White consciousness.

In a similar sense, Black people have changed, too. Many Blacks held overarching and stereotypical views of White people as "the man" (including White women) and the creators of all things bad that happen to African Americans. This led many African Americans to be suspicious around White co-workers and authority figures (with good historical reasons). Fortunately, the vast majority of White people are good (mighty White of me to say that). Yet our cautions and suspicions over time have led many of us to oversimplify and typecast White people as arrogant and authoritative and privileged. This stereotyping and the resulting negative micro-level acts of discrimination toward Whites rob both groups of the chance to live and laugh together.

Cultural Cringe

When we see Blacks enacting what might be considered to Whites "negative" behavior (whether Blacks personally think any specific act is negative is another point), we experience what is called "cultural cringe," or embarrassment. When someone Black performs an outlandish act—like mock tap-dancing—deemed appropriate or acceptable *within* the confines of a Black group, we can laugh with the individual. But when the same act is perpetrated in mixed company, we might cringe. We might feel demeaned. Laughed at. The side effect from cringing is regret that the bad behavior by one of us likely forges a deep resentment toward all of us. Dave Chappell's departure from *The Chappell Show* was a result of noticing Whites were laughing at him *and* Black people. That epiphany raised questions for Chappell about the appropriateness of his comic act of making fun of stereotypical African American behaviors. He turned down a $50 million-dollar contract with *Comedy Central*, thus cancelling the show.

Part of the embarrassment with Black cultural cringe is our own angst and social projection that White social "others" don't truly understand Black behavior within our own cultural context and will therefore, uncritically, look down upon our entire culture as *the same*: Less than Whites. We can be accused of over-thinking matters, but that is the nature of living in a country where under-thinking social situations for Black people can result in social suicide.

All cultures experience some form of cultural cringe, though maybe not to the degree Black Americans do. A cricket radio commentator noted on a broadcast during a lazy Saturday afternoon that New Zealand had experienced a good deal of cultural cringe in the past when visiting England for Test cricket matches. Former wicket-keeper-turned-announcer Ian Smith recounted how England and New Zealand teams were introduced in the hallowed grounds of Lord's—home of international cricket and a highly dignified place, even by British Standards. The

English team was announced by a gentleman speaking the Queen's English with the perfect accent of a man of royal standing.

Thereafter, a New Zealand announcer took the microphone and began speaking in the native "She'll be right, mate" Kiwi accent, and the jarring nature of their own clipped, sharp "Kiwi twang" set against the backdrop of upper-class England in such a sacred sporting place had them all deeply embarrassed. They cringed at how simple and common they appeared next to English upper-class respectability. They also were keenly aware of being judged by Englanders as "commoners from that far-off colony" somewhere down near Australia.

Whether team impressions were true to how the English felt was beside the point; Kiwis cringed at *possibly* being judged. I lived in New Zealand from 1996–2010 and struggled with the hard-to-understand accent of Kiwis verses the familiar accent of English ex-patriots living there. I knew exactly what—and how—the New Zealand cricketers felt.

Many African Americans will feel the same way about all manner of Black expression that might embarrass, such as youthful saggy pants (as noted earlier), hats turned to the side (with the "just bought this" sticker still on), overly colorful clothing or shoes, hair weaves, gold-plated teeth, blatantly foul language, cornrowed hair, tattoos on athletes, and end-zone dancing. The 1990s show *In Living Color* fronted by the Wayans brothers made their mark off of mocking Black urban expression primarily as showcased in and around Los Angeles. Included in the cringe moments was (1) the entire Raider football team conducting a choreographed end-zone dance to "Disco Inferno" at the L.A. Coliseum, and (2) two Black "Run DMC"-dressed gold-chain wearing brothas on a private White golf course with a ghetto-blaster blaring from their pimped-out golf cart. The brothas used pool cues to sink their putts.

Indeed, Black comedians have always poked fun at Black urban behavior—as well as the stiffness of the White middle-class. Middle- and upper-class Blackness is teased just as well, so as not to imply that one class (or race or ethnicity) has a monopoly on "bad" or "good" behavior. We are all cringe-worthy. My White students visibly cringed when I told them, "I'm learning more and more about White culture every day. Why just yesterday I saw on TV a family fronted by some little White girl named Honey Boo Boo Child—and I was transfixed by White culture yet again."

A Black middle-class has emerged that is distinctly different from White middle-class culture (and Honey Boo Boo-type working-class White culture) and the isolated Black middle-class of pre-1970s America. Contemporary Black middle-class folks appear far more in touch with class politics, social issues, and the embracing of cultural roots rather than White behavioral norms. This is a direct effect of many Blacks (1) who were once "lower-class" moving into the middle-class ranks, (2) a direct effect of hip-hop music and politics heard by youth while growing up, (3) campus politics and integration across class and cultural lines at universities, and (4) humor directed at past middle-class people thought to have "sold themselves out" to attain the American dream of the suburban home surrounded by Whiteness.

"Appropriate" social behavior is an extremely sensitive issue for Blacks. If not careful, Blacks can be labeled "sell-out" for demanding other Black folk act "with dignity" in front of White folks. Worse, Blacks can be called "Uncle Tom" for "over-the-top" mimicking of White behavior patterns to gain favor and social rewards at the cost of their own dignity as they do the delicate dance of assimilation. On the other extreme, Black folks who fully express themselves without regard for the impressions they might be drawing are said to be "bringing the race down," or worse, "ghetto."

He Hate Me, They Love Me

Does America hate or love Black athletes? The answer is, of course, both. Many of today's NCAA football stars might marvel at the fact that at one time Black players were banned from playing alongside White players in universities and the NFL. In fact, the way "the game is supposed to be played" originates from the early days of both the NCAA and the NFL when leagues were all-White in terms of players, coaches, media, owners, administrators, rule-makers, and to a large degree, stadium fans. While the accounts of sportsmanship's early days are covered in detail in Chapter 6, I want you to know that football, baseball, and basketball on all levels changed in the 1950s into what has become a multicultural sporting arena with significant numbers of African American players. And with this mixture have come cultural differences in behavior patterns and conceptual language styles both inside and outside of the lines of play.

To be sure, fans and coaches, owners and administrators, media and athletes all see the cultural differences on display on game day. The conflicts within that love-hate relationship of Black athletes show in media comments, fan grumblings about showboating, and cultural cringe by both Black and White alike. Most of the celebratory behavior we observe—at least the celebrations that are most penalized in football—are by Black players. The NFL banned end-zone celebrations in principal in 1984, though periodically relaxing the rules to allow players their occasional jump into the stands to celebrate with fans. In what appears a contradiction though, the NFL bans taking off the helmet on the field but has no problem with John Madden's NFL video-games, which feature the latest, up-to-date end-zone dances, braided hair, do-rags, chants, and poses to television cameras and crowds by athletes. Athletes even change their dances and hairstyles and notify the Madden programmers!

The NCAA, by comparison, does not allow student-athletes to take off their "hats" on the field of play nor any expression in the end-zone whatsoever—not even a spike of the football. In a creative twist to spice up their new league, the now-defunct XFL not only allowed expression but went so far as to condone individualized names on player jerseys, which led to the famous name on the back of one player's jersey that read, "He Hate Me." This was a cringe-worthy moment if ever there was one for the Black middle-class, the other group (of which I am now a part of) that definitely has a love-hate relationship with the Black athlete.[3]

This might even be a multiple-cringe moment: (1) Black player chooses Ebonics moniker, (2) Whites play along and put the poorly phrased name on his jersey, (3) player is happy, (4) announcer's poke fun at him at every turn, and (5) Blacks cringe at the ghetto phrase and wince each time his name is mentioned and he is teased by media. Or in my case, *laughed* each time I heard *He Hate Me* mentioned. I laughed at the cringe. I knew how great the athlete must have felt to have his individuality and his jersey so talked about (and hey, many of us *remember* that name, and Rod Smart was eventually good enough to turn pro in the NFL).

Rod "He Hate Me" Smart might have been implying that "I am so good that he [the opposing cornerback] hates me. He hates having me on the other side of the line—on the other team—making catches. He simply hates that I exist. Hate is all he can think of when going against me. He *hate* me." My Microsoft Word software does not allow me to type "hate" without an "s." The name He Hate Me is not ironic in the least; if anything, it is hyper real. Smart is telling it like it is. Nothing wrong with a sprinkling of Black expression on our uniform. As a matter of fact, advertisers have begun to love Ebonics and Black lingo also.

Ever heard the phrase, "We do chicken right!" Ebonics in marketing is the ever-growing influence of Black culture and expression on the commercial landscape. Black cultural language, phrasing, and "cool" are becoming more apparent every day in commercials, billboards, promotions for shows, and comedy routines. It is as if Jim Crow figures (White men dressed in Black face who performed in front of genteel White audiences and allowed to show the emotional extremes many Whites were socialized out of showing in public) are really no longer needed to appease White sensibilities. Black people are now front and center.

Commercialism is now marketing the hyper real—telling it like it is. Raw unsanitized language, in many cases; watered down, in others. There are many examples across America's visual and verbal landscape. The Golden State Warriors played the Toronto Raptors for the NBA Championship in 2019. While the Warriors theme was a strategic nod to their fans, "Strength in Numbers," the Raptors opted for the Ebonics flavored phrase, "We The North."

Raise your hand if you have heard any of these phrases on television or radio or in contemporary films: "pimped-out," "keep it on the down-low," "off the hook," "she's all that," "she's got it goin' on," "props," "shout-out," and "hatin." These are just a few phrases and words I heard while watching random television shows—over *one week. White* television shows. This type of common usage of African American "urban" phraseology was not nearly so prevalent when I left the States for New Zealand in 1996. We might be seeing a shift in who gets to determine what is appropriate (or at least cool). Not that this should be any surprise.

In New Zealand, Maori and Samoan have long looked to African American culture as the popular culture with which to identify. I once asked a Maori woman why she and others knew so many African American Motown songs I had never heard of. She thought a good while and replied, "When we pick up a guitar, we play those songs because they were the B-side to the 45 records we used to buy. We played the popular A-side so much that we wore it out. So, we had nothing left but the B-side, and we learned that, too." White kids in suburbs all over the U.S. have for years looked to Black urban style as the ultimate in cool and swagger. Here, B-side stands for Black side.

It could still be argued that even though White advertisers have picked-up on what is cool, they—in the end—still determine the approved standards. But "Black speak" is being taken up more and more as a common vernacular among the White middle-class, which says something for the acceptance across both culture and class. African American norms—or urban-based language and behaviors—are finding a home outside of urban culture, and at a rapid pace since the Internet and hip-hop explosion of the late 1990s. I think the racial disconnect is lessening as youth merge "cool culture" with "Black culture."

Part of going "mainstream" is giving up ownership. We may have "invented" (and still own the patent) on a phrase, a fist-bump, a dance-style, or hairstyle, but we no longer have sole usage rights to the (now) bit of cultural swagger, however misused or misunderstood. Part of obtaining "full citizenship," as we finally did in 1964 after protesting for civil rights, was getting some of our cultural practices mainstreamed. This same process of merging with the whole of U.S. and having fragments of one's culture infused has happened to all cultural groups since 1776.

While some Black critics will see Whites mimicking Black culture as watering-down, I see that as part of the bargain. Part of what we have been fighting for since Blacks first arrived on North American shores in 1619 is equal inclusion—and infusion. Both viewpoints are correct. This inclusion is merely happening a bit late for Black culture and style. It is no wonder we are leery of acceptance of part of our whole. We are not used to it.

My Autobiographical Position

This autobiographical remix serves to place me *within* the research instead of *outside* of it. Though at times in the text I am keen to keep objective balance in my critique of sport and culture, I am a sociologist concerned with the subjects and the outcome of the research. Where my objectivity fails me, I try to check myself. I have written elsewhere about the everyday Vernon Andrews thinking someone White was racist—only to find out that it was *me* who formulated a stereotype based upon misunderstanding behavior.[4]

While traveling through Nebraska on the way to Wisconsin in the early 1990s (as a graduate student), I stopped to get coffee one evening. The Hillbilly-looking White guy left the counter to go to the kitchen for the coffee. He took too long. He returned with my cup, but I decided he didn't like Blacks and had likely spat in my coffee. No way I was going to drink that to-go cup. I was about to head outside to "accidentally" dump it, then return for another cup. I handed him my money and he gathered the change as two Black guys walked past and called him a friendly pet name and laughed about seeing him the next day. They were all good friends. The White guy had no problems with Black people, turns out. As they walked out and he handed me my change, he even told me, "Sorry I took so long—I made you a fresh pot."

I don't like being wrong about something as serious as racism. I know how bad it feels to be called sexist for some random act out of context. I work, therefore, to first assume the best out of people. They might actually be racist, but I now look for more than superficial evidence.

Neither do I like having to experience the mental anguish we Black people have to go through to work out "truth" in these scenarios. I experienced far less stress living in New Zealand, as I was, people noted, an "*American*!" No grabbing of purses as I passed, rarely a locked car door while crossing the street, and nary a nervous woman next to me on an elevator.[5] Women know what I mean. At night, in the dark, women have to "work" to process men who walk past them. Ninety-seven (or so) percent of the men would *help* if they saw a woman being accosted. But women don't know who represents friend or foe. They have to have their guard up against every *potential* threat.

So, while I am immersed in the topic of expression and cultural difference—enough so that I have conducted academic and personal research on the subject since 1989—I am always guarding against wading too far into the White guilt or Black victim pool. I do think many Whites have good reason to feel guilt (or at least shame), and I also think lynch mobs and racist Jim Crow laws gave many (my parents and grandparents and beyond) the right to feel like victims. I also think many of us are ready and willing to move to the next stage of racial, cultural, and ethnic enlightenment. Whatever place that might be, it involves a whole lot of listening, storytelling, and on occasion, red-in-the-face disagreement.

This area of scholarship has also been the cause of countless people getting up in my face about the bad behavior of Black people. As noted earlier, many Black people over the years likewise have scolded Black athletes (or rappers or truants) over "bringing the race down." I, myself, have cringed at Black people over the years who I feel "made us look bad as a people," whatever that hyper-vigilant phrase means. Whether they are twelve-year-old kids who feel no shame at cursing loudly or talking back to adults in a mixed-race mall, drug dealers who intentionally try to get neighbors "hooked" on products (much like cigarette and pharmaceutical firms do), or athletes so hyped they get up in the face of disinterested athletes in order to intimidate. I don't like those who disrespect, those who prey on others, and those who act like bullies. We all live with our flaws. I am working on mine.

But I am slowly coming to the place where I believe what I think or feel does not matter in the overall picture, and that just because my parents raised me a certain way does not mean it was the "right" way. It just means I had my parents and you did not. You had yours. *Shame on you for having your parents and not mine.* This appears to be the general sentiment of many in society. But everybody is just a little bit different.

I am careful to target my cringing at Black folks, not White or Latino or Asians. But I don't like Whites or Latinos or Asians who bully or prey on others either. Across the board dislike. Cringing happens as a result of realizing that "negative" acts by those in our in-group might be detrimental to us by out-groups holding stereotypical views. Thus, I dislike Blacks *more* when they perform the above acts (what I might consider negative) as I am member of the greater Black community. On the matter or talking back to random elders, I remember how we behaved as kids and how we knew our boundaries and were taught to respect our elders. This is a personal attitude that obviously varies from individual to individual. In many ways, how we critique athletes is an echo of how we ourselves were raised.

As an adult I expected that Black teenagers would treat me with respect. On rare occasion, they have fallen short. I am now the adult with outdated views of the present and harkening back to the "good old days" with my own flaws of selective perception of the past and a fantasy that I have somehow paid my dues and have earned the respect of youth. This colors my social lens. But this perspective also allows me a sense of knowingness about how middle-class sensibilities of Blacks are not always based on simply looking down on others. The larger picture shows our interconnectivity.

There is a genuine sense that African Americans are losing something—something we can't quite put our finger on. Maybe it is a continuity that had at its roots a respect for one another right up the age continuum—and certainly along the race continuum. There has always been Black-on-Black crime, but there was more often than not a respect for the elderly and a general desire to build something better, together. The "I gotta get mine" culture leaves many folks over the age of fifty quite stunned at the loss of community and the "we are all in this together" love shared by many Black folk of my generation. "Help your brotha or your sista" was a social pressure we did not always live up to, but we sure as hell recognized.

Our athletes lead the way. This book is not only a call for Whites to begin to walk in our collective Black moccasins, but a call to arms for Black youth—athletes especially—to see how we are connected not only to sport or our "fellas," but also to our White, Brown, red and yellow brothers and sisters—and especially to our greater African American diaspora.

We are all still in this together. And rather than fight against the cultural cringe that youth might create by the behavior I might personally dislike, I'd rather fight for your right to express yourself. Just like you want to. Within the rules—or around the rules.

A key moment in my past shaped my concerns for the freedom of expression of so-called lower-class Blacks, or to my way of thinking, Blacks of minimal means who do not have strong social advocates to help fight their particular battles. I had an advocate who taught me the meaning of standing up to the "powers that be" for the right of self-expression. She is the reason I fight for the rights of others.

The Slave Ship as Art: Picking Your Battles

My family, in 1963 Oakland, California, in every respect could have been considered middle-class (except the part about family income). I was five years old, heading to kindergarten for the first time, and we had a nice new pink Cadillac. We also had one of the first color televisions on the street, and after getting it all hooked it up with the rabbit-ear antennae, neighbors poked in to have a look at our cutting-edge technology.

My entrepreneurial father held down a full-time landscaping job at the military base and on the weekends, in the basement, preached for a small congregation. Kathryn, my three-year-old sister, was stunningly beautiful and the apple of my father's eye. My mother played the piano for the church and loved gardening, so she planted seven different fruit trees on our property. But four short years later in 1967, it all came crashing home: Epilepsy for mom, divorce, welfare, and bare survival.

Many times my mother asked the neighbors for food because food stamps and seventy-five dollar child support did not cut it. My mother would cry endlessly, play the piano at midnight when depressed—which was *always*—and beat us weekly and for any random reason—dishes not washed, garbage not out, out after dark, teacher complaint, room messy, talking back, breaking a window playing kickball. No discussion, just whippings with any implement available—switches from peach trees, extension cords, phone cords (we had those back then), and hot water bottles. Whatever.

This type of parenting was common for Black families in the 1960s and 1970s and dated back to slavery days I suppose. To some extent those parenting patterns have faded in the 1980s and 1990s as I think the Black middle-class has learned the negative effects of this tragic bit of our history, and many families I know now rule with a strong voice, glance of the eyes, and the ever-present *threat* of bodily harm.[6]

But through it all, in those dark days of the late 1960s, my mother held it together as best she could. That she took out her aggression on us is what psychologists refer to as "projection," or displaced aggression. In truth, many Black and White families dealt with the harsh realities of divorce in the 1960s and 1970s when either the husband or wife had had enough. Be that as it was, times were not all bad. There was one time, specifically, that shines and is one reason for my defense of the underdog.

Before my father left, he and my mother decided Kathryn and I would both go to college, and the best way to procure this dream within financial reason was to purchase the *Negro Heritage Library* (an *Ebony Magazine* publication) from a travelling salesman (I would later, during my college summers, also sell books door-to-door). I loved those books and spent time by the fireplace looking at our tragic slavery and Jim Crow past. I was fascinated by the rows of slaves on the bottom of the slave ship and how neatly and organized the whole matter seemed.

From pictures, things didn't look too bad for the passengers. Of course, those sketches did not show blood, sweat, flies, mosquitoes, nor the stench and mayhem that no doubt lived in those horrific cabins. Never mind all those unsavory details. I thought this would be a fantastic bit of art to sketch and take to the annual parent-teacher spring evening in the student cafetorium at Horace Mann Elementary School.

Keep in mind, this is 1968 Oakland: The Black Panther Party was on the rise, Martin Luther King Jr. had just been killed, and Oakland was neatly situated smack-dab between all types of disruptions in Berkeley and San Francisco and the anti-war movement. And the Raiders had just lost the Super Bowl to the Packers. Things were hot. My picture of the slave-ship cabin was also hot—so hot it was decided by my teacher that it did not make "the cut."

Dejected, I crept home and slid onto the sofa to watch TV, only to have my mother ask, "Why do you still have your picture? Isn't it going up on the wall for the PTA meeting tonight?"

I mumbled a dejected phrase or two under my breath, something like, "Teacher said I can't put my picture on the wall."

"Why not?"

I did the universal kid thing and hunched my shoulders and said, "I don't know."

But she did. And thus it was time for war. She picked her battle, and this was it. There had been a racial disconnect—and I didn't even know it.

Calmly, with a few curse-words under her breath, she went to the bedroom, put on her dashiki, combed out her afro, put on some African beads for good measure, and said, "Come-on; we're going up to that school right now." It was on.

I cannot sit here and tell you with any accuracy what my mother said to those powerful White folks, Ms. Warren and Principle Parrish, in the main office. It was a closed-door session. I *can* tell you of my mother's reputation for dealing with people—"old school." Her large Louisiana family believed if you saw somebody else's kids doing wrong, you whipped them. I had seen my mother chase Donald Pipkins—the biggest bully around the neighborhood—off our porch with a shoe in her hand, smacking him upside the head.

Poor Donald had just hidden on our porch atrium in a hide-and-seek game and Mom came home thinking she had caught a burglar. She cursed like a sailor while hitting him, all the while her piercing green eyes were indeed piercing Pipkins as she held him with one arm while he desperately tried to pull away. Hide-and-seek was now a contact sport.

"There but for the grace of God go I" would be the words I'd use now to describe poor Donald's situation. Back then I just thought, "Oh Shit!"

Mom took special pleasure in parceling out a beat-down. She'd make us pick our own switches (who *does* that?), and if we dared pick a small one, she'd pull one from her stockpile of hickory-cured switches behind her bed. Poor Donald never lived it down as the "Boy who got beat by an old lady." Not your ordinary old lady.

So, as Mom came out of the campus main office on that day in 1968, she had *that* look on her face—like Donald Pipkins was on her porch all over again. Principle Parish patted his balding head with a handkerchief and poor Ms. Warren, despite my crush on her, looked very pale—like she'd been at a funeral. She didn't even look me in the eye.

My picture, turns out, *was* going up on the wall. Oakland Miracle!

That event in the principal's office stuck with me. Mom fought for me. Mom fought for the principle of the freedom of expression of my "art." Mom "had my back" even though, in some sense, my pathetic art was not worth half the effort. She had turned around, confronted the expression police, and policed *them*.

The fruit punch and chocolate chip cookies in the cafetorium never tasted as good as they did that night. Everyone treated my mother and me with uncommon respect and dignity, even if they did not really mean it. Such is the nature of concession after victory.

Momma didn't care if they *really* liked us—she just wanted them to do the right thing and treat us with respect. She might have thought, "They'll have time to like us later and probably like themselves more," knowing, upon reflection, they did the right thing—however reluctantly at the time.

Change can be like that. And this is why I defend those who are told they have no right to bring their expression to the party. Even if I don't share their style, and even if most don't think it is worth half the effort. We need to continually confront the principal in his office and test the theory of democracy and the freedom of expression. Any time and everywhere.

Notes

1. For those reading this book deep into the future, believe it or not, the Raiders used to play football in Oakland, California. If the electric grid is down in the future, just ask grandpa about it.
2. Capital Times, Wisconsin, Fall, 1989.

3. He Hate Me is the moniker used by former Las Vegas Outlaw Running back Rod Smart. He came up with the name when he first joined the team and was placed on 3rd string. Rod still used the name for autographs in the NFL, where he played as a kick returner for the Carolina Panthers. "He Hate Me because I just scored a touchdown on him," would be one usage of the name in a sentence. (From the Urban Dictionary, entry by Sean, January 19, 2004: http://www.urbandictionary.com/define.php?term=he+hate+me).
4. Please see Andrews, 2003: "Self-Reflection and the Reflected Self."
5. Ibid.
6. I forgave my mother for the beatings. I mentioned to her that awful part of my past—and she had completely forgotten. She apologized, saying, "I did the best I could."

3

The Illegal Use of Black Expression

Before & After Muhammad Ali

Valrey's Twist

Late one Friday afternoon I wandered into Fremont High School and up to the silver cyclone fence that separated the stands from the track field. I was an eighth grader from nearby Alexander Hamilton Junior High School, it was hot, and this was my first high school athletic event. I don't remember any White people being in the stands. In this part of Oakland, being White and being here, in the heart of the 'hood', represented a special type of bravery. An array of Black males and females talked loud, gestured at the other side of the track, and anticipated the final race. I soon saw why.

Three hundred and thirty yards into the race—the 440-yard, four-man relay—the home team, Fremont High (seven blocks from my doorstep) was winning. Fremont and Castlemont, two of the hard-core Oakland flatland schools, were the toughest rivals in East Oakland. These schools had the best athletes and the extreme sports pride, or so it seemed to us on the Oakland streets.

Valrey started out about two lengths behind. He paced himself and did not seem in the least bit panicked about losing. My own arms and legs would have been flailing in every direction trying to keep up. But Valrey was cool. His head was level and he looked confident. In a mere five seconds, Valrey was breathing down the neck of the Fremont track star at the final turn. And then Valrey ran even faster—and won the race.

Valrey, African American (and half Japanese), had a very different concept of sports conduct than our White forefathers, because mere victory was not enough on this day for Mr. Valrey, who later became a medical doctor. This was not a signature win—yet. Crossing the finish line first was *simply winning*. Sports in expressive Oakland were not simply about winning or losing, but how you played the game. Valrey—Black Rayban sunglasses and all—not only knew how to play the game, he knew what Castlemont Knight *and* Fremont Tiger and fans wanted: They wanted Valrey to cross the "Ts" and dot the "Is" of individuality, spontaneity, and celebration.

So, in the spirit of customer satisfaction, Valrey passed the grandstand and decided *grandstand* was not such a bad concept. He smoothly twisted his lean golden-brown six-foot tall body around, ran backwards toward the finish line, gazed over at the Tiger opponent who was flailing his arms as he struggled to keep up, tipped up those 1960s cool Black sunglasses to politely show his eyes, waved goodbye to his hustling opponent, twisted his thin body back around to face the finish line—in wonderful expressive control—and gracefully glided past the screaming fans to victory, arms-raised in forever-remembered East Oakland glory.

The place rocked. Knight fans raised their arms and hands to the sky, winced seemingly in pain at how precise the mastery of the moment was, slapped some very hard fives into each other's' burning palms again and again and again until all nearby partners were acknowledged. It was a religious moment if there ever was one in Oakland sporting lore. The crowd's physical, verbal, and psychic expression ran so deep it appeared that the fans themselves had won the race and were enjoying the victory celebration. Purple and white pom-poms waved and Knight Pride soared. To the victor go the spoils: Expressive celebration was that spoil.

After a few dazed moments, Tiger fans realized the expressive miracle they had seen and gave due respect to both Valrey and Knight supporters in the crowd by an exchange of a few slapped-hand fives, slow nods, and "brotha got down" whispers. It was as if Jesus himself had just executed a perfect 360-degree slam-dunk, such was the awe of the fans.

All Black folks agreed they had witnessed something special, something almost spiritual in its impact on this day. Perfectly executed, high-risk improvisation in a moment one could win or lose. And to have the nerve, the gall, the power to put yourself in a position to perform an act that was thought-out well in advance! Premeditation! (Or so it seemed to me. Could that have been spontaneous?) Well, that spoke to all of us who previously felt that no amount of pre-planning would keep us out of harm's way in Oakland from "the Man."

Pre-planning anything as an African American at times appeared to be arrogance: "I will achieve this!" In the face of many who said, "Yeah, right—are you bigger than the White man? Are you bigger than God? Bigger than fate?" Yes, there was arrogance in pre-planning as if your dream were actually going to happen. There is both community pride and a "laugh out loud" chuckle whenever an athlete pre-plans an expressive event, and then pulls it off. It is also the essence of cool: "He worked, he planned, he achieved, he showed us the blueprint of his plan by displaying for all to see in the end-zone and on the rim," or in Valrey's case, at the "finish line."

And in these few defining moments at Fremont High School, speed—coupled with a risky display of skill and creative genius—gave birth in my mind to a paradigm of expressive African American behavior that became normal not only in a sports context, but in many daily contexts where some sort of skill or creativity could be displayed. I began to see Black life not as an ordinary walk in the park, but as an opportunity for individuality, for expression, for a signature that said: "I grew up tough, I survived, I worked hard to get here, I won, and I'm feeling good. Let me show you how good I feel!" I learned to look outside my own life for moments when athletes would transcend mere sporting victory (because I wasn't transcending anything on the sidelines). I looked for creative genius and athletic talent that was larger than life. In some way, these expressive acts, if executed as sweetly as a Dr. J drive to the hoop, gave me hope in an uncertain White world.

And just like that, my decision that day to wander up and witness all the commotion brewing at Fremont High School was my sliding-doors moment. I say sliding doors in reference to the film of the same name starring Gwyneth Paltrow, which shows what could happen in an alternative universe if but for one door sliding shut on the subway train before Gwyneth enters. That one door shutting changes everything. Had Valrey simply trotted across the finish line as if it were was no big deal, like he had been there before, and that this was simply a walk in the park, then it is 100% certain that this book would have never been written.

That moment crystallized in my mind the crazy notion of sport as entertainment. That moment gave me no alternative but to choose the rival Castlemont High School instead of my local high school, Fremont. That moment later led me to travel around the world viewing sport and interviewing fans and athletes. Coupled with my mother's encouragement to discover and defend the subtleties of culture, that moment has inevitably led to me study this topic for over 30 years and finally complete this book.

Reflected Glory

I immersed myself in sport viewing and sought out expressive heroes like Muhammad "Float like a butterfly" Ali, Clyde "The Glide" Frazier, Earl "The Pearl" Monroe, Julius "Dr. J" Irving, and later, Michael "Air" Jordan and Steph Curry. I looked for athletes who—in the act of executing at a pivotal moment in the game or race—would strike a pose, bust a move, or sign their name on the field. I admired athletes who added a little spice to the mix. I knew they were winking at me—at us—at those who could appreciate a moment reinvented at will. Like all my older friends that day at Fremont High School, we knew we couldn't do what Valrey did. Later in life, knew I could never "Be like Mike" or pretend "I am Tiger Woods." Those people were different from me.

And that was the beauty. I was not like them. Or more straightforward, they were not like the rest of us. The fact that we curled up on the sofa and whispered, "I could never do that!" gave us the necessary separation to appreciate the difficult artistry of their skills and expressions. But right underneath the surface of distance was the emotional connection to Black athletes via our common cultural past that made us like first cousins, at least in my mind, and thus gave me some psychic connection to their greatness. Their greatness was somehow a reflection of me and the possibility that I could transcend our tattered African American past. Greatness seemed the only way out.

Reflected glory is the sociological phrase for people who feel good because their team wins. Their glory is our glory. In this sense I share in the successes and glory of every Black expressive athlete, from Jack Johnson and his flowing purple robes right up through Mr. Valrey, on past Deion Sanders and Kobe Bryant, and even with two non-American Black folks, Jamaican sprinter Usain Bolt and Greek-African NBA star, Giannis Antetokounmpo, and finally embracing expressive women who have jumped into the celebratory expression frame, Venus and Serena Williams—in the far more constrictive sport of tennis (their clothing pushed the expressive boundaries), and right up to future African American improv stars who have yet been born.

Shaking, Baking, and Risk-Taking

Of course, risks are involved in expressing during the act of triumph. Sometimes a hoopster will make an unnecessary fancy pass that badly misses the mark, injure a wrist trying to slam-dunk a ball into the rim or over the end-zone goal post, or otherwise fall on his collective expressive ass. If the athlete does not score as a result of such a screw up, and as a direct result the team loses, dire consequences will ensue, not the least of which would be perpetual ridicule from friends and foes.

One athlete I interviewed, Wisconsin wide receiver Tony Simmons, an African American from Urban Chicago, and voted one of the most expressive on the Wisconsin team in 1996, says the worse fate is that the failed act is *never forgotten*:

> … what if you did a back flip but didn't land on your feet? Now, you've scored but [you've embarrassed] yourself at the same time. Because I've seen people score. They score, they run around, boom, they fall. They embarrass themselves right there, and that's what you get for trying to showboat, do you know what I'm saying? Yeah, everything has a drawback, because you can do a back flip and not land on your feet. Now you've just embarrassed yourself. People are looking at you, and now they're laughing at you, and you hope to get up from there … I would say, 'hey, you landed on your head—at least you could land on your feet.' People remember stuff like that: 'hey, it was a nice play and all, but you still fell on your head.' Some people don't remember the stuff you did before that. They remember the stuff you did after.[1]

Teasing serves the purpose of (1) easing any obvious embarrassment the player may have had initially, (2) bonding teammates, and (3) replacing a burst of player ego with a dose of humility. Here humor can ease pain and serve as either a deterrent for future expression or a warning to practice in advance. Opinions about failed or successful acts are extremely complex and dependent on our deep cultural understanding of the act, the actors, and the context. Social and interpersonal rewards for successful execution of expressive acts vary by individual and team and fans, as do social and interpersonal punishments. Which means you consider the context and person when an expressive effort fails. Then you work from there. Mostly, you have some fun at their expense. "Here, let me help you up, Tyrone. Did that hurt? Because it looked like it hurt. Don't worry about it. Nobody saw you. Except everybody at the party. Never moonwalk with steps behind you. And for the record, I'm laughing *with* you—not *at* you. Just so we're clear."

The Problem: Different Conceptions of Sportsmanship

Since the eighth grade and that day at Fremont High School, I have noticed, as do many people who watch sport on a weekly basis, that Black and White athletes often differ in the ways they express elation or joy on the field of play, in addition to other subtle differences in style. Many Black athletes not only dance in the end-zone, hang onto the rim after slam-dunking, or pose for fans in expressive moments, but also engage in a little more talk, wear their shoes or sports clothing with a bit more individuality, and sport various hairstyles considered "radical," from Afros in the 1960s and 1970s to Jeri-curls in the 1980s (certainly cringe-worthy), to cornrows, dreadlocks, and long braids sticking out from under the helmet in the 1990s through 2020.

Individuality in clothing or tattoos or hairstyles is a significant marker of difference for many Black athletes striving to be noticed. To be sure, there have been expressive White athletes over the years, also—from longhaired student-athletes like UCLA's Bill Walton, to those who wore fancy moustaches and reveled in quirky personalities. Brian Bosworth even sported a Mohawk in his collegiate and professional football career with Oklahoma and the Seattle Seahawks, respectively. "Pistol" Pete Maravich was as showy with the basketball as any Black athlete of the time (and since), matching Earvin "Magic" Johnson for showmanship in passing and equaling Reggie Miller, Ray Allen, and Stephan Curry for long-range shooting (without the 3-point line).

Indeed, Maravich spent much time with Black athletes learning their "open" styles of playing. Maravich's father, a coach at Louisiana State University, even had son Pete spend time in urban centers playing hoops before attending LSU as he felt the Black style of basketball was "the wave of the future." Mark Gastineau of the New York Jets virtually invented the concept of the "sack dance." These cases of White expressiveness appeared to be exceptions to the rule of the middle-class norm of humility, whereas the Black athletes who were expressive seemed to be more in line with Black codes of individuality. Both assessments, while close, miss the mark.

In truth, both Black and White athletes are humble, team oriented, and low in expression. And at other times, both Black and White athletes are not humble, not team oriented, and highly individual in their expression. Black and White athletes show their humility in similar ways while they show their individuality in different ways. And what is not team oriented for White observers may be part of the team framework for Black athletes. Yes, we can be both *high* in individuality and *high* in team orientation.

Hobey Baker, discussed in Chapter 6, was humble, team oriented, *and* an individualistic football player in his day. He always heaped praise on his teammates and the other team, never wanting any credit: Humble and team oriented. Yet Hobey Baker ran back punts—if you can believe this—with no helmet on so fans could see his blond locks and good looks: Individualistic. Ali chose the round he would knock you out, and even put it to verse: Brash *and* individualistic. Ali lost his first professional fight to the tough Joe Frazier and noted that he'd probably be a "better man" for the loss: Humility.

Curtis Mayfield has a song entitled, "Don't Worry: If there is a hell below, we're all gonna go." We're all a combination of good, bad, selfish, altruistic, arrogant, humble, and fiercely individualistic. This, for better or worse, is the American way. Of course, the "situation" we express these practices in, like sport, are what gives many of us with a lack of cross-cultural understanding reasons to criticize and what also leads to overbearing rules.

Professional Athletes as Expressive Models for Behavior

Professional athletes were extremely important models back in the day (1960s–1980s) for Black kids learning how to "move and groove" on the field or court and also models for "style" and how to dress and look cool in the hood. All of us running around my neighborhood in Oakland were quick to mimic what we saw athletes do or wear on TV or what older kids in the neighborhood told us was cool. One trend was to wear white "tube socks" with multiple-colored stripes. We'd mix and match colors, coming up with our own signature color coordination of stripes. We just knew we were *all that* (and a bag of chips).

Not until I recently reviewed Nelson George's *Elevating the Game* did I find that Wilt Chamberlain initiated the striped-socks trend in the NBA. Chamberlain also initiated the headband and wristbands, other trends we followed indirectly through observing older guys in the neighborhood and at school, guys who probably followed professional sports trends more closely than the neighborhood ragamuffins.

Given the many types of expression in sport I witnessed after Valrey in East Oakland, I thought it very natural to play team sport and show individuality and entertain the crowd a bit. But as I watched games on television or read newspaper accounts of contests in the 1980s, a pattern of negative discussion emerged regarding Black celebratory expression that did not match my own positive experience in my family, among my friends, in my neighborhood, in Oakland high schools, or among other Black people I knew. Of course, not all Black athletes were expressive and not all Blacks approved of expressive behavior.[2]

Black stylistic behavior was also manifest in how African American athletes wore their uniforms on television and how they talked to teammates and opponents on inner-city basketball courts.[3] Black athletes even seemed to talk to the media in a different way—often taking questions literally and answering interviewers in a far less humble manner than their White counterparts. A question such as "Will you win tonight, Cassius?" might be met with a reply of, "Yes—because I am the greatest!" Black athletes seemed to pay less attention to soft-pedaling around questions. To be sure, I am not talking about all of the Black athletes I have observed but certainly not just the occasional Muhammad Ali, Thomas "Hollywood" Henderson, or Draymond Green.

For every outspoken Black athlete, at least eight others went about their business from week-to-week without much fuss. We all have a combination of factors in our unique lives are the catalysts for our respective styles of behavior. And though very expressive folks get the bulk of positive social attention in small groups, families, and at various African American functions, these same individuals often get the bulk of negative attention from media, fans, and rule-makers.

For this reason, the book highlights the exploits—and exploitation—of African Americans on the higher end of the expressive scale. For those Black athletes who are more extroverted and flamboyant, along with hardworking and athletically driven throughout their lives, the idea that one would suddenly act humble when confronted with a celebratory moment goes against their individual personalities. Extreme humility as a psychological weapon was probably not the way they, as young Black urban athletes, made it to the top of their trade. Why change now?

The media interpreted Black athlete behavior in a much different way than my friends and I read Black behavior. My concern about misinterpreted Black behavior grew over the years: Did White fans and media simply not understand what they were seeing? Did they not realize that celebratory expression, individual style, and improvisational risk were a large part of the fun of sport? Or was my interpretation of Black behavior unique and not shared or experienced by many other Black Americans?[4]

I believe, simply put, Black people express themselves in sports and life in ways that both converge and diverge with White behaviors.[5] Black folks might define sportsmanship or have knowledge of sport that is different from mainstream knowledge.[6] I think African Americans have an unspoken understanding of their own forms of expression that for many Whites represents a foreign language of the body. But deconstructing the component parts of the foreign language requires a far more rigorous approach than casual observation. The same difficulty is true in trying to understand the complexity of how African Americans and European Americans learn in-group behaviors. These questions require more than an individual understanding of sports expression. For these reasons I include interviews with both Black and White athletes later in the text.

Football is a sporting terrain, like basketball, where a range of behaviors is apparent. Baseball players, in contrast, show far less exuberance or extreme joy during games. The one moment that baseball players express themselves to an extreme is during arguments/fights on the field. Celebration is not penalized, per se, but repercussions in baseball (after, say, a slow home-run trot) include getting hit by a fastball for "showing up" the pitcher.

One reason for lower celebration levels might be because the adrenalin level in baseball is not as continually high as in basketball and football, and also because baseball players do not carry the ball. Or maybe because baseball is a non-contact sport and a far more conservative sport that does not tolerate individuality. There are, therefore, fewer opportunities in baseball to individualize movement or improvise play. There is also a conservative player's code against exuberance until the game is over, with the exception of home runs and pitcher strikeouts. But one had better be careful after a home run.

A story about superstar Babe Ruth "pointing" before a home run illustrates the fine line baseball players draw with any type of showmanship. Baseball legend has it that the famous slugger Babe Ruth, in the 1932 World Series that pitted the New York Yankees against the Chicago Cubs, pointed his bat toward the flagpole in the centerfield stands at Wrigley Field. Which might strike you as arrogant. On the next pitch he hit a home run to the exact spot. Baseball players often even the score, but this was not the case:

> Charlie Root, who managed Des Moines's baseball team in 1950, was Babe's victim—and the "point" of the legend always made the old pitcher furious … He admitted that Babe, before his second homer, made certain gestures in answers to hecklers in the Cub dugout. Ruth held up one finger after the first strike and two after the second—both called. Also, Root said, Babe had a habit of swinging his bat out with one hand as he took his stance. "But," Charlie explained, "he did this before every pitch. If he had really pointed, everybody who knows me knows that Ruth would have been on the seat of his pants on a knockdown pitch … Ruth himself never said he pointed." In a 1944 interview with John Carmichael of the Chicago Daily News, Babe said: "Right now I want to settle all arguments. I didn't exactly point to any spot, like the flagpole … I just sorta waved at the whole fence."[7]

Babe knew the unwritten rules in baseball against anything that bespeaks of individuality or personality or standing out as a player, though many still assert their individuality at points and turns. Notice that baseball now allows players "walk-up" music before they bat. Coco Crisp, in Oakland, has been known for his personal walk-up music and his 2013 dance "The Bernie Lean," which fans do when he comes up to bat in tune with the music.

There is one White athlete, Bryce Harper, who crystalizes the idea of the difference in baseball regarding expression that he sees as holding the sport back. Harper sees the fun in individuality as the frame for his argument:

> Baseball's tired … It's a tired sport, because you can't express yourself. You can't do what people in other sports do. I'm not saying baseball is, you know, boring or anything like that, but it's the excitement of the young guys who are coming into the game now who have flair. If that's Matt Harvey or Jacob deGrom or Manny Machado or Joc Pederson or Andrew McCutchen or Yasiel Puig—there's so many guys in the game now who are so much fun. Jose Fernandez is a great example. Jose Fernandez will strike you out and stare you down into the dugout and pump his fist. And if you hit a homer and pimp it? He doesn't care. Because you got him. That's part of the game. It's not the old feeling—hoorah … if you pimp a homer, I'm going to hit you right in the teeth. No. If a guys pimps a homer for a game-winning shot … I mean—sorry.[8]

Oh Mr. Harper, my new hero, is not done yet. He is just getting started. Now he's going to pull in other expressive athletes from other sports to ride shotgun on the Celebration Express Bus …

> If a guy pumps his fist at me on the mound, I'm going to go, 'Yeah, you got me. Good for you. Hopefully I get you the next time.' That's what makes the game fun. You want kids to play the game, right? What are kids playing these days? Football, basketball. Look at those players—Steph Curry, LeBron James. It's exciting to see those players in those sports. Cam Newton—I love the way Cam goes about it. He smiles, he laughs. It's that flair. The dramatic.[9]

Oh my. Harper gets it. But wait, there's more from another reviewer of Harper's commentary, *CBS* sportswriter Ken Axisa, who agrees with Harper's assessment:

> There is very much an old school mentality still prevalent throughout baseball. The "act like you've been there before" mentality, where any on-field gesture is considering showing up your opponent. It is tired. This is a game. It is supposed to be fun. Over the last few years MLB has made an effort to attract younger fans to the game. You know what attracts younger fans? Players acting like kids

> and having fun. Puig's bat flips and Harper's hair flips and Fernando Rodney's arrows take a pretty monotonous game and make it exciting. No young fan is going to appreciate a player with a business-like approach … Expressing yourself is frowned upon in baseball and that's a damn shame.[10]

Young writers, like many at *ESPN*, are slowly moving in the direction of "more is better" regarding expression. As these are large television networks, it is not lost on me that expressive athletes benefit the bottom line of teams, advertisers, and media conglomerates. Fans are more apt to watch the news if expressive athletes have been playing. I have zero evidence for this assertion. But fans certainly turn out at the ballpark or stadium or arena for expressive players like Brett Favre, Steph Curry and Bryce Harper. It helps to be good.

For all of the expression in and around the end-zone, professional football has very specific written rules against celebration. And, whereas basketball and its rules against verbal sparring may very well be racist,[11] the rules do not include a component regarding celebration, except for extensive hanging on the rim.[12]

The rules about celebration and football appear to come from a White middle/upper-class historical reading of the purpose of sport and the rules of sports conduct. Rules about appropriate forms of expression and sport conduct are in the rulebooks of both the NCAA and the National Football League. The cultural values underlying rules on good sportsmanship are embedded in a deeper historical context. European culture, values, manners, and civility give insight into how current rules have been recreated from past values of appropriate public behavior. European-centered historical accounts about the *right* way to behave—versus *different* ways of behaving—is a dominant group account of what is appropriate and condoned as fitting behavior. In contrast, Valrey's twist represented *his right* or legitimate way of behaving.

Politics and Sport

> "What they don't know is the bullshit, the drama, the guns, the armor, the city, the farmer, the babies, the mamas, the projects, the drugs, the children, the thugs, the tears, the hugs, the love … the problems, the things, we use, to solve them." *Who We Be*—DMX

Sport may not have been political for the majority of U.S. Whites until 1980 when the USA boycotted the Soviet Olympic Games, but sport was always a political institution for Black athletes, given segregation and exclusion over the painful years of the early and mid-twentieth century. Sports fans around the world were excited, amazed, and perplexed when Cassius Clay, Olympic Gold Medalist, broke from his White ownership syndicate, announced himself as Muhammad Ali and a member of the Nation of Islam, and later denounced in the loudest possible way his contempt for American racism and his conscientious objection to the war in Vietnam.

We praise him now for his moral fortitude, but many, both Black and White, viewed him as a traitor to Christianity, his race, and to the America that had "given" him the money and "freedoms" he complained about. That shift in Ali's life from "Black humility" to "Black expressive" to "Black revolutionary" certainly woke some White folks up. Come to think of it, it woke Black folks up, too.

No one previous to Ali (or since) had stood up to the sports establishment so brazenly and had asserted his negritude/Blackness so loudly. There were many other African Americans in the 1960s fighting for social rights in public, such as Malcolm X, and also Black expressive athletes who struggled in the distant past, such as Jack Johnson, but the combination of beating on White people in the ring, denouncing White people outside of the ring, and saying, as James Brown would later say in song, "I'm Black and I'm proud—and sick and tired of this system of things," was, at the time, revolutionary talk. And considered very bad sportsmanship.

Jack Johnson: The Original Bad Sport of the Twentieth Century

There are good sports—and we tend to agree on what good sports behavior is—and there are bad sports; yet we all differ on what makes a bad sports man or woman. Is roughness bad? Is aggression good? We could argue for hours. But back in the day, there was no doubt *who* was bad and *what* kind of bad behavior he participated in. This opinion seemed to overwhelm White sports enthusiasts. And racists.

The *first* bad sportsman in the twentieth century was Jack Johnson, a Black man who reigned as a heavyweight boxer and White antagonist in the time of both Walter Camp and Hobey Baker (1905–1919), two exemplars of U.S. sportsmanship featured in Chapter 6. American sports fans, the press, and boxers vilified Johnson for, primarily, *boxing while Black*. Or, I should say *winning while Black*, as nobody would have cared if Jack Johnson was an over-weight tomato-can getting a *beat-down* fight after fight.

Johnson, in his bravado, set the paradigm for future Black athletes in terms of *what not to do.* Black athletes who wanted general American approval (read: White acceptance) post-Jack Johnson had to be in essence the *opposite* of Johnson: Don't be politically "Black," respect Whites, never talk back, be humble—especially in victory, stay away—*miles away*—from White women, and show the proper respect to America, the U.S. government, and the flag. This is the antithesis of Jack Johnson, who could be labeled the father of bad sportsmanship—the model to which "none should aspire" and the posterchild of arrogance and ego and pride and over-indulgence. And that was just what Black people thought. I see Jack Johnson as the bravest man in American at the time. He did what no other Black man at the turn of the century dared to do—speak Black truth to power.

If there were five pictures on a wall, coaches back then—both Black and White—would point to Walter Camp, Hobey Baker, Jesse Owens, and Joe Louis, and say, "Do like they did. Be like them." They'd look to Johnson's dart-ridden photo and say, "You see what happens when you are an arrogant athlete and a bad sportsman? Don't be like him."

Jesse Owens, Joe Louis, and Jackie Robinson exemplified this contrary model of sports assimilation and indeed did succeed as "cross-over" (to White acceptance) stars. We should not disparage any of these three great athletes for doing what they had to do to win public favor. They lived in different times and did their political dance with Whiteness. It would be easy today to brand the three above Black athletes as "sell-outs" for catering too much to the will of the many racists of the time.

Their *gentlemanly humility* in the face of horrible social acts by *arrogant fans and commentators* helped pave the way for Cassius Clay to emerge and later to reframe and reinvent himself as Muhammad Ali at the peak of the Civil Rights Movement. And though we now admire and adore Ali and can acknowledge his moral struggle with racism, power, war, and religion, in his time Ali was the social villain: He was Jack Johnson reincarnate—or rather, the model *son* of bad sportsmanship in the twentieth century. He was the anti-Hobey Baker; the man most parents wanted their kids to dislike.

Ali: The Greatest Bad Sport

Muhammad Ali was loud, talked about his opponent in negative and demeaning ways, used the media even as the media was using him, was arrogant in naming his rounds of defeat of an opponent, and appeared to break every unspoken, humble, sportsmanlike rule Walter Camp and Hobey Baker had painstakingly constructed—or had constructed for them by a willing media and public.

Muhammad Ali also stands alone, in an ironic juxtaposition, as the biggest contemporary fighter of the norm of socially imposed humility on all Black citizens who participated in integrated institutions and society. That is, *Black people had little behavioral choice outside of humility in integrated social situations previous to Ali's time.* It was "be humble, or else!" Humility and self-deprecation are admirable traits in athletes and talented individuals that make us all feel better about ourselves. These concepts are significant because, as Americans, we have the freedom to choose between humility and arrogance. We can *choose* to be humble in the face of our great success. And average citizens can frame successful people as not too distant from themselves. We admire those who make us feel better.

But if Black athletes and Black citizens are forced by social norms to be humble in all interracial scenarios and live in perpetual fear of speaking their minds or acting contrary to those norms, then what you have on display is a false humility and a code of conduct that has as its master, Jim Crow, and its servant, Black athletes and other Black citizens, terrorized in public and private by otherwise upstanding White gentlemen and gentlewomen. Muhammad Ali said, "No more" to false humility and head bowing. Playful arrogance and Black power were his new calling cards. Ali was about to paint his canvas Black, like Jack Johnson before him.

In essence, looking back to the 1930s, 1940s, and 1950s before Ali, what we had were second-hand humble Black athletes; athletes who were confined by their skin color to behave in ways that they did not choose as much as it was chosen for them by the norms of the day and the delicate dance they had to do to survive, let alone thrive in sport. If humility and grace are enacted at gunpoint, then what are we really admiring? Like Plato's shadows on the cave wall, what we are looking at are shadows of selves and not the true individuals acting out of self-structured codes of conduct. I do not think either Walter Camp or Hobey Baker would approve of a post-modern culture that muzzled individuality and the freedom of expression.

But they also would not have approved of Jack Johnson's extreme showmanship. P.T. Barnum, though, would have loved Jack Johnson. Jack Johnson was the "Greatest Show on Earth" in sport at the time. Ali, indeed, borrowed some of Johnson's arrogance and showmanship, and the pre-fight hype and love/hate emotions that White wrestler Gorgeous George aroused in crowds, and Black cultural traditions of bragging and boasting and rhyming as a way to sell tickets for a fight.[13] Bragging and boasting, in this context, is tricky when trying to interpret across culture lines. Suffice to say that during Jim Crow times a Black person bragging or boasting about what he could achieve—or his exploits—was taken with a grain of salt and often said as a joke among Blacks. Ali might have been joking, but with an edge.

We knew who had the true power in society, and we knew who could wield it unmercifully at the drop of a hat or badge. The Black body and voice were highly regulated by police during Ali's time—and everyone else who deputized themselves as "behavior police" back in Jack Johnson's day. So, it is "ha-ha—laugh out loud" funny when someone Black bragged, much akin to a man bragging about being the "boss" of the house when his male friends knew his wife ran the home, the kids, and everything therein. But we humor our friends by listening and nodding while we bite our tongues and hold back tears of laughter. This is a necessary context to delineate, because Black "loud talking" is often misconstrued as *real* and heartfelt.

Loud talking is no more real than when "false-humility" constrains a White athlete or coach before a big game to pronounce, "The other [insert team, pitcher, quarterback, or coach] is better than we are." We know they think better of their own team and their chances at victory, yet they hedge their own bets downward. Likewise, it could be construed as "false-arrogance" when a Black athlete or everyday citizen brags about how good he is and that he could indeed "be the champ." Which is why people laughed at Ali from a young age about such matters:

> Soon, Clay would hook up with Angelo Dundee, his cornerman for life. "This is a new kind of person," Dundee told boxing scribes, "a special case where you can't give orders." Clay flourished under the easygoing Dundee, who taught him subtle technique as he mapped a road to the title. "I'm gonna be the champ!" bragged Clay over fallen opponents, and everybody would laugh.[14]

Similarly, though in a much more developed time in his career, Jack Johnson wore long flowing purple robes and bragged and boasted, which upset the status quo of humility, all the while winking at the Black people in the back rows, who probable laughed saying, "They actually believe Johnson's lip!" Robert Lipsyte comments on Ali's use of his lips and overall "show" to sell seats:

> It was Ali, first as Cassius Clay, who brought bodacious black style to the global village as a way of talking his opponents off balance and publicizing his fights. He sold real tickets along with wolf tickets. The cultural commentator, Nelson George, has pointed out that Ali's descriptions of himself as "pretty" was the "mack talk" of pimps and his assigning animal names to his opponents—Sonny

> (the Big Ugly Bear) Liston and Floyd (the Rabbit) Patterson—was in the African tradition of elevating oneself by dehumanizing one's enemies. George even saw Bundini Brown, Ali's assistant trainer for uplift, as a kind of Mr. Interlocutor from the minstrel shows. (Robert Lipsyte. Pro Basketball; The Art of Trash Talk Not Limited to a Court.[15]

Ali was certainly the father of contemporary sports expression to Black athletes. Yet Ali was also the father of bad sportsmanship to many Whites. Ali was easily the most hated—and loved—sportsman of the twentieth century. Why was Ali hated? After all, in his earlier days he was revered much like Hobey Baker, as the model of what an athlete (especially a Black athlete) should be: Quiet, respectful, endearing, and deferential to the media and elders. The early Cassius Clay was similar to Hobey Baker—he did his talking in the ring, though he was considered quite a joker and good-natured braggart. And further, he was not yet political, which eventually changed the tide of how people framed him.

When asked about racial issues in the Jim Crow South upon arriving home from the Olympic Games in Rome with his gold medal and American flag in 1960, Ali noted that there were qualified politicians and others who could better answer those questions. Hobey would have been proud of a humble answer like that. But what would transpire over the next few years in America would change Ali, change boxing, change the nation, and for the sake of this book, change the impressions people had of Black expression in and around sport.

Ali, the Nation of Islam, and Flawed Heroes

How could anyone's persona change so much during the height of his popularity so as to alienate both Black and White fans in America?[16] Yes, many Black sports fans and citizens alike despised Ali, but for different reasons that had little to do with poor sportsmanship. White notions of how Black athletes should behave were well-entrenched with the role models of Jackie Robinson and Joe Louis, who had both learned the lessons of the bad-ass Jack Johnson of the early twentieth century: Speak quietly and do nothing to upset the racial status quo.

Ali's story is a complex one and deserving of larger treatment throughout this text as he represents a rise and fall from grace—and then a rise again. America made many changes in the social order between the time Ali started boxing in the 1950s right up to his redemption in 1996. His fall and vilification happened, though, soon after he left his boxing syndicate and intertwined his fate with the Nation of Islam:

> In the early 1960s, Ali, then Cassius Clay, burst into public view as a loud-mouthed showboat, a skilled boxer with dubious and insufferable claims to greatness. (How little did we know?) He joined the Nation of Islam, then widely perceived as a separatist sect of black militants. And in 1966, he defied Uncle Sam with his celebrated quip, "I ain't got no quarrel with them Vietcong." Ultimately, he faced his darkest hour when he refused induction into the armed forces, instead choosing exile from boxing and a long court battle. (John Stravinsky, The Long Reach of Muhammad Ali). [17]

The Nation of Islam represented Allah and not Jesus, and for Black Christians—who had long held beliefs in the by-and-by (more in Chapter 4 on Black Christianity)—this was sacrilegious and racial suicide. "Why hast though forsaken us?" Black people seemed to ask. He was speaking a language (Islam) of The Nation that was unfamiliar to Black people. Ali sent many Black people cringing and running in the other direction. Ali was thus, by many, considered to be "ruining" it (the chances at social equality) for everyone else. Not that this was Ali's burden to change on his own.

Ali as the "Big Bang" for Black Sporting Expression

And thus the die was cast for Black athletes to mimic and live up to the Ali persona of self-love, Black love, religious freedom, ego-centered self-expression, celebration, psychological warfare (later repackaged by the media as the more negative "taunting"), self-promotion for monetary ends, and clothing artifacts as individual style and norm-crashing. About the only "in your face" thing he didn't engage in was shaving his head, preferring instead the Afro hairstyle that was in itself a political statement in the 1960s.

His continued resistance to social power as embodied in the White-run institutions of the penal system, the military establishment, the draft board, the boxing syndicates, and the federal government—at the expense of his career, his livelihood, his means of supporting his family and religion—was a bold expression of local Black power that sent a shockwave through the Black community. All had to question their own commitment to social values, the Black power movement, family, and just how far we would be willing to go to fight for a cause. Many knew they were in no way prepared to sacrifice as much as Ali was sacrificing for the race, their jobs, or their families. There were some things were more important than racial pride. Eating, for one. And you can't eat unless you have a job.

But, lo and behold, with the advent of the Black Panther Party and other movements and social upheavals in the 1960s, many Blacks began to see Ali as a hero of sorts and a leader—someone ahead of his time. Even the military servicemen fighting in Vietnam who at first chastised and disliked Ali for his negative stance on the war and "draft dodging" began to see him as a prophet of sorts.

And, in truth, that is what Ali represented to Black people—a modern-day prophet living by a religious and social code none of us knew anything about. Ali was willing to sacrifice everything for a higher purpose. We are not supposed to say that word "prophet," but that is what many felt. He lived in a time of other prophets named King and X, and he was the only one who survived the 1960s.

Slowly but surely, with Ali setting the example, other athletes didn't feel so constrained by the tight rules, codes, and restrictions on their behavior. Olympians were protesting with clothing—sunglasses, Black socks—and with their fists. Athletes across college campuses also began to protest—with beards, mustaches, Afro haircuts, dashikis, and Afrocentric jewelry. Campuses and power structures began fighting back by instituting rules that *forbid* facial hair and long hair.

These rules, of course, were for all athletes, not just African Americans. White athletes were upset because they had to cut their long hair—which was also a protest of the older, more conventional system of things. Hippies and the hippie lifestyle, exemplified by people like UCLA Basketball star Bill Walton, promoted freedom of expression also, which included experimentation with drugs, sex, and devaluing both money and bodily conventions like short hair and no facial hair.

White athletes, caught in the middle of social revolutions just like Black athletes, had to make tough social choices. Compromise and cut your hair or challenge the system? Many athletes, both Black and White, challenged the status quo and lost the battle. Many were kicked off of teams, thus ending careers, and others were blacklisted. Athletes—both Black and White—were learning the high price of living up to the social justice in sport and society stance set in motion by Muhammad Ali.

End-zone celebrations in professional and collegiate football followed soon after in the early 1970s. No, end-zone dances were not political in the traditional sense. There were no raised fists or Black gloves after touchdowns. Ali broke the door down, but people ran into the house and did what suited their individual fancy.

The case of Thomas "Hollywood" Henderson is novel because he was expressive on the field and on the sidelines, and because he played for "America's Team," the Dallas Cowboys. He frequently contested the control of his behavior by the Cowboys, which management and beat writers generally deemed unsportsmanlike. "Hollywood" was considered individualistic, and therefore, not a team player. You can't be both, history has taught us. Ali never played on a team sport so never contended with this criticism.

Henderson challenged the notion that he could not be an individual in the context of team-oriented football: "There's a difference between being a team player and being a company man. I said what I thought and I gave everything I had on the field for the Cowboys … I just wanted to play the game and do my thing."[18] Henderson wanted to play the game in line with team goals and ideals about winning and working together but drew the line at "doing any—and every-thing the boss wanted." Hence his notion of falling prey to being a company man.

"Hollywood," as the nickname implies, saw the game as performance. To control behavior was not the domain of the owners or coaches, in his view. This all goes solidly against the grain of tradition in football, and indeed sport in the USA. Employees in most industries are paid to work, remain silent (unless spoken to), cause no trouble, treat co-workers respectfully, and return safely home to family. We do it in our jobs; why shouldn't athletes?

Yet, as we all know, expression and outspokenness and bragging and boasting and challenging management, coaches, umpires, and referees happens daily. And while obviously the home fans pay less attention to player indiscretions if the home team wins, opposing fans are often not so apt to let individualistic players off the hook. The end-zone dance, while loved at home stadiums (Icky Woods, Deion Sanders, and Chad Ocho Cinco are three good examples from the 1980s, 1990s, and 2000s, respectively), tends to be booed when performed in front of the opposition. "You can score a touchdown, but don't dance in our house" is a common sentiment among many, if not most, football fans and players alike.

The earliest end-zone dance anyone seems to remember was by Elmo Wright, wide receiver for the Kansas City Chiefs in the early 1970s. He performed a high-knee kick for about five seconds once he entered the end-zone. This type of end-zone expression was later (1984) banned from professional football. Below is the NFL's official interpretation of, and response to, expressive behavior in what they call "gridiron" football in New Zealand. The people evaluating the behavior this time are on the National Football League's Rules Committee. We are left asking: What is normal? What is sportsmanlike conduct? Do sports conduct norms change over time? All of these questions are of primary concern in this book.

The league attempts to define appropriate and inappropriate forms of expression in 1984 for athletes such as Hollywood Henderson and Elmo Wright in their writing of rules against celebratory behavior:

Figure 3.1. Ickey Wood's dance was moved to the sidelines by the NFL, but it still motivated his fans and his Cincinnati Benglas. Source: Rick Stewart/Getty Images Sport/Getty Images

> The Committee is unanimously opposed to any prolonged, excessive or premeditated celebration by individual players or groups of players. Antics such as unrestrained dances, wild flailing of arms and legs, simulated dice games, 'high-five' circles in the end-zone, imitations of gun-fighters, and similar behavior are deemed to be contrived exhibitionism that has no place in the sport and should be penalized five yards for unsportsmanlike conduct. There is no intent here to prohibit normal reactions in emotional situations. When they expand, however, into prolonged and unreasonable demonstrations, they are perceived as attempts by players merely to draw attention to themselves and can easily provoke opponents.[19]

The league is trying to make a case for keeping the game at high standards of decorum. Never mind that TV commercials that promote NFL games highlight athlete expression; that commercials for Campbell's soup or car insurance or beer use athletes and coaches in full expressive mode to sell products. Commercial interests love expressive athletes like Aaron Rodgers and his "Discount double-check" celebratory expression. Is the reason the rules exist because of the presumed values of people in the Midwest and southern "fly-over" states who are solidly against Black cultural expressive-styles?

What, then, explains the Midwestern state of Wisconsin, the expressive Aaron Rodgers, and the "Lambeau Leap?" The "Leap" was allowed as an NFL-sanctioned bit of expression that involved primarily Black players jumping into the laps of primarily White, bratwurst-and-cheese-curd-eating, fans. This was legal when dancing was illegal.

According to the rules committee, certain acts are simply not "normal." Who's view of normal? —remains the question.

The Committee is careful to note that not *all* expression need be stifled. Just those acts that are prolong and appear premeditated at the time of the ruling. Which, for some reason, means you can't take your helmet off while on the field of play. The main goal might be to prevent players from provoking others by the act of drawing attention to themselves. We should not do things—like use expressive forms of behavior that are foreign to the rules committee—that might upset traditional White people, like those folks who impose rules on expression. This is the official notification that the use of Black culture on the football field shall be penalized. The "illegal use of Black expression" is thus implied by celebration rules and language. The racial disconnect in sport grows more apparent.

A Brief History of End-Zone Drama: Rulemaking and Rule Breaking

It often appears athletes have an agenda of their own and are intent on bending and breaking the rules, in the end upsetting coaches, owners, fans, and other players. The rules of on-field celebration—and the breaking of those rules—have been a cat-and-mouse game between the league and players over the years. Are players simply defying the rules and the norms? Might they be oblivious to sportsmanship and the team ethic? The rules will continue to shift. The most recent win has been for the athletes. But I predict more changes. Here we go:

1. Players began spiking (slamming the ball down hard to the turf) the ball mid-field after a nice catch, to the chagrin of referees who had to then hustle after the ball. The Rules Committee (primarily the team owners) imposed a rule that implies 'no spiking on the field of play.' Got to control the herd.
2. Players were thus content to spike the ball 'off' the field of play—in the end-zone—and sometimes added in a dance, wave, or gesture to the

crowd, teammates, the television camera, or opposing players. The Rules Committee had good reason to huddle-up and come back with new rules as they noted that not only did celebrations provoke opponents, but in the end started fights. For good measure, they noted celebrations were too long and delayed the games. Never mind that games were becoming longer due to play stoppage for more "TV Time-out" commercial time. The Rules Committee thus said no dancing in the end-zone.

3. Icky Woods of the Cincinnati Bengals then decides in 1989 to take his dances to the sidelines, behind the home team's bench, directly facing the crowd. The Rules Committee scratched their collective heads and declared, "No dancing will be allowed on the sidelines" (presumably because it wasted valuable fan time).
4. The players—always alert to a new opportunity—decide to do their dances or moves or gestures in the act of running *before* they reach the end-zone in order to escape celebration penalties. Players also scored touchdowns and then stopped and posed for the cameras or crowd—legs spread, hands on hips—quickly, I believe, to avoid the "prolonged" rule, or pose without a dance, to avoid the "excessiveness" rule, and pose without teammates to avoid the appearance of "premeditation." There are more permeations and changes in rules and morphing of expressive strategies by players each year in the NFL. All sorts of mayhem. In 2014, the league decided to ban slam-dunking over the goal post. In 2018 the League relaxed the rules. And if fans complain, the owners will put their badges back on and again police Black athletes. This disconnect will go on and on. Power concedes nothing without a fight. But the freedom of expression will test power to the end, fighting all the way.

On occasion—rare occasion—there are college athletes who express in the end-zone, and there are strict rules that disapprove of certain forms of sports conduct, which are far stricter than pro rules. You cannot even spike the ball in college—anywhere at any time. In this amateur arena where more traditional rules apply (is pro sport more geared for entertainment?) the players do not receive salaries, only the promise of a four-year degree (unless they are cut) sandwiched between their years of football eligibility. The NCAA stated, in 1995, that:

> The NCAA Football Rules Committee has exceptional pride in the Football Code … These guidelines form a harmony of agreement between coaches, players, game officials and administrators that places each contest in an environment

> of fairness and sportsmanship. Players will express excitement over a great play but must never address remarks or gestures to opponents or spectators, nor may they spike the ball or throw it into the air. Choreographed or delayed spectacles have no validity in football and detract from its honored traditions. Enthusiasm without exhibitionism must be the goal for the 1995 season. Specifically prohibited acts and conduct include: (a) Pointing the finger(s), hand(s), arm(s) or ball at an opponent, (b) Baiting or insulting an opponent verbally, (c) Inciting an opponent or spectators in any other way. (d) Any delayed, excessive or prolonged act by which a player attempts to focus attention upon himself, (e) Removal of a player's helmet before he is in the team area ... or spiking the ball to the ground ... Flagrant offenders ... shall be disqualified. If a player commits two unsportsmanlike fouls in the same game, he shall be disqualified (NCAA Football Rules). (For recent rules additions please see the endnotes.)[20]

The above elaboration on good and bad sportsmanship points backward to "honored traditions" and the "football code." The traditions and codes they speak of have been initiated in the USA by one man, the father of American Football, Walter Camp. Camp serves as an anchor for any discussion of conduct in football, and a peak behind the historical curtain later in Chapter 6 at the man who begat the current mythology serves our purposes well in uncovering a modern model for what good sportsmanship consists of. If we are ever to forge a hybrid notion of sport in the U.S.A. that includes many perspectives on sports culture and behavior, "We've got to go back before we can go forward. Know your history," my mother once told me. Many times.

Body Expression in the 1970s: Gettin' Black

With the 1970s came more inclusion of African Americans in a variety of social institutions, often initiated by forceful political hands and socially loud mouths. Black people learned in the 1950s and 1960s that shouting loudly was a new social privilege. For White people, shouting was, of course, always a social right. But for Black folks the idea of public shouting anywhere around White people in the South during Jim Crow times (roughly 1865–1965) was a crime punishable by a swift kick in the ass. We decided to try on our newfound social privilege in a variety of social spaces and institutions. And we liked it.

Turns out Whites didn't like it when Black folks got loud—or as we say in the "hood," "got Black." When it comes right down to it, it really means "get loud and angry like we are not supposed to and never were supposed to around White folks because of that looming slap across our face or swift kick in the ass." Because, given U.S. social history and arrogance, what we are really doing is mimicking what Whites have *always* done—we are actually exercising our right to "get White" on somebody. Of course, we always "acted a fool" around each other, but that was mostly about getting loud and silly.

"Getting Black" is a specific social style of behavior situated in social spaces occupied by White people and ignited when Black people feel they have been wronged and want to "right" the disrespectful situation. This is the precursor to the "Act Up" movement within the gay and lesbian community designed to disrupt the normal proceedings of meetings and social spaces in order to politicize the moment. Either way, "getting Black" by "acting up" is usually accompanied by anger, finger pointing, hand on hips, head bobbing and weaving, and some reference to both race and respect. In my experience, Black women are far more skilled at this craft than Black men.

Whites Not Tickled with Elmo

Muhammad Ali, as noted above, was the first athlete in modern times in the domain of White sport to express himself to the level of major annoyance to White audiences. And that was just with his mouth. The idea of someone expressing a strong cultural emotion with the body was sacrilegious in sport. Of course, Little Richard had come along in the 1950s and invented rock and roll, body in full swing, and was later mimicked by Elvis Presley. These gyrations were not being tolerated, though they later would be, in the late 1950s and early 1960s when Ali made his way onto the scene with his dancing in the ring and later, his flashy red tassels dangling from his white boots.

Athletes were supposed to respect their opponents and respect the sport and not cause the competitor any embarrassment or shame. This was the American sport ethic—to be held in the same high esteem as religion. No minister would dance in the pulpit, would he? No choir would gyrate or get out of hand? No congregation would shout and move away from their seats and "act up" and "show out" would they? We are all dignified, aren't we? You've obviously never been to a Black church in Oakland—or other urban or southern setting. In Chapter 4, we will explore in more detail the interrelationship between Black church expression and sport. There is plenty of body expression in and around Black churches and neighborhoods.

After 1965, African Americans took the newly acquired high ideals of Civil Rights cautiously to heart and began acting as full participants in all that society had to offer in the way of regional mobility, economic gain, voting rights, higher education, and the freedom of expression. It is no wonder the first NFL spike of a football was in 1965 by New York Giant Homer Carroll Jones.[21] And then along came Elmo Wright, a wide receiver for the Kansas City Chiefs, who decided he'd take his newfound social freedom of expression right into the end-zone during the game. Football was never the same.

Elmo Wright started "showing out" right there in the end-zone in front of all the cameras and fans of the National Football League. Tradition in the nation's most rugged sport had just begat another tradition. Mr. Wright's end-zone dance was not flashy. He resembled someone speedily running in place. His end-zone expression, dazzling to us at the time, would be fairly tame today. Elmo Wright's dance resembled the high-knee thrust of a marching band member, except neither of his feet touched the ground at the same time. It was simple, but it was exciting and different and made us watch in anticipation. Though Whites may not have been pleased, I believe most simply looked the other way, possibly seeing it as a "one off" occurrence: No need for control. No racial disconnect yet.

Black folks, or *Negroes* as many still called us back then, were not supposed to act like this in public around White folks, which is what made it all the more fun. How about that: A Black athlete spontaneously showed some expressive joy and emotion and showing out without any shame or apology for his Blackness. It was a small moment in national history, but significant for neighborhood Black boys.

The secret Black handshake was no longer tucked neatly into our back pockets and we arrogantly slapped each other "five" hard on both hands so hard it would sting. Years of pinned-up expressive emotion flowed forth. Young folks in my family had previous to this been told that once you go work for The Man you have to become *like* The Man—as White as your pride would allow. Matter of fact, you had to act White to even be *considered a candidate*. We were made to feel that we had to sell our cultural souls in order to achieve in the White world beyond Urban America. There are, of course, parallels with women (of all shades) in the workplace conforming to the male norm of expressive behavior, language, style, and even political opinion.

The loss of the cultural self would usually show up when Black folks like me who had left for a long period of time came back to the urban Black church. We seemed stiffer, more ill at ease in the setting, more aloof. Matter of fact, we acted much like the White people who would occasionally attend Sunday services.

Maybe that is where the myth of losing one's cultural swerve, swagger, and cultural soul at the hands of middle-class America (while away at college) began. One can never be sure.

I would not have felt the same emotions had Elmo Wright been White. The act would not have had a *cultural* impact on me or the other kids in my neighborhood. I would not have felt the same pride in the player or the same social awakening if the subversive act and local empowerment had been by anyone other than a Black player. I was fourteen years old, playing street football, and thereafter mimicking everything I saw him, and later, Billy "White Shoes" Johnson, do.

That's what kids do—we see it in sport, and we bring it to the streets. In that way it might be a completion of the circle, as many Black athletes learned their sport and attitude toward sport from the street. Certainly, Billy Johnson did. Billy "White Shoes" Johnson took expression to an entirely different level, holding the ball aloft in one hand while doing the "funky chicken" with his knees moving outward and then inward while bent, again and again. He was funky and fun. Way funkier than me.

College Football Expression: The Case of the Roadrunner

In 1972, a collegiate athlete named Rufus Ferguson at University of Wisconsin-Madison adapted a dance called the "roadrunner shuffle." The roadrunner portion of the title referred to his nickname earned by his quickness as a high school athlete. Rufus would run through holes cleared by Wisconsin's massive front line and make his way around and by people with speed and agility. If he scored, he would hold the ball high, slightly bend both knees, and do a bit of an Irish River Dance knee-kick from his heels forward. He'd then hug the linemen and run back to the sidelines.

He was the first NCAA Division I athlete to do an end-zone dance of any sort (at least according to local lore). I tracked down Mr. Ferguson and asked him how people responded to his dancing. He noted that the fans loved it, his fellow players loved it, and so he kept doing it. I was surprised Rufus had gotten away with his expression for more than one game. Something was changing in America in the early 1970s if predominantly White Wisconsin was embracing an expressive Black athlete. What did the team's power authority, the coach, think?

"The coach did not like it," Mr. Ferguson, the owner of a sprawling Ford car and truck dealership in Pennsylvania, responded.

As far as I knew, when White people in power did not like something, they enforced a behavioral "adjustment." Not so, in this case. Mr. Ferguson, when pressed, issued forth this assessment of the situation:

> The coach did not like me dancing in the end-zone, but I was scoring, we started winning, fans started coming to games, and we started making money for the athletic department. Which meant that the boosters and alumni loved it. And so the alumni told the coach to back off and allow me to dance if I wanted to. Because the Badgers were filling the stands at Camp Randall with people for the first time in a long time and the alumni, they just loved it. And, basically, what the Alumni says, goes.[22]

How is it that Badger fans—predominantly White, rural, and protestant—loved Rufus and his dance? This seems counter-intuitive, given that White Americans from Midwestern small towns are thought to be less expressive and more conservative than most. So will the real White, middle-class protestant male please stand up? Where is he? Is he the generic White fan in the stands in Madison cheering for Rufus? No. Is he the head coach of the Badgers?

Maybe. The coach *represents the ideas* and *enforces the ideas* of White middle-class society, but without the power to enforce his own tastes in this instance with the Badgers. Leroy Butler invented the "Lambeau Leap"—a Black man in upper Wisconsin jumping into a stadium crowd full of drunken White men and women—and they loved it.[23] "What the alumni says, goes," as Mr. Ferguson reminds us. It also appears that what the fans say, goes: The NFL does not fine or penalize players for the Lambeau Leap (though they considered it for a minute).

Figure 3.2. Mosh pit in Green Bay as fans enjoy Packer Donald Driver doing the "Lambeau Leap." Source: Dilip Vishwanat/Getty Images Sport/Getty Images

The NCAA Videotape and Long-Standing White Traditions

The NCAA has produced videotape called "A Tradition of Teamwork," produced after instilling rules against celebratory behavior in college athletics early in the 1990s. They might as well have called it, "How to Police Yourself—Especially if you are Black." The rule, enacted in circa 1993, was first dubbed the "Miami Rule" because the NCAA and media specifically targeted the Miami Hurricanes as the chief offenders of the high standards of sportsmanship in amateur athletics. The Hurricanes, who count the among their former players the likes of Michael Irvin and Ray Lewis, were often given to expressing themselves after catches, tackles, and touchdowns on the field. These acts appeared to draw attention to the athlete but also to rally the team and demoralize opponents.

The first college football game I ever attended in Wisconsin was against the Hurricanes in 1989. I remember it clearly. The Hurricanes won in Madison, 53-3. I was demoralized. But like a lemming I followed fans onto the field after the game to do the "chicken dance" with the band in the infamous "Fifth Quarter." I became ecstatic. The loud chant from Wisconsin fans as we ran onto the field was "We scored first!" I learned that day that it was okay to celebrate small victories. The game was over. There is always a nugget of pride to be had—even if someone *was* dancing in your end-zone.[24]

The Hurricanes had a string of national championships (1983, 1987, 1989, 1991, and later in 2001) and were thus often on national television. As fate would have it, their most successful leader over the years—and a man who was very emotive himself—was a coach named Jimmy Johnson. He wasn't your average coach. He allowed his players their freedom of expression. And they performed. But in 1992, the NCAA had enough and established the "Miami Rule," as it was called, that disallowed any acts that "draw attention to the individual and not the team." Transgressions such as finger pointing, crowd baiting, spiking the football into the turf, or booty-shaking were now off limits and punishable by a fine. I get it. Sometimes players go too far.

The NFL had also established rules, in 1984, which were also anti-expression and based upon reviewing acts by "The Smurfs" of Washington and Mark Gastineau of the New York Jets. So, the NCAA was following in the restrictive policing footsteps of its bigger football brother.

The videotape by the NCAA speaks to "honored traditions" and "normal behavior" that we have *all come to agree* is the "appropriate" way to behave. No amount of individual dancing or prancing about "will be tolerated," because this type of behavior "is not normal, not natural and does not flow down from the honored traditions of amateur and gentlemanly behavior."

Vince Dooley, head of the rules committee at the time and athletic director at Georgia Tech, is the voice and face in the camera speaking to athletes and speaking for *all who have played* and closely observed sport from the lofty perch of morality and virtue and the highest democratic ideals of equality and egalitarianism. He is speaking not only to Black athletes, but also to White athletes, which of course follows in a long tradition of not *intentionally* targeting or profiling individuals but making the laws equal in their effect on lives.

Dooley is speaking to a generation of young Americans that were raised in the 1970s and 1980s on Michael Jackson's twirling, leg kicking, and crotch-grabbing pop music; raised with the funk tracks of George Clinton, Parliament, Funkadelic, and Bootsy Collins; and raised with the soul of James Brown and Aretha Franklin and funk music sampled to provide the background tracks for rap music that blared on schoolyards, courts, and around neighborhoods and in homes on videos via "music television." Vince Dooley was speaking via the stern video not to passive Black and White youth of the 1950s, but to individualistic and opportunistic and expressive youth like Deion Sanders (of Florida State) in the 1990s. Quite a challenge.

The flashy clothes and celebration of self-expression that happened in Black culture in the 1970s spilled over into the 1980s and gradually the sports world became a place where athletes became not only sportsmen and women, but also entertainers and entrepreneurs shaping themselves into marketable commodities. Of course, they had come to realize that whether or not they marketed themselves, they were still commodities for the teams and schools they played for. They knew the amateur ideal, as touted by the NCAA, was no more than a smokescreen that allowed collegiate sports to justify the billions they were making while compensating the athletes with scholarships, dorms, food, and less-than-minimum-wage "pay."

American sport, somewhere between 1972 and 1992, grew to become work *and* entertainment for Black athletes in predominantly White stadiums across the country while at the same time becoming a social space of control. In the Negro Leagues, sport had always been entertainment and fun, never given to the aggressiveness and violence that is part of the "normal" playing of hockey and football in North America.

After Elmo Wright, more and more Black athletes began to treat sport as a place for expressions of joy and culture, and "in-your-face" psychological warfare that was later repackaged as "taunting." Historically, taunting was evident on the streets of any Southern city on any given day (between 1865 and 1965) when Whites disagreed with Black behavior, however humble Blacks might appear. That brand of taunting was sanctioned by police and the court system. Whites were not complaining about taunting, so long as it was them doing the taunting. Years later we took our expression to the arena, the only place we would be allowed to stand up to White folks, though more of that is happening these days.

We got our groove on in the 1970s and, halfway through the 1980s, the NFL decided enough was enough and put a stop to the "nonsense." And, with a shrug of the shoulders and a finger pointing to rule number "167.8, Section D" Whites can simply say, "Sorry, it's in the rulebook."

This feigned apology is a way of distancing rule-makers from power. The distance happens in the form of pointing to the *rule* rather than pointing to the power that can *change* the rule. The blame is placed on the *unchangeable rule*, rather than on the rules committee that has the power to adjust or eliminate the rule.

When we allow those in power to distance themselves from their own dominance by pointing to rules rather than arguing for rule changes, we are complicit in the buy-in that rules can never be changed. Rules are *not* commandments on stone tablets that cannot be altered lest our entire democracy come crashing down. Unless, of course, those in power decide to "upgrade" the rule when it suits monetary goals. Or a compromise to appease athletes who might morph into social activists.

The implicit *rule behind the rules* is that "If a rule has been in place for many years, there is no reason and no way to change it, regardless of how much you complain." And further suggestions to "change tradition" are simply insubordination.

But, on occasion, when it suits the ends of league officials, rules are changed for "the betterment of the game," "progress," or some such justification that trumps the previous notions of tradition and history and amateurism. There is a powerful golden rule in America, and it is: "*He* who has the gold makes the rules." This is the overarching power of rulemaking that all of us across classes, genders, sexualities, abilities, races, and cultures have conceded as "Just the way things are." But be warned that when rules are "loosened" because of public opinion, this is often a smokescreen.

Power knows that loosening the rules makes people happy and quiets the unruly masses. But the unruly masses should take matters one step further: Eliminate the rule or law, whatever it is. The right to spit on the street, to marry interracially, to buy a beer after dark, to have consensual wild sex with your husband or wife on a Sunday, whatever the rule is—if it is time-worn and of a bygone era, but is still on the books—get rid of it. Or it will surely bite you or someone you love right on the ass on any given Sunday. And I'm not simply talking about touchdown dances.

Because, sure enough, when the tide shifts and power wants to point anew to any rule, or misogynistic or homophobic or racist law, as archaic and ancient as it might be, they will. And you and I will be trapped.

Notes

1. Tony Simmons, Univ. of Wisconsin-Madison, 1996. Personal interview, p. 41.
2. What about Blacks who respond negatively to expressive celebratory behavior … even the very idea of discussing these topics with a White public, as I am doing here? To be fair, there are at least two objections to my line of research and this very public discussion of Black culture. One line of comment follows the (1) "I hate white folks thinking that all we like to do is play football and dance—we're reproducing stereotypes that may negatively affect the race" line, and the other, the (2) "why can't we just play football and shut up" critique. The latter comment is an assimilationist stance that carries along with it the sentiment that Blacks should behave like Whites in order to gain acceptance. To some degree, those critics are right. You cannot allow yourself the luxury of pretending everybody is down with your "new look" just because it's "fly" in your neighborhood. I get that. I lived that at Hewlett-Packard Company. I do not concur with the specific "just act white and it will be alright" theory of behavior. We've done that against our will many times. I do, however, understand the former sentiment and feel I need to address this here as I have been asked by both Blacks and Whites about my research "reproducing stereotypes." My question is: What stereotypes do you think Whites have? What will eliminate them? Certainly not avoiding the topic of difference, which I do believe exists re self-expression. This battle is often a class-educational level clash in Black culture, with those of us who are academically inclined fighting the hard fight for rights on one end and feeling that lower-class, more "expressive" Blacks feed negative White imaginations. My answer is that just because one chooses to express does not mean the behavior is negative. I believe the battle is better fought when we attack the stereotyped and negative casting of our behavior rather than silencing yet another Black nonverbal cultural voice.
3. Shirts untucked, baggy shorts in basketball, multi-colored socks, hats turned "to the back" are all examples of this bodily expressiveness of style.
4. In this paper I use the terms United States and America interchangeably, aware that I am excluding Canada, Central and South America. My intent is to break the monotony of one referent rather than to exclude.
5. I use the term "White" to describe both a social formation of power and as an American racial category.

6. "Sportsmanship" and "sportsmanlike" conduct are sexist words that hearken back to the days sport was for men and not women, White and not Black. With so many social changes (1996 was the "year of the woman" at the Olympic Games) since the inception of the word, it is no longer useful to describe a "players' code" of behavior because the term is based in White male behavior patterns. The term, therefore, is initially used in the text with quotation marks. But the archaic term is still useful as it describes a mindset and knowledge that I will be critiquing, so you will occasionally see the term sans quotation marks. In essence, there is no Sportsmanlike conduct with a capitol "S," but many knowledges of playing sport and many knowledges of conduct befitting of sport. I therefore often use the phrase "sport conduct" as an alternative to sportsmanship.
7. Bryson, 1989, pp. 7–8.
8. Keown, T. 2016. "Sorry—not sorry." *ESPN The Magazine.* March 10.
9. Ibid.
10. Axisa, M. 2016. "Bryce Harper: Baseball 'a tired sport, because you can't express yourself.'" *CBSSPORTS.COM.* March 10. https://www.cbssports.com/mlb/news/bryce-harper-baseball-a-tired-sport-because-you-cant-express-yourself/.
11. I refer to Cashmore (1990) for a working definition of racism: "A set of beliefs or ideas based on the assumption that the world's population can be divided into different human biological groups designated 'races.' Following on from this is the proposition that the 'races' are ordered hierarchically, so that some stand in a position of superordinacy, or superiority, to others. This is a classic type of racism; nowadays, ideas of superiority are often veiled in arguments concerning culture, nationalism, and ethnic identity. Quite often, these contain connotations of racism that are not specific, but only inferred. When ideas, or beliefs, about racial superiority are translated into action, we speak in terms of racial discrimination or simply racialism" (Cashmore 1990: 81).
12. Hanging on the rim is prohibited except in cases where players are observing where they might land. Hanging on the rim is generally considered celebratory expression by some, and showboating by others. Hence, the rule.
13. Please see "The Full Story of Muhammad Ali—World Documentary Films." https://www.youtube.com/watch?v=P3HYPkfd2v8&t=387s.
14. Stravinsky, John, 1997, p. 2.
15. Lipsyte, Robert, 1994, p. 8.
16. Tiger Woods may be the only other athlete in his prime to achieve this feat in 2009 after his multiple affairs.
17. Stravinsky, John, 1997.
18. Henderson, T. and Knobler, P. 1987. *Out of Control.* New York: Simon and Schuster. P. 243.
19. Pierson, Don. 1991. "Icky rule is proving to be sticky for NFL." *Chicago Tribune.* March 24, p. 8.

20. NCAA Football 2013–2014 Rules & Interpretations

FR 92 RULE 9 Conduct of Players and Others Subject to the RulesSECTION 2. Unsportsmanlike Conduct FoulsUnsportsmanlike ActsARTICLE 1. There shall be no unsportsmanlike conduct or any act that interferes with orderly game administration on the part of players, substitutes, coaches, authorized attendants or any other persons subject to the rules, before the game, during the game or between periods. Infractions for these acts by players are administered as either live-ball or dead-ball fouls depending on when they occur. (A.R. 9-2-1-I-X)a. Specifically prohibited acts and conduct include:1. No player, substitute, coach or other person subject to the rules shall use abusive, threatening or obscene language or gestures, or engage in such acts that provoke ill will or are demeaning to an opponent, to game officials or to the image of the game, including but not limited to: (a) Pointing the finger(s), hand(s), arm(s) or ball at an opponent, or imitating the slashing of the throat. (b) Taunting, baiting or ridiculing an opponent verbally. (c) Inciting an opponent or spectators in any other way, such as simulating the firing of a weapon or placing a hand by the ear to request recognition.(d) Any delayed, excessive, prolonged or choreographed act by which a player (or players) attempts to focus attention upon himself (or themselves). (e) An unopposed ball carrier obviously altering stride as he approaches the opponent's goal line or diving into the end zone. (f) A player removing his helmet after the ball is dead and before he is in the team area (Exceptions: Team, media or injury timeouts; equipment adjustment; through play; between periods; and during a measurement for a first down). (g) Punching one's own chest or crossing one's arms in front of the chest while standing over a prone player. (h) Going into the stands to interact with spectators, or bowing at the waist after a good play. (i) Intentionally removing the helmet while the ball is alive.RULE 9/CONDUCT OF PLAYERS AND OTHERS SUBJECT TO THE RULES FR-93(j) Dead-ball contact fouls such as pushing, shoving, striking, etc. that occur clearly after the ball is dead and that are not part of the game action. (A.R. 9-2-1-X) PENALTY—Live-ball fouls by players: 15 yards [S27]. Live-ball fouls by non-players and all dead-ball fouls: 15 yards from succeeding spot [S7 and S27]. Automatic first down for fouls by Team B if not in conflict with other rules. Flagrant offenders, if players or substitutes, shall be disqualified [S47]. 2. After a score or any other play, the player in possession immediately must return the ball to an official or leave it near the dead-ball spot. This prohibits: (a) Kicking, throwing, spinning or carrying (including off of the field) the ball any distance that requires an official to retrieve it. (b) Spiking the ball to the ground [Exception: A forward pass to conserve time (Rule 7-3-2-f)]. (c) Throwing the ball high into the air. (d) Any other unsportsmanlike act or actions that delay the game.NCAA Football 2011–2012 Rules & InterpretationsFR 87 RULE 9 Conduct of Players and Others Subject to the RulesSECTION 2. Unsportsmanlike Conduct FoulsUnsportsmanlike ActsARTICLE 1. There shall be no unsportsmanlike conduct or any act that interferes with orderly game administration on the part of players, substitutes, coaches, authorized attendants or any other persons subject to the rules, before the game, during the game or between periods. Infractions for these acts by players are administered as either live-ball or dead-ball fouls depending on when they occur. a. Specifically prohibited acts and conduct include:1. No player, substitute, coach or other person subject to the rules shall use abusive, threatening or obscene language or gestures, or engage in such acts that provoke ill will or are demeaning to an opponent, to game officials or to the image of the game, including but not limited to: (a) Pointing the finger(s), hand(s), arm(s) or ball at an opponent, or imitating the slashing of the throat. (b) Taunting, baiting or ridiculing an opponent verbally. (c) Inciting an opponent or spectators in any other way, such as simulating the firing of a weapon or placing a hand by the ear to request recognition. (d) Any delayed, excessive, prolonged or choreographed act by which a player (or players) attempts to focus attention upon himself (or themselves). (e) An unopposed ball carrier obviously altering stride as he approaches the opponent's goal line or diving into the end zone. (f) Removal of a player's helmet before he is in the team area (Exceptions: Team, media or injury timeouts; equipment adjustment; through play; between periods; and during a measurement for a first down). (g) Punching one's own chest or crossing one's arms in front of the chest while standing over a prone player. (h) Going into the stands to interact with spectators, or bowing at the waist after a good play. PENALTY—Live-ball fouls by players: 15 yards [S27]. Live-ball fouls by non-players and all dead-ball fouls: 15 yards from succeeding spot [S7 and S27]. Automatic first down for fouls by Team B if not in conflict with other rules. Flagrant offenders, if players or substitutes, shall be disqualified [S47].2. After a score or any other play, the player in possession immediately must return the ball to an official or leave it near the dead-ball spot. This prohibits: FR-88 Rule 9 / Conduct of Players and Others Subject to the Rules (a) Kicking, throwing, spinning or carrying (including off of the field) the ball any distance that requires an official to retrieve it. (b) Spiking the ball to the ground [Exception: A forward pass to conserve time (Rule 7-3-2-e)]. (c) Throwing the ball high into the air. (d) Any other unsportsmanlike act or actions that delay the game.NCAA Rules & Interpretations 2009–2010FR 122 RULE 9 Conduct of Players and Others Subject to the RulesSECTION 2. Unsportsmanlike Conduct FoulsUnsportsmanlike ActsARTICLE 1. There shall be no unsportsmanlike conduct or any act that interferes with orderly game administration on the part of players, substitutes, coaches, authorized attendants or any other persons subject to the rules, before the game, during the game or between periods. a. Specifically prohibited acts and conduct include: 1. No player, substitute, coach or other person subject to the rules shall use abusive, threatening or obscene language or gestures, or engage in such acts that provoke ill will or are demeaning to an opponent, to game officials or to the image of the game, including but not limited to: (a) Pointing the finger(s), hand(s), arm(s) or ball at an opponent, or imitating the slashing of the throat.RULE 9-2/ CONDUCT OF PLAYERS AND OTHERS SUBJECT TO RULE FR-123(b)

Taunting, baiting or ridiculing an opponent verbally. (c) Inciting an opponent or spectators in any other way, such as simulating the firing of a weapon or placing a hand by the ear to request recognition. (d) Any delayed, excessive, prolonged or choreographed act by which a player (or players) attempts to focus attention upon himself (or themselves). (e) An unopposed ball carrier obviously altering stride as he approaches the opponent's goal line or diving into the end zone. (f) Removal of a player's helmet before he is in the team area (Exceptions: Team, media or injury timeouts; equipment adjustment; through play; between periods; and during a measurement for a first down). (g) Punching one's own chest or crossing one's arms in front of the chest while standing over a prone player. (h) Going into the stands to interact with spectators, or bowing at the waist after a good play. If committed while the ball is alive, these fouls are treated as dead-ball fouls. 2. After a score or any other play, the player in possession immediately must return the ball to an official or leave it near the dead-ball spot. This prohibits: (a) Kicking, throwing, spinning or carrying (including off of the field) the ball any distance that requires an official to retrieve it. (b) Spiking the ball to the ground [Exception: A forward pass to conserve time (Rule 7-3-2-d)]. (c) Throwing the ball high into the air. (d) Any other unsportsmanlike act or actions that delay the game.NCAA Rules & Interpretations 2007 FR 122 RULE 9 Conduct of Players and Others Subject to Rules SECTION 2. Noncontact Fouls Unsportsmanlike ActsARTICLE 1. There shall be no unsportsmanlike conduct or any act that interferes with orderly game administration on the part of players, substitutes, coaches, authorized attendants or any other persons subject to the rules, before the game, during the game or between periods. a. Specifically prohibited acts and conduct include: 1. No player, substitute, coach or other person subject to the rules shall use abusive, threatening or obscene language or gestures, or engage in such acts that provoke ill will or are demeaning to an opponent, to game officials or to the image of the game, including but not limited to: (a) Pointing the finger(s), hand(s), arm(s) or ball at an opponent, or imitating the slashing of the throat. (b) Taunting, baiting or ridiculing an opponent verbally. (c) Inciting an opponent or spectators in any other way, such as simulating the firing of a weapon or placing a hand by the ear to request recognition. (d) Any delayed, excessive, prolonged or choreographed act by which a player (or players) attempts to focus attention upon himself (or themselves). (e) Obviously altering stride as an unopposed runner approaches the opponent's goal line, or diving into the end zone when unopposed. (f) Removal of a player's helmet before he is in the team area (Exceptions: Team, media or injury timeouts; equipment adjustment; through play; between periods; and during a measurement for a first down). (g) Punching one's own chest or crossing one's arms in front of the chest while standing over a prone player. (h) Going into the stands to interact with spectators, or bowing at the waist after a good play. 2. After a score or any other play, the player in possession immediately must return the ball to an official or leave it near the dead-ball spot. This prohibits: (a) Kicking, throwing, spinning or carrying (including off of the field) the ball any distance that requires an official to retrieve it. (b) Spiking the ball to the ground [Exception: A forward pass to conserve time (Rule 7-3-2-d)]. (c) Throwing the ball high into the air. (d) Any other unsportsmanlike act or actions that delay the game.

21. Known as "Rhino" to his teammates, he wore uniform number 45 in New York. Having seen players such as Giant teammate Frank Gifford and Green Bay Packers star Paul Horning celebrate touchdowns by throwing the ball to fans in the stands, Jones decided to come up with his own post-touchdown maneuver. In a 1965 game, he scored a touchdown and threw the football down hard into the end zone. He called the move a "spike," and modern post-touchdown celebrations, including "touchdown dances," are said to have evolved from Jones' invention of spiking the ball. http://en.wikipedia.org/wiki/Homer_Jones_(American_football).
22. Rufus Ferguson, personal conversation, 1992.
23. Leroy Butler's "The Leap," which is also known as "The Lambeau Leap." The former Green Bay Packer safety is credited with having started the phenomenon at Lambeau Field, used whenever a Packer crosses the goal line. "20 years later, the Ickey Shuffle still lives … in contest form." By *Ryan Greene* · September 10, 2008 · 12:28 PM http://www.lasvegassun.com/blogs/sports-unlv/2008/sep/10/20-years-later-ickey-shuffle-still-lives-contest-f/.
24. The Wisconsin Badgers made up for the Miami Hurricane loss (in my mind) by beating them in three straight bowl games in 2009, 2017 and 2018.

4

The Interwoven Fabric of African American Sport, Church, and Community

The Birthplace of the Black Aesthetic

> It is a story of the public presentation of the black body, a search for the cultural imperatives that have influenced the ways in which African Americans have clothed themselves, styled their hair, and communicated meaning through gesture, dance and other forms of bodily display ... within the confines of an oppressive social system, African Americans have been able to develop and give visual expression to cultural preferences that were at variance with those of the dominant group.[1]

I sat down to dinner with Dr. Harry Edwards, considered by many to be the father of sport sociology, in 1991 after his rousing speech at the University of Wisconsin-Madison. I was a budding graduate student studying the NCAA and NFL celebration rules and queried him on his thoughts. After a few moments, he commented that if I were to seriously write about the topic, I had to include the Black church as a central aspect of African American cultural style today. I later took Dr. Edwards up on his advice and researched the connections between church, community and individuality in Black culture. This chapter is the result of that conversation.

Years of observation and research around the Black church since 1991 have led me to the conclusion that African American religion, sport, community, and social rituals are all interconnected. But you knew that. Yes, the Black church has served as the institutional conduit and transfer-point of cultural ways of singing, shouting, preaching, and testifying. Yes, it is true that the church has traditionally been the place Black people felt free to express. This freedom included expression with the body, fanciful clothing styles (stop by a Black church on any given Easter Sunday), hairstyles, big hats, shiny shoes, loud voices, jumping, shouting, singing off-key, waving handkerchiefs—and all manner of expression that had to be tucked away in our churches from slavery onward.

Many Black congregations over the decades have taken "make a joyful noise unto the Lord" quite literally. Given the importance of the Black church to the Black community from slavery up through the Civil Rights Movement, it should be no surprise to find that African Americans rework religious ritual into cultural ways of ritualizing in everyday society. Desegregated sport, especially after the Civil Rights Movement, allowed African Americans from Earl "The Pearl" Monroe, Julius "Dr. J" Irving, Michael "Air" Jordan, Venus and Serena Williams (why don't more female athletes have nicknames?), and NBA star LeBron "King" James to both succeed at the game while embodying the African-American dream of the freedom of cultural expression.

The focus in this chapter is on African American behavior patterns and social rituals with deep roots in the Black church. Ministers, congregants, and choirs forged unique modes of expression in the Black church that spread into surrounding communities. Ordinary rituals in everyday behavior forged in and around urban and rural Black churches serve as the framework that informs contemporary athletes who ritualize in sport. The Black church, though still strong, no longer leads the way for Black social expression, however. The new churches of African American expression are stadiums and arenas all over America.

Three rituals flow from everyday life and Black religious life into both professional basketball and football: (1) the ring/circle ritual (African born), (2) the call-and-response ritual (church born), and (3) the individual creative-expression ritual (community born).[2]

Though both male and female create and continually rework Black expressive rituals in churches and neighborhoods across America, the bodies most prevalent and controversial in popular sport are African American male. As the WNBA grows in significance, we will begin to notice more Black women performing expressive individuality and leading group expression on teams. This trend is evident in NCAA women's hoops where emotion and energy and camaraderie run high. The ring/circle is evident both before and after women's NCAA games, especially during March Madness. Given that, my research notes will highlight the far more controversial expression and target of rules and social animosity, Black males.

Four examples of these types of expressive rituals have made their way into popular culture via sport: (1) Pregame circular rituals designed to both harmonize and "fire-up" teams before play begins, (2) LeBron James' pregame powder-toss, (3) creative slam-dunking in basketball, and (4) end-zone celebrations in professional football.[3]

The Ring and Circle in Sport

If any doubt existed about the convergence of sport and religion, behold the naming of National Basketball Association (NBA) player LeBron James as "King James" and "The Chosen One" that we all bear "Witness" to. James emerged into the professional ranks straight out of high school in 2003 and was drafted by his local team, the Cleveland Cavaliers, for whom he played the first six years of his career. Though James later took his talents to Miami Beach to play for the NBA Heat, then went back to Cleveland, and then Los Angeles to play for the Lakers, I'd like to focus on his years as an NBA player and leader of the Cavaliers, where he first made his mark.

The two honorific religious titles alongside "witness" were used by Nike to promote James in billboard ads, television commercials, and with symbolic branding on basketball shoes. ESPN, ABC, and TNT, which all feature NBA games, highlighted James in slow-motion mythic commercials. Couple media and advertising worship with Cleveland Cavalier fans that used to bear "witness" t-shirts and we begin to see how James was viewed as much more than a star athlete. In a sporting sense, he was viewed as the second coming of Michael Jordan—"chosen" by birth to excel to new levels of greatness. And where we have greatness in sport, or music, or religion, we usually have rituals of some sort.

We all engage in rituals throughout our week, and for many people rituals surround watching sport. We get together to watch football at home or at bar with friends, sit in the same seat, drink the same beer, and wear our special mojo sweatshirt. All are rituals designed to give some order, meaning, and good luck to the proceedings.

Ronald Grimes notes, "Ritualizing transpires as animated persons enact formative gestures in the face of receptivity during crucial times in founded places."[4] That is quite a mouthful, but if broken down, we can see what Grimes is getting at regarding the athletes who perform for us each week. If naming "King" James "the chosen one" is any indication, then fans, advertisers, and media are certainly receptive to the formative gestures I highlight below and later in the essay. The "crucial times" are games—and the "founded places," arenas.

LeBron James, Michael Jordan, Kobe Bryant, Steph Curry, James Harden and many other contemporary Black athletes since Muhammad Ali all developed their own individual styles of play—and can thus be considered the "animated persons" Grimes notes above. On occasion, some performed acts by athletes become ritual. One act is the ring or circle ritual teams engage in as they prepare for the game to begin, most notably in football or basketball.

By way of example, LeBron James stands in the center of a circle of his teammates and dances, chants, and sings as they all support him via the outer ring. He smiles, snaps his fingers, chants, and gestures. Other teams in professional basketball and football also engage in this now common ritual.

Football's New Orleans Saints also engage in the ring/circle ritual, with the White quarterback Drew Brees leading the chant. Just because Black athletes might have initiated this ritual, being Black is not a prerequisite for leadership, especially if one's nickname is "Breesus," a combination of Brees and Jesus. That said, Gena Caponi notes the African roots of this Black cultural practice:

> In the majority of cultures across Africa, group rituals were performed in a circle, dancers danced in a circle, and individuals performed solos in the center before returning to the surrounding circle of community. The circle helped to keep everybody involved, active, and interdependent. In addition to the circle, African rituals used … individual improvisation and stylization … interaction or call-and-response … Taken together they form the basis of most African cultural expressions—the basis of African aesthetics.[5]

At many Black wedding receptions, guests initiate a "ring dance" by forming a circle while dancing and singing in unison, and then one-by-one join the circle, performing an improvised dance move or their own signature move—often to laughter and chants—then return to the outer ring. (The "Soul Train" line is a variation on this theme.) Individuality is supported, and the more exaggerated the dance move or gestures, the more laughter and support by the group. The circle gets loudest when a child jumps in and dances wildly and "shows out." Roger Abrahams discusses Black ritualization around the ring in play and games:

> Each player is encouraged to show off in some way, either through some kind of individualized dance step … or through strutting, teasing, flirting, and wiggling, with everyone else clapping, commenting, and joking in support. This is the point. For while the player is at the center he or she is never alone, rather there is constant commentary and support by the ring.[6]

Black athletes have transferred common ritualizing in the ring to professional basketball and football via the circle of community before games. Athletes are never separate from the team or the crowd; they perform *for* the crowd and team. This is part of the larger ritual of call-and-response in Black culture in general, and the Black church, specifically.

Ritual in Everyday Life

Legend has it that former President William Howard Taft—at 300 pounds the heaviest President in history—inspired a baseball ritual quite by accident:

> In 1910, as a game between the Washington Senators and the Athletics wore on, the rotund, six-foot-two president reportedly grew more and more uncomfortable in his small wooden chair. By the middle of the seventh inning he could bear it no longer and stood up to stretch his aching legs—whereupon everyone else in the stadium, thinking the president was about to leave, rose to show their respect. A few minutes later Taft returned to his seat, the crowd followed suit, and the "seventh-inning stretch" was born.[7]

They did the same the following game until the "stretch" became a ritual across America. We've added another ritual to the seventh inning, post 9/11 trauma and recovery—the singing of "God Bless America." These are everyday sports rituals in our lives that often go neglected and relegated to the storage bin titled "things we do—though we don't know why we do them." Rituals, big and small, inhabit our daily lives. Like our morning bowl of cereal in our special bowl alongside our favorite coffee and mug.

We are all just a little bit different from one another. If you check your life closely, you will notice habits or customs formed over the years that often have no beginning reference point: Rituals slowly came about and took shape as we took shape. My brother, Bill, recently became quite grumpy because we drank all the coffee as we prepared our pre-Rose Bowl breakfast of grits, bacon, and eggs. He *had* to have his coffee *with* his meal, "Not ten minutes later!" I reminded him to take his "meds" (though at the time I didn't know if he took meds—he does!).

Though I joked with my older brother, his breakfast ritual had provided a sense of normalcy and comfort over the years. And that is often how we view rituals if they are not our own—silly and unnecessary. For Bill, this regularity was normal and comforting, as other people might view their personal rituals.

When we think of a "real" ritual, we center on larger historical/social occasions —such as Passover or Sunday Mass or singing the Star-Spangled Banner at a baseball game—and tend to overlook the smaller behaviors like the seventh inning stretch, which Robert Grimes describes as "ritualizing."[8] We forget the little things. We forget that smaller actions, "ritualizing," are what lead to social actions that eventually become rituals.[9] So think, for a few moments, about how rituals originate. They originate in small, everyday acts that eventually gain momentum and become "normal." Rituals are not acts cast in stone and given to us at birth (okay, maybe some social rituals, like playing peek-a-boo with kids). But think of everyday actions as openings or opportunities for ritual to evolve, or as Grimes notes, "ritual creativity," which may lead to ritual.[10]

It may come as a small surprise that African Americans have created an entire arsenal of ritual creativity that we apply to everyday social situations and private occasions. We have lived a completely different and complex socio-historical ecosystem alongside other racial and ethnic groups in the USA. The crux of this book highlights the dilemma of keeping these rituals "in the closet" verses outing them for scrutiny in larger society. Hence the book title's subheading, "Racial disconnect in sport." Expression leaves one open to all sorts of criticism.

Black creative rituals are surprisingly okay to many Whites and others in larger American society. To others less forgiving, Black ritualizing is fine as long as it *remains* among Black Americans—or only shows up in tiny doses on stage or screen. More and more, youth of all persuasions (as I learned observing New Zealand Maori and Samoan youth) are appreciating the many corners of Black cultural expression in public.

That said, African Americans differ regarding the appropriateness of displaying Black cultural ritual in front of White people.[11] As noted earlier, many African Americans cringe when we act out among Whites. For many, Black body rituals and expression are only "illegal" if you get caught doing them out in plain view of everyone. Both Blacks and Whites typically brand African Americans who participate in ritualizing in predominantly White public spaces as "ghetto" and "street." But individualized expression is more than simply anti-social behavior.[12]

What appears as resistant social acts (or clowning) by Black athletes are ritualizing instances that often become part of the American social fabric—like the fist-bump or the high-five or even the funky worm. Initially these gestures are thought of as meaningless cultural acts.[13] The same can be said of many words and phrases in Black culture (listen to ESPN SportsCenter or Charles Barkley and crew on TNT) that have now worked themselves into the everyday national sporting lexicon and broader American language.

And just like White people always suspected, there is an ongoing visual/verbal conversation between African Americans that centers on verbal and nonverbal cultural style. We can speak to each other without saying a word. On the other hand, we can talk all we want about a topic, but cautious cultural eyes can notice that our gestures might contradict our words. These behaviors and assessments are learned through interaction and social reprimand or praise. As John Edgar Wideman notes on African American expression, "Our stories, songs, dreams, dances, social forms, style of walk, talk, dressing, cooking, sport, our heroes and heroines provide a record ... so distinctive and abiding that its origins in culture have been misconstrued as rooted in biology."[14] Wideman says that African American rituals get passed on to the next generation through "stories, songs [and] dreams."

African American ritualizing is a way of existing in the world that is passed down generation after generation through cultural expression in music, dance, sport, games, play, and religion.[15] Religion is the center-most institution in Black history where people learned and transferred expressive behaviors. And one need not attend church on a regular basis in order to learn Black religious expressive practices.[16]

Black Church Ritual

The Black church has always been the one American institution that has been free from White entanglement. As Albert Raboteau notes, the influence of this Black-controlled space was crucial for community development:

> As a center for social organization, economic cooperation, educational endeavor, leadership training, political articulation, and religious life, the ... church exercised unrivaled influence in many black communities. It was ... the one institution that African-Americans controlled.[17]

The Black church serves a broad purpose for African Americans.[18] The Church can serve as a community center and social gathering place, festival and anniversary site, and a place where major rites-of-passage such as baptisms, weddings, and funerals are held. People meet their spouses in the church, raise their kids in the church, sing in the choir, and seek fellowship. Others, like me, play in Church sports leagues.

It is the *how* of doing church that separates this Black institution from its White counterpart, though this was not the original intention of gifting slaves with Christianity. Critics of slavery point to Christianity as a means by which slave-masters could maintain peace on the plantation. Reverend Calvin Marshall, in 1970, counters with the resistant nature of an empowered Christianity:

> Long before there was a college degree in the race, there were great black preachers, there were great black saints, and there were great black churches. The man systematically killed your language, killed your culture, tried to kill your soul, tried to blot you out—but somewhere along the way he gave us Christianity, and gave it to us to enslave us. But it freed us—because we understood things about it, and we made it work in ways for us that it never worked for him.[19]

How did African Americans transform church rituals to fit their ends? Blacks took Christianity and used it to communicate hope, to communicate perseverance, to communicate inevitable justice (which they needed to hear, given the stark injustice of slavery), to communicate sorrow with song, relieve stress with shouting, and to express artistic individuality by preaching with style, singing with style, dressing with style, and even moving and dancing in the church with style. African Americans used this one meeting place as an arena for Black expression, especially in the Jim Crow South.[20] And thus a vehicle for Black expression and ritual was born.[21]

Black Ministers and Style

The identity of the Black minister was intimately tied to his (rarely *her* before the Civil Rights Movement) ability to use his creative expressiveness—within the context of the church ritual of preaching—to bring about an emotional release from audience members. Albert Raboteau discusses the distinctive style of Black preaching as "the chanted sermon,"[22] and notes that this style is not inclusive of all Black ministers, and that indeed some White ministers follow this style: "The chanted sermon is as much a staple of African-American culture as spirituals, gospel, blues, and tales."[23] The chanted-sermon style is marked by Black ministers who can "perform," in the best possible sense of the word. Spontaneity is key as is their level of creativity, intensity and humor. G. S. Holt elaborates on the chanted sermon:

> The ritual begins with the preacher "stylin' out," which the audience eagerly awaits ..."Stylin' out" means he's going to perform certain acts, say certain things with flourish and finesse ... The preacher walks, body swaying from side to side, slightly bent, from one side of the pulpit to the other ... He waits until

he gets to one side, stands straight up, and makes a statement about sin ... with a strong sense of melody and rhythm.[24]

If ever an original ritual existed in African American culture, it was the expressive way of the Black preacher in synchronicity with his (and more recently, her) Black congregation. Sermons were never a monologue, but a dialogue between pastor and flock, which sets up the cultural expression in modern society (between sports stars and fans, among others) of call-and-response that Grace Sims Holt describes:

> The verbal exchange between preacher and audience throughout the service is accompanied by a variety of counterpoint. When the preacher makes his charges of sin he may shout or whisper, point a finger, lean on the pulpit, pause, or look long and hard at the audience, letting the words sink in for effect ... The white handkerchief, wiping the face, pausing to get a drink of water, and changing to a shaking voice all signal to the audience that the preacher is really going to get down and preach; the spirits of the audience lift ...[25]

The pastor's personal expression is grounded both in tradition and his or her own "signature" style that involves everything from how she yells or sings during a sermon to how he wipes the sweat from his brow. The early gestures and movements by the pastor are part of the build-up. The audience is aware of each movement as part of the nonverbal communication, part of the pastor saying, "I'm tired, but this is so worth saying that I will fight my fatigue in the name of the Lord."

My father, the Reverend Dr. David V. Andrews, was well known on the west coast as an orator and teacher of other pastors in how to give sermons. I saw first-hand the importance of the pastor's leadership and skill at moving people emotionally and spiritually. Sunday was a special day, and the pastor had better deliver. I asked him once, "How do you prepare for your sermons?" He replied,

> I study extensively during the week—the bible, ancient history ... and then on the day of the sermon, I walk to the pulpit, pray, and then sit and watch as the congregation enters. I relax. I watch how people move about and how they shift in their seats, and this informs me as to what they need to know today. I adjust my sermon and add and subtract what I feel is necessary at that moment.[26]

Reverend Andrews tuned-in to his audience. His congregation in effect guided his level of call-and-response during the sermon. Given the exalted status of ministers and the church in the Black community, it is little wonder then that these call-and-response ways of interaction have flowed from the pastor to the choir, throughout the church, and right down the steps into the Black community. There has always been a strong receptivity by Black congregants to not only the message of healing earthly wounds, but also receptivity to the personal enactment—the form of delivery that has become sacred ritual in African American culture, as Grimes describes:

> Ritualizing is enactment in the face of imagined, socially experienced, or mythologically construed receptivity. For ritualization to occur, the surroundings must expose a vulnerable (vulner = wound) side . . . in order for ritualizing to gestate. The more deeply an enactment is received, the more an audience becomes a congregation and the more a performance becomes ritualized. "Sacred" is the name we give to the deepest forms of receptivity in our experience.[27]

Thus, we could consider Black ministerial ritualizing as a performance to a deeply receptive congregation steeped in historical wounds. These styles of interactions are sacred on Sundays, to be sure, but interaction styles are also sacred rituals in the Black community. And as there is diversity in American society, there too is diversity in both Black and White church-going rituals. It might appear that from a common past might flow a singular style of expression in African American culture. This is not the case. There is a range of ways individuals choose to express in any given social situation. Your parents, your personality, religious affiliation, neighborhood, financial status, and whether or not your sports team won its playoff game on Sunday might all affect how you behave at the cocktail party on Thursday night.[28]

I want to be clear: The Black church is primarily an opportunity for congregants to cleanse themselves of worldly pain and suffering, seek forgiveness for sins, and commune with others. But in ways uncommon to White congregations (White Pentecostals and middle-class Blackness notwithstanding), the Black church has served as a safe haven for creative expression. All this expression and the transference into Black everyday life is summarized well by rhythm and blues guitarist Johnny Otis, who noted:

> I never had to instruct my horn players how to phrase a passage . . . The music grew out of the African American way of life . . . the emphasis in spiritual values, the way reverend Jones preached, the way Sister Williams sang in the choir, the way the old brother down the street played the slide guitar and crooned the

blues, the very special way the people danced, walked, laughed, cried, joked, got happy, shouted in church.[29]

The texture that adds character to the African American way of life are the day-to-day practices that have forged distinctive ways of living that are ritualized and reinvented with each new generation. While reinvention happens in Black churches, Black homes, and playgrounds, ritualization certainly happens weekly on street-corners and all around the Black community.

Ritual in the Black Community

Two key social rituals/social norms are learned in the Black church and transferred into everyday life: (1) The call-and-response interaction between all parties in church, and (2) the free-flowing acceptance of bodily expression by church members. The choir is especially important to this process of call-and-response and emotional catharsis, as is the minister.[30] What is the perfect outcome for the congregation?

The perfect outcome for the congregation is a catharsis, a moment of emotion that crystalizes in the soul and dances with the choir, the minister, and other congregants. The choir and minister must "perform" to their peak to bring forth this strong emotion and release in the pews. The church "performer" who distances him- or herself from the audience—who performs as if no one is watching—does not gain broad acceptance in the African American religious community.[31] This is also true, to a lesser degree, in sport.

The Sunday emotional release and expressive communion with the body in the sacred space of the church has resonated with the Black community since Christianity was introduced to the slaves. The Black church, with its choirs, usher boards, deacons, ministers-in-training, and musicians has always served as a community center as well as a place of worship; this was the original *Black Facebook*. For Maori in New Zealand, the Marae (community meeting house) serves a very similar cultural purpose. This is where we shared what happened the past week, what we felt about our kids or our husband, how we felt about The Man and our jobs, and asked for help from our brother or sister member. In this cultural portal, this physical and psychic space, locals met once or twice a week, exchanged stories, testified, supported each other, and listened to some heartfelt preaching and gospel singing.

African American expression moved from church to community and influenced many other aspects of life. The Black preacher is such a staple of life in Black communities that African American male comedians are almost required at some point in time to mimic the expressive Black minister. The same could not be said for White comedians and White ministers—with the humorous exceptions of Rev. Jim Bakker, his wife Tammy Faye Bakker, and the Reverend Lovejoy on *The Simpsons.*

Similar to the Black church-community interweaving, Robert Orsi talks about the rich flow of community life as he sought to understand how the family-centered culture of Italians in Harlem (from 1880–1950) influenced all other aspects of local Italian society. In essence, the extended family was what he termed the "domus." But the family domus extended its reach throughout the community. There was a natural interweaving of the domus and the community, which is as natural as the interweaving of the church and the African American community.

Orsi notes that life in Italian Harlem was very public, and that life on any given street consisted of women leaning out of buildings, men sitting on stoops, and children playing in courtyards. Local kids and adults alike had to behave (much like in my Oakland neighborhood growing up) because people monitored and policed each other, in essence serving as an extended family.[32] There was no sharp distinction between extended family and the intimacy of the community.[33]

Let's rethink the domus (or extended family) of African Americans as the Black church and the larger community as the closely watched streets and the urban chorus surrounding the domus.[34] And whereas Orsi's Italian family-centered domus sees priests as outsiders (since priests are celibate and do not have families and thus are not central), the Black domus sees the pastor as exactly the opposite—the center of life, culture, history, and hope. In this way we can better understand the connectivity between the Black church's expression and its influence on Black culture in the greater community.

Taking It from the Church to the Streets

Regular church attendance has diminished among African Americans, especially among poor and Black youth.[35] Given more social choices since desegregation in the 1960s, African American people are becoming more secular and less religious, and in some instances more individual (and less "church") in their spirituality.[36]

So, while there are arguments on the increasing intermittent nature of modern Black church attendance, African Americans have found many other public spaces in which to enact ritual behaviors, including corporate functions, picnics, bowling leagues, and the like.[37] Catherine Bell notes that it "has become clear that secularization does not entail the progressive demise of religion in general but a transformation of its form."[38] One arena African Americans enact ritual expressive behaviors in is professional sport.

What is the connection between the Black body performing in church and the Black body performing in stadiums and arenas? Expressive ministers and congregations certainly influence the greater community, but motivation still has to exist to perform Black ritual in White spaces. The Civil Rights Act was the official social blessing African Americans needed to begin socially expressing years of denied freedom in public spaces. African Americans began an association with the *body* as public, alive, expressive, and as divine temple, as Albert Raboteau notes:

> In a society chronically split between body and spirit, African American ritual exemplifies embodied spirit and inspired body in gesture, dance, song, and performed word. In worship the human becomes an icon of God … the person is of ultimate value as image of the divine.[39]

Raboteau implies that *African American ritual* inspired Black creativity and individuality with the body. And that this inspiration speaks to being in touch with something deeper and spiritual and—if someone is very good at expressing—something divine.[40] In church, our verve and inspired singing or testifying translates into being in touch with not only ritual but also a spiritual force. That same spark of embodied spirit that flows into creative ritualizing with the body in the Black community is what Black athletes carry with them into collegiate and professional sport.

Black bodily expression in integrated settings can carry costs as well as individual and group-level rewards. Many African Americans learn that watered-down Blackness (more in tune with White behavior norms) in a society controlled by Whites might lead to promotion.[41] But in a heavily commodified and commercialized marketplace, sometimes the opposite is true for Black bodies. Sometimes the Black expressive body is not only a reflection of the Black community and Black expressive history in and around the church, but a means to an end. In the second half of this chapter I want to take up the complexities of African American ritualizing in the context of professional sport.

LeBron James and NBA Rituals

LeBron James engages in two ritual acts that embody the call-and-response of the Black church and community: (1) the powder-toss in front of the crowd before a game and (2) the slam-dunk. Though it is said that Michael Jordan, and later Kevin Garnett (formerly of the Timberwolves, Celtics, and Nets) were the first to throw powder up in pregame ritualizing, James chose to take the powder-toss to an entirely different level—to ritual form.

Before the game begins, he takes a hand full of talcum powder (used to keep hands dry during the game) in front of the scorer's table, faces the crowd, and then tosses the powder high into the air. With feet and legs together, arms spread wide at right angles with upward palms and head tilted back, he appears every bit as Jesus on the cross.

Is James blessing the sacred space? Is he sprinkling metaphorical holy water? Or is he offering himself up as the "chosen" to entertain? In keeping with his anointed status as "King James," he might also be calling out, "This I do for you."

To be sure, it *is* only talcum powder, but it is the symbolism of the act that is important. The powder-toss is highly suggestive of a religious ritual and was so loved by Cleveland fans that they also, at times, had been given confetti to join in on the expressive act. As LeBron released the powder high into the air, fans also tossed up their handfuls of colorful bits of paper. This acknowledgement of the crowd as part of the game is call-and-response behavior that breaks down the "fourth wall" between audience and performer, akin to what Black ministers do when they interweave congregants' life-dramas into sermons.[42]

LeBron James also loves the slam-dunk. His style is to clutch the ball way behind his head in his outstretched arm before crashing it home into the basket—an emphatic slam-dunk over the opposition. James, like others in the NBA, watches the crowd go wild and then stops for a brief moment to scream at the top of his lungs in *response* to the crowd. Thus, LeBron's call (the slam), the audience's thunderous response (cheers), and James' reaction (the scream). The slam-dunk, in and of itself, has become a ritual in American sport, and the "Greek Freak" Giannis Antetokounmpo has perfected the post-dunk yell on the court.

The slam-dunk in basketball is the single most individualistic and expressive act of "performance while scoring" in any America sport, while the end-zone dance (discussed below) is the most individualistic and expressive act "performed after scoring" in America. African American athletes have taken slam-dunks and end-zone dances to ritualistic heights. Gena Caponi notes the controversy of both slam-dunks and end-zone celebrations:

Figure 4.1. LeBron James breaks the fourth wall between players and fans. He becomes a *fan of fans*. Source: Christian Petersen/Getty Images Sport/Getty Images

> In some cases, the "in-your-face" style was so intimidating that rules were changed to eliminate it. The NCAA banned the slam dunk in 1967 because of Kareem Abdul Jabbar's (then Lew Alcindor) performances for UCLA, and the move didn't return until Julius Erving ("Dr. J") and others helped popularize it in the American Basketball Association (ABA) of the 1970s. Likewise, professional football has banned "excessive celebration" after touchdowns . . .[43]

Tulane University scholar Joel Dinerstein ironically terms White rules about excessive celebration as the "illegal use of Black culture."[44] I highlight Black expression as a subset of culture in this work but do feel the two are intertwined and (somehow) a cause for White concern and a racial disconnect as we slowly integrate society.

We have crossed racial divides by allowing Blacks access to more neighborhoods, schools, institutions, and public places. Allowing Black culture to come forth in all its expressive colors is our next challenge. Sport is a great institution for testing just how far we have come. And how far we have left to go. If the popularity of slam-dunk is any indicator, we are moving closer.

The slam-dunk is a significant ritual in ways that still defy explanation. When a slam-dunk is performed with individuality and creativity, it is the ultimate in expressive brilliance in the Black community, akin to a great sermon ending on a high note or a jazz band reaching their conclusion with a swirling crescendo. It is a moment of truth—the one play that can send the crowd over the top in ways that no other basketball sporting moment can. (In baseball, a grand slam and in-the-park home run are high moments, as is a football interception for a "pick-six" or a kick-off return for a TD.) In these moments of elevation, time can stand still. Only a split-second or so, to be sure, but there is a stoppage of time in that one moment of brilliance that many have witnessed elsewhere with choirs, musical performers, ministers, and with Black and White athletes over the years.

The brilliance and resonance of these acts are what transfer expressive ritualizing to the next generation. The epitome of this expressive moment is embodied in the logo for "Air Jordan"—the silhouette of the outstretched arms and legs of Michael Jordan leaping to the basket for a slam-dunk in mid-flight that adorns Jordan's clothing line and many of Nike's basketball shoes.[45] We go from what was once a ban on slam-dunks to billions of dollars earned by Nike for shoes and apparel that promote the dunk in addition to the slam-dunk competition before the NBA All-Star game every year.

In 2011, Blake Griffin took matters to an entirely religious level at the All-Star game at the Staples Center in downtown Los Angeles. Before he executed his slam-dunk over a Kia car (later used in a major ad campaign), Kenny "The Jet" Smith introduced Griffin in the fluctuating tones of a Baptist minister. After his introductory sermon whipped the crowd into a frenzy, Smith then introduced a full gospel choir that sang in preparation for Griffin. And next, Griffin performed his air-defying dunk flying over the Kia. There we have it: The merger of religion, sport and culture. The slow-motion version of the dunk was used in the Kia ad.

John Edgar Wideman describes a player's brilliant slam-dunk as executing a "move so spectacular that glory reflected instantly on all of us because he was one of us out there in the game and he'd suddenly lifted the game to a higher plane ... he needed us now to amen and goddamn and high-five and time-out."[46] Wideman's reaction explains exactly what happened when Valrey executed his twist for Castlemont High School in Oakland noted in Chapter 2. Key for me in Wideman's quote is the "amen" as it implies the spirituality in the moment the act is conceived and performed.

Likewise, Caponi references what composer Olly Wilson calls the "soul focal moment" in Black music performance, where the player performs the unexpected to such a level that he or she "elevates the community through his or her individual effort, and the community bursts into spontaneous applause, responding as one body."[47] This is classic Black church call-and-response, where collegiate and professional athletes and everyday individuals jump in and act—fusing self and community with their daring performances. Valrey ran, performed, and ignited.

Grimes notes that we should look at the rhythms, the unique styles and gestures of these moments, and not take them for granted.[48] Black expression flows and changes and takes new shapes and often has no obvious "intent" as it were. Creative gestures have no deep and hidden religious meaning to athletes who perform them. Rather, the ever-changing uses of gestures are symbolic of a dialogue with Black expressive practice that flows from neighborhoods, homes, playgrounds, and the Black church. We need to observe the nonverbal culture of African American expression and gestures and reconceptualize them as symbols of cultural communication rather than toss them away as "meaningless" behavior.[49]

White Tradition vs. Black Ritual in Sport

African American ritualizing in traditionally White collegiate and professional sport has embodied controversy. As noted in earlier chapters, there were always implied codes of conduct—referred to as "sportsmanship"—that were in play during the Twentieth Century before Blacks ever entered the top levels of sport in America. These "sportsmanship" codes conflict with many African American expressive codes and interaction norms.

There has always been an undercurrent among Blacks that public displays of expression might confirm Whites' thinking of African Americans as "primitive" and only capable of communion with the body, rather than as complex and conscious individuals.[50] Given historical criticisms of Black behavior and prevailing images of the "Sambo," "Coon," and "Happy Darkie" by Whites, this critique is warranted.[51] White objections center on the uselessness of the action ("Is that necessary?") and the lack of humility ("Why don't you act like you've been there before?"). The NFL's policy toward Black player expression, noted in Chapter 2, echoes the above sentiment and recalls the "ring" component of end-zone celebrations:

> The Committee is unanimously opposed to any prolonged, excessive or premeditated celebration by individual players or groups of players. Antics such as unrestrained dances, wild flailing of arms and legs, simulated dice games, 'high-five' circles in the end-zone, imitations of gun-fighters, and similar behavior are deemed to be contrived exhibitionism that has no place in the sport and should be penalized five yards for unsportsmanlike conduct.[52]

Further, there are codes of conduct in collegiate sport that have been in place for a number of years and that look at individual creative expression (whether by

White or Black) as a gesture of poor sportsmanship. As noted in earlier Chapter 2, the NCAA ruled in 1995:

> Players will express excitement over a great play but must never address remarks or gestures to opponents or spectators, nor may they spike the ball or throw it into the air. Choreographed or delayed spectacles have no validity in football and detract from its honored traditions.[53]

While at some point in time everyone involved might have agreed on behavioral norms—such as in the 1930s and 1940s when teams were all-White and Black athletes were banned—the NCAA and the NFL are now heavily populated with African Americans, many who are steeped in their own traditions, norms, rituals, and ritualizing. Bell argues that groups with oral traditions (such as African Americans) are much more flexible than textual based "literate" societies, and that this can cause conflict:

> In an oral society, the embodiment of tradition can flexibly change to keep pace with the community and win people's assent as remaining true to tradition and appropriate to the current climate. Ritual can change without necessarily being very concerned with change as such. In literate societies with written models, however, change itself easily becomes a problem that is viewed as a threaten (sic) to tradition and authority ... In other words, in literate societies change can be very untidy.[54]

Black athletes may well be "untidy" while working within an expressive community that diverges and thus disconnects from traditional White values. Many African Americans (and many Whites, also) might well view end-zone celebrations as normal behavior, as reasonable, and as acts that draw attention to themselves as part of a larger ritual of community-in-the-round that need not provoke opponents. Jonathan Smith speaks about the tension between codes of conduct, such that "Ritual is a means of performing the way things ought to be in conscious tension to the way things are."[55] When we as Americans oppose one set of norms in favor of another set of values based primarily in "tradition" and without any critical analysis, we reaffirm—in this case—White privilege. Things should stay the way things are. Change is untidy.

Thus, rather than view Black creative expression in the end-zone as embarrassing, arrogant, or stereotypical, the freedom of athletes to ritualize creatively show us how limitless the body's capability for joy and spirituality in the moment can be. Maybe expressive "calls" to the audience by Black athletes are not intended to alienate teammates or embarrass and humiliate the opposition, but possibly cultural rituals or expressions that are an outcome of different histories and ways of using the body. The global transmission and acceptance of African American music in addition to dance styles, youth slang, and clothing style, says something about the resonance of Black culture.[56] If we employ a broader vision of the crowd's response and reactions to Black performers, there might be no stigma:

> From another perspective, while the slam dunking and one-on-one competitions may temporarily distract attention from a team organization, they nevertheless take place within a larger organic community that is following every nuance, a community that in each action, each comeback is being resurrected, strengthened, and dignified.[57]

The notion of a Black organic community is important. Black ritualizing veers us away from the neatly trimmed formality of institutional America, especially as found in American sport and perpetuated by archaic rules and traditions. Remember, the NFL is currently hovering around 70% African American. In truth, expressive ritualizing by African Americans in Black churches and communities were no problem for American society until the ritualizing began to creep into professional sport and White public spaces after desegregation.

Gaining Our Rituals, Losing Our Religion

The dispersal of Black folks away from each other in urban neighborhoods and churches threatens the continuity of stories passed down and traditions of verbal and physical expression: The ritual of Black life.[58] Indeed those rituals and rites and ways of behaving and talking and walking and all those good and bad qualities that come from being raised within an interwoven community, or an "enclave" similar to Orsi's Italian Harlem, might be slipping away. This is an unforeseen consequence of obtaining equality of movement in American society since 1965. African Americans, like previous ethnic groups that slowly saw their American ghetto streets dissolve, want to preserve culture while taking full advantage of social opportunities down new avenues.[59]

Part of what gave rise to Black creativity was our fight against subjugation and our general underdog social status. What happens when the future for African American culture looks brighter? What happens when middle-class status and movement away from the Black community shifts the color and ethnicity of our neighborhood friends, our co-workers, our spouses, and even our pastors?[60] What happens to the underdog status when the occupants of the White House are Black? For me, the growing diversity of Black culture and community settings predicts a shift in Black cultural expression in the future. Rituals will surely live and die as they are needed or lose resonance.

For now, and into the near future, fans from all cultural groups will continue to resonate with Black athletes' expressive "calls" to audiences. Before Black expressive rituals become obsolete, we can continue to enjoy athletes communing in the ring-circle with one another before games building camaraderie and we can enjoy slam-dunks and end-zone dances in the knowledge that long-suffering Black social humility has as least some reward in contemporary America.

If we are lucky, we can catch a glimpse of giddy and soulful Black joy in a local church, a local Black barbershop, or on a sacred playing field in any city in America.

Notes

1. White and White, 1998, p. 2
2. I do understand that each of these expressive forms could be considered *African* precursors to African American life.
3. A broader study might include greeting rituals and congratulatory rituals such as the fist-bump made famous by Barack and Michelle Obama (Andrews & Majors 2004).
4. By naming him LeBron "The King" James and "The Chosen One," marketers are also eerily bringing forth Ray Allen's portrayal of Jesus Shuttlesworth in Spike Lee's film *He Got Game*. The film is a critique of basketball—and collegiate and professional sport in general—and its exploitation of African American athletes.
5. Caponi, 1999, p. 9.
6. Abrahams, 1992, p. 104. Anthropologists, Black nationalists, sociologists, historians and geneticists have debated the presence of Africanisms in African American culture at least since the turn of the 20th century. See Caponi 1999, Herskovits 1941, Floyd 1995, Gilroy 1993, Holloway and Vass 1993, Thompson 1966, 1983, Rickford and Rickford 1976, Glazier 2001 and Capone 2007 for discussions of the complexity and controversy surrounding Africa/African-American cultural and religious relations. See Gerrie ter Haar (1995) for African ritual in Amsterdam.
7. Emory, 2009, p. 1
8. Grimes, 1982, p. 61.
9. Traditional ways of looking at ritual held that rites "originated but cannot originate," which is, Grimes notes, a conservative fallacy (1982, 61).

10. Grimes 1982, p. 61.
11. Please see Kochman, 1981, for more discussion of Black behavior in White social settings, specifically classroom settings.
12. See Jones, 1986.
13. See Grimes 1982, p. 62.
14. Wideman, 1990b, p. 43.
15. See Caponi, 1999, p. 7.
16. By way of analogy, a child of Catholic parents need not be Catholic him or herself—nor have ever been to a Catholic church—in order to have had Catholic *ways of being* infused into his or her life processes.
17. Raboteau, 1995, p. 79–80.
18. See Battle, 2006.
19. Marshall, in Holt, 1972, p. 331.
20. See also Holt, 1972, p. 332.
21. Raboteau (1995) notes that Black Christians rejected the notion that Christianity was a White man's religion and instead noted that "… Christianity and slavery were antithetical. Christianity was not false; the American version of it was. (61)"
22. Raboteau, 1995, p. 41.
23. Ibid, p. 142.
24. Holt, 1972, p. 334.
25. Ibid., p. 336–7.
26. Dr. David V. Andrews, personal conversation, 1980.
27. Grimes, 1982, p. 62.
28. Hanna (1997) comments on what she has observed in relation to dance and the Black church, implying that there is neither an essential Black church nor a Black way of being:

    … dancing is not innate among Blacks; middle-class Afro-Americans (sic) often move like Whites. So do Africans who are educated in British or American settings as I discovered in my African fieldwork. Some do not know how to dance. Furthermore, as there are Black churchgoers who "feel the spirit," as their manifest body movement bears witness, there are also middle-class Black churchgoers who are as physically restrained as their White counterparts (1997, p. 382).
29. Otis, 1993, p. 117.
30. Burnim (1985) notes, "When the expectations of the black congregation or audience are met, performer and audience merge: they become one. The personal interpretation of a given gospel selection generates a sense of ethnic collectivity and spiritual unity" (p. 157).
31. Olly Wilson (1992) knows that the audience is seeking solidarity, release, "… And that the expected goal is a point in the performance when the expressive power of the performer is so overwhelming that it demands a spontaneous response from the audience" (169).

32. Please see Edward K. Braxton (1998) for a discussion of religion and culture in the context of a Black barbershop, another center of the Black domus.
33. Orsi, 1995, p. 92.
34. Bell (1997b) notes that involvement in a "highly ritualized community is often based on an interest in ethnicity as a framework of community, identity, and a sense of tradition and belonging" (270).
35. See Hunt and Hunt (2001), Clemmitt (2007), and Ramirez and Brachear (2006), for more on Black church attendance among African Americans.
36. Catherine Bell (1997a) notes this would not be the first time secularization gave way to different affiliations: "In a secular society, people have many more choices about what to believe, how to act, and where to affiliate and devote their energies. The existence of these choices puts greater emphasis on the individual as the basic unit of the society and less on the family or clan or group as a whole." (P. 199)
37. The growing secularization of society leads to conjecture on what replaces church-going rituals and rites. Please see Barry Stephenson (2003) for a discussion of how boys and girls fashion their own rites of passage and Takahashi and Olaveson (2003) for a discussion of the ritualizing of dance and music and the influence of DJ's on youth.
38. See Bell, 1997a, p. 202.
39. Raboteau, 1995, p. 190.
40. Ernest Olsen (2001) notes "The Pentecostal church has an exuberance of music, preaching, and prayer that clearly demarcates the denomination's presence in the Tongan Islands." (p. 14)
41. Milton Gordon defined cultural assimilation as a "change of cultural patterns to those of the core society" (Gordon 1964, p. 71).
42. See Goffman, 1959.
43. Caponi, 1999, p. 4. Please see also Stallybrass and White (1986) for an extensive discussion of "transgressions and the attempt to control them" (p. 160).
44. Dinerstein, J. In "Introduction: The case for an African American Aesthetic." Caponi, 1999, p. 4.
45. Media commentators suggested during the 2009 playoffs that the "Air Jordan" slam dunk leap be the new "logo" of the National Basketball Association, replacing the iconic 1960s image of Los Angeles Laker Jerry West.
46. John Edgar Wideman, 1990b, p. 395.
47. Caponi, 1999, p. 5.
48. Grimes, 1982, p. 66.
49. See Grimes 1982, 66. Please see also Andrews and Majors, 2004, on African American nonverbal culture.
50. See also Dubois, 1903.
51. Please see *Ethnic Notions* (1986) by Marlon Riggs on the historical images of African Americans and also Weisenfeld's (2007) study of how Hollywood has stereotyped Black religiosity.

52. Pierson, 1991, p. 8.
53. NCAA, 1995.
54. Bell, 1997, p. 204.
55. Smith, 1987, p. 37.
56. See Raboteau 1994, for further discussion of the global acceptance of African American music.
57. Caponi, 1999, p. 6.
58. Hunt and Hunt, 2001.
59. Please see also Steinberg, 1989, and Hraba, 1994.
60. Black mega-churches are one recent invention that acts as a "glue" of dispersed African American communities.

5

Some Blacks Don't Dance & Some Blacks Don't Shout

> De La Salle wide receiver Cameron Colvin dedicated his final high school performance to coach Ladouceur on Saturday, catching two first-half touchdown passes in the nationally televised U.S. Army All-American Bowl in San Antonio. "Coach Ladouceur is a great mentor, philosopher and always keeps our heads on straight," Colvin told the [*San Francisco*] *Chronicle*. Asked if he had a message for coach Ladouceur, Colvin said: "Tell him thanks for all he's done for me. Tell him that I love him. And tell him to get better."[1]

Athletes are almost stereotypically given to saying, "Coach was like a father to me." Coaches have a profound effect on how male and female athletes behave and express themselves in sport. Mr. Colvin's last phrase above—"And tell him to get better"—refers to Bob Ladouceur's recovery from a mild heart attack that hospitalized the forty-nine-year-old powerhouse De La Salle coach before the big game. My interviews with collegiate athletes point out that both parents and coaches serve as strong mentors and as major influences on the verbal and physical expressive behavioral styles and attitudes of young athletes.[2] And many athletes have expressive styles that differ from both Muhammad Ali and many other expressive athletes. Many, like Al Toon, are simple and low-key personalities both on and off the field. This chapter explores the thinking and logic that informs their behavior and attitudes.

While my primary focus in this chapter is on Al Toon, I want to reach back into my archives on athletes, parents, and coaches—interviews I conducted in 1994–1995—to compare and contrast with Toon's experience and to add additional flavor from a time when the rules were just coming into being at the collegiate level. This data from six Black athletes is not generalizable to the whole of America by any stretch, but is instructive as we get to peek inside the heads and homes of Black male athletes during a time when they first began grappling with "right and wrong" expressive behavior in high school and college sport.

Some students are from single-parent homes, some from two-parent homes; some from the suburbs and some from urban areas. This small mix can serve as a backdrop for what may be happening in homes today as students prep themselves for playing at the next level.

Monitoring My Black Body

> … Within the social divisions of our team you see that and it's just that some people have been raised in all-White communities which basically [is where] America takes to set their standards with … In all-White communities they may listen to their music at volume five and they may take their hats off at the dinner table and stuff like that. Where in another community it may not go that way, you know. [Blacks] may listen to it at volume ten and they may like to dance and hang out and have a good time … It's not necessarily done that way in [the White] community but society tries to teach you that this is the right way and everything else is not … (Terrell Fletcher, former Wisconsin Badger and NFL Running Back)[3]

I like my music at volume five, like White people. Or maybe like old people. Either way, Fletcher (above quote) points out some subtle differences in standards and is quick to point out that socialized differences don't imply a right and wrong way, just that White ways are more socially acceptable. Black athletes may play sport with the volume turned up a bit higher at times. Still, other Black athletes prefer the music of their bodies to be in the background, more of a "White noise": Non-distracting.

Celebratory expression and social rules critiquing athlete behavior are constant media talking points when "excessive" behavior leads to penalties, fines, brawls, or expulsions from games. Negative discussions of celebratory expression among athletes, coaches, media, and fans often revert to reviews of the lack of good sportsmanship and how athlete "X" may not have learned "appropriate behavior."

The blame for "X" not learning how to "correctly" behave is usually attributed to parents and coaches, as ex-NFL star and Wisconsin Badger Terrell Fletcher noted above in his interview. Fletcher also observes Black and White home life and implies that economic status (middle-class, poor, rich) may also play a part in what people approve of in their homes.

While I don't subscribe to the "blame the parents" way of criticizing athlete sports conduct (sometimes youth do exactly the *opposite* as parents instruct out of spite), it's instructive to understand some of the processes involved in athletes accepting mentoring from parents and coaches in their early years. I sat down with twelve athletes on the Wisconsin Badger football team to find out (1) their opinions on celebratory expression in public and in sport, and (2) their ideas about expressive athletes and celebration rules. I interviewed six Black and White athletes who were considered high in on-field expression and six athletes considered low in expression as judged by two sports editors on the student newspaper.[4] This team had just recently won Wisconsin's first Rose Bowl ever.

Their answers are not a one-size-fits-all flesh-colored Band-Aid. Every parent is just a little bit different from the next. Parents ideas about appropriate behavior clash across the twelve young athletes. This leads, naturally, to a diversity of behavioral styles and attitudes. And while this result was anticipated, an unexpected result of interviews was that low-expressive Black athletes accepted expressive athletes and generally had little problem with "over-the-top" behavior. Even though low-expressive athletes did not engage in high-end celebration, they did not see the celebration as the problem as much as the retaliation (players fighting) or penalties by referees. I discuss the Black athletes and their various views in this chapter and discuss White athlete views later in chapters seven and eight.

Diverse Styles of Play

Since the integration of sport, scholars have analyzed racist tendencies by White players, fans, and coaches.[5] Similarly, many current scholars fight the good fight regarding discriminatory practices in sports that target Black athletes.[6] One goal is to legitimize (or de-stigmatize) Black behavioral practices that differ from middle-class White norms.[7] The various expressive styles of African Americans are a function of many different family proclivities, forms of religiosity, levels of neighborhood and work integration, and the growing socioeconomic diversity of Black culture. Each NBA and NFL team displays a wide variety of Black behavioral and verbal styles, which should come as no surprise. As we see later, White athletes vary even more in how they express themselves and think about the celebrations of other Whites.

If You Ruled the World

"Traditional sportsmanship" has given way to (and has likely always had) a variety of local sporting cultures. We expect cultural differences in other vocations and institutions—such as different "corporate cultures" and diverse behavioral norms across university departments—but many still see sport and sportsmanship in narrowly defined, static "traditional" ways. We would never expect Apple, Google, or Facebook employees to think, dress, and behave like IBM, General Electric, and Rockwell employees. The corporate culture of these groups of companies are miles—and years—apart.

My job as a corporate PR manager was to train new employees in Hewlett-Packard Company history and the "HP Way" of behaving in the workplace. We wanted our employees to think for themselves and to talk to each other every morning and afternoon at intervals (10 am and 2 pm) about work and life. HP would set out coffee and donuts and ring bells to entice and remind people to mix and mingle. For a Silicon Valley rules committee of executives to come together to explain to companies that there needed to be one set of rules—no donuts and coffee! —would have been absurd.

To have a consensus, on the other hand, of company employees at HP about what rules to keep and what to jettison is quite another story. The beauty of a variety of institutional cultures is if you don't like one culture, you can quit and join another corporate team, university department, or marriage—you can always push the "eject" button. Quite often we perform better in an environment where our style is a compliment to the new institutional setting.

This happens to athletes who move to teams with different cultures and coaches and veteran athletes. Want to grow a beard? Then you can never play for the New York Yankees. They don't allow any facial hair. Want to be an outlaw on the football field and wear any kind of hair you want? The Oakland Raiders (yes, I said it) would have loved you.

But there is no opting out of the NFL and NBA if you want to play top-rated talent at the highest possible salary. Rules apply to everybody everywhere at all times forever and ever, amen. No consensus. One size *will* fit all. And no backtalk. Parenting by policing at its best.

We expect athletes from various ethnicities, economic conditions, religions, and personal backgrounds to act in narrowly defined, similar ways. To be fair, many middle-class African Americans like myself see Black youth culture as overly expressive in terms of clothing and style. That's the same way people thought about me and my platform shoes and nine-inch afro when I was eighteen years old. But now I am an old fart. I know that. This is how narrowly I will think until I get more education about fifteen- to twenty-five-year-old behavior. I know my personal ideas are a narrow definition of ethnicity and expression. But I want to ensure that you are aware that not all Black folk are "over-the-top."

Chill Athletes

Many Black people are quiet, shy, humble, and not outward in showing their emotions. This chapter highlights those athletes because with all the talk in this book about expression and ministers and choirs and behind-the-back passes, one might get the impression that all Black people wake up in the morning, have a cup of coffee, a bowl of Cheerios, then run to the driveway, slam-dunk a few, hang on the rim, and scream loudly before driving off to work.

Earl Campbell, Walter Payton, and Barry Sanders shared not only a common African American male heritage, but also shared a similar quiet, non-expressive demeanor on the football field during their NFL careers. For every celebratory athlete like Billy "White Shoes" Johnson or Thomas "Hollywood" Henderson, there are many athletes who successfully perform and are very quiet about it.

Unfortunately, the less-expressive Black male athlete is pointed to as behaving "appropriately" by those who mock the "poor sportsmanship" associated with physical and verbal expression of players like Deion Sanders, Michael Irvin, Terrell Owens, or Richard Sherman. This overemphasis on one Black man's acceptable social behavior pitted against another Black man's challenge to decorum harkens back to house/field slave comparisons, however inadvertent or well-meaning. This is an attempt at social control. "Why don't you act like those good Negroes?" African Americans are guilty of this behavioral "thought crime" as well as many Whites. We point to successful, low-expressive Blacks as role models.

Many African Americans fear that challenges to institutional rules and codes of conduct are destructive to Black life-chances. For the individual, they might be right. Too many challenges will get you demoted, fired, or blacklisted in many work settings. In contrast to this Black traditional (survival) view, traditional White critics see both the conformity and rules "everybody has to live by" as fine. We all have to learn how to behave appropriately.

This review of less-expressive Black athletes in no way lessens the continued need to critique the power relationships, policing, and control apparent in media, rules committees, and the predominantly White public scrutiny of Black celebratory behavior as "unsportsmanlike." But taking stock of the development of less-expressive athletes can shed light on the often-neglected lower ranges of expression, in the end shedding light on perspectives Whites—and African Americans—have taken for granted. In the first few years of this study, I, too, neglected to consider that most athletes, indeed most African Americans, are moderate in terms of public displays of celebration or expression. I was the quietest guy in church. Never moved an inch.

Parents, Coaches, and Sports Expression

Daryl Carter, an African American and former University of Wisconsin (UW) linebacker from Milwaukee raised by a single mother, began his interview by discussing the strong link between family style and expressive tendencies. He notes that how an athlete expresses himself depends:

> On what you were raised to believe is good and what's bad, or what's acceptable in your family or not acceptable. Maybe some families would think it would be outrageous to dance or something. They might think that's embarrassing. But my family wouldn't think that way, they'd say, 'He's having fun out there. He's doing what he likes to do'.[8]

Carter was considered more expressive than most of his Wisconsin Badger teammates, though his expression is moderate when compared to other collegiate athletes. In his experience, expression is equivalent to "fun."

Michael London, another former UW football player, partially sides with Carter. London, from a middle-class two-parent home in Sicklerville, New Jersey, and who played both as a defensive cornerback and offensive receiver, was not expressive and was generally conservative in his views of athletic celebration. His view is more lenient toward "spontaneous celebration," noting that the NCAA has gone too far in its attempt to control players:

> Almost anything flamboyant they put a regulation [on it] or flag you for it … I think it takes away from the excitement of the game … it's just spontaneous and you make a big play … of course you're going to be happy and celebrate … but you almost feel like you have to look over your shoulder when you celebrate. You can't really get your true expression. It's good they put some regulations [in], but I think they may have come a little strong, [they] really nit-pick.[9]

What I question is both the NCAA and the NFL definition of "spontaneous." We are left with the conclusion that The Committee is recreating White upper- and middle-class norms of the body in their hidden definition. What we need is a cross-cultural definition of spontaneous. We might all be better served, at the very least, by committees comprised of various social groups who could then debate celebration rules. They could also render their own angles on the term, though eliminating the hard-to-pin-down word "spontaneous" altogether might better serve everyone. There can be no definitive assessment of an act as "spontaneous" or not, as London's confusion reveals.

London is not confused, though, about the role of his family. He notes his family was always very vocal and expressive, and that he learned early in life to verbally express himself with his parents, whom he greatly respects: "My father and I have a bond that's so tight ... just from watching my father growing up, I would say he would have to be a role model ... my number-one role model." London senior stressed to his son that he be his own person, not a follower, and London says candidly in the interview that he does his "own thing" and that he strives to be "original." That originality has always stayed "in bounds" and well within the rules for the low-expressive London.

In Carl McCullough's neighborhood not even mild forms of individual celebration were tolerated. McCullough, former UW Badger and a Texas-born running back raised by a single mother in a tough urban neighborhood, moved "up north" to Minnesota to attend high school, to get away from crime, and to be raised by a disciplinarian uncle. The low-expressive player notes that:

> Down South [Texas] we really don't celebrate. Like I said, everything's a team effort. It's okay to celebrate as a team but as an individual that's a different story ... you won't ever see a dude in the end-zone doing something, you know, running through a crowd, whatever. It's a big difference down South than it is up North. When I moved north to Minnesota, I noticed that. How much difference [there] was in the attitudes and everything.[10]

McCullough emphasizes that his focus is always on the game and that celebratory expression and crowd involvement by players is a "waste of energy ... that's just not me at all."

Carter, much like McCullough in his personality and demeanor (both quiet and intense), says little about his Milwaukee neighborhood, other than saying it was violent. Carter notes a mentor, and only in passing, primarily because he says he didn't look up to anyone as a role model. As the oldest son, he was on his own and without much guidance or structure to his life. His first mentor was a high school coach at Milwaukee-Washington High School, Greg Levin. Levin was the first person who "set parameters on me. Mom let me do what I wanted."

This is likely the case with many young men and women who eventually enter collegiate sport.

Reggie Torian had two parents and a sister to influence him. Though his parents were divorced the year he was born, discussion of his father strongly suggests active parenting. Torian's father was an All-State athlete in Illinois and worked in the Chicago area as a professional singer. Reggie describes his father as a mental man, a philosopher: "His words have meaning." The words that resonate most are words spoken just as the junior Torian was reaching his all-state potential. These words solidly place the father in the role of mentor and socializer: "He sat me down and he just told me one line … 'Be humble in victory and gracious in defeat.'" Torian senior could well be aware (through his former high school coach?) of social norms and historical traditions surrounding sporting behavior. Torian senior's advice is nearly exactly the phrasing the NFL and the NCAA hearken back to from 1949:

> Sportsmanship: The ethical code embodied in sport at its best. It includes fairness in action and attitude, abiding by the rules, refusing to take an unfair advantage, courtesy toward the opponent, modesty in victory, graciousness in defeat.[11]

Torian senior was not short on advice and strongly influenced Reggie's code of living (steeped in religiosity) and ways of relating to sport: "We all win by losing … you can never win if you never lose every once in a while … keep it modest, keep within yourself … be gratified that you're even out there competing … the Lord giveth and the Lord taketh away." Reggie listened to the forewarnings of his father because Torian senior, he noted, had experience in life *and* in sport.

Torian Junior was also prompted to anticipate life outside of sport and to consider what might happen if he did not "make it." This mentoring came via his mother. She questioned his dedication to sports and suggested he reverse the order of his commitment from sports to books: She "… kind of made me think. I can hurt myself, I can break my leg, I can pull a hamstring, and I'll be done with athletics." In addition, Torian's mother encouraged him to get good grades, get his high school degree, and get a job.

She accepts her son's athletic ambitions, while ensuring that his dreams do not overtake the practicality of living day-to-day if those dreams are not achieved, as she must have seen with many Black boys and men in the area. I think this is great parental advice needed by young people with high athletic ambitions. She was stressing to always have a fallback plan because of the extremely low (less than one percent) chance of a good high school athlete making it to the professional level.

In addition to being the sole provider in the home, Torian's mother served as a guidance-counselor of sorts regarding her son's future, surely earning additional respect and love from Reggie.

Mentoring, then, happens at many moments during our lives by people we love and who love us. The conditions that have these mentoring moments influence our future behaviors and attitudes appear to be driven by our resonance with the individual giving the advice. The resonance appears to be conditioned upon a combination of love, respect, or admiration in either the home, in society, or in sport.

Think about your parents and what they taught you. For those of us blessed with a parent or two to raise us, their words echo through our minds whenever we evaluate the behavior of others. If I am at a table and people prop their elbows up, or blow their noses, or chew with their mouths open, I wince—knowing I might have been slapped. This translates in my mind to "That behavior is unacceptable—and I wish they would stop!" But that's really my mother speaking. I have had to learn to say, "Well, they were raised differently. Maybe I have to learn to look away. Or that everyone is a little bit different. Especially our parents." Or simply decide to leave the table. I work hard not to think in absolutes such as "My mother was right, and their mother was wrong!" That doesn't much get me anywhere. Besides, I do many things others don't like. I complain about my food in restaurants. Dates have looked at me and said, "My father would never tolerate sending food back. You eat whatever you get. You don't complain. Period!" Parents are important in shaping how we see the world, for better or for worse.

Kevin Huntley, a former defensive player at UW, speaks very highly of both parents as his role models. The primary influence on his behavior, he believes, were his parents who treated him as an "individual" at a young age. He says his mother treated him as older than he was, giving him many responsibilities and talking to him as "a person" rather than as a child. He notes that as he grew older, he "learned to respect" his parents for that aspect of their relationship.

He attributes his low level of excitability in sport and life to his being an only-child and not having anyone his age around the house to share things with. He had friends at school, but remained "laid back" and continued to keep emotions within. That was simply the "type of person" he was. His attendance at schools where he was the lone African American may also have affected his social expression; standing out in a potentially hostile environment is rarely a good idea.

Carl McCullough also attended a school in Saint Paul that had an extremely high population of White students, but this does not appear to have inhibited him. Like Torian, McCullough notes that his mother played a key role as a model of strength. "She raised me very well," he says. She was strict and exercised "tough love," reprimanding him physically when he did wrong. "If I messed-up, I'd get a whoopin. She'd yell at me. I never took it personally, though. If she's happy, she'll let me know she loves me." Tough love alone, though, does not suffice as a survival mechanism in many neighborhoods. Hence Ms. McCullough's call to her brother Tim to take young Carl under his wing in place of McCullough's (then) recently murdered father.

Tim was—like Reggie Torian's father—a star athlete in Minnesota. McCullough glowed as he noted "He'd come home, we'd go outside and play football ... Tim was sort of a coach and a mentor ... 'Always room for improvement,' he said." Tim was the man who brought McCullough "down to earth" and taught him to take criticism, to give one hundred and ten percent, and "not to 'showboat'... you'll be *noticed* by your performance."

I highlight the word "noticed," because it appears an important characteristic for future success (beyond great athletic performance). It begs the question: Do some parents coach kids in the various ways of getting "noticed," such as increased expression in celebratory situations? Is getting "noticed" key to getting a collegiate scholarship, a possible professional career, a television commercial, or a shoe contract? What might be the various ways one can get "noticed" on the field?

Carter, McCullough, Torian, Huntley, and London emerge from their environments with mentoring about appropriate physical and verbal conduct in sport. Verbal and physical expression appear to be an outgrowth of attitudes formulated by relationships to mentors, coaches, and/or parents. Hence, Carter states that he would never do anything on the field of play to make himself or "the family look bad." These athletes appear to have taken the role of the parent/coach "other" in constructing their physical expressions.

Indeed, another former UW athlete, the more expressive receiver Tony Simmons, at one point in college had to explain to his mother—who loved his touchdown dances in high school so much she verbally chastised him once when he opted to "do nothing"—why he could no longer express himself in the end-zone after touchdowns in college: "Mom—they say don't showboat!" "They" were the Wisconsin Badger football coaches, and at least one Black athlete had taken the coaching and mentoring to heart.

A Note about Former UW Coach Barry Alvarez

Reggie Torian disclosed that two coaches had an effect on his behavior in sport. One was a high school coach who yelled and showed his anger if Torian did not perform to standards. Torian took this to heart and generally likes coaches who put themselves into coaching emotionally. He seems to have been affected particularly by former UW football coach Barry Alvarez. The main lessons he learned from Alvarez were: (1) to respect the coach, (2) to not degrade yourself, (3) to not perform any acts that might degrade a coach, and (4) to not be an individual on the field drawing attention to yourself. This obvious coach-centric set of lessons by Alvarez took the focus away from the individual and emphasized the coach and team.

Torian discussed an incident early in the 1993 Rose Bowl season where a player from the University of Nevada scored a touchdown and pulled mock pistols out of a mock holster and fired them at the Badger crowd in Camp Randall Stadium. Alvarez was furious after the game and lectured the players on acts of bad sportsmanship, asking what lessons such behavior was sending to the younger generation. Alvarez also told players they did not have to taunt to get attention. "Above all else," Torian recounts, upholding their stature as UW football players was key. Torian admits to being affected by the lecture. He recounts how he had previously thought of sport and expression:

> ... Before I came to this university, I used to watch NFL football players and the collegiate football players—high steps, [spiking] the ball, [players] taking their helmet off, and I thought that was cool. I was like, hey, are you supposed to do that? Coach Alvarez said, 'No, we do not do that here. We do not bring attention to ourselves as individuals. We bring attention to ourselves as a team.'[12]

Alvarez no doubt had his own agenda, one which includes maintaining tight control over player on-field behavior.[13] One possible motivation could be the NCAA rules that stipulate a penalty for "unsportsmanlike conduct" if players show "excessive" individuality on the field in acts of celebration. Whatever the case, Alvarez had a set of coaching rules that he was intent on players knowing. No problem with that. You go to UW to play football; you buy into the complete system. The coach is in charge of this process. This steers some toward and some away from schools like Wisconsin.

A Meditation on Social-Expression Theory

Torian's father is Black, and Alvarez, his coach at Wisconsin, is White. Torian followed the advice of both. Most of us, through daily necessity, have become more aware of how our words and acts affect other cultures and genders. When we assess our own social behavior, as Cooley in 1902 reminds us, we do so by reflecting on what "others" think about our behavior. Those "others" in social institutions have significantly shifted since Cooley wrote, and far more women, African Americans, Asian-Americans, Latinx, Native Americans, and immigrants are part and parcel of daily life in neighborhoods, offices, schools, and on the internet, which means that there is possibly more "reflection on the others" taking place.

Social psychologist John Hewitt puts forth that there is a "dawning of consciousness" when an individual gains an awareness of the world. People become self-consciously (or double-consciously) aware of their reflected actions. We come to understand that our actions can cause pain, hurt, embarrassment, or shame. Our behaviors or words can also cause joy, elation, awe, and motivation for others to excel. We are part of an interactive society.[14] When we learn to control and target our actions, we can gain an important social advantage over those who only behave without regard to the feelings of others or who otherwise do not know they can monitor and strategically use expression.

This is a key point, and I want to be clear. African American athletes often are not aware of the impressions more conservative folks (or simply others who are low-expressives) have of their expressive behaviors. Many might act never knowing the hurt they may cause. I don't think this is okay. I would much rather have it that individuals understand the multiple reactions to their actions. I would much rather have athletes "choose" their actions well aware of the views of others and the possible sanctions. In choice there is strength. And I would much rather the *rules and sanctions and policing* were altered to include alternatives to White middle-class norms.

On that same track, Whites who criticize Black (or expressive) White athletes without any knowledge of cultural norms outside of their box are not choosing, either. They are acting without consciousness of any but their own narrow parameters of right and wrong. They, too, need to be aware of the harm, hurt, pain, and shame they may cause by stigmatizing others.

I am not siding with expressive Black athletes nor with Whites who are offended by expressive Black athletes. I have a deep empathy for those who express their joy on the field of play and empathy for those who might feel shamed in front of family or friends by an overly expressive athlete of any color or stripe.

George Herbert Mead would suggest that we all—fans, athletes, coaches, administrators—leap in social awareness from the "play" developmental stage of acting out roles to the "game" stage—taking on roles of others and their assessments in social situations.[15] Taking on the role of the other—and learning the social situation of people not like ourselves—would benefit all in the sport superstructure.

Erving Goffman first suggested in his 1959 book, *Presentation of Self in Everyday Life*, that we move and act in ways to add coherence both to our roles (father, daughter, aunt, uncle) and to ourselves in the roles. If you are a professor, for instance, you attempt to maintain some consistency between the knowledge of what your role is and your behavior in that role. I wear jeans, a tweed jacket, a White buttoned-down shirt, Converse All-Stars and a sweater-vest to class when I teach.

These clothing acts I perform so as not to disturb or upset the "audience" and to convince students of my authenticity. If, on the other hand, a professor was severely disciplined because of her style choices, she may begin masking her feelings of anger, frustration, and a loss of selfhood. This is much the same reaction Willie Sims commented on in Chapter 1 when his coach, Steve Yoder, called Sims' expressive actions "street" and "retarded."

Erving Goffman (1959) notes people in social roles strive to negotiate between the human/expressive self and the perfectly socialized self that knows "appropriate" behavior.[16] If, by chance, an impressionable and expressive athlete like Sims is penalized or chastised for celebratory behavior—deemed a social error and "inappropriate"—by a mentoring parent or coach, it might bring great pain. His behavior has stepped out of line with his mentor. In these instances, athletes are perhaps taught anew about how to manage impressions when in the public eye:

> In other words, we must be prepared to see that the impression of reality fostered by a performance is a delicate, fragile thing that can be shattered by very minor mishaps. The expressive coherence that is required in performances points out a crucial discrepancy between our all-too-human selves and our socialized selves. As human beings we are presumably creatures of variable impulse with moods and energies that change from one moment to the next. As characters put on for an audience, however, we must not be subject to ups and downs … a certain bureaucratization of the spirit is expected so that we can be relied upon to give a perfectly homogeneous performance at every appointed time.[17]

Our society teaches us that athletes must maintain a "front" of personal detachment and must not respond emotionally to the opposition, referees, fans, or media. The tight confines of the social role of "athlete" instructs that we must be above it all. The game must appear not to be too important—certainly not more important than tight-lipped non-expressive behavior. I find the concept of "bureaucratization of the spirit" especially poignant here, given our next subject, Al Toon, and his reliance on "credible" performances. Emotional displays that are out of line with a coach's concept of proper team spirit would require an athlete to systematically learn how to "manage" or bureaucratize those behaviors and impressions.

Many athletes who feel expressively constrained might argue that the homogenized ("there is no 'I' in team") nature of play that is demanded is a killing of one's "off-stage" spirit. For many African American and White athletes, no distinction exists between how one behaves in life and how one should behave on the field of play. Goffman notes that for certain social roles, expressive coherence between two domains is significant. Consistency in behavioral style is a hallmark of post-Civil-Rights Black America in stark contrast to how African Americans relaxed and acted "off-stage" around other Blacks in contrast to "tomming," hat in hand, around Whites in Jim Crow times.

Many African Americans I've known hold it as their highest personal value consistency in their behavior from situation to situation— "keeping it real," as the kids say. Yet, however student-athletes might act around their peers, collegiate and professional football adherence to coach-instilled White middle-class norms and expectations of the role of "collegiate athlete" is vital.

The expectation is that the non-expressive behavior exhibited on the field is consistent with the humble behavior one should exhibit off the field. Put another way, we are expected to bring the same decorum we practice off the field—to the field. Through social discipline, then, we are told to adopt a mask of our expressive selves—keeping the spirit in check in certain social roles. This applies to everyone, Black or White, Latinx or Asian, male or female, trans or otherwise Q+. But adhering to White, male, middle-class, heterosexual norms makes self-consistency more difficult for some than others.

Athletes are always negotiating between various selves: A "real" internal self, a self in everyday life situations, and a sporting self. The sporting self looks for cues from others (coaches, parents, teammates, and peers) as to the appropriate behavior for the given situation. Some athletes do not look to others for cues. Life becomes especially difficult when athletes negotiate between the expectations of parents and coaches, which might clash if the parent is Black and the coach White.

Yet with friends at a party, the athlete might refer to peers for behavioral cues rather than the advice of parents or coaches. Other social role models such as church ministers, entertainers, and politicians all add to the mix of our distinct behavioral choices. Black ministers, politicians and entertainers are often fond of breaking down the "fourth wall" as noted in Chapter 4. Many Black athletes pretend there is no wall—or that the social wall of conformity is designed to be scaled. Valrey, our track star from Castlemont High School in Oakland is one such athlete who scaled the fourth wall with no shame.

Sport Sociologist Gary Sailes, in an examination of performance orientations of Black and White basketball players in pick-up basketball, notes that he had to discard data from his study after continual interaction of Black players with courtside researchers:

> The recorders were not only visible to the players, but dialogue took place between the recorders and some players. However, only the African American players appeared to be curious about the presence of the recorders. When they learned that game statistics were being recorded on their pick-up games, they insisted the recorders watch closely as they played. Although the white players did make curious glances at the recording team, no verbal discourse took place at any time. It became necessary to discard the original data and to observe the games from a position not visible to the players.[18]

Sammy Davis Jr. noted that once he left his house, he was on stage. Player-fan interaction in sport reflects traditional call-and-response patterns evident in many Black communities, as I noted in Chapter 4. Consistency of identity across social roles might be important for all athletes. Black athletes who interact and are more expressive might be acting to maintain a consistent personality.[19] They simply may be keeping it real—shrinking the distance between themselves and the adoring crowd. Expression may indeed be a desire to create intimacy among players and fans in massive arenas and stadiums around the country.

Indeed, in the 2000 movie *Gladiator*, the lead character, Maximus Decimus Meridius (played by Russell Crowe), asks a Roman crowd, "Are you not entertained?"

The athletes noted above have background similarities yet distinctly different family/coach backgrounds. While each is different from the other, they all share common traits with how Al Toon, former Wisconsin Badger, was raised to see himself in sport and the social world. I sat down with Al Toon in 1996 to review his career.

Al Toon: A Case Study

Al Toon is a former team captain of the New York Jets and a former All-Pro NFL athlete. He was universally liked by his teammates, the opposition, and Jet fans—a hard group to please. Like other athletes herein, Toon's behavior and attitudes are directly linked to his home life, and more importantly, his mentoring by a White coach who prepared him for his transition to college and helped solidify his concept of acceptable public behavior.[20] Al Toon was raised in a very low-key, non-emotive family, "without a lot of physical affection … pretty vanilla." He lived in a predominantly Black neighborhood in Newport News, Virginia, where his parents were laborers in nearby shipyards.

The middle child of three siblings, all separated by one year in age, Al Toon's sporting career began in high school. He ran for the state champion track team and played receiver on his football team. By his own admission Toon was a painfully shy adolescent who found it hard to make friends. Even today he admits to being reclusive. He says he knows that his behavior can be misconstrued (as, I am guessing, arrogant). He also notes there has always been, if nothing else, a consistency to his behavior, because his

> … personality never changed from day one. But being reclusive, somewhat shy, [I] didn't talk to too many people because I was painfully shy growing up [which] made it difficult for me to develop relationships outside the family. Having friends wasn't a goal or something I consciously went out and did. But that was just me, I think, and who knows why I was like that … It could have been because of my family … there was not a lot of physical interaction, emotional displays…[21]

Toon was introverted, self-conscious, and aware of others and their impressions of his demeanor in high school. His personality and disposition toward others *was* shaped primarily by his home life and "low-key" family. As models for expressive social behavior, his parents would represent the low-expressive end of the spectrum. As noted previously, low-expressive parents do not necessarily beget low-expressive children, as many youth become exact opposites of their parents. But the context of the home is key. This is where we learn how to behave. We eat our Rice Chex in our crib and watch what our parents say and do as they whiz past. They give us, by their behavior, license to mimic what we observe in them. Toon's home was reserved emotionally and physically, and his behavior definitely reflected his parents.[22]

Mentoring and Credibility

Toon's philosophy of expression and sportsmanlike conduct, of how he "chooses to run his life and social and private persona," were shaped by a critical meeting with a White high school football coach. This talk with Coach Nuttycombe proved to affect Toon's life fundamentally. Here is where Toon experienced a dawning of consciousness:

> My football coach, I sat down with him. He sat down with me on many occasions just helping me plan and look at the future and develop a direction where 'you would always maintain your credibility and always have respect for other people, because once you lose your credibility it's very difficult to get it back.' I'm in his government class … After class, 'Al, come over here, I want to talk to you. We need to talk. You're getting ready to leave to go off to [Wisconsin] and you're a nice kid, you've done well, and academically you're doing well, and I need you to think about these two things.'[23] And the word that he wrote down I kept in my wallet … It stayed in my wallet for probably seven or eight years—was the word "credibility." He wrote it out on a piece of paper and I kept it in my wallet forever. And I thought about that word all the time. And what it meant and how it applies, and it does—it applies to every life-situation.[24]

Toon obviously has a deep respect for his coach and sees Nuttycombe as a mentor and confidant. Toon believes his personality shifted as a result of the conversation. Or did it? It might be that Toon's life may not have changed significantly, but the focus he gives to this "article of faith" galvanizes his way of looking at life.[25]

On the point of memory, *Seinfeld's* Cosmo Kramer once described a crucial moment in his life with the term "memory burn," to emphasize the fact that the moment would forever be etched in his psyche. It appears Toon's conversation with his coach was also a memory burn and is sincere, especially given the level of detail. Toon was at one and the same time analyzing his past and tracing his vivid memory of his own life-course.[26] As to the possibility of socially desired responses and omitting relevant information, Toon does not appear suspect, but there is no one-hundred-percent certainty.[27]

For Toon, credibility becomes his primary goal at age eighteen. What Coach Nuttycombe meant and what Toon interpreted as "credibility" may have differed, of course. The Oxford English Dictionary defines the adjective "credible" as "capable of being believed," and "worthy of belief or confidence; trustworthy, reliable," and finally, "of good repute."[28] Again, we confront the idea of the "audience" of the credible.

For a rapper or urban Black athlete with a big-money contract, "street cred" or respect among people from one's neighborhood is most important. I suspect Nuttycombe did not have street cred in mind. Nuttycombe most likely wanted Al Toon to instill confidence in (powerful, White?) others that he could perform in roles on and off the field.

In order to gain the confidence of others one must, it would seem, continually perform with others in mind. But what would be Toon's motivation for gaining the confidence of others? Is Nuttycombe suggesting that in life—and specifically the infrastructure of sport in America—those who are credible have a better chance at success? Nuttycombe may have been offering a path for Toon to achieve outside of Newport News, Virginia, in the broader world, and possibly, in the White world of University life in Wisconsin. Robert K. Merton suggests that people adopt the values of a group to which they aspire to belong. Owning the other groups' values eases the adjustment to the other group.[29]

When someone else tells us in advance how to negotiate an upcoming life-change, like leaving high school for a far-away college, or leaving college for the NFL or NBA, we are getting what is called "anticipatory socialization," as in "here's what to anticipate ... here's what will help."[30] African Americans, like everyone else, must be credible in the mind of the powerful other in order to gain institutional acceptance. The powerful "other" in America is most often White men with middle-class normative values. Street cred may give way to institutional cred.

Thank goodness there are many White coaches, like Pat Riley, Chuck Daily, Steve Kerr, and the Zen master himself, Phil Jackson, and many others in the pros and college sport, who have a strong understanding and love of Black cultural values and expressive practices such that what many see as a detriment becomes a source of energy to be aimed through great coaching toward hard work and achievement.

This brand of socialization—initiated by a mentor—comes before a passage from one membership group to another. Toon was making a passage from high school to college, from the South to the Midwest, and from racially mixed Newport News to predominantly White Madison, Wisconsin. It is no wonder, then, that Toon was heeding the advice of Nuttycombe—this represented the greatest transition in his life. Toon may have been in a bit of fear as well as nervous anticipation about his future in an unknown place. Life-chances at higher levels of social interaction in the U.S. signal to some African Americans the need for cultural conformity as well. The NFL has an entire seminar to prepare rookies for life in the NFL. Most of those rookies are African American.[31]

Credibility and Identity

What does Coach Nuttycombe mean by "credibility?" Maybe the Coach saw credibility as the way athletes achieves success inside and outside of sport. We know Toon took the coach's word and ran with it—applying the concept to "every life-situation." Toon's insight was crucial to the formation of his self-concept and identity. Coach Nuttycombe appears responsible for a major shift in Toon's conception of himself and the social world. But Al Toon had parents, too. Had his parents already taught him about credibility, though possibly said in a different way? Toon answers this question:

> [My coach] sat me down. My mom didn't sit me down, my dad didn't sit me down, no one prior to that had sat me down. He sat me down in his classroom after class, and said 'Okay, this is what we need to do. This is what you need to think about.' [That conversation] influenced my whole life.[32]

Toon's life was influenced (and possibly consumed) thereafter by a desire to achieve credibility. Toon monitors his behavior in order to maintain consistency across social situations. He notes, in the third person, "Al Toon on the field is no different from Al Toon off the field. My philosophy is the way I carry myself, the way I go about things—they don't change."[33] Consistency of self—which appears important to Toon's idea of public credibility—has evolved from a slip of paper to a "philosophy" of life.[34] Others who desire to maintain consistency across social situations, and who just so happen to be highly expressive, face the near impossibility of transferring their consistent behavior to college sport.

Toon has an epiphany. His philosophy and attitude in public and private life is concretely displayed by "the way I carry myself" and "the way I go about things."[35]

Toon thus becomes what social psychologists would term a low self-monitor. Self-monitoring is the tendency to look to the social context for cues to guide your actions. Low self-monitoring is the tendency to look instead to one's own attitudes for guidance about how to behave.[36] For instance, high self-monitors would be very cautious about talking politics on a first date; they constantly work to fit themselves into all situations so as not to make waves. Low self-monitors would jump right in and take swipes at politicians or laws they thought were unethical; like Toon, they would not waver regardless of their environment. One is cautious and wants to be "appropriate," and the other wants to make sure they are "keeping it real" and not masking any feelings or putting up a false "front." In this sense, there are self-monitors who are both high and low in self-expression, and our theory needs to also account for not only high and low self-monitors, but high and low-expressives who exhibit their high or low monitoring in very different ways.

The Delicate Dance with Whiteness

This is a delicate dance—monitoring our behavior to fit social situations. African Americans didn't survive long as slaves if they "kept it real" and spoke their minds. Same for African American behavior during Jim Crow times. Being smart about "the situation" meant looking at how people reacted to your behavior. If you were a slave and a father wanting to provide for your children, then you just had to suck-it-up and keep your attitude about the overseer and his whip in your back pocket. You lived to die another day. I therefore don't want to privilege either side of the self-monitoring scale, high or low.

Of course, Black people in America aren't slaves anymore, and formal Jim Crow codes don't exist anywhere. High self-monitoring among African Americans today is often looked upon as "selling out" or "kissing up" to The Man, while high self-monitoring among Whites is viewed quite oppositely as being strategic. This concept of "selling out" also applies to women and Q+ individuals (closeted or not) in institutional settings. If you don't like the off-color joke someone told about women, how do you respond if you want to "move up" in the company without being criticized for not having a "sense of humor?"

This happened to me within my first few months of working for the international corporation Hewlett-Packard Company in Silicon Valley in 1983. During a department dinner function at a local winery, we gathered around a wine list to make some selections. The older, inappropriate White male yells a good old-timey joke aimed at me across the room, "Hey Vern, you'll love the wine list—it has Ripple on it!"

"Ripple," as it was thought back in the 1960s, 1970s, and 1980s, was the chosen wine beverage of Black people, especially poor Black people. It was bad, sweet, three-dollar per-bottle wine with a Kool Aid-type flavor. What was my response? Just like the slave in the field, I sucked it up and lived to die another day. That wasn't a battle worth fighting. The red faces from the fourteen White people in the room would fight that battle later. They were more embarrassed than I was. But make no mistake, it hurt me to be put down—and not be able to respond—in front of my new peers.

I was a high self-monitor, dancing with Whiteness in a new world with new hope fraught with old stereotypes. I didn't want to prove that "All Black guys from Oakland will get ghetto on you if you attempt to humiliate them." This was, after all, a PR department. I had to show I could handle a tough communication moment. Like Toon, I was aware of the situation and aware that my credibility was at stake, as many African Americans, women, the poor, lesbian, gays, bisexuals, and trans people do on an hourly basis in businesses throughout the country.

Social situations are always tricky. Having a game plan that steers you toward credibility helps you stay "in the ballpark" in social scenarios. If you are credible in multiracial social situations you stand less chance of getting stigmatized, demoted, or fired.[37] You have to prevent a racial disconnect.

Toon, Race, and End-Zone Expression

Al Toon has no problem evaluating the behavior of both Blacks and Whites in sport. Toon never discusses racial situations he may have confronted, though that does not mean he has never confronted racism or is not keenly aware of a racial audience in the stands or in other arenas. Through our conversations and observing him in public, my impression is that his attitude about maintaining consistency crosses racial lines. In essence, people—Black or White—do not appear to affect his self-presentation or behavior. There appears to be no "double" to his consciousness, no Black or White "audience adjustments" he makes.[38] He and I are quite different in this regard.

I certainly give a conference talk very differently in front of a room of Whites verses African Americans. I don't think Toon would make the same adjustment in comfort level. He is a warm human being, certainly. But I believe he would keep his stone-faced matter-of-factness to any group, any gender, and maybe even any age level.

Given his equal treatment of audiences, Toon is still aware of the racial dilemma concerning fellow athletes, specifically about our topic, celebratory expression and sportsmanlike conduct. He has observed a general pattern of expression differences between Black and White players on the issue of spontaneous versus choreographed end-zone celebrations. One of the main components of the NFL's rule on celebration in the 1990s is that players should not exhibit "excessive, prolonged, or premeditated" behavior.[39] Toon doubts whether Whites and Blacks see the situation and behaviors in the same way:

> I think [African] Americans are typically more animated about expression, and I think it's just translated onto the field of play in whatever sport. I think that in general … Caucasians, I think they are a bit more reserved in expression. I think even with what some people may consider "excessive celebration," I think that's spontaneity. It may seem like it's premeditated but I think it's spontaneity in certain cases. [Players say] 'That's the way I express myself'.[40]

There is no doubt Toon is aware of race and racialized viewings of expression in sport, and by implication, the ambiguity involved in older White (and Black) referees determining the situational intentions of much younger Black players. What is premeditated to one is spontaneous to another, though most would concede Terrell Owens' use of a Sharpie pen pulled from his sock to sign a ball after a touchdown required a bit of foresight. But that act wasn't celebration, that was exhibitionism. Terrell Fletcher, quoted earlier, appears to echo Toon's sentiments about cultural environments and expression, noting:

> Those [blacks] who have been taught the other way, you know … it works the same way because those [Black] people look at the other [white] group … and be like, 'They're square, they're just chipper' … That's just a division that's gonna be; it's always gonna be as long as there's two different classes of people. As long as there's two different ways of teaching it's gonna be that way. And who's to say what's wrong, or right?[41]

Given that Toon sees African Americans as more spontaneous and expressive than Whites in social settings in and out of sport, how does he account for his own expressive style? By his own admission, Al Toon's expressive style while playing for the Wisconsin Badgers and the National Football League's New York Jets was very conservative. If anything, Al Toon would avoid expression and expressive people in or around the end-zone. In a lighter moment during the interview, he confessed his modus operandi: "Ninety-nine percent of the time my expression was a one [out of five].[42] I'd drop [the ball] on the … ground, or if a ref was around, I'd toss it to him." He said he did occasionally give a few high-fives, but no head-butts. He commented:

> No, never did that. I would actually run away from those guys because half the time they'd hurt you—diving on you and kicking you … I kept running usually, I never stopped until the excitement died down. I'd run through the end-zone and I'd make a big loop and I'd never stop and I kinda kept going … I'd keep running and never stop.[43]

Consistent *protection* of self seems to be the theme here. And, ironically, if he ran away from his teammates in college football today, he would be penalized for "unsportsmanlike conduct."[44] Toon was extremely quiet when he scored, quiet during the game, and quiet after the game—maintaining a leadership role on the team by, he feels, "example." He also showed up on time, says he practiced hard, was a perennial all-pro, and was the NY Jets Most Valuable Player for three years in a row, noting in the interview that he is the only Jet player in history to have accomplished that feat.

Toon's attitude supports my hypothesis about celebratory expression: African Americans tend to support/condone celebratory behavior more readily than Whites—even if their own individual behaviors are conservative. This might be due to Black communities that generally allow a broader range of acceptable behaviors.

In a similar sense, I would expect White Americans to more readily embrace/condone traditional codes of sports conduct as these norms were likely more prevalent in their environments. In point of fact, there is broad acceptance in both socio-cultural groups of the concepts of "expressive freedom" and "sportsmanship." That said, those terms are defined differently within those social/cultural groups and also differ among the poor, middle-class, and rich within both groups.

Conclusion

What appears most significant in the lives of the young Black men featured herein is a sense of respect, admiration, and care for the mentor giving them advice on how to adopt new behaviors. That advice could be about verbal and nonverbal communication patterns, individual expression, or toward coolness and humility. People who garner the respect of youth extend beyond parents to include coaches, uncles, and in the case of Al Toon, a coach/civics teacher in high school. There are no doubt many other people—including ministers, counselors, former athletes, and idols—who ultimately influence student-athletes with decision-making on and off the field. In the case of Al Toon, the advice received from his influential coach was an epiphany that led to a shift in how he viewed the world.

One major question for future research is: What leads youth to respect adults? More specific: What aids Black males in respecting adults? These questions have no doubt been asked by many parents and coaches, and not only of Black student-athletes. All other ethnic groups have the inevitable parent-adolescent coach-athlete frictions and disagreements. Given the narratives from athletes about the influence of significant others in their lives, there must be a key mechanism at work that has student-athletes shift adults from the role of "parent" or "teacher" or "coach" to role model or mentor. What is this process? Can it be recreated?

I need to re-emphasize here that my intention is not to reproduce the athlete behaviors I discuss in this chapter. Given the diversity of athletes, a variety of styles of play make for a better, more entertaining NCAA, NFL, NBA, or MLB. Also, improving the player-coach-parent-teacher relationship has its own benefits outside the arena of expression, sportsmanship, or sport.

These select interviews with athletes are limiting in that they only represent those selected to attend the University of Wisconsin. More analysis of African American athletes at other universities, in other sports, women, and those with differing sexual orientations would greatly expand our knowledge of African American social psychological processes. The concept of double-consciousness—observing the Whiteness in the institutional setting while conscious of one's own Blackness in the eyes of others—would seem to loom large for African American self-monitoring in the future.

For those inclined to view Black behavior as stereotypical and highly expressive, this chapter should point to there being no "essential" African American culture. Diverse behavioral patterns of African Americans are evident herein. Expansion of our definitions of what is "normal" is what I am pushing for, along with the social inclusion of many voices in the construction of our rules about behavior in sport—and society.

Notes

1. Stevens, 2004, p. 2.
2. I employ (sociological) social psychological frameworks of the "self" as an analytic tool throughout the analysis. This frame works well as a means of assessing the variations of athlete internal/social motivations on sports expression—and the influence of parents and coaches—along their life-course. One additional motivation for this analysis frame is that social psychologists have historically not included African Americans as central to their research. There is thus a general lack of social psychological analysis of Black lives in the broader field. Elsewhere (Andrews 2003) I have sought to employ social psychological interpretations of African American cross-national racial experiences to begin to redress some of those critiques.

   Moghaddam et al. (1993), noting the need for more general research in cross-cultural social psychology, have commented also on the need to move beyond White college students as generalizable research subjects. Other scholars, notably Hunt et al. (2000) have done an extensive review of the general lack of application of social psychological principles to people of color, specifically African Americans. To that end, this chapter helps to bridge that gap by adding to the literature on social psychology and people of color.

Sociologists and psychologists in the broad field of social psychology focus on relationships between the person and the social world by focusing on the internal processes of individuals in social settings. Athletes perform in an often-intense social setting with hundreds of thousands of observers all varied in their own sociological backgrounds. And though Gordon Allport (1968) didn't have sport specifically in mind, he might as well have as he defines social psychology as "… an attempt to understand and explain how the thought, feeling, and behavior of individuals are influenced by the actual, imagined, or implied presence of others" (p. 3).

The focus of social psychology is on the internal workings of individual cognition. How do we process the information we receive? What are our resulting social actions? Social psychology provides an important avenue of analysis of athlete processing of knowledges of sporting conduct from significant others.

3. In Andrews, 1996b, p. 50.
4. The research method employed in data gathering was an intensive, structured interview process, which also included open-ended questions at the end of the interview. Questions were formulated to probe four major areas of concern: (1) athlete on-field expression, (2) opinions on the expression of other athletes, sportsmanlike conduct and sports conduct rules, (3) athlete expressive socialization from parents, mentors and role models, and (4) athlete demographic information. The five sections totaled 50 questions.

   The first section—self-reflections on expression—sought to find out how athletes expressed themselves verbally and physically on the field during times of excitement. The second section was intended to probe athlete opinions about celebration rules, celebratory expression and "talk" on the field. I also wanted to know if there were unwritten rules, or a "players' code" that might act as a mechanism to promote desired sports conduct as distinct from "written" rules. The third section was an attempt to find out what expression was like around the home and the neighborhood. I wanted to know if physical expression was encouraged or not, if athletes had role models and mentors while growing up, and if they had collegiate or professional teams or athletes they liked and disliked.

   My hope was that these questions would elucidate more deeply-seated emotions and attitudes held about sports and on-field expression. When players mentioned key facets of experience with a parent or coach I would veer away from the set interview questions and probe deeper.
5. For instance, see the literature on coach "stacking" by sporting position by Loy and McElvogue, 1970; Curtis and Loy, 1978; Leonard, 1978; Lavoie, 1989; Smith and Seff, 1990; Leonard and Smith, 1997; Smith and Harrison, 1997; and Margolis and Piliavin, 1999.
6. Please see Simons, 2003; Andrews, 1996; Majors and Billson, 1992; George, 1992; Dyson, 1993; Sailes, 1998; Kochman, 1981.

7. Please see also Duneier, 1992, and Jones, 1986.
8. Daryl Carter, in Andrews, 1996b.
9. Michael London, in Andrews,1996b.
10. Carl McCullough, in Andrews, 1996b.
11. Cummings, P., 1949, p. 420.
12. Reggie Torian, in Andrews, 1996b.
13. A Chicago story parallels the Alvarez incident: "But it was also at this point that the white coach felt obliged to step in and … 'clean it up' by extending the customary white compliments and credits to a 'defeated but valiant opponent.' The coach interpreted (or at least responded to) the black team's boasting in accordance with white cultural norms … This violated the white norm that one should be charitable to the opponent one has just defeated. Because of these violations, the white coach felt the need to step in and re-establish the dominance of white decorum rules" (Kochman, 1981: 72).
14. See Hewitt, "The organism that minds itself is aware of itself as a part of the world, and has gained an important capacity for control over its own acts" (Hewitt, 1991, p. 46).
15. Mead, G., 1934.
16. Goffman, E. 1959. *The Presentation of Self in Everyday Life*. New York: Doubleday Anchor Books.
17. Goffman, E., 1959, p. 56.
18. Sailes, G., 1998, p. 128.
19. One's self-defined identity is a key component of behavioral patterns, and Scheier and Carver (1980) theorize that people's identities are determined by unique life circumstances and individual variations in approval needs. Internal versus external expectancies also differ by individual. We will therefore approach any situation with a cue of responses infinitely different from another person on our own team, let alone our own cultural group.
20. In our push as scholars and educators to fight for more Black and Brown role models and mentors, we might need to become more cognizant of the variety of ways White role models and mentors affect Black/Brown behavior patterns.
21. Al Toon, in Andrews, 1996b.
22. "The context in which the child's initial sense of self develops and basic identities, motivations, values and beliefs are formed" (Gecas, 1990, p. 165). Gecas comments that though much of parental socialization is intentional, such as teaching children roles, values, norms and beliefs, much of what a child learns will be "inadvertent, unintentional, and often unconsciously produced by parents" (Gecas, 1990, p. 173).
23. Toon, in a later conversation, amended this to "one" thing Nuttycombe wrote down.
24. Al Toon, in Andrews, 1996b.
25. Given the gravity of Toon's statement and significance he places on Nuttycombe, a word of caution is that of course interviewees can give socially desired responses and

omit relevant information. Bradburn (1983), in discussing the interview process and subject responses, cautions that interviewees can give socially desired responses, omit relevant information, and err due to faulty memory (p. 291). This certainly applies to all the athletes I interviewed, but my feeling is that Toon was the clearest of anyone as to who he was—and how he got that way, with his noted exception about "who knows how" he got that way. The reader is left in each case to discern which athletes they believe.

26. Indeed, Toon was observing his own "biographical memory," a term Schwartz (1999) says occurs when we examine critical episodes that helped shape our lives. Further, Schwartz notes that this memory is "a social process ... as we look back, we find ourselves remembering our lives in terms of our experience with others" (Schwartz, 1999, p. 15).
27. It has been noted that in the United States we live in an "interview society" (Atkinson and Silverman, 1997; Silverman, 1993) and have an inherent faith that our research results are trustworthy and accurate—as long as we have not somehow biased the respondent. Extensive precautions were taken to protect against inserting bias in my prepared questions—and the framing of follow-up questions. I would hope the interview bears out conclusively that no bias slipped-in nor were there any leading questions put to Al Toon. My own credibility, in the end, is left up to the judgment of the reader.
28. OED, 1971, p. 1154.
29. Merton notes that people may be seeking to aid their "rise into that group and of easing [their] adjustment" once they become a part of the group (Merton, 1957, p. 347).
30. Merton suggests that through anticipatory socialization mobility-minded people engage the social structure by sometimes taking on "the values of the non-membership group to which they aspire" with the hope of finding "readier acceptance by that group" and therefore to make "an easier adjustment to it" (Merton, 1957, p. 347).
31. Banaji and Prentice (1994) note that more substantial changes in the self-concept are documented during periods of life transition. Similarly, Deutsch et al. (1988) note that new identities are formed during transition stages, while Ethier and Deaux (1990) comment specifically on ethnicity, finding that the more ethnic identity represents a threat to the new environment, the less strongly we identify with our ethnic group.
32. Toon, in Andrews, 1996b.
33. Ibid.
34. Denzin (1989a) would add that these moments often occur during the interview process, and that they represent "those interactional moments that leave marks on people's lives [and] have the potential for creating transformational experiences for the person" (p. 15).

35. Swann (1983) might suggest that Toon is exhibiting stability in self-concept and identity by behaving consistently in the situations and audiences he encounters. This consistency is backed by exhibiting strong, central self-beliefs also activated across social situations and audiences (Fiske and Taylor, 1991).
36. Please see Snyder, 1979, for an extensive discussion of self-monitoring. He notes, "High self-monitors use social cues to regulate, control and monitor verbal and non-verbal behavior. On the other hand, the expressive behavior of the low self-monitoring individual is controlled by their internal affective states and stable attitudes as opposed to being constructed to fit the social situation" (Snyder, 1979).
37. Biddle and Thomas (1966) note there are expectations and norms in any given social situation and, furthermore, that treading far from those norms during performance of a social act will lead to evaluation and possibly sanction by "others."
38. Please see Adell (1994) and Dubois (1964) for broader discussion of the issue of double-consciousness and Blacks having to at one time observe the social other and race across situations. See Wiggins (1997) for the relationship between sport and the double-consciousness of Black athletes in American history.
39. NFL, 1990.
40. Toon, in Andrews, 1996b.
41. Fletcher, in Andrews, 1996b. Please see Norbert Elias' (1978, 1982) discussion of cross-cultural manners and civility.
42. Toon rated his expression as a "one" on a scale of 1 to 5, the highest expression being five.
43. Toon, in Andrews, 1996b.
44. If Al Toon exhibited the same behavior in college football now, he'd be penalized. It is against the rules to run away from teammates who are trying to celebrate a "team" achievement. The act of separating yourself from teammates, much like soccer players do when scoring a goal, incurs a 15-yard penalty and is deemed "unsportsmanlike conduct" by the NCAA as of 1996.

6

Good & Bad Sportsmanship

Walter Camp, Hobey Baker, & Muhammad Ali

Sportsmanship is only broken down into two categories: Good and bad. Good sportsmanship is generally considered positive interaction with teammates, officials, coaches, and opponents, verbal and nonverbal support, encouragement or praise to all players on the field, shaking hands after the game, helping someone up, and complimenting others for good plays.[1] This does beg the question—do you say to the opposition, "Nice end-zone dance, Terrell," or "Nice double-pump 360-degree slam-dunk over my teammate, Kobe?" Probably not in the heat of battle. Probably never.

Bad sportsmanship, on the other hand, could be classified as negative behaviors such as arguing with coaches or teammates, retaliating with abusive language toward fans or opposing players, starting fights, intentionally causing injury, yelling at referees or umpires, or refusing to play anymore if you don't get your share of the ball (in basketball, football, or soccer).[2] When you are playing with the neighborhood kids, the worst form of sportsmanship we are all familiar with is a kid taking his ball and going home when things don't go his way. This might very well be the only universally agreed-upon act of bad sportsmanship. We can generally agree, for the time being, that many in the US consider all of these acts … *bad* sportsmanship.

Are athletes who dance in the end-zone bad sports? If so, then how do Black athletes mentally reconfigure socially unacceptable bad acts to be acceptable? Are players who strut after an interception or sack of the quarterback exhibiting bad sportsmanship? Is the person who slam-dunks to entertain (when the game is out of reach) a bad sport? In general, is the overly expressive athlete a bad sportsman and a bad sportswoman? If Venus and Serena Williams dance around the court waving to the crowd after a grand-slam doubles victory instead of first addressing the losing players, is this bad sports*woman*ship?

It would appear that many behaviors classified under celebratory expression are socially unacceptable or bad. Many athletes and fans somehow reconfigure these acts as "good" or acceptable. Further, how would other acts be considered in terms of sports conduct, such as a coach yelling at a referee or umpire? Or a team owner, such as Mark Cuban of the Dallas Mavericks, yelling at (then) Denver Nugget Kenyon Martin's mother in the stands, "Your son is a thug!"[3] History shows us that sports conduct has been contested for centuries.

Sports Conduct and Boasting in the Ancient Texts of Homer

The thickest and most intimidating book I ever read as an English undergraduate was *The Iliad*, by Homer. I loved it. I was fascinated by the skill and athletic power of Achilles—and by the high esteem both his countrymen (and women) and his rivals held him in. He was Michael Jordan, Muhammad Ali, Aaron Rodgers, and Hank Aaron all rolled up into one heck of a fighter. Turns out, Achilles had a high opinion of himself also, much like Ali. Many contemporary fans feel that athletes bragging during a game or boasting about themselves or their prowess against an upcoming opponent is another form of bad sportsmanship. If this were the case, Achilles, it appears, would have been penalized fifteen yards with a loss of down. He may have even gotten his own reality TV show.

Case in point: Though Achilles observes the sporting competition from a luxury box while eating hot dogs and sipping beer, he wants to let everyone know that if he were competing, he'd surely open up a large can of whoop-ass. He states: "Now if we Achaeans were contending for the sake of some other hero, I myself should take away the first prize to my shelter."[4] In other words, "I am not competing—but if I were, everybody knows I would win … right?" Achilles, the non-competitor, still demands status recognition by his peers. No one disagrees with his claim that he, indeed, would come out on top. This is akin to Michael

Jordan saying, "I am a judge in the slam-dunk competition this year, but if I was competing, everyone knows I would win, right?" Indeed, the NBA likely did ask Jordan to step aside so other young Turks could make a name for themselves amongst fans around the league.

We need to consider Achilles' bragging and boasting in the context of his times, as Allan Guttmann reminds us that sport is "a human universal, appearing in every culture, past and present. But every culture has its own definitions of sport."[5] Sport in ancient times served different purposes to what we see today:

> Physical performances (hunting, dance, runs, processions, combats, mock warfare) were elements of rites of passage, mating displays, festivals, and rituals of community—fields of play on which status was defined and social orders were re-constituted. Sport of various types allowed communities to incorporate physicality and aggression therapeutically.[6]

Then again, maybe we also see sport today as a rite of passage, a mating ritual (many couples have come from college and corporate intramural co-ed leagues), a means of defining status in society (amateur ideals and professionalism come to mind), and given the nature of violence that is always lurking in contact sports, maybe sport does serve as a way to therapeutically work through our aggression through contact and physicality. Many weekend warriors also say they play for the passion of competition, and Donald Kyle notes also that though academics tend to privilege the mind over the body, "The physicality and passionate competitiveness of the Greeks and Romans cannot be denied."[7] Unfortunately, one man's passionate playing is another man's "showboating."

For instance, here is one Homeric old-timer letting all-comers know he is not going to go down easy:

> Who can oppose me?… I am the one who is strongest/and most skilled in athletics and trials of strength. That my name be established into distant days …/ That my name be spread wide in the land /That I be eulogized in all the lands /I, the runner, rose in my strength, all set for the course … I resolved to traverse it as if it were [but a distance] of one "double hour."/Like a lion that wearies not of its virility I …[8]

You get the idea. Kyle goes on to note Homer's characters are more inclined to "hubris than humility" and that Homer's "heroes usually were eager to demonstrate their talents in contests … Boasts and challenges claim that individuals had won, could win, or will win different events."[9] Robert Lipsyte echoes Kyle's notions of Homer's boastful characters, and notes that contemporary characters can match with their own boasts:

> Three of the greatest trash talkers in the history of sports—Muhammad Ali, Henry Kissinger and Marge Schott—made encore performances recently as if to remind the current designated mouths that there have been giants in the field. Call it Homeric boasting, bench jockeying, psyching out, trash talk is the latest label for a line of hostile chatter that goes back at least to Cain putting down Abel before eliminating him from the race.[10]

Lipsyte goes on to lay out the boasting and "trash-talk" of each named person, careful to note that this type of brash behavior is nothing new and indeed part of human history going way back. Homer might be reflecting the sport of his time, where "Ancient games, both sports and spectacles, were communicative performances" between viewers and viewed, actors and audiences.[11] Apparently, both athletes and spectators appreciate attention at contests: The spectators see the athletes struggling, and the athletes realize that people have assembled to watch them.

Even further, Tertullian said that spectacles were places for "Seeing and being seen."[12] Dramaturgy, noted earlier, is life viewed as a "stage." We all continually perform. The theater has four superficial "walls"—a frontstage, back-stage, stage-left, and stage-right. Irving Goffman says some performers break down the "fourth wall"—the wall that separates performer from the audience.[13] This would appear to be the case in ancient Rome and Greece where one can hope to see and be seen:

> Ancients did not consume their sport and spectacles passively and anonymously in dark movie theaters, or sitting in easy chairs watching television in their homes. They had to attend events and pay close attention. Ancient spectatorship simply was more public and interactive.[14]

The ancients can make a case that, indeed, their own brand of sports behavior was contextual and specific to their own situations, offended no one intentionally, and were well within the boundaries of established protocols. We have to rethink our definition of "appropriate behavior" to consider the society within which sport is played, lest we be too quick to judge our ancestors.

Howard Cosell shaped his career around an athlete who interacted with the audience and media continually, Muhammad Ali. Cosell reminds us to be wary of sport as decoupled from the society within which it occurs:

Figure 6.1. Many loved him, many hated him, but Muhammad Ali was the essence of expression. Source: Don Morley/Allsport/Getty Images

> I learned early on that sports is part of life, that it is human life in microcosm, and that the virtues and flaws of the society exist in sports even as they exist everywhere else. I have viewed it as part of my function to reveal this in the course of my pursuit of every avenue of the sports beat.[15]

In the end, what is revealed is that bragging, boasting, and otherwise acknowledging one's own prowess at sport is more traditional than we might have originally thought; bragging and boasting was acceptable sports norm in some ancient societies. Why not today? Much of the dissention comes from not only our protestant-work-ethic notions of humility, but also our inherited/adopted ideas of sportsmanship from England.

English Traditions of Sportsmanship and Fair Play

Where did we get our notions of sportsmanship and fair play? It is safe to say our ideas of what is good and bad sports conduct originated in England. Ikuo Abe, in a study of the history of sportsmanship, traces the roots of the word "sportsman" back to England in 1677, where Nicholas Cox first used the word in *The Gentleman's Recreation.* The first usage was "sports-man" and referred to a "man of pleasure," and later, in *The History of Tom Jones*, "sportsmanship" was synonymous with "skills" on the field of play.[16]

Early uses did not refer to ethical behavior, a player's code, or appropriate conduct. The use in an ethical context was in 1949 in Parke Cummings' book, *The Dictionary of Sports.* This modern usage is the one echoed by both the NFL and the NCAA as they hearken back to:

> Sportsmanship: The ethical code embodied in sport at its best. It includes fairness in action and attitude, abiding by the rules, refusing to take an unfair advantage, courtesy toward the opponent, modesty in victory, graciousness in defeat.[17]

The above ethical definition likely arose at the turn of the twentieth century, as Abe estimates there was a fifty-year time lag between the first usage and placement in the dictionary. The usage of the word thus underwent a change over time from referring to sportsmen as people "fond of hunting" or "skill" in sport to the current usage of sportsmanship as "a person who behaves generously in defeat or victory," or generous behavior befitting a good sportsman.[18]

There is also a brief mention of the concept of "amateur," first used in 1784 as "one who has a taste for anything," or "one who cultivates anything as a pastime," to the usage in England of the word "amateur" in the late eighteenth century and then to the word "amateurism" in the late nineteenth century. The current usage of amateur has its roots in the 1901 definition:

> One who cultivates a particular study or art for the love of it, and not professionally: In general terms, one who plays a game for pleasure, as distinguished from a professional who plays for money—nearly every game has its special definition to meet its own requirements.[19]

This is a perfect fit with Walter Camp's idea of the gentleman sportsman. The connection of sportsmanship to the ethical nuances of sport thus came about in the 1890s, and at the same time the concept of amateurism began to be tied to sporting activities. In a cross-cultural note, Abe cites Japanese dictionaries as responsible for acceptance of the term "sportsmanship" in Japan, though Japan had a different understanding of modern sport and adapted the term to fit Japanese traditional culture and attitude. Japan did not simply accept the concept and all its particulars.

I flew to Japan in 2007 and visited Tokyo to observe baseball. The Sebu Lions game proved to be an eye-opener for this American. As an avowed stadium rat, one of my hobbies is visiting ballparks to observe local customs and practices and critique the stadium. My first stop is for a stadium hot dog and a local beer, and I then evaluate once plopped into my seat. I went against custom, settling for the most popular dish, noodles. I slurped noodles and saw how the Japanese, at least here, humbly cheered for their team in the oddest way I'd ever seen. They rotated their cheering.

When the home team batted, their fans stood and cheered and had a large drum banging out beats. When the opposing team batted, the home team sat silently and watched. The opposing fans stood, chanted, clapped, and went wild, until the third out. Then they sat down. This was completely foreign to me, once again, and I eventually engaged in conversations with locals about what was going on (another habit, though more sociological). Baseball might have started in the USA, but its practice overseas in Japan reflected local culture. I moved to sit right in the thick of the most rabid fans, sort of the "Black Hole" in the end-zone where hard-core Raider fans sit. I was deep in the mix.

I'll spare you all the details but suffice to say that the Japanese drums were loud, the fans loyal, the beer good, and the balloons we all set adrift in unison, quite inspiring. Yes, different from the USA, different from New Zealand, but no less interesting or exciting. Different country, same sport, different customs.

No way I was about to grab the microphone and say, "Stop! Time out! You are practicing the sport all wrong. I don't know what this is—but it is not baseball! You don't know what you are doing! Here, let me teach you! Yell at the umpires, drink far too much beer, taunt opposing players, and whenever possible, fight with opposing fans! Have you lost your minds! I'm about to report you to America!" No. I'm humble. I'd never presume that the way I practice anything is the way everyone should. The difference in how the Japanese play baseball (no arguing with the umpires or fighting) and practice fandom (no nastiness) is what makes them, and us, unique.

But it turns out the Olympics were not Japanese, but rather a ripe sporting institution for both teaching amateurism and (one idea of) sportsmanship, and telling everyone that indeed there was one way to do everything—the right way:

> However, it is not deniable that some time after the second half of the nineteenth century, a 'sportsmanship' movement arose as a world-wide ideological movement, diffusing the 'game ethic.' In other words, the conceptual changes of 'sportsman' and 'sportsmanship' reflect not only the export of English public-school game ethic from the second half of the nineteenth century, but also the international diffusion of Pierre de Coubertin's 'Olympism' from the end of the nineteenth century.[20]

Indeed, Jan Cameron addressed the International Olympic Academy in July of 1993 and commented that the ethics of sport have a gendered and English background, noting that: "The form of sport which was considered legitimate was determined by those in control, usually dominant men and, in the case of British colonial sport, the English 'mother country.' It was clearly their ethics and values which determined fair play."[21] Cameron says traditions were started and perpetuated by the powerful who have control over rulemaking and what is considered fair play.

Cameron says further that politics, ideology, power, and sports are often bedfellows, and that neither the beginnings of the notion of how sport should be played nor current ideas about fair play are random or condoned by all. She notes that: "... sports, and their rules, are controlled by a very small elite. As such, sport is a very useful and increasingly important vehicle for conveying the ideas and values of those in power."[22]

Cameron later states that sport is infused with dominating ruling-class ideas of fair play and good manners, in the end representing dominant power in action. In addition, she notes—and this is a point I discussed with her in New Zealand—that fair play is cultural and contextual, and that officials need to look more at the circumstances or intent of actions versus whether or not one ideology considers it "unfair."[23] She also suggests consulting athletes about fair play, allowing those who engage in sport to enter the debate. This is a point critical for both collegiate and professional rules committees to consider. Inclusion of diverse voices in rulemaking is key. And not simply the voices of athletes, but fans, referees, women, gays and lesbians and transgendered athletes, most importantly the differently abled, retired athletes, and folks from a variety of ethnic and cultural backgrounds in the USA. This is what democracy looks like.

Abe says the "ethicizing process" of sport needs to be analyzed from a cross-cultural viewpoint, and he calls for a universal, integrated value system of sportsmanship. A universally agreed-upon value system of any kind—let alone involving sport—would be a miracle in this day and age of cultural, religious, and national differences. The least we can hope for, though, is agreement on bad sportsmanship on a case-by-case basis, one rule at a time.

We need rules. "Chaos" is what we play in the street or backyard or in the park or in the alley as kids ... making up the rules as we go along. When new kids enter the game, they can discuss the rules and suggest upgrades. Kids play, kids make the rules. Modern sport is complex and very much in need of rules and refinements as society shifts and competition morphs from one generation to the next. What is needed is constant refinement as new kids—and cultures—enter the game. College football decided early in the last century to set down rules and codes of conduct with which to organize play and prevent chaos on every down.

The Early Football Rules on Expression, Emotion, and Individuality

The NCAA Football Rules Committee was established in 1916. One of the first things that this new NCAA Rules Committee did was to publish "A Code of Football Ethics," and thus a "plea for high standards of sportsmanship."[24] This is aimed at the individual player, and tackles a number of practices and behaviors that it deems "unsportsmanlike tactics," including talking to officials or opponents in an abusive or insulting way:

> The football code is different (from the rules). The football player who intentionally violates a rule is guilty of unfair play and unsportsmanlike tactics, and, whether or not he escapes being penalized, he brings discredit to the good name of the game, which it is his duty as player to uphold.[25]

In 1916 the "Code" was published as a guideline for sportsmanlike conduct, but over time the NCAA would need a code of enforcement with which to make it effective, hence the making of rules, like the conduct rule passed in 1975: "[The] Use of gestures or acts which provoke ill will, now a non-contact, 15-yard penalty-foul."[26] Not only did gestures and acts provoke ill will, they provoked fights. The biggest offenders were the individual celebrations by football players, most often after scoring a touchdown.

Walter Camp

Violence, toughness, and rugby in the USA went hand-in-hand in the old days, even after the game had taken the shape of what is now "gridiron." Until 1906, football was vicious and violent. So violent, in fact, that in 1905 President Roosevelt got involved so as to preclude more deaths to players around the country. The man most consider to be the father of American football, Walter Camp, was the innovator who in 1905 formulated the sport we know today. He is, in essence, the "William Webb Ellis" of American football.

William Webb Ellis is the famous Englishman who, during a soccer match in 1823, picked up the ball (highly illegal and no doubt unsportsmanlike, however innovative it might have been) and began to run with it, so the story goes. This single act led to an all-new sport, rugby, first played in the city where it all happened and that bears its name, Rugby, England.[27]

The NFL as we know it today evolved from rugby and that very moment of unfair play. Turns out Walter Camp played in the first ever Yale-Harvard rugby match in 1876, and thereafter captained the team in 1878, 1879, and 1881. To say Camp shaped the game is an understatement, as he moved the game from a backyard rugby brawl to a game that had a set number of plays, first downs, strategic positions on the field requiring different skills, a new points system for touchdowns and kicks, and the all-important "Webb-Ellis" touch: Walter Camp invented the forward pass.[28] Without Camp we'd still be kicking the ball around or tossing it backward as they still do in rugby. Not that there's anything wrong with that.

With no forward pass we would never have seen the likes of Roger Staubach, Aaron Rodgers, Joe Montana, Kenny "The Snake" Stabler, Warren Moon, Peyton Manning, Tom Brady, Drew Brees, Cam Newton, Andrew Luck, Brett Favre, Warren Moon, Doug Williams, Russell Wilson or Patrick Mahomes II. Nor would we have seen their spirals caught by Fred Biletnikoff, Jerry Rice, Sterling Sharpe, Larry Fitzgerald, Odell Beckham Jr., or any number of great receivers. The quarterbacks and receivers produce much of the excitement of American Football and passing is more or less how we define the difference between gridiron football and the game of rugby union. But Walter Camp was also known for something else that shapes how we play the game today. Many feel his ethos of sportsmanship was his greatest contribution:

> It is for his qualities as a human being, his unselfishness, his sincerity, his leadership in the interests of sportsmanship and fair play—these are the facets of Walter Camp that made him respected and admired in whatever group he gathered.[29]

Walter Camp could be said to have invented our modern U.S. idea of sportsmanship. He believed in the concept of fair play and referred to athletes as "gentlemen." He believed in playing the game within the established letter and spirit of the rules, and that fans can and should engage in "jolly fun" but should steer clear of the "vicious element." On how you should treat your rivals, he notes:

> A gentleman is courteous. It is not courtesy upon a ball-field to cheer an error of the opponents. If it is upon your grounds, it is the worst kind of boorishness. Moreover, if there are remarkable plays made by your rivals you yourselves should cheer, conceal any chagrin you may feel at the loss it may be to your side, but be courteous to appreciate and applaud an exceptional play by the opponents.[30]

Walter Camp would obviously be very, very upset at the fan behavior in contemporary American sport. He'd likely roll out of his casket and begin policing the NFL like a boss. Fans jeering the opposing players, waving banners while the opposing player shoots free throws, standing and cheering the home pitcher if the last opposing batter has two strikes on him—all of these acts are unsportsmanlike in Camp's eyes. In addition, Camp would suspend former NBA coaches Pat Riley and Chuck Daily for promoting ungentlemanly violent play in their athletes. Camp would also approve of the controversial one-year suspension of Coach Sean Payton of the New Orleans Saints for his team (purportedly) awarding "bounties" for injuring opposing NFL players.

Camp would love, on the other hand, singing the national anthem, having a home-run hitter do a curtain-call, group prayers on the field after the football game, and boxers hugging after a well-fought and bloody match.

Why should we care what Walter Camp thinks? Sure, he saved the sport by creating new ways of playing, but does that mean he should be the exemplar when it comes to sportsmanship? Do we trust him? Why should we? He loved the sport, but so did Al Davis, owner of the dreaded Oakland Raiders and scourge of the NFL (may the Brooklyn native rest in peace). In short, I think we look to Camp because he is the father of American Gridiron football. As they say, "Father knows best." We respect what he stood for and that he gave so much for his sport. Heck, he invented the concept of choosing "All American" athletes, which he started doing in 1898.

Camp chose every All-American team from 1898 until 1924. He died in 1925, but not before serving on nearly every rules committee involving football, as Guttmann notes: "Walter Camp, who played the game for Yale, was for forty-six years the dominant force on the rules committee that—step by step, year by year—turned rugby into American football."[31]

Of course, they *had* to listen to Camp. From 1885 through 1889, Camp's Yale team won forty-six straight games in the Ivy League. Nice win streak. And oh, by the way, Camp's teams opened up quite a "can"—they won scoring a total of 2,018 verses the opposition scoring only twenty-nine points.[32] How did his teams become so dominant, and in turn allow him to so dominate the ethos of football?

Camp loved specialization, and made sure his players trained for specific positions, unheard of in his time: "Division of labor … has been so thoroughly and successfully carried out on the football field that a player nowadays must train for a particular position."[33] Camp was a revolutionary. Camp was a winner. He said, "Things should change." That's why we look to Camp for how the game should be played—he won. And he was the primary mover in re-shaping and saving our game—his game. All due respect to Walter Camp. He earned it.

As the modern father of the game, we respect him and what he achieved and what he attempted to leave behind for us—a game that could be enjoyed for the next one hundred years. But like all fathers, we listen to some things they say and look the other way when we want to do it our way. "That was fine in your time, Dad," we say as teenagers, "but this is a new day—we want to do it our way. Times have changed." This is the teenage logic we use when we put forth rules that run counter to what our forefathers would have liked. Or, we simply look the other way (and smoke that cigarette at your friend's basement party).

This is how we can allow for fan interaction via booing, fan taunting, premeditated cheers to throw off the opposition, stadium music that demeans an opponent, or loud noise and flailing arms in order to make someone miss a field goal or free-throw. We simply look at winning as the ultimate goal of sport, and our price of admission allows us to freely express our emotions as we see fit—toward the opposing team, a player, a coach, a referee, or an opposing fan sitting down front. Anything—and everything—goes. We could care less about Walter Camp at these moments of emotion.

When we pay for our tickets and enter the turnstiles at a sports venue, we rightfully feel we have paid for the freedom to express ourselves as *loudly* as we want *at whom* we want and *when* we want.

Challenges to people while exercising their game-time freedoms can lead to arguments, fistfights, expulsion from the stadium, or all of the above. And though these game-situated ideals of our freedom of expression run counter to how we might behave *outside* the stadium, we ever so subtly reconfigure our actions as justifiable given that we need—*deserve*—an emotional release through sport. Further, times have changed since 1906 when Walter Camp and "gentlemanly times" ruled our consciousness. Finally, if my rowdy expression does not directly *hurt* anyone, then all is fair in love and war.

This is what we would explain to Fiona in New Zealand—that she is following an antiquated set of codes that will not get you a win *nor* will it get you to the emotionally joyous/depressed state American fans reach when experiencing a win or a loss. Fiona would love Walter Camp and his ideas about being a fan because Camp's codes of fan conduct mirror her society far more than contemporary U.S. society. Indeed, Fiona sadly notes that New Zealand fans are becoming more and more like U.S. fans, especially given the amount of ESPN football, basketball, and baseball games that are piped-in each week via satellite television.

Camp speaks directly to fan behavior and athlete behavior but does not address all the changes (how could he?) and complexities of modern sport. My obsession with expressive celebration leaves me wondering how he might reflect on current sport. That is, we know what Camp says about good sportsmanship, and we know what Camp says about bad sportsmanship, but what would he say about the messy stuff in the middle—such as individual expression?

There were no end-zone dances in his day. And no expressive Deion Sanders or Richard Sherman-type cornerbacks, or any Tiger Woods-type golfers pumping their fists after sinking a long putt. Come to think of it, there were few Black athletes allowed to play sport. But wise Mr. Camp had seen glimpses of individuality and expression, which gave rise to these comments:

> After winning a race or a match, there is no reason why a good, healthy lot of young men should not do plenty of cheering, but there is every reason why they should not make their enjoyment depend on insulting those who have lost. You cannot take your hilarity into a corner and choke it to death, and no one wants you to; but gratuitous jibes and jeers at the crestfallen mark you as a man who does not know how to bear a victory … Finally, to non-contestants, I want to say a word regarding "celebrating." Primarily, do not, I beg of you, do anything because it looks smart. Enjoy yourselves, but do not try to "show off."[34]

I added the last quote about *fans showing off and celebrating* as Camp feels strongly about this: You should rightly feel ashamed if you have ever participated in post-game celebrations in front of opposing fans (including your spouse, who loves the Dallas Cowboys). I also want to put emphasis on his remarks about expression, as Camp is setting up a general way—an *understanding*—of being in and around sport that is respectful of others, while still giving in to the emotion of the moment. Enjoy yourselves, he notes, but do not "show off."

We can extrapolate the non-contestants Camp mentions to his feelings on contestants-as-athletes regarding showing off and celebrating: Don't. And we can be certain that Camp would not condone Seahawk Richard Sherman's post-game comments after the 2014 NFC Championship game. Camp would likewise not approve of Eric Crabtree refusing to shake Sherman's hand after the contest was over—or Crabtree pushing Sherman in the face.

What Camp would have frowned upon was Sherman thereafter running around the field with his hands around his neck giving the "choke" sign to the Forty-Niners. I said aloud to the group I was watching the Super Bowl with, "I disagree. I don't think the 49'ers choked. The Seahawks had the better record. The Seahawks had home-field advantage. The 49'ers were driving for the victory.

Sherman just made a great play, but the 49'ers didn't choke. Every loss is not a choke." Then, later, I thought about it. Sherman was reacting to Crabtree's snub, refusal to shake his hand, and push in the face. His anger came out even more once interviewed by Erin Andrews.

I can imagine what Crabtree would have done had he scored on the play. He likely would have danced like he'd won the Super Bowl. So couldn't we use the same logic to justify celebratory behavior that we use to justify fan expression? Could we not turn a blind-eye to Camp and say his advice is outdated and old-fashioned? This is where we begin to question the NCAA rules committee and the NFL when they both speak of time-honored traditions. Which traditions are time-honored, and which are old-fashioned? How do we justify keeping some remnants of our sporting forefathers while tossing others?

We are in the game of continually re-visioning our sport in America as the years pass. But it might be a bit disingenuous to bow down to Walter Camp as our guiding light one day (re: players and celebration) then look the other way and backslide on other days (re: fan expressive behavior). You can't have it both ways without being hypocritical.

Who knows, Camp might even say that if we are to allow extreme celebration and expression in the stands that we have to logically allow it in our high-performance emotional athletes. That, possibly, athletes should be allowed to celebrate—that they should not take their "hilarity into a corner and choke it to death"—quite a strong visual analogy for allowing verbal, physical, and emotional release during games. Which types of release? "Normal" types, of course.

We can only guess the particulars he was thinking of both on and off the field. Camp is keen to let us know that emotion is a strong part of the mix of being both a player and a fan and he does not want people to lose the emotion. "Don't be afraid of enthusiasm. A man without it is a man without purpose."[35] So, then, how do we show our enthusiasm and emotion in ways that do or do not demean an opponent, Walter?

If Camp is indeed saying that polite clapping or cheering is the honorable way to support one's team and the best way to acknowledge a good play by the opposition, might he also say that much of what fans and players do today is beyond the pale? If we agree that times have changed, do we selectively choose to allow fans their range of emotions both physical and verbal and yet deny players those same liberties? What might Walter Camp say about two codes—one for fans and one for players?

It would appear he holds a similar code for players—gentlemen—and fans: Don't embarrass the other team and don't embarrass yourselves by going "over the top" with your excitement, he says. What we do as athletes and fans—how we respond to the knowing of this edict—says much about what we think of Walter Camp. Or at least the ethos of Camp, as most contemporary fans have never heard of him, let alone his sportsmanship ideals. Or maybe it says more of what we think has changed in sport and what sport should allow. Certainly, sport back then was not geared toward "entertainment" as it is now.

Amateur Ideals

Indeed, Walter Camp, turns out, did not want athletes to play for money. The "amateur ideal" was his theme: You do "not want your boy 'hired' by any one. If he plays, he plays as a gentleman, not as a professional; he plays for victory, not for money."[36] Times have indeed changed, it seems. The amateur ideal no longer exists in collegiate sport or in Olympian sport, for gentlemen *or* ladies. College players receive tuition, room and board, and stipend money on which to live.

On occasion, rare occasion, collegiate players receive money, cars, and other fringe benefits by virtue of signing with or staying with a University sports program. (But you didn't hear that from me.) My guess is those doing the under-the-table giving may very well consider themselves alumni who hearken back to the time-honored traditions of a different set of committee rules: He who has the gold makes the rules. The boosters who break the rules likely consider themselves upstanding, rule-abiding citizens.

In the years since the 1984 "commercial" Olympics in Los Angeles, designed by Peter Ueberroth to turn a profit, Olympic athletes are allowed to "have a life" so to speak, and earn money. This also allows countries to put their best athletes forward.[37] In contemporary Olympics, professional basketball and hockey players can play for their country, as can professional tennis players, soccer stars, and track and field athletes.

Professionalism in post-modern sport has eclipsed anything Walter Camp might have imagined. Players such as Kobe Bryant, Kevin Durant, Steph Curry and LeBron James are more important to their franchises than the coaches, especially given their huge salaries, the revenues they generate, and their teams' success on the court. The NBA, NFL, and MLB franchises, Camp would be saddened to know, speak of revenues in the hundreds of millions of dollars. Professional Golf, NASCAR, and "professional" (WWF) wrestling also rake in more money than Camp could imagine. I think Camp might have a cardiac arrest sitting ringside at a WWF "Battle Royal" given their extreme showmanship, expression, and celebratory behavior, though he might indeed enjoy the spectacle for its intended purpose as entertainment.

Most important for the Camp analysis, though, might be the amateur ideal still clung to by collegiate sports. But even collegiate sport can no longer claim true amateurism, given the billions of dollars earned (primarily basketball and football television contracts) by the National Collegiate Athletic Association (NCAA) every year. Collegiate sport and its rules about eligibility, fraud, illegal payments to players, and rampant cheating via recruiting has been called "unsportsmanlike" not only in conversation, but indeed in the title of a book by former NCAA executive director (1951–1987) Walter Byers.[38]

Given that sport has moved in unheard of directions since Camp's death in 1925, we have to concede to the ravages of time some of his finer points about athlete pay, fan behavior, and player behavior. The question will remain: What is the baby to be kept and what is the bath water to be thrown out? What lessons do we keep from Camp's era about sportsmanship and professional football? Who decides?

Before revisiting Muhammad Ali's version of sportsmanship, we need to discuss one more historical figure, a mythical "ideal" for our contemporary framing of the model gentleman/sportsman, the ever-popular Hobey Baker.

Figure 6.2. Steph Curry merges talent, athleticism and 3-point celebratory expression with fan-friendly fun in the Bay Area. Source: Mike Stobe/Getty Images Sport/ Getty Images

Hobey Baker and American Sportsmanship

What an amazing human study. Most sports fans would never have heard of the Princeton star hockey and football player born as Hobart Amory Hare Baker (January 15, 1892—December 21, 1918), most known as "Hobey" Baker. Baker, an amateur athlete of the early twentieth century, is the only member of both the College Football Hall of Fame and College Hockey Hall of Fame. While the Heisman trophy is given to the top collegiate player of the year, college hockey's annual award for most outstanding player is named in his honor. If you do know who Baker is, this is likely the extent of your knowledge. His story is so complex and layered that his ethos and personality still resonate ninety years after his death.

He was, indeed, a Muhammad Ali-type figure whom people admired and loved to be around—as much for his physical gifts as an athlete as for his physical beauty. Indeed, the term "man crush"—depicting the feeling heterosexual men feel when awed by the beauty and talent of another man—would surely have been invented earlier with Hobey Baker's emergence had male homophobia not been so deeply entrenched in early twentieth century society.

For now, let's focus on Hobey Baker as the exemplar of sportsmanship referenced when sportswriters bemoan the lack of "sportsmanship" in contemporary sport or grow nostalgic for a time when men were men (and not gay), sport was White (and male), and everyone (women) knew their place in society.

My cynical tone is not directed at Hobey Baker and his persona, but rather those who would use the most brilliant athlete of his era as the norm to which all others should be held accountable. Hobey Baker would not approve of the comparisons between him and others. He would surely want to be remembered as a gentleman, a fair sportsman, and a man who played to win—with respect to the letter and spirit of the rules. He was indeed the perfect athlete on and off the field. The late Ron Fimrite notes this in his 1991 *Sports Illustrated* article on Hobey Baker:

> Through his Spartan example, he imposed a code of behavior on athletes, particularly college athletes, that was accepted, if not faithfully observed, for the better part of four decades. It is now, alas, as forgotten as the dropkick. In the Hobey code, for example, a star player must be modest in victory, generous in defeat. He credits his triumphs to teamwork, accepts only faint praise for himself. He is clean-cut in dress and manner. He plays by the rules. He never boasts, for boasting is the worst form of muckery. And above all, he is cool and implacable, incapable of conspicuous public demonstration. No room there for the Icky

> Shuffle. The Hobey code—unspoken, for to speak of it would be another form of muckery—was far-reaching in its time ... Hobey was the gentleman-sportsman, the gifted amateur in the English tradition he so admired ...[39]

While Fimrite holds Baker up as a model of good sportsmanship to athletes of our times, Fimrite also uses Hobey as a stick to smack (or police) what Fimrite feels is *bad* sportsmanship. Icky Woods is "Exhibit A," the former Cincinnati Bengal whose name is synonymous with the rule that banned end-zone and sideline celebrations. Playing Icky off of Baker is the equivalent of asking, "What would Jesus do after scoring a touchdown?" He certainly would never taunt the opposing player or do a back flip in the end-zone. Not even in a game between the Nazareth Saints vs. the dreaded Jerusalem Herders. "Therefore, Icky, you are wrong," is the sentiment Fimrite attaches to Icky Woods regarding Bakers' Jesus-type characterization.

First of all, we don't know *what* Jesus might have done in the end-zone. His expression might depend on what the score was, whether he was at a home game or on the road, who his coach was, and what the cornerback said to him before the play. We know he was from a poor neighborhood, so that might color his expression, as would his parents (Mary and Joseph) and their style. Finally, if he was up for free agency at the end of the year, Jesus might have been angling for more publicity. But I digress.

My point here is I do not think Baker would approve of being used in this way—as a foil or a model against which all others should be judged. He might say, "Every man and woman has to decide who they are—but they should play the sport with decency and respect for fellow athletes, male or female, regardless of class or color."[40] Baker might see the dissing of other athletes in his name as "the worst form of muckery."

Hobey was born into wealth, so he knew another lifestyle and swam in company far different from the average "Spartan" athlete. But Baker's family also fell on hard times, and after his parents divorced, Hobey's older brother was forced out of the costly boarding school they both attended. Likewise, there was only money for one Baker to go to Princeton, and so it was Hobey—and not his brother—who would get in. So, even though he was born into wealth, he knew of adversity and would probably empathize with those not born of his public standing. Be that as it is, Baker stands out as the model for the idealized athlete—great, modest, handsome, and above all an adherent to a code steeped in the English traditions of gentlemanly behavior and amateur sport that has nothing to do with money and greed.

There is a saying, "Things aren't like they used to be—but then again, they never were." In other words, maybe our idealized past isn't as perfect as we now reflect on it. We exaggerate the good about the past. We look back with rose-colored lenses. White Wonder Bread was better than brown whole wheat bread and typewriters were better than computers. Or maybe not. Truth is, Hobey followed this English code, but not many others of the era appeared to give much credence to the "gentlemanly code" of our forefathers. Indeed, rough play was probably more the code of the day, as noted earlier in commentary about the potential banning of the sport previous to Baker in 1905.

The soft-spoken but adept Hobey was a target every time he stepped onto the ice, and it is noted that he only received one penalty in his career—for slashing against Harvard in hockey. And he was such a believer in fair play that he found it hard to believe someone would intentionally harm another to win a game.

Baker was a gift to sport and to humanity, and he is indeed a model for not only athletes but also sports writers and administrators, who indeed could benefit from his model of personal integrity, which is in the end what we are discussing here. Hobey did not break the rules—he didn't attempt to gain an advantage at the expense of another. He didn't put a good shooter on the free-throw line instead of the guy who received the foul, as contemporary coaches have. He didn't toss a chair across the floor of the basketball court in order to intimidate the referees, as one great coach has. He didn't smash his racket in the finals of a grand slam tennis match because he was upset at a call that did not go his way, as some tennis greats have. And sure, Hobey did no end-zone dancing when he scored. Or did he?

Baker was the archetype F. Scott Fitzgerald drew upon in *The Great Gatsby*, and also an athlete who, while playing football, refused to wear a helmet … the only man out there who wanted his face, his golden hair, seen by all. As Jeffrey Hart notes:

> I had never heard of Hobey Baker until I began doing research on Fitzgerald some years ago, yet Hobey Baker is a powerful figure in the background of Fitzgerald's fiction, and a major figure in Princeton's tradition. As one sports writer recalls, "The whole atmosphere was electric when he was playing. Everyone would just stand up when he got the puck or caught a punt. Never wore headgear in football and I remember that great shock of blond hair—Hobey standing waiting all alone. He was the only player on the field you looked at, the only player you saw …"[41]

Hobey Baker, the bigger-than-life figure who stood only 5′ 9″, seemed to enjoy being admired. That, or he had a death wish. No sane man runs screaming down a field head-on into traffic with no head gear on, leather or not. Baker still lives on as our model of a man who was a bit different from his peers in an era that also was a bit different from ours:

> Baker's ability, as great as it was, was topped by his sportsmanship and he is perhaps known more for this than his playing skills ... was counted on to always visit the opposition's locker room after a game. Opponents as well as teammates loved him and his tremendous celebrity never occurred to them ... Newspaper[s] began to feature stories on him and while he cooperated with the press, he never went overboard ... [He was a] "glorious representative of young American manhood"... Baker's era of our nation's history will never be seen again. It was a time of confidence, almost arrogance, of determination ...[42]

Such is the awe Baker is held in even today. Teamed with Yale's Walter Camp as the father of American Football and sportsmanship, Baker is certainly cast as American sports' most favored son of sportsmanship—the model not in words, but in deeds. This title of father and son of sportsmanship is both well-deserved and well-earned by both Camp and Baker.

The Ali-Baker Remix: Humility and Flawed Heroes

What would Hobey Baker make of a man and athlete and rebel such as Cassius Clay, later known as Muhammad Ali? In contrast to Baker, Ali spoke of knocking people out in certain rounds and punishing them. This is certainly not what the White Jim Crow press of the time wanted to hear nor what Hobey Baker would have said. To be fair, the press was listening with both ears and speaking openly about what the newly titled Muhammad Ali was saying (like sports broadcaster for ABC, Howard Cosell), and writing with genuine inquiry into what Ali was going on and on about, as was Robert Lipsyte and later, Mike Marqusee:

> There are some who have discovered belatedly and with shock that Ali was an imperfect hero. Perfect heroes, however, are not only implausible but also useless. They can only be admired, not imitated. Ali's flawed humanity reminds us that role models are always incomplete and contradictory.[43]

Marqusee (may he rest in peace) might be echoing sentiments shown in the USA media toward Hobey Baker. Is Hobey Baker perfect? Yes, for his times he was. Is he useless? Perhaps for our times, he is. He can, though, be admired. Imitated? No. "We all fall short," as my Christian friends and family would say. We can always ask ourselves "what would Hobey do?" in this situation or that situation on the field or in the clubhouse. There might be much gnashing of teeth as we could never reach his heights and indeed could begin to despise Baker's revered "perfection."

We can always use him as a great historical figure worthy of study and admiration, but we need to be extremely careful when holding him up as a model with which to either compare contemporary athletes or as the standard we set when reviewing contemporary conduct rules. This is what Marquese, above, might be referring to when noting athletes like this are "useless."

What would (muscular) Jesus do if he was taunted and punched while recovering a fumble? We assume that he would simply "turn the other cheek." In truth, we don't know. There was no football in his time, his team wasn't behind by three points in the last quarter, and we don't know how aggressive his coach was. We are very sure of what Ali would do if punched. He'd punch back. Is Ali wrong? Were our parents wrong for teaching us to stand up for ourselves when bullied?

Expression is nuanced, situational, and context driven. What we might have done thirty years earlier in high school football we might not do in a recreational league to gain advantage. Time—the era we are living in and our own age—also plays a factor in how we evaluate what is or is not appropriate. Hobey Baker would be different if he were born today because he'd face completely different sports scenarios and would grow up playing Grand Theft Auto on his X-Box.

In competitive instances we might all—including Baker—fall prey to our base instincts and fight back, forever regretting our actions if they came at the wrong time. Zinedine Zidane gave a head-butt to a player as retaliation for a family insult and was eliminated from the France vs. Italy 2006 World Cup final in Paris, a moment he and French fans will forever regret. When we experience forgettable moments like those (in the heat of intramural sport) our flawed human heroes are the ones we look to for redemption. Ali, as such, would be the "flawed humanity" athlete Marquese would have us recall.

As we teach kids to play sport, we might look to the Hobey Bakers of the world to show us the way the game can be played and loved. When we want to teach them a lesson or two in how to rise, once fallen, we would have them look at Ali. If we also want to show them how their athleticism is but one facet of their humanity and that sport can also be about everything from intimidation to politics to religion and commercialism, then Ali is indeed our man. Comparing historic amateur athletes and their behavior to contemporary professional athletes and their behavior is not a fair parallel construction.

Indeed, Baker and Ali are probably more alike than we would ever care to admit, though they at times appear to represent opposite ends of the sportsmanship continuum, which has humility and arrogance as its bookends. Baker and Ali are complimentary *and* competing models of sportsmanship. They would have most likely admired each other, each in his own way. Both were considered beautiful physically, both were gracious to fans and admirers, both liked to be admired, and both were supreme athletes—the best by far in their sport in their time.

Taken together, they represent behavioral models contemporary Black and White athletes can mirror and admire. White administrators, rules officials, and media cite Baker as the model, while Black kids—urban, suburban, and rural—and many White kids appear to look to Ali as a guiding light. His humility and weakened physical condition in his later years only heightens the man who once was king.

Earlier on, while making his comeback, Baker—as well as Camp—would have appreciated Ali's rise from the ashes and his supremely humble and human moment after the first Frazier fight:

> By 1970, with public sentiment for the most part returned to his corner, the ex-champ was at last back in the ring. A favorable Supreme Court decision on his draft-evasion case was imminent, as was his first loss—to Joe Frazier in the now legendary "Fight of the Century" at Madison Square Garden. Afterwards, the now "officially" former champion was humble, yet self-assured in defeat: "Just lost a fight, that's all. Probably be a better man for it. I had my day. You lose, you don't shoot yourself."[44]

Ali would have appreciated Hobey Baker being the only man on the football field without a helmet so as to allow, as the mythology goes, him to show his "blond locks to the crowd," as noted earlier. Ali loved the blond Gorgeous George and modeled his showmanship on him. Bill Esposito emphasizes the showmanship of Baker, too. This quote, similar to the first, takes a turn at the beginning and mirrors what many consider Ali to be—a showman. Interesting how the words showmanship, showboating, and sportsmanship are all akin:

> Baker was a player who continually brought a crowd to its feet, whether he caught the puck on the end of his stick, or picked an enemy punt out of the air. He was not, it was written, a showman, but he did everything with a sense of showmanship because it was natural to him ... He didn't wear any headgear, either on the gridiron or on the ice, and with a shock of blond hair topping his strong frame, he was the only player out there, someone said, for the crowd to look at. As George Frazier noted, "It is part of the legend, and not the least true, that he was as handsome an undergraduate as his college ever had."[45]

Ali and Baker, for my money, would have sat down and had a great discussion about how much people admired their charisma, how much people admired how they performed their sports, and how fans and media alike admired their athletic bodies. Reporter Robert Lipsyte comments on a reporter who waxes on about people admiring Ali:

> Vacationing white collegians, male and female, are more reserved, but stare at him with a hot covetousness that seems nearly universal. It was a sportswriter, Jim Murray of Los Angeles, who summed it up best with the frequently quoted, "I'd like to borrow his body for just forty-eight hours, there are three guys I'd like to beat up, and four women I'd like to make love to."[46]

In many ways these two very different role models—Baker and Ali—have become the standard-bearers for White and Black cultural sporting norms, respectively. And given the contradictory nature of humans and athletes, there are cases where White athletes were brash or expressive (Pistol Pete Maravich and Mark Gastineau come to mind) in sport—similar to Ali's flashiness—and where Black athletes were quiet, soft-spoken, and more in line with Hobey's code of conduct (Barry Sanders and Kawhi Leonard come to mind).

These complexities and contradictions point up the ever diversifying work place called contemporary sport in America. The development and trajectory of these differing codes point in the direction of cultural convergence in the future, where Black and White codes merge and interplay and reconfigure according to personality and broader cultural patterns of the times verses long-ago heroes and superstars, though they too have helped in shaping our norms.

What is key here is how we grow to be who we are as individuals, how our individuality is shaped by our neighborhoods, coaches, and role models, and what people make of us when we do whatever we do. Whether we initiate a fight with a little baseball "chin music" or with a flourish of our arms held high after hitting one deep into the seats in baseball; whether we slam-dunk over a hapless opposing player with one hand behind our head or shake-and-bake them out of their sneakers on the court; whether we punch a player in a pile-up after a fumble, or whether we do a Michael Jackson moonwalk after scoring in the Superbowl: We do what we do for a variety of reasons, some cultural, some personal, some racial, and some for attention and financial gain. And sometimes, an end-zone dance is just an end-zone dance. Nothing more, nothing planned, nothing intentionally harming to others.

Because everybody is just a little bit different

Notes

1. Please see: Wandzilak, T., Carroll, T., and Ansorge, C. J. 1988. "Values development through physical activity: Promoting sportsmanlike behaviors, perceptions, and moral reasoning." *Journal of Teaching in Physical Education*, vol. 8, issue 1, p. 13–22.
2. Ibid.
3. I was surprised by Cuban's statement to Martin's mother as I watched him storm off the court after a hard-fought playoff loss to the Denver Nuggets. He has for a while been my favorite team owner, quite the Maverick himself. He later (maybe too late) apologized for his actions to both Martin's mother and Kenyon.
4. Kyle, D. 2007. *Sport and Spectacle in the Ancient World.* Maine: Blackwell Publishing, P. 59.
5. Guttmann, A. 2004. *Sports: The First Five Millennia.* Amherst and Boston: University of Massachusetts Press, P. 1.
6. Kyle, D., 2007, p. 37.
7. Ibid., p. X.
8. Ibid., p. 28.
9. Ibid., p. 56.
10. Lipsyte, G., 1994, p. 8.
11. Kyle, D., 2007, p. 56.
12. Ibid., p. 18
13. Goffman, Irving. 1959. The Presentation of Self in Everyday Life.
14. Kyle, D., 2007, p. 18.
15. Cosell, in Lipsyte, G., 1994, p. 415.
16. Please see Abe, I. 1988. "A study of the chronology of the modern usage of 'sportsmanship' in English, American and Japanese dictionaries." *The International Journal of the History of Sport*, vol. 5, issue 1, pp. 3–28 (p. 3).
17. Cummings, Parke, 1949, p. 420.
18. Abe, I., 1988, p. 9.
19. Ibid.
20. Ibid., p. 25.
21. Cameron, J. 1993. "Fair play and playing fair: The context of good manners. Paper presented at the International Olympic Academy Session for Educators." Olympia, Greece, p. 4.
22. Cameron, J., 1993, p. 5.
23. Ibid., p. 6.
24. Falla, Jack. c1981. *NCAA, The Voice of College Sports: A Diamond Anniversary History, 1906–1981.* 1st edition. Mission, KS: NCAA, p. 53.
25. NCAA, 1916, p. 54.
26. Waldorf, J. 1975. *NCAA Rules Committee Chronology of 100 Years, 1876–1976.* Shawnee Mission, KS: The National Collegiate Athletic Association, p. 26.

27. Webb was "rather inclined to take unfair advantage at football. The incident where Webb Ellis picked up and ran with the ball in his arms during a football match is supposed to have happened in the latter half of 1823." http://www.rugbyfootballhistory.com/webb-ellis.html.
28. Guttmann, A., 2004.
29. Camp, W., no date.
30. Camp, W., 1893, p. 166.
31. Guttmann, A., 2004, p. 143.
32. Ibid.
33. Ibid.
34. Camp, W., 1893, p. 166.
35. Ibid., p. 165.
36. Camp, W., 1989, p. 167.
37. The USA Basketball "Dream Team" made a farce of commercialism in 1992 in the debate about sponsors, Reebok vs. Nike logos on uniforms and tennis shoes. Nike athletes simply draped the American flag over the Reebok logo.
38. Byers, W. c1995. *Unsportsmanlike Conduct: Exploiting College Athletes.* With Charles H. Hammer. Ann Arbor: University of Michigan Press.
39. Fimrite, P. 1991. *Sports Illustrated*, p. 79.
40. It needs to be acknowledged, delicately—and to take nothing away from their accomplishments, that the time period both Hobey Baker and Walter Camp played football in and around were also times of extreme racism regarding the participation of African American athletes in professional sport, especially football, baseball and basketball. Though this does in no way diminish the achievements of both stars, it does frame the absurd argument that everyone should behave like them. Truth be known, African Americans of the time period were both *quiet and humble* when behaving in White institutions and around White citizens. This was a very different sociological time period within which to live and achieve, and sadly, many talented African American athletes were excluded from the joy of playing sport with their contemporary White peers like Baker and Camp.
41. Hart, 1983, p. 1194.
42. Esposito, B., 2007, p. 30.
43. Marqusee, M., 2000, p. 297.
44. Stravinsky, 1997, p. 3.
45. Esposito, B., 2007.
46. Lipsyte, G., 1975, p. 252.

7 How White People Think

Well, certainly not *all* White people. But I know how at least six white people think through intensive interviews. And while that is not enough White people to generalize about all White people, I'd like to present this data as a 1990s "time capsule" of sorts—a picture of how some rural and suburban White parents raised kids to think about social behavior. Those kids likely have kids of their own now and are raising them in likely a more open fashion—redefining those social norms given their collegiate, mixed-race team backgrounds. Below is a discussion of what White athletes think about their bodies in the context of sport and society.

I've studied and lived, mostly invisible, amongst White people since 1976. Though I was aware, generally, of how White people thought about expression and body movement and sports conduct, hearing White athletes verbalize how they frame behavior in and around sport was a revelation. I suspect that many of us Black folks who have worked hard to figure out White people will say, "Of course!" when reading a random response below that is self-evident. I suspect for those not familiar with White people yet—namely Black high school athletes about to enter college—this might come as an education about a unique culture. Yes, White people have culture. And, compared to Black culture, White culture is quite unique and diverse.

This must appear odd—four chapters on White people in the middle of a book on Black expression in sport and society. What is more, the next two chapters deal with the micro-level of White culture where I go right into their homes and chat with their parents and their coaches, in a sense. But there are two specific reasons I've chosen to do a close reading of White cultural norms in and around families and neighborhoods. One is that African Americans are always judged against this norm of civility and humility, so why not find out where it comes from here in the USA? Why not do justice to White voices and White ways of knowing the world? Our ideas are not better than theirs, as I say throughout this book. And their ways of doing things are not better than our traditions. But on the whole, White ways are different. I don't need an academic citation for you to get that generality. I am curious as to where our racial disconnects begin.

I present the White athletes mostly without my own commentary, on occasion jumping in to stress a point or two here and there. What I want you to be aware of, going in, is the symmetry of rules, parenting, coaching, and lifestyles in White, mostly rural, communities. I believe these settings are the "norms" of White cultural backgrounds and attitudes about life and expression. This is in sharp contrast to Black urban voices and communities, where I believe most African Americans get their attitudes about life and expression. These two norms clash—and dance together—in sport. I hold no bias against how Whites were raised and view the world. Many Whites, it seems, feel that everyone should have been raised the same way, by the same parents, in the same neighborhoods, and with sports ideals from coaches who are different in many ways from us.

In addition to wanting to show the "White side" of the ledger of expression in sport and society, I want to show Black athletes—and Black everyday folks like myself who have to work in and amongst Whites—how we are viewed by the "other." I think it is instructive to know how people see us. The "knowing" doesn't need to make us shift our behavior to appease Whites, but knowing how others see us in social situations can certainly impact how we decide to act. I'd rather have us choose from a set of situational options rather than think, "I'm sure they see the world exactly as I do. I'll behave like I've always behaved." I don't think narrow, unexamined thinking or behavior serves anybody. I am not demanding self-consciousness in and around Whites, no more than I'd want Whites to be self-conscious in and around Black folks.

But I would want White people to be aware of the language they use, the humor they use, the inferences they make, and the tone they take about social issues concerning Black folks. That's called being "conscious," and as we all know, the best kind of White people are conscious White people who don't patronize or freeze-up around us but are comfortable in their own skins and are quick to praise and slow to criticize us. They know our history and know their role in that history.

In a similar sense, I hope this small slice of White knowledge of behaviors, expression, sportsmanship, and such informs us and offers an option. The option isn't between "being Black" and "selling out." We sometimes fall into that unconstructive framework. Rather, I'd want my son or daughter or cousin to say, "Hmmm, I could go with what I've gone with—in the past—or adjust to this situation and get the job." Or get the contract or get to know her parents or get the grade in class. Whatever the situation, it is better to be armed with options instead of a one-size-fits-all mentality.

By way of example, I sought out Dr. Yvonne Smith, an African American sports sociologist and mentor (then) at Michigan State, to discuss my upcoming job interview with Canterbury University in New Zealand. I asked her two questions about physical expression. I noted (1) my earring and, (2) my shaved, shiny, bald head. I wondered if I should change anything in my appearance before the interview. She said,

> Hmmm. I like your bald head. Looks great. But many White people associate bald-headed Black men with "inmates" and "radicals," so I'd recommend you grow your hair out until you get the job. Then you can go bald again after a few months. They'll be more comfortable with you and won't see you as a threat. But you can keep the earring.[1]

I took her advice. I got the job. I never shaved my head again, but I kept the earring. I benefitted from having an alternative option. I was still Black. My shaved head didn't make me Blacker. And with my earring on, I still thought I was cool. Which is all that really mattered, anyway.

As you read, just consider how others might see you in a game, or in an office, or in a relationship in that first conversation with her/his parents. Always be aware of the social other critiquing your moves, decisions, and verbal and physical expression. Make your choice from a base of knowledge—whatever choice you make. You don't need to conform, but I also don't want you to be surprised when the "other" takes offense at your actions. Challenge their offense, but don't be surprised. That is my reasoning behind these chapters on Whiteness. Wisdom in our decisions is a better option than ignorance. This likely sounds patronizing to anyone above the age of thirty, but even we old heads can learn a thing or two. White people change their views, and as they do, they often become more racially connected. We need to keep changing, too.

Here is an (almost) unfettered review of athletes' impressions of Black sports behavior while tensions and rules were running high and being challenged in the mid-1990s. I think ideas have shifted toward a more positive review of expression, but I've decide to include these few interviews from the 1990s rather than interview anew because these voices shed light on many (still) strongly held rural beliefs.

Introduction to the Student-Athletes

There were six White athletes selected for interviews, three coinciding roughly with higher expression and three with generally lower expression than their teammates. These levels in on-field expression made by judges do not necessarily coincide with athletes' self-reports of their expressive style or level, to be sure. The three who were ranked highest were quarterback Darrell Bevell and linebackers Eric Unverzagt and Pete Monty. The three that were ranked in the lower range are Matt Nyquist, tight end, and offensive linemen Steve Stark and Gerald Wunsch. Below is a brief introduction to the athletes, which includes basic background information to give context to their views on celebratory expression and their attitudes.

Bevell, Unverzagt and Monty

Darrell Bevell grew up in Scottsdale, Arizona, in a predominantly White community where he often played football against Black athletes. He and his parents are Mormon, and Bevell has done a three-year mission in predominantly Black areas of Cleveland, Ohio. Eric Unverzagt is from a small town on Long Island, Central Islip, where he played football on a virtually all-Black high school team and grew up around people from many cultural backgrounds, predominately African American. His parents raised him in the Lutheran church. Pete Monty is from a small town in Northern Colorado, Fort Collins, where he was raised in a two-parent home (as were the other five White athletes) and socialized by a father who was a high-school coach and former center for the Notre Dame national championship football team of 1968.

All athletes were from middle-class families, based upon self-reports of parental employment. Darrell Bevell was raised in a predominately White community but had contact with many Black athletes while growing up in an around sports.

In contrast, Eric Unverzagt was raised in a predominantly Black neighborhood and school system. Pete Monty was raised in an all-White small town and had little contact with Black athletes in his town or on the playing field. I will be interweaving the life-experiences and expressive attitudes and behaviors of these three athletes throughout this chapter with the experiences of the other three less-expressive athletes described below.

Nyquist, Stark, and Wunsch

The three athletes ranked lower in expression have a more "rural America" profile, as all are from small Midwestern towns. Matt Nyquist is Scandinavian and from Cokato, Minnesota, an all-White (one hundred percent) town with a population of 2500 located fifty miles West of Minneapolis. Steve Stark was raised in Rockton, Illinois, about a mile from Beloit, Wisconsin. Rockton is ninety percent White and also has a population of 2500. Gerald Wunsch grew up in Wausau, Wisconsin, a larger town (est. 50,000) in northern Wisconsin that is roughly eighty percent White (in the mid-1990s), though much Whiter when Wunsch was growing up.

All three athletes were raised in two-parent, religious, middle-class homes where both parents were employed. Stark and Wunsch are offensive linemen and Matt Nyquist is a tight end. How did these athletes adjust to playing on mixed-race teams? Their transition was mandatory given the philosophical approach to socializing athletes instituted by Coach Barry Alvarez. Very progressive, I believe.

Barry Alvarez's Race Philosophy at Wisconsin

Barry Alvarez was officially hired to be head coach at the University of Wisconsin on New Year's Day, 1990.[2] The school has been successful in football ever since. So much so, that Alvarez took over as athletic director in 2004. Other coaches around the country have asked how the Wisconsin "turnaround" happened and how other schools bent on success could mimic the Badger approach.[3] Solid recruitment of great athletes—with the inducement to play "right away" (without sitting on the bench for one or two years behind a stockpile of great athletes)—was no doubt one method. But there are two recruiting and socializing techniques that bear our attention.

One technique is the recruitment of athletes who are race-tolerant and the other is the social incorporation of Black and White athletes in their first year at Wisconsin. This has little to do directly with sportsmanlike conduct, celebratory expression, or rules, but it has everything to do with interpreting the attitudes of team players about racialized expression and race in general.

Alvarez (while head coach) recruited players who would likely be tolerant of race differences and who would be able to work side by side with others. Players commented that UW gets a "pretty good mix" of athletes from around the country, not just Wisconsin, Illinois, and Minnesota, neighboring states. Alvarez was called a "great recruiter," one who could point out a guy "who's going to have trouble, troubles hanging out with White guys or hanging out with Black guys" (Monty). Alvarez recruits "good people" who will be able to "adjust and bend and conform with the team" (Monty). Monty notes that team chemistry is vital, and that if the team recruits a Black player who has had problems with Whites in the past it is "going to make it hard for our team to come together."

The team enculturation begins at the Holy Names Seminary in Madison during the August preseason training session. Athletes live together for a brief period of time during the summer, sharing living quarters. Alvarez has the players live with athletes of another race, such that:

> When you're freshmen they'll put you with a Black or White guy ... and that breaks down everything ... you get to understand where this guy is coming from a little bit more than if you where just paired with another White guy ... freshman seminary I was with Carl McCullough.[4]

This background into UW integration practices shows sport administrators are aware of the racial problems that could occur if athletes of different cultural, class, and locational (rural, urban) settings are brought together without considering sociological difference. I like the conscious thinking about racial connectivity.

I caution that the UW integration process might serve to mute interviewed White athletes verbalizing extremes in attitudes regarding behavior considered "Black" or "White" for fear that they might be being negatively labeled.

Time to make sense of the athletes' opinions and behaviors surrounding sporting conduct, including attitudes about on-field self-expression, sportsmanlike conduct, mentors and role models, sport rules and regulations, and race and expression. I label each section with a major theme that evolved from interviews.

Controlled Expression

Team quarterback Darrell Bevell epitomizes the themes proclaimed by White players about on-field behavior. The primary philosophy underlying all of his expressive actions is "Never Let them See You Sweat," a popular tag line from an antiperspirant commercial. In his own words, "Don't let them see you getting down but don't really let them see you get too excited either (Bevell)."[5] He says he learned this philosophy from both his father and the (then) UW offensive coordinator, Ray Childress. The primary purpose of the controlled-expression philosophy is to not let the opposition know they are "getting to you," mentally or physically, for fear that they might realize some specific tactic is working and therefore repeat their actions.

This "never sweat" philosophy is physically manifested by Bevell with an even-keeled emotional control of body language, maintaining a "poker face," not showing any frustration, and not yelling at teammates. The key objective is to prevent the opposition from saying, "We're getting to him, we'll keep hitting him, they're going to fall," and, let's "get them out of their game plan" (Bevell). Bevell notes that he thinks he was told this philosophy because of the position he plays—quarterback—which might be an especially vulnerable place to attack in a defense's strategy of preventing offensive movement of the ball.

End-of-Game Expression

Unverzagt notes the theme of control in the context of end-of-game expression. This theme can be summarized as the idea that any premature celebration by athletes may lead to overconfidence and thus letting one's "guard down," a loss of focus and game control (and possible defeat). His philosophy might best be summarized by a popular sport saying, "It ain't over until the fat lady sings." That is, there is little reason to celebrate until the game, the playoffs, or the season is over. He comments that:

> I mean any time we win a game, I'm probably one of the happiest guys in the locker room and I let everybody [see] it. You know, you can't be scared to show your emotion after the game is over … anything can happen during a game. I mean obviously you get excited when a big play happens, like an interception or touchdown, and you show your emotion there. But I'm showing my emotion more towards the other guys … I try and keep calm … I try to keep it a little bit more controlled because you got 80 to 90 plays in the game.[6]

Big-Play Expression

These statements emphasize the overarching theme of White expression: There is a time and a place for proper expression. The time is after a big play—a theme three players shared. Monty shares this, saying that he gets excited when he makes "a big play, an interception, or tackle for a loss" (Monty). The type of expression, or "proper" form of expression, seems to be spontaneous, quick tension-release.[7] Bevell says he motivates others by giving high-fives, pounding fists, jumping up and down, and yelling and screaming at fellow players.

Team Celebration

This Badger phenomenon started during the first Alvarez Rose Bowl run (fall 1993). The celebration is primarily between the offensive linemen and the running backs. The celebration consists of linemen running after and catching the running backs in the end-zone and roughhousing with them for a while (exactly what Al Toon hated and feared). The act was initiated for two reasons: (1) because the offensive linemen were excited after a running back scored and (2) because the running backs typically are the ones who score and get the spotlight, and the linemen wanted some of that glory because they helped accomplish the goal. Gerald Wunsch explains the beginning of the tradition, noting that running backs, after a TD, always "get the spotlight, they get the camera … it started our Rose Bowl year" (Wunsch).

Wunsch is conscious of the fact that it is the offensive line that plays a large part in the effectiveness of running backs, and that celebration in the end-zone—the spotlight—is a reward, of sorts, that should be shared. Wunsch's excitement at the moment of a touchdown is much like a valve releasing steam, or maybe more like "a little switch that I turn on and off … I try and stay as calm as I can" until he gets on the field (Wunsch). Once on the field, and specifically in the end-zone, he just goes "crazy," noting that the hard work warrants a reward—a celebration—a team celebration:

> I do ridiculously stupid things after we score a touchdown because I get so excited … I jump on piles, beat up my running back … we have fun … the lineman gets to do a lot of work and he doesn't get the rewards like Carl [McCullough] and Steck [Stecker]… you know, [we] get a couple of bunny punches when we get in there. That's our reward for getting in the end zone. They get to do all the dancing and all the fun stuff.[8]

Wunsch later notes that in spring [training], "we'll chase them around and they'll run away from us and of course they're faster … we're just goofing around being a bunch of kids" (Wunsch). The physically rough end-zone-activity expression of "love pats … of showing the guy we care about him" is reciprocal, for Wunsch says the running backs do "the same thing to us. It's our way of celebrating 'cause we can't showboat at all … those guys can't spike the ball" (Wunsch).

So, in addition to all the other reasons for team celebration, one also seems to be in response to the NCAA generally putting clamps on individual celebration. Wunsch happily notes, "There's no rule against everyone getting in there and having fun" (Wunsch). One drawback to Wunsch doing even more celebrating—diving into the stands like Green Bay Packer players—apart from the rules, is that he is exhausted by the time the team reaches the end-zone. That, and the fact that he is fairly large, even for a football player, at six feet six inches, 330 pounds. There are not many, college or pro, who are bigger. He notes that when you've been blocking the whole drive and then get into the end-zone and do a little celebrating, by then "you're just like 'thank you,' okay, let's go back." I mean when I get done I'm just beat, I need a break" (Wunsch).

Stark, another offensive lineman, shares similar expressive tactics with Wunsch, except he calls the team end-zone celebration "moshing," and notes that the behavior sounds "kind of stupid," but includes "hugging" and "high-fives" that encourage "more unity and more team spirit" (Stark). He says that if he ever scored a touchdown that he would "go nuts. I've never scored a touchdown so it's kinda hard to say what I'd do," but notes later that as an extreme case, he might spike the ball (Stark). Coaches' comments and his "team" perspective temper his celebrations:

> Honestly, I probably wouldn't do any big celebration. Just because I know my coaches would not approve of it … you got to think about the team when you do things like that. I don't know exactly how the rule works but I know they've taken some scores back because of [celebration].[9]

A final word or two on Matt Nyquist, who plays the closest position on the field to a lineman, but who catches passes and scores an occasional touchdown. By far the least expressive of the White athletes, Nyquist says he tries to keep expression to a "minimal reaction," and that he is not a "big jump around, slap a high-five" kind of guy, settling for "a big hug," or in high school after a touchdown simply shouting, "Yes!" (Nyquist). He learned his de-emphasis on physical expression from his father and from his high school's team philosophy:

> It was 'don't celebrate, don't show your emotions, score, go back to the huddle, play,' and we never ... [expression] was more discouraged so I'd score a touchdown and ... I never celebrated at all. Just walk back to the huddle and run the next play ... when I was in high school ... I thought it was unsportsmanlike to be celebrating, showing off that I made a touchdown ... there was no jumping around—'oh, I got a sack!'[10]

Nyquist said his severe dyslexia underscores his lack of expression and hurt his self-confidence in high school because he was always put in the "dummy" classes (Nyquist, p. 28). He took a lot of razzing from other kids. In addition, his teachers met with his parents and told them he was not a good enough athlete to get a college scholarship and was certainly not smart enough to make it into college: "That made me less expressive. It wasn't really lack of self-confidence in my athletic ability but more what people were going to say if I was overly cocky" (Nyquist).[11]

Nyquist's response to his dyslexia is a cautionary note to everyone that we should never rely too heavily on race, class, gender, and region as the *sole* explanations for behavior or attitudes. Individual personality, contact with others, or individual situational variables quite often creep into (or are avoided in) group-level analysis that might explain unique behavior. Nyquist's dyslexia might be a major factor in shaping his behavior and his overall perception and attitudes about the expressiveness and sportsmanlike conduct of others, as we shall see later.

Team and Teammates Over Individuality

Darrell Bevell considers the Wisconsin Badgers a group that celebrates as a team, versus other schools like the University of Miami that celebrate more as individuals, with "guys who like to stand out for themselves" (Bevell). Bevell deviates a bit from the norm of his fellow White athletes by condoning some extreme forms of individualized expression. His attitude is that the team's primary purpose is to win and that every person is important to the team including those who celebrate in ways he would not himself (Bevell). I thought at this point in the interview that I had to push the scenario to test his philosophy. I presented a scenario in which receiver Michael London had scored a touchdown and did an end-zone dance—no penalty called, but an obvious individual celebratory act—beyond the rules. He says:

> Well, if [Michael London] was shaking butt, people would probably be laughing ... I had something to do with getting the ball to him. All those linemen had

> something to do with giving me time to get the ball to him. So everybody knows they had a part of it, you know, and everybody could celebrate in their own way, and shoot, if he's 50 yards down the field—I mean he's going to be able to react to the touchdown before [us].[12]

Both Unverzagt and Monty share the team-over-individual theme, and in much stronger words. Unverzagt notes that he is specifically against acts that draw attention to the individual over the team after big plays, noting that if you take off your helmet and you screech across the fifty-yard line, "you're showcasing yourself" (Unverzagt). This is unwarranted individual attention that "takes away" from the team and de-emphasizes the help others had in the play. He carefully notes that players who dance can also be team players, but that this different style of play and way to show your "emotion" are generally not acceptable to him (Unverzagt). Unverzagt offers an alternative, such that if you take off your helmet when you're celebrating with your team, then the act is okay, for football is a team sport and "you didn't get to the end zone by yourself" (Unverzagt).

Monty also believes that individuality on the field can be taken too far and detract from the team philosophy. Athletes who take off their helmets and wave to the crowd or camera are taking away from the team, versus players who "add to the team concept" by coming back to the offensive linemen to celebrate after the touchdown. Celebrating with the team, again, keeps the fabric together and "fires up" other teammates in the emotional struggle of the contest. Celebrating with teammates reinforces the team concept, and Monty feels the player would not have scored that touchdown or been able to celebrate if "You didn't have those other ten guys up there for you … it's a team thing" (Stark).

This makes sense if I am an offensive lineman doing the hard work up front. I recall working for Hewlett-Packard when John Young, then CEO, would give his speech about the state of HP around Christmas time. He would comment about how well sales and profits were over the loudspeakers as we all listened—with one hand on the calculator. Then he would announce the profit-sharing percentage—and we would all calculate how much our bonus checks would be for the holidays. This was HP's way of acknowledging that the group was truly responsible for the company's touchdown. John Young guided the ship, it is true, but he passed along the praise—and spoils. This is the same logic linemen have. It makes sense to me, especially if I am a lineman.

Stark feels that when a person "separates" himself during celebration, when he breaks off and celebrates on his own, it does not promote team unity. When an athlete, though, involves the whole offense, then "that's normal. I don't think it really takes away from the team concept" (Stark).

Stark's definition of a good sport is "a player who respects his teammates, respects his opponent, yet has confidence in himself, his abilities, and doesn't do anything detrimental to his team, his opponent, or the sport" (Stark).

While terms like "respect" and "detrimental" might be left to individual interpretation, respect for team, teammates, and even the opposing team is a view of the sport that Stark appears to gear his own actions around and also assess the "sportsmanship" of other players. He feels players should constantly seek ways to include others and add excitement to the game and team versus separating and individualizing behavior.

Gerald Wunsch goes as far as saying that Wisconsin recruits players who are fun, energetic types of people who bring to the Badgers the "team atmosphere we want" (Wunsch). Wunsch agrees that if players start celebrating too much it's not a team sport anymore:

> Because I'm an "O" (offensive) lineman and everything I do is based on team. That's the nature of my position. I'm not going to get recognition for what I do. Maybe a pat on the butt from Carl [McCullough] or Steck [Stecker]… that's all I want, you know.[13]

The Limits of Celebratory Expression

But these players did not want to impose severe limits on celebration. Steve Stark mentions that all players should be allowed to express themselves, and that if a guy feels he needs to do an end-zone dance, then "make it short so it's not a delay of game" (Stark). He does say, "It has to be policed a bit. You just can't let it get out of control." Wunsch also draws a soft line between acceptable and unacceptable behavior, noting that (then) fellow Badger—White freshman Sam Okey on the Badger basketball team—dunks the basketball and shows individual emotion and style, which can be positive. He comments that an Okey slam-dunk brings the team emotionally together: "I sit back and watch basketball. If Sam Okey comes in and does a tomahawk dunk over a guy, he sees his teammates just get jacked!" (Wunsch).

The resulting team enthusiasm validates dunking the basketball, even if it is "in your face." But Wunsch also says he can be the police officer: "If a guy goes too far, I'll say something." This is the player's code at work. In the context of the game moment, and celebration, one player—from either team—can police the situation and make a comment as to what might be going "too far."

By far the most intriguing and opinionated athlete regarding the celebration styles of others is the Scandinavian from Minnesota, Matt Nyquist. From his early days in high school, Nyquist thought that celebrating in college football was not fundamentally sound:

> It wasn't sportsmanlike to celebrate. I mean that's just what all our fans thought. All our coaches thought ... that's the way our town was. That's the way our people liked it. That's just kind of the way it was.[14]

Which is a way of saying that if everyone did it and agreed to it, it's fine. Just like me growing up in Oakland. Where conflicts and disconnects arise is when someone new comes into the neighborhood—or someone from the neighborhood moves away to a place with a different view, like college and possibly the NFL.

Nyquist is okay with acts that help you "win the game" and condones expression if you are "legitimately excited." But he draws his line in the dirt with the celebrations of Deion Sanders: "Getting all the dancing in the end zone and stuff, the Deion stuff, I don't agree, that's unnecessary ... you should never take the ball and put it up before you get to the end zone because you're taking unnecessary chances to lose the ball" (Nyquist). Nyquist is speaking about players who begin celebrating in the NFL before they get into the end zone and then, unexpectedly, lose the ball and thereby lose the touchdown. It happens more often than you'd think. And we hate when it happens to a member of our team and laugh when it happens to an opposing player: "Ha! That ought to learn ya!"

Nyquist backs up his strong views with comments on how celebrating—especially premature celebrating—can hurt a team. Here he paints a picture of celebration as poor sports training and also risky behavior. He is aware of the fact that people express because it gets them excited and pumped up about the game. But he cautions that emotional displays can detract from the ability to play the game. He goes on:

> If you're worried about high-stepping, you're not thinking about what you're supposed to be thinking about. You're supposed to be getting into the end zone first and foremost and if you're high-stepping on your way in, you're taking extra chances. If people fumble, that's unacceptable. There should never be a mistake like that made. You should always be cradling the ball.[15]

Nyquist is also a policeman of sorts. He will not tolerate trash-talking, saying, "I'll talk back, I'm not just going to sit there and just take it. If people start dishing it out to you, you've got to stand up for yourself. There's a certain level of stand-up you gotta do, but you can't initiate that kind of thing." He also monitors the behavior of others on his team, and should the situation arise, he might comment: "Get yourself off the field. You know, we don't want to see that. That's unnecessary. I would be mad at one of my teammates for going into the end zone and [doing] a little dance."

So, while the others have moderate attitudes about the expression of others on the field, Nyquist has far stronger convictions against individual celebratory behavior. I asked him later in the interview about what might happen if he's drafted by the Dallas Cowboys (he wasn't), who had both Deion and Michael Irvin—two very expressive pro players—on their team. I suggested that, considering his strong views, he might have to sit both players down and have a talk about controlling their excessive expression. In a lighter moment he smiled and solemnly said, "Deion, I don't think that's appropriate here. There will be no more of that as long as I'm around here." To this he gives the reply of both Michael and Deion back to himself: "Here, let me help you pack your bags."

Nyquist is aware that his views are strong, and at the end of the interview clarifies his stance by saying that he doesn't despise people who celebrate, it is just that when players "take it to a new level it does bug me." Turns out other White student-athletes have impressions of Deion Sanders.[16]

The Unusual Response to Deion Sanders

Deion Sanders epitomizes the highly talented, expressive athlete of the 1990s. Most athletes had an opinion about him. The White athletes surveyed had similar feelings about Sanders. The themes centered on Deion Sanders as an athlete who could "talk the talk and walk the walk"—one who can brag and back it up on the playing field. The sentiment is that Sanders is an extremely arrogant and flamboyant player, but one who has earned the right to talk and boast by constantly performing at a level far above other athletes. Unverzagt says Deion is a mellow guy, laid back, and a player who is so comfortable with his abilities that once during the heat of battle Deion was asking an opponent how his wife and kids were:

> You know, he can say a lot because he can back it up. You know, there's very few people who can back it up on a consistent basis like he can. He's one of the few who can. I can't think of another. He can definitely walk it and he can talk it all he wants.[17]

Unverzagt notes that Deion's behavior is allowable because he is an entertainer and plays professional football verses NCAA football. When Deion scores and dances, it's "entertainment" for the fans. He goes on to say that Deion is obviously showcasing himself, but when he dances "a lot of guys are around him." Unverzagt sees Deion's individuality in a team-oriented context.

Bevell echoes the "pro football as entertainment" by Deion, noting, "the people love it, and that's what he's there for, you know. They paid to get in, let them have some excitement." Stark and the others uniquely contextualize Deion's behavior, downplaying his obvious individuality and playing up his ability to often create a team fabric where there was none—or little—before his arrival. Stark notes:

> I think Deion has respect for his teammates too even though he, you know, he obviously likes to showboat a little bit. Everybody knows that. But I think that, I think if you listen to him talk ... he never puts down his teammates or says 'we would have won' or 'because of this guy,' and I think that shows respect for his teammates. He gets involved with the team celebration too. You know he does his little dance and the team's there and they celebrate.[18]

Verbal and Physical Taunting

Wisconsin's victory over UCLA in the 1994 Rose Bowl involved the biggest physical fight the team has had in my seven years of viewing UW football. Four players were tossed from the game, two from each team. Much of the team loss of control was due, no doubt, to the intense competition and national attention the game commands, but it is evident here in Bevell's remarks that the verbal conduct of UCLA—and the probable counter-talk by UW—led eventually to sparks flying:

> There's a point I think where you could be talkative, then there's a point I think where you go past that and it starts being bad sportsmanship. There's some ribbing and all that, you know, to fire yourself up. I would say UCLA in the Rose Bowl was a very dirty team and very bad sportsmen. It started from the second they walked onto the field.[19]

Expression that leads to physical harm or altercations is where Bevell, Unverzagt, and Monty draw the celebratory line. Bevell cites a specific form of physical expression—after the quarterback is sacked—as behavior that is unsportsmanlike. He has never had any problems with linemen celebrating over a sack of the quarterback, except "if they're standing on you, or when they get up they push off of you, kick you. The sack is fine. You know, go celebrate, get your sack, but you don't have to do the extracurricular" (Bevell).

Monty notes that some forms of physical expression are aggressive and uncalled-for, as in the cliché, "cheap-shot," which is when a player is hit from behind or blind-sided after the whistle has blown and the play is supposedly dead. He notes in his statement: "Guys that want to start talking trash … there's no reason for that. But in a game where guys are cheap-shotting and the referees aren't keeping control of the game, then I think some things get out of hand" (Monty).

In one specific game in 1995 against Iowa, Monty noted, "Those guys cheap-shotted more than any other team that I've ever played in my life. The play was out of bounds and some guy cheap-shotted me in the back." Unverzagt also notes that athletes need to get away from "the taunting and the pointing the finger," noting that this is a form of "putting yourself in the spotlight," and not team oriented.

College Football as Amateur Sport

Wunsch emphasizes his conception of the purpose of college versus pro football by noting the monetary outcome some players appear to worship:

> We really stress team so if you got any sense in your head they [coaches] don't want you singling yourself out. Not going out and doing a dance and taking off your helmet and throwing [the football] in the stands … and doing a head-spin and doing the Icky Shuffle, you know what I'm saying? [Then] it's not a team. It's a bunch of guys running around the stake of who can make the most amount of money, you know, setting themselves apart and I don't think that's good.[20]

Constant attention to one's accomplishments outside of the realm of the team could lead to disharmony and the questioning of the athlete's "purpose." I file this alongside coaches who constantly want athletes to skip class and go to the weight room and train for "the team" when in the end a better team record means the coach can leave for a higher salary the following year. Each emphasis is done in a team context, but each person might have been looking out for number one.

Wunsch goes on to say that professional sport is different from college football, for what college is attempting is to make football a "pure sport." Making players "just players" is the theme, not "superstar figures." Wunsch feels the NCAA is trying to make football more team oriented by "trying to instill team concepts.

They don't want anyone showboating or taking themselves away [from] the team concept." It is possible that the Badgers have read the NCAA's team writing on the wall, socialized its athletes, and thus responses I've gotten are a direct result of that socialization.

It is also possible, as with Al Toon earlier, the philosophy given by coaches turns out to resonate with some more than others. Nevertheless, Badger team philosophy on celebratory expression is parallel to NCAA dictates on acceptable forms of expression. These dictates—at least the interpretation through athletes—appear to stress non-individualistic and non-monetary ends for participation in football at the collegiate level.

Nyquist notes that it is tough to celebrate in college currently because every celebratory act is going to get called for a penalty—"that's their [NCAA's] emphasis the last couple of years which has really cut back on [celebration]." He also recalls there used to be "a ton of celebrating with the helmets off and the dancing," but that the new rules put a stop to these forms of expression by players.

Professional football in contrast allows athletes—for various reasons—more freedom to express. But the key distinction that society (and governing bodies like the NCAA) makes between the amateur and the professional is a monetary distinction. In college, you play for fun and for your team, not for money or the thought of the later reward of money. In the pros, you play for your team, your personal statistics, and later, the monetary reward for both team and individual success—as negotiated by the player's agent.

For many college athletes, one reason to play is for a scholarship, or if you are lucky, college sport is for team-level enjoyment and satisfaction. For the few, there is the hope of a professional career and the subsequent payoff. Steve Stark echoes this reality:

> If this wasn't fun, I wouldn't play. And I still have fun playing. That's why I want to try out for the NFL.[21] And if I didn't think it was fun, I wouldn't do it. I mean I think some players today don't play because they are having fun. They play because maybe it's a way to get through school, maybe it's a way to make some money.[22]

This last insight may point up one of the most significant reasons for attitudinal and behavioral differences between Black and White athletes regarding the issue of celebratory expression in college football. What we may have are divergent career reasons for pursuing sport and divergent definitions of fun within the context of sport.

Grace in Defeat

One of the key tenants of Walter Camp's version of sports conduct is that one should take defeat with honor and dignity. Hard feelings, while stirring in our stomachs, must be put to the side while we shake hands with the team we love to hate. This can test the very best of us. The ability to put the game behind and revel in the joy of competition with your sister or brother is a challenge. To do it with a smile and sincere congratulations is probably an action only someone like Jesus could pull off. Though I do wonder if Jesus would have shaken Richard Sherman's hand if he were in Eric Crabtree's place—and knew he wasn't going to the Superbowl. Wisconsin's White athletes have learned over time to be graceful in defeat.

Bevell associates grace in defeat with good sportsmanship. As an athlete, "you got to be man enough to go over there and shake the guy's hand," implying that once the game is over a truce is called and athletes ought to be able to part on good terms after the war. Unverzagt echoes the sentiment of his fellow Badger by emphasizing not only "after the game" behavior, but the attitudes about how one should conduct himself during the game:

> I think sportsmanlike conduct is if you lose and you can go over there and congratulate the other player and say 'you guys did a good job today—you deserved to win.' Or if you're on the field and someone makes a good play against you that knocks you down or beats you for a touchdown … you can get all pissed but you're like—'good job.'[23]

Monty notes that a good sport is one "who is always encouraging people, helping an opponent off the field, saying "good effort" on this play. Someone who just enjoys the game and takes it for what it is." Socioeconomic class level could very well determine for athletes what the game "is"—or what it represents. For many poor Blacks and Whites, "it" represents a chance out of poverty for their family. For many who only hold slim aspirations for turning professional, "it" might represent a game—a chance to compete and show one's talent and resolve. In this sense, hard feelings do need to be put to the side.

I tell my students this all the time when they "earn" a "C" grade. No hard feelings. Shake hands. Even if your scholarship will now be revoked. It wasn't personal. Problem is, for many students, it is personal. I think of the education process as a learning experience where sometimes you win and sometimes you lose (by earning that "C" grade). That's what "it" is all about. At least for me, the professor. It makes sense in my world. But I understand the student's situation, too.

They have higher aspirations. They might not be inheriting money. Their grades might mean everything. College is their chance. Learning for the sake of learning might be a good working theory of education for me, but not for them.

I can sense the frustration collegiate athletes have with players who are looking for higher honors and more attention. That can cause dissention on a team if people work at what seem to be cross-purposes. But after the game, the player's code has usually been to "let it go." Leave any animosity on the field.

I watch NFL football games and marvel at how many players mix and mingle and shake hands after a stunning loss. Of course, this didn't happen in the old days—and a few team owners have noted how they don't like all the fraternizing among players.

But players are now all in the same union, move about from team-to-team, and admire each other. I think I prefer the inter-team camaraderie verses the bad blood that has players fight after games. I like good attitudes in my students, too. And I work hard to realize my students and their professor are sometimes at cross-purposes. It is easy for a privileged professor to say, "Don't worry about your grades."

Player, Fan, and Media Interaction

Steve Stark notes that at the beginning of the 1995 season, with the new and stricter NCAA unsportsmanlike conduct rules in effect, some fans' attitudes about college football shifted. He says some fans felt that it took a little away from the game, that maybe the game was not as fun (Stark). He also says there are other fans who feel dancing and celebration should not be a part of college football. Nyquist notes that cameras at a football game affect player behavior, such that some athletes just "go out there and do stuff just to get extra TV time, to get on the camera, to get attention drawn to themselves." And the media usually obliges.

Nyquist also feels the National Football League may have compromised its mission somewhat by allowing individual expression. He says college has struck the right balance between unnecessary acts and penalized acts. The NFL has not made the connection, "because they think the dancing and stuff attracts fans." One last note from Nyquist is on Christian Laettner, former player on the Duke Blue Devil basketball team and the NBA Minnesota Timberwolves (Nyquist's' local team). The media image of Laettner affected Nyquist's impressions to the point of hating Laettner at Duke, stating that Laettner "talked and talked. He ran a mile a minute at the mouth" (Nyquist).

Although most references to taunting and coded language about "that element" creeping into sport target Black athletes, many White fans and athletes do look beyond the race issue and focus on the "act" they don't appreciate. There can be equal opportunity dislike of some expressive behavior regardless of who offends. Oddly, I find this refreshing.

Gerald Wunsch talks about his dislike of television and player-fan interaction. He first makes it clear that the television cameras have an effect on athletes. He does not like the effect. First, players often take their helmets off on the field, an act he feels is never warranted. Second, "when a guy gets in front of a TV camera and starts showing his face off … that's a little ridiculous" (Wunsch). Wunsch then notes that the Icky Shuffle is primarily an expression of happiness and that Woods "wants to be on TV. I mean people wanted Icky Woods to score so they could see him do the Icky Shuffle."

He goes on to condone a specific celebratory act, though, and that is the reciprocal interaction with fans after touchdowns. That is, if a player scores a TD and points to the student section (which would receive a penalty flag for unsportsmanlike conduct in college), that's fine (the fan acknowledgement, not the penalty). It is akin to the player saying, "Hey, thanks. We're here to put on a show for them, and we make them feel like part of the show. The more you make them part of the show, the more they like coming." Again, player-fan interaction gets a fifteen-yard penalty in the NCAA, whether or not Wunsch thinks it is cool.

The fans, to Wunsch, are everything. He makes the point, long since forgotten by many collegiate and pro players and administrators, that there is no game without fans. There is a reason to celebrate when people are in the stadium. No people, no celebration. He gives a game sequence and touchdown scenario to emphasize the point, such that if there is no one in the stands, "you walk out, you throw a ball, you score a touchdown, you throw the ball up in the stands to empty stands, who cares?" Indeed, Mr. Wunsch.

He finishes by noting that "you can sit there and do your little dance in front of no one and no one will care." It certainly begs the point: Are the fans' opinions important?

The White athletes are not shy about how they feel about their sport and sportsmanship. They vary in what they think about expression, fans, and people like Deion Sanders. What I find most interesting is that they interact, practice, play, and live with African American athletes who might disagree with their opinions but still manage to function as a working unit. Well enough, in the previous year, to be Rose Bowl champions.

Notes

1. Smith, Y., personal conversation, 1996.
2. Barry Alvarez was interviewed for this study but declined to be quoted.
3. For more on the Wisconsin athletic department turnaround, see Rick Telander's (1994) book on the UW turnaround, entitled *From Red Ink to Roses: The Turbulent Transformation of a Big Ten Program.*
4. Monty, in Andrews, 1996b.
5. I use numerous quotes from athletes in the next two chapters. In order to avoid repetition I will cite the page number of the quote and refrain from also mentioning the athlete by name. In all cases the cite refers to the athlete most recently mentioned in the text. The special case is where I might note that Darrell Bevell feels comfortable around Black athletes like Tony Simmons, but he feels "… Daryl Carter is difficult to understand." Here, the quote (fictitious) belongs to Bevell, as is obvious, and not to Tony Simmons. Where there might be any confusion, I use the name in parentheses.
6. Unverzagt, in Andrews, 1996b.
7. I make a distinction in type of expression. One is celebratory, usually involving joy-release. The physical behavior usually involves a sense of happiness and might include dancing, some improvisational gestures, high—or low-fives, or other expressions of extreme joy. I classify tension-release as behaviors such as head-butting, the hitting of teammates, quick fist-thrusts, and other such show of aggression-type behaviors. These "ideal types" can be hard to detect at times or even overlap within the same individual on the same expressive occasion.
8. Wunsch, in Andrews, 1996b.
9. Stark, in Andrews, 1996b.
10. Nyquist, in Andrews, 1996b.
11. Nyquist (April 1996) signed a free-agent contract with the NFL's Houston Oilers.
12. Bevell, in Andrews, 1996b.
13. Wunsch, in Andrews, 1996b.
14. Nyquist, in Andrews, 1996b.
15. Nyquist, in Andrews, 1996.
16. "Deion" is a single-name phenomenon in sport, much like "Bo" (Jackson) was and like Madonna, Prince and Elvis are in music. For that reason, and not disrespect, the players and I will often refer to Mr. Sanders as Deion.
17. Unverzagt, in Andrews, 1996b.
18. Stark, in Andrews, 1996b.
19. Bevell, in Andrews, 1996b.
20. Wunsch, p. 17–18, in Andrews 1996.
21. Stark was drafted (April 1996) by the NFL's Houston Oilers.
22. Stark, in Andrews, 1996b.
23. Unverzagt, in Andrews, 1996b.

8

White Homes, Rural Settings and Reflections on Celebration Rules

The Players' Code

Rules are necessary in order to compete in sport. We have to have rules that everyone agrees to before we can be expected to determine who won or who lost a contest. We have to agree on the type of ball to play with, the length of the field or court, and the timespan within which the game will be played. Much of what else is decided is arbitrary. Many of those arbitrary rules are a product of conceptualizations of the players' code. Here is where I think much of the on-field conflict resides when we talk about cultural differences in expressive behavior.

The players' code is an interpretation of how the game should be played based on concepts of "fair play" rather than the rules of governing bodies. The players' code varies for each sport, but a couple of common codes are that (1) you never intentionally try to hurt another player, or (2) you never give a player a cheap shot—hit him when he's not looking. We shout as kids, "Hey—that's not fair … and that's not cool … you can't play anymore," when someone breaks the neighborhood kids' code. We learn how to play together and set up a structure for the game that everyone must agree to. But later in life, the testosterone, adrenaline, and money kick in. We may break the players' code (in the adult version of the kids' game) for our own ends. This is akin to breaking the gunslingers' code of the old West when you shoot someone in the back. Simply put, it was not considered the honorable or "manly" thing to do.

Breaking the players' code is a far worse offense than breaking a game rule and often has long-reaching ramifications for the player who breaks the code. Claude Lemieux broke the players code in the 1996 hockey playoffs as a member of the Colorado Avalanche by hitting a player on the Detroit Red Wings from behind as he was leaving the ice. The player suffered a broken jaw. Opposing players vowed revenge next season, and it was feared Lemieux would receive abuse from other players around the league. So, while a "good hit" is fine, the cheap shot is a violation of the code.

Another code violation is strikebreaking by athletes. The baseball repercussion in the mid-1990s after the baseball strike was to not speak to players who had crossed the picket line. Blaming a player for a loss to the media is another breach of the code.

While I believe there are many overlaps in how Black and White players code appropriate behaviors, I believe the key differences between the groups is how they construct what is coded as acceptable versus not acceptable celebratory behavior: Black and White athletes have fundamental differences in how they construct the players' code, which is the major cause of friction on the field in the three major sports in America. In baseball, watching the trajectory of your own mammoth home run is within the players' code of conduct for Black and Latino players, but a breach among White players.[1] Generally speaking, of course. Because, Bryce Harper.

For the non-White player, the stadium consists of thousands of people admiring the act. For the White player, there is only the batter and the pitcher, so any act of celebration by a batter is, to this line of thinking, directed at the only other person in the stadium, the pitcher. Words are exchanged, family lineage is discussed, threats are made, fingers pointed, and on occasion, there are fisticuffs.

Basketball is a major sport where conflicts over interpretations of the players' code are rare given the high percentage of African American athletes at many colleges and at the NBA level. "Trash-talking" and slam-dunks and "street-ball" used to do battle with the functional, control-oriented type of traditional White play. Indeed, urban street ball informed behaviors many Black athletes took into college and later, the NBA. Darcey Frey spent many months in and around Coney Island observing Stephon Marbury and other young basketball talent. He notes in more than one place how the young inner-city players and fans take pride in playing the sport in a way that is unique and expressive, and noticeably in stark contrast with traditional style:

> But he soon discovered it was also possible to cry out like some herniated weight lifter, ream the ball through the hoop, and then, as he hung from the rim with a fiendish look, listen for the urgent, swelling, seashell roar of the crowd rushing in from the bleachers, howling their delight. 'One more second on the rim, young man, and you've got yourself a technical,' the ref would warn as soon as Tchaka had landed on the firm earth. But Tchaka would grin and shake his head and point out—most reasonably, in light of the still-whooping fans—that monster dunks were precisely what the crowd came to see.[2]

Much like Valrey's twist in Chapter 3, Tchaka's improvisation was an expressive play to the crowd, well within Black boundaries of acceptable behavior. "The crowd is here to be entertained and I am, therefore, an entertainer" is the scenario for Valrey and Tchaka, along with others like Earl "The Pearl" Monroe, Julius Irving, Walt Frazier, Michael Jordan, Serena Williams and the Harlem Globetrotters. There is a racial/cultural make-up of the players' code which spans athletic competitions from track and field to football and covers expression with the body and expression with "artifacts" such as do-rags, hats tilted to the side, tattoos, and other clothing and body statements.

Notice Florence Griffith-Joyner's multi-colored, one leg-in one leg-out running tights in the late 1980s and 1990s, the long fingernails and braids of Gail Deavers, and the flamboyant outfits of Jackie Joyner-Kersey. Venus and Serena often challenge the dress norms in conservative tennis. This is a physical expression embedded in the larger African American code of acceptable behavior. Many Whites do learn the code and also engage in their own forms of individual expression, but rarely live "stylized expression" as part of their larger social context.

One noticeable exception was the young White student-athlete from Mercer College who danced after the stunning defeat of Duke in round one of the 2014 NCAA March Madness tournament. He danced, twisted, twirled—then stopped to look into the camera, perfectly—then kept going. The pause was key—pure African American blue-eyed genius. I watched live and knew I had seen something rarely seen in USA sport—Whites coopting African American celebratory style for an extended time period in front of the cameras. With no shame. High five to you, young bold White guy. Mr. Kevin Canevari, you have just completed your cross-cultural internship on the Nae Nae dance.[3]

What is important to cross-cultural understanding is that these codes are what we are born into and dependent on the city and street we grew up on and tempered by what our parents tell us, what our coaches mentor, what (or how) our ministers preach, and what our heroes model on television. There is no good or bad. There is difference. It is therefore important to understand the differences and similarities of codes of both Black and White players—and that athletes breech the codes of the "other," and on occasion, adopt the codes of the other.

White Codes

One of the major unspoken tenets of the White players' code appears to be that a player should never "show-up" another player. That is, a player should never show extreme happiness when he succeeds. He should show humility. White players interpret extreme happiness as a personal affront to them. It is about them: "The home run is not about you being happy—it is about me giving up a home run in front of everybody and feeling very, very bad. Don't make me feel worse by being happy or showing off! Everybody is watching!" The White player feels bad enough because he threw a "pick-six" interception or threw a home-run pitch. To dance in football or to "admire your handy work" in baseball (slowly watching your home run leave the park) prolongs or exacerbates the agony of a player in full view of one's teammates, coaches, fans in the stands, family and friends, and millions of viewers if the game is televised.

"Showing-up" another player is another sign, according to White codes, that (1) the coach has been lax in instilling appropriate behavioral norms, (2) the athlete's parents did not teach proper manners or the civil way to behave, and worse, (3) that the athlete (if Black) is acting like a "street nigger." (If I must say that word, it has to be with a lower-case n.) If the athlete were only socialized to "better understand how things are supposed to work, we would not have problems" is the general sentiment. While it is common for everybody to blame the parents for a kid's behavior (I do it every time I go to the mall and see ballistic children), coaches also bear the direct blunt of breaches in the code via team penalties or opposing players' repercussions that can injure an athlete. So where did White codes originate?

As noted in Chapter 6, the humble, self-effacing amateur athlete that best exemplifies this White upper-middle class code is the early twentieth century Princeton sports star Hobey Baker who played both football and hockey with grace and charm and with no thought of harming others in words or deeds.

The White players in this study echoed this general sentiment when discussing athlete expression, sportsmanlike conduct, and attitudes about football rules and regulations. The themes embedded in answers support the argument that these knowledges are strongly held beliefs in White culture that permeate not only sport but how life is played, what is valued, and thus what is condoned and accepted. Likewise, what is reprimanded.

As noted above, there are many overlaps with Black and White players. Common themes were to "respect your teammates and the opposition," to have "parents as primary role models," and that "ambiguous celebration rules need refinement." Players I interviewed were strongly against fighting, cheap shots, and excessive taunting.

These themes strongly suggest a players' code—which is a proxy for each group's definition of sportsmanlike conduct—that includes hard work and respect, and in addition include notions of "not worrying about monitoring the behavior of others but making sure your own house is in order," "never aggressing against someone else's joy or celebration," and "never taking expression to the point of embarrassment for you or your teammates, but do what you gotta do—it's all good."

This is an "understanding" rather than part of the coded discourse of White America, and therefore not common and not often taught or mentioned in the media. There are negative terms, though, that many Whites—and some Blacks—note in this study as terms depicting expressive behavior: Showboating, hot-dogging, and "hamming" it up are three such terms.

Since White-player codes see expressive individual celebrations and "sticking-out" as overall undesirable, it is no wonder there are negative and not positive word associations. Blacks, on the other hand, are constantly reinventing dances, walks, moves, dunks, and such to further argue the case that coolness of movement is desired and condoned. It appears that what we have come to is a society where sports celebratory expression is restricted to the "unchained exuberance" of Whites and attempts to "chain coolness" as expressed by African American athletes.

White Role Models

Opinions and ideas about social topics and institutions do not form in a vacuum. We are products of not only our individual personality and our racial-cultural social histories, but we are also a conglomeration of our unique experiences—the social situations we have been a part of, what we've watched on television, or the experiences with key individuals like parents and coaches, who have given us advice through conversation or helped or otherwise aided our character development. I asked questions during my interviews about the home, the neighborhood, schools, and the media. The primary themes that emerged from the interview data were the role of "the father as mentor" and "professional athletes as role models."

The role of fathers stood out prominently in the text, primarily because three athletes' dads served at some point in their lives as their sports "coach." Two athletes made mention of the expressive behavior of their mothers, who both were far more emotionally and physically expressive than their husbands, though no discussion of moms as role models or mentors emerged. Professional athletes—called "classy" and "humble"—emerged as people closely watched on television while growing up. Two sub-themes that emerged from the interviews were "bonding" with fathers (and others) and "consistency" in behavior on and off the field, both to be included in the analysis of mentoring fathers.

The Father as Mentor

White athletes emphasized their fathers, more than anyone else, as being most responsible for their expressive behavior and attitudes. The athletes described their fathers as conservative and humble, not given to much physical expression of joy, though anger and frustration on the sidelines was noted. Pete Monty notes that his father—and high school football coach—was always quiet at home when watching the Denver Broncos on television with his family (they lived a short distance from Denver in Fort Collins, CO). Monty's mother, whom Pete described as very sociable and talkative, would be screaming at the TV, while the father remained silent and controlled.

But on the sidelines during a game, Monty's father, whom he describes as a very "humble man," would be "throwing his hat, yelling at the refs" and not in as much control (Monty). Monty's father is low-keyed and keeps to himself, and a person whom Monty admires and "looks to for resources." Monty senior has a lot of resources to draw upon, as he played starting center for the 1968 National champion Notre Dame football team and has served as a high school football coach for many years.

Darrell Bevell's father likewise was the head football coach in high school. Bevell's father was described as "conservative," did not mind expressive celebration, though he thought there was "no need" for certain types of celebration. He did make rules about other forms of physical appearance, such as disallowing hair that stuck out the back of one's helmet. Bevell senior emphasized that football is a team sport and though some people stood out, there "are other people helping," and Darrell goes on to show his acceptance and incorporation of this attitude by commenting that these ideas are "something that I believe, too, when he told me that."

Bevell receives an even stronger dose of socialization from his mentor/coach/father, as he is about to be interviewed at home in Scottsdale, Arizona, for the first time ever about sports. This highlights the perspective-shifting moments athletes often commented on, such as when Al Toon shifted his on and off-field life one day when a coach stressed "credibility." Thus, Bevell comments:

> My father definitely was trying to get a sense of team … I'll never forget the first interview that I ever was supposed to give … my dad says 'there's a newspaper man in here,' and he said, 'Compliment your team, compliment your coaching staff, and don't brag.' [Those were] the three things that he told me … and that's something that I always try to remember … you need to remember that it's a team sport.[4]

Eric Unverzagt's father did not stress the team aspect but did tell him that grades were important and gave the impression that Unverzagt was free to express himself. One example of this is early on in Eric's career as a Pee Wee football player when Eric's father was his football (and later, baseball) coach:

> I remember when I was seven years old and he [my father] was like 'the first time you score I want you to spike it.' I was like 'okay.' And this is in Pee Wee football. So the first time I score I spiked it … and I got a 15 yard penalty.[5]

Of course he got flagged. That Unverzagt senior instructed his son to spike the ball is fascinating enough. That Unverzagt followed his father's behavioral advice without question is what we do as kids. We listen to our parents (for the most part). No wonder Unverzagt was ranked the highest in physical and verbal expression of the White players on the 1993 Badgers—his parents are to blame. And maybe, just maybe, the fact that he grew up in a predominantly African American environment where social sanctions for expressive celebration were less severe, than, say, rural Minnesota, accounts for his style.

Long Island has a broad array of racial and cultural groups and is located right next to the most densely populated urban area in the United States, New York City. This location likely gives way to a wider array of behaviors than a small midwestern town might. When I asked Eric Unverzagt what his mother would say if he did the "Icky Shuffle" in the end-zone, testing the limits of his family tolerance, he commented first that his father would think he was "pretty excited," and ask, "Well, where the hell did he learn how to do that?" His mother would not care, he says, as long as he was just out there playing: "She just enjoys watching me play, so if I did an end-zone dance or ran out there buck naked—she'd still be excited no matter what."

Bonding

The issue of communing with nature in rural, pastoral, timeless settings could be expected, as three athletes are from small Midwestern communities. The setting for bonding rituals were hunting or fishing expeditions, or darts, pool, and beer with Dad or a coach. No athletes expressed any such bonding rituals with their mothers, though Gerald Wunsch did speak of both parents as best friends, having fun vacations, and occasionally shopping with his mother "just to be with her" even though he didn't necessarily enjoy shopping. He does mention all-day fishing while on these vacations with family and friends, but I am not aware of the role of the mother on these trips, though I suspect from his statements on their family's closeness that Mom was an active participant in many rituals. He does describe his father as his best friend, with whom he is comfortable drinking beer, along with shooting darts and playing pool at bars. He describes one particular bonding ritual that is his favorite way to pass the time—fishing with the guys:

> I'll sit out there with my dad and my buddy and we'll sit out there all day and just talk. It's just one of my favorite things to do, sit out on the boat. Just the camaraderie with my friends and my family. It's just about the relaxing.[6]

This type of bonding for a kid from Oakland is completely foreign. I don't doubt that many in Oakland take fishing trips, sit out on boats, and bond over beer. I wish I had. I imagine my worldview would be very different. I imagine the pace of life would be slower, more in tune with the seasons, and much more predictable. My harsh urban reality was very different.

One day I stood with four other twelve-year-old boys one block from my house looking down at a man who had multiple gunshot wounds and was bleeding out—now *that* was unpredictability. A boat and a beer sound like much better options for many of us who entered Wisconsin after likely seeing life in far worse conditions. I envy Wunsch and his camaraderie and his bonding in such a serene setting. And I see far better his perception of the meaning of sport in his—and others'—lives.

Just like Gerald Wunsch, Steve Stark is a big outdoors person who bonded with his middle-school basketball coach over fishing and hunting in Illinois and Wisconsin.[7] Out of this union they became close friends and the teacher/coach became so much of a role model that Stark himself desires to be a teacher and coach. Patience and hard work were the specific, tangible concepts Stark says he learned from "one of the bigger role models that I have had." Matt Nyquist says it was more fun—and more competitive—playing soccer and basketball with his dad,[8] where he carefully observed his father's behavior and summed up that "my biggest role model was my dad. I wanted to be a lot like my dad" (Nyquist).

Consistency

Pete Monty often participated in hunting and fishing rituals with his father and a local ex-pro player who served as a mentor. One of the key qualities Monty noted as admirable was the consistency of personality over time shown by Jeff Donaldson as he turned professional and later retired to live a normal, Fort Collins life (more on Mr. Donaldson, later). Other White athletes say they admire parents or others for their consistent behavior. This appears to be a proxy in some cases for "no deviation" regarding behavior. The key terms that foreshadow a note of "no deviation" are "always" or "never" or "being himself." These are also instances when interviewees noted qualities they themselves strove to acquire.

Nyquist cites his father as his primary sportsmanship socializer, noting also that his father would "absolutely never, ever, ever celebrate," or show any emotion or reaction or excitement, even after beating his son at hoops in the driveway or making a great play during his own college football career. Nyquist's father viewed celebrating as negative. Matt acknowledges admiration for his father and says that behavioral decisions were each son's choice rather than dictates from Dad. While I don't question that each child had decisions to make, the loss of a parent's love is so crucial to childhood that, unless a child is in outright revolt mode, we tend to mimic the desired behavior of parents we love and admire.

Steve Stark stresses that his parents are accepting of his decisions, being sure not to push him into sports or choose his college for him. They gave their opinion, told Stark he'd have to live with his own decision, and refused to make his decision for him. There is a consistency in their approach to him and his decisions, traits I believe he admires and desires to emulate:

> And my parents have been like that about everything. They didn't make me play sports. My dad encouraged me when I was younger to get into it and since then he's been involved, and he coached me when I was younger, but he never forced me to keep playing. I think they are very accepting.[9]

"To thine own self be true" could be a sub-theme running throughout this section of the interviews, with Wunsch's parents telling him that consistently being honest was important and accepted in the family, and that you must always be fair and tell people what you think. "And that's one important thing my parents taught me. That's the way I was brought up. I'm close with my parents. We always express how we feel."

Professional Athletes as Role Models

My expectation was that athletes would have many stories of their professional television warriors to tell, especially when it came to whom they admired and why. I also expected that they would talk of a hero who they let go as a role model because of the athlete's association with drugs, alcohol, bar fighting, a rape trial, a contract hold-out, or a player trade. But no one had a story of such a "fallen from grace" role-model story.

Two people Wunsch sees as role models are so not because of their behavior, per se, but because of their consistency of behavior, for their ability to be expressive of their honest emotions and not to waiver from those views (obviously a close fit with his own upbringing and personal philosophy). Those two professional—and pop-culture—athletes are Charles Barkley and Dennis Rodman. This is not what I expected.

One of the more telling statements about Barkley is that he's his "own individual" who has earned Wunsch's respect because you either "like Charles Barkley or you don't, and he doesn't care, and he's not going to change for anyone" (respect for a low self-monitor). Wunsch characterizes Rodman as an individual:

> And no matter what anyone says or what he does he's himself, and whether he's doing it [physical expression, hair-dying, cross-dressing] for hype or not, he's just being himself and he's stepping outside of what people call normal in society. I think that it is important that people go out and step out of bounds and do what they want to express themselves. A lot of guys aren't what they really want to be, you know what I'm saying?[10]

I think I know. The logic here is that it is better to be self-consistent than be liked by others. Wunsch, like the rest of us, wants to be liked, but sacrificing self is not an option. Extreme behavior—as long as it is part of their character and they can "walk the walk"—is tolerated in both Barkley and Rodman, though Wunsch notes he doesn't agree with everything these athletes say and do. But there is a respect that is the residue of being one's "true self," much as was the case with the acceptance of Deion's dancing and expression if he could "back it up."

Athlete experiences with coaches, fathers, and media athletes shape early impressions of acceptable behavior and personal attitudes about others that shift or are reinforced in week-by-week observation of athletes on the field and on television.

The most extensive discussion of a professional athlete as role model was by Pete Monty, who speaks about a long-term bond with former NFL strong safety Jeff Donaldson.[11] Donaldson, who is White, played for Monty's father in high school before his pro career, and afterward returned to Fort Collins to live. The relationship between Donaldson, Pete, and Pete's father was straight out of *Mayberry RFD*, with the three of them often fishing, hunting, and generally engaging in rural male-bonding activities. The theme throughout Monty's extensive discussion of Donaldson was stability and humility, as highlighted by a cross-section of his discussion:

> [Donaldson] has always been a man who I've looked up to, not because of his athletic ability, but because of who he is and what he does. He always stayed true to himself. When he went and made a bunch of money in the pros, he's always still Jeff Donaldson. It never changed him and you know he could be driving around a big fancy car, but he drives around in a little beat-up pick-up truck. I've always respected Jeff for being modest and being humble about it. He's always kept his family real close to him and his religion and he's never tried calling attention to himself, and I think that is something I really respect.[12]

It could go without saying here that Donaldson was a hero for Monty, but a hero not needing to have hoopla surrounding him. For Monty, Jeff was an average guy with an average life with exceptional talent and resources. It would seem that Monty would model his own behaviors after those of his role model, given the attraction to Donaldson's lifestyle and attitude about material wealth and popular success.

Most of us never come face-to-face with the challenges of stardom (I certainly have not). I regret not asking him if he would model his own behavior after Donaldson's if he ever turned professional, though my sociological assumption is that he would answer in the positive.

Monty later mentions Julius Erving, professional basketball star, as a community man who has done a lot for the game of basketball, who "draws attention to his teammates more than he does to himself," and who in many ways is "similar to Jeff Donaldson." Michael Jordan is another admired athlete, who was someone whom Monty "had posters up all over the place" when he was growing up. Monty thus includes here two Black athletes—athletes with extreme talent and expressive "slam dunk" celebratory behavior—as players whom he admires for their modesty and team play.

Likewise, Eric Unverzagt chooses Marcus Allen, a Hall of Fame Black football player as a role model because he's "someone who doesn't seem to celebrate that much, just goes out there [for] fourteen, fifteen years and he's still getting the job done. He's someone who does not showcase himself [and is] a team player."

Unverzagt compliments Deion Sanders also on being a role model, noting that despite his bragging, Deion's off-field life is exemplary, and when combined with his talent gives Deion the right to "say whatever he wants. I mean obviously he's a great role model, he has a family, and he doesn't drink. He's a pretty clean-cut guy."

Bevell keeps with the theme of "all-around good guy" as role model in the high-expressive category as he describes his role models—all quarterbacks—Danny White, Roger Staubach, Joe Montana, and Steve Young, the last two he describes as "classy guys." He readily admits, though, that the two Dallas Cowboys—White and Staubach—are his favorites, saying, "Those were the two—the people I really looked up to. That's why I wear number 11, Danny White," noting that his reasons for admiring White and the others are "the things that they do off the field—that's why I look up to them." Bevell does mention an athlete he does not look up to or consider a role model and that is Dennis Rodman:

> I look at a guy like Dennis Rodman and that's a situation where I'm baffled. Because I appreciate what he can do on the court, but off the court I don't understand why he has to ... I mean I know he's expressing himself but sometimes it's just, I don't know.[13]

These athletes keep a keen eye on their role models (and anti-models) and how they conduct themselves on and off the field or court. Athletes note certain values cherished over others, with the most important being family, humility, acting with class, not indulging in conspicuous consumption, and "team players" as central themes to model.

It is not enough to be a good athlete. What you *do* speaks louder than what you say. The implication is that a professional athlete speaking loudly may even be a cause to jettison him or her as role model, the notable exceptions being Deion Sanders, Charles Barkley, and Dennis Rodman.

Attitudes about College Football Rules and Regulations

White athletes fell into two camps regarding the 1995 celebration-rule changes. The high-expressive athletes generally disagree with the extremity of the 1995 rules, while the low-expressive athletes understood the "best possible intent" of the rules.

Bevell says the celebration rules were designed to get the game focused "on the team, and not draw any attention to yourself, you know, go off in a corner and dance, go over to the stands. Some guys would kneel and pray." Bevell later notes that he understands the intent of the rules—"getting back to team"—but tempers his remarks with an analysis from the expressive athlete's perspective: "They want it to get back to the team, but I don't think you're saying 'look at me, look at me, look what I did,' I think you're just celebrating."

Bevell here points up the important issue of the intent of behavior, citing an athlete's intent while expressing may not be "self-exposure and anti-team" as much as sheer celebratory joy after a big play. He has complicated the issue of the league's interpretation of what constitutes "team" and "anti-team" celebration. He says things are not so simple as the league would have it.

These athletes, though, generally think the 1995 rules were "ridiculous" (Bevell) and "bullshit" (Unverzagt), Unverzagt noting that "… the NCAA overdid the rules." Monty notes that athletes have a right to celebrate more than normal during big games or after big plays. Bevell recalls a conversation with teammates about the absurdity of the new rule's subtext of "drawing attention to yourself." Here he recounts the possible big-play scenario:

> We were making jokes about it [the new rule]. Like what happens if you break away for a 75-yard touchdown and you beat the guy by 25 yards? You got to slow down because you're drawing attention to yourself. You know, you're getting too far away from everybody! That's how ridiculous the rules were.[14]

To complicate matters, Unverzagt notes inconsistency in how officials sometimes call or don't call penalties when rules are broken, noting in his confusion that he doesn't know "what the hell to do now," apart from being sure he leaves his helmet on. He goes on to note, as does Bevell, that college football is emotional and that it is difficult to control what happens on the field, with athletes having to concentrate to insure they did not break rules. Bevell says that he feels players are excited when they score but they have to "monitor" their behavior for fear of breaking rules.

Monty, who feels monitored behavior "takes away from some of the excitement that that player is experiencing," also discusses the feeling of "being watched." If he has to "sit there and think about what he's going to do after his touchdown and make sure that he doesn't have a flag thrown against his team," that takes away from the fun aspect of the game. Bevell does note that players receive warnings of sorts from game officials, who have said to players celebrating after touchdowns, "Break it up, break it up. You're getting close to getting out of hand! Hurry it up, hurry it up!"

NCAA Anti-Celebration Rules Strict—But Necessary

The low-expressive interviewees—as opposed to the three White high-expressive athletes—all agreed that, in general, college rules about expression and celebration were much the same as rules in their respective high school conferences. Wunsch says that his high school and conference "had the same ideals in mind." Team celebration—and not individual forms of celebratory expression—appear to be those ideals, judging by statements in both the NCAA videotape and player comments. These players felt individual celebration after a big play was getting out of control. There was a need for the NCAA to step in and remind athletes of those "ideals."

Fighting was often a consequence of talk on the field, and the NCAA included "taunting" within its reconstructed definition of good sportsmanship, thus penalizing players for unsportsmanlike conduct of the were involved in "excessive" talk or finger pointing or handing the ball to the opposing player or dropping it in his vicinity. Matt Nyquist summarizes the issues above and explains why the new rulings were necessary:

> The [NCAA] made a big enough deal about it—told all the teams about [rules]. It takes away a lot of the celebrating, which is unnecessary, I think. As far as college goes, I think they're trying to take unnecessary [celebration] and make it illegal. And they're doing a pretty good job. The new rules really cut back on the fighting. I think they're [the NCAA] actually getting pretty good as far as taking away celebrating, especially this last year. They've really cleaned things up a lot and I think it's pretty good.[15]

Steve Stark concurs, saying, "Expression has to be *policed* a little bit, you know. You just can't let it get out of control." Wunsch takes a much harder line on individual celebration, similar to teammate Nyquist:

> A guy doing a dance, I don't think that should be allowed. A guy doing things that aren't really natural in excited situations. I don't think a guy in college football should be able to run and start pulling fans over or hugging fans. I mean

> sometimes a running back gets excited. But I think a guy that intentionally goes over there just to make a scene isn't good. Extended individual celebration I don't think should be allowed. I mean, a guy that takes off his helmet and goes in front of the TV and starts saying 'hi mom and dad' and all that, then I'd agree with [a penalty].[16]

The Helmet Rule Is Good, But Needs Refinement

Whether noting the necessity of NCAA celebration rules or saying they were "bullshit," both high-and low-expressive White athletes then criticize the broad interpretation of the "helmet rule." The rule is, simply, that players cannot take off their helmets on the field of play—they must be on the sidelines. Any player caught taking the helmet off on the field will be penalized fifteen yards. The rule was implemented primarily to curb celebration after big plays, when athletes would take off their helmets and streak to the sidelines. This was thought to be drawing unnecessary attention to the individual who made the play and not stressing the team aspect of the game.

The three Florida Division I teams, Florida, Florida State, and Miami were most known for helmet-less expression. Those three teams, coincidentally, were also always vying for both state supremacy and national supremacy in football, as all three were perennially ranked among the top-ten teams in the nation (Florida State won the national championship in 2014). Some thought college and high school athletes were being influenced by the expressive behavior of the Florida teams.

The initial 1990s NCAA celebration rule was nicknamed "The Miami Rule" after the University of Miami's expressive athletes. Unverzagt cites the University of Miami as one of the schools that "overdid it," primarily with taking off their helmets after a good play.

The problem arises in the interpretation of the rule by referees. White athletes note that the rule is well intended. "I think it's a good rule if you're doing it [taking helmet off] with the intent to celebrate. It's not hard to leave your helmet on," Nyquist says. Monty says that when players take off their helmets, these individual acts generally take "away from the game." Nyquist goes on to slam the rule, though, commenting that "I don't think it's a good rule, overall, and the way they have been enforcing it. It has to be with the *intent to celebrate* if you're taking your helmet off," that should draw a penalty. Therein lies the key to dissension about this rule.

Some White players feel that calls were being made—or could be made—for anyone taking off their helmet, even away from the cameras after a bad play. Stark says, "That's part of the rule I don't agree with. If you're taking your helmet off as you leave the field, I don't see how that's going to draw attention to yourself." He cites a case where a quarterback was upset leaving the field and removed his helmet before reaching the sidelines, which drew a penalty. Stark says this is a bad interpretation of the rule. Wunsch is even less forgiving, saying the rule is "absolutely insane. I think it's the stupidest rule there is."

Steve Stark also had comments on the "grey area" of referee rule interpretation, but his strongest comments were saved for his criticism of the NCAA. Stark feels the NCAA, in its rule-making policy, is dictatorial—"this is it, this is what's going to happen," inflexible—"they should have taken more time to integrate rules," and unconcerned with the input of athletes or fans—"if they went to the players and asked what they felt was acceptable and they asked the fans what they thought was acceptable" that would be better. Stark says, "The NCAA makes rules sometimes just to make rules. They have a couple of new rules every year."

His advice, interestingly, is that the players and fans should be polled. If the NCAA has "time to come in and drug test us, I think they could probably send a few people to interview [us]. Maybe interview five or six people from each team—they could get a really good understanding of how a team feels about expression." (Hence, this study.) Stark spells out why he thinks it is necessary to understand the player: "It's not the NCAA's game. It's our game. We're the ones who play the game. We should be happy with the game." Though I doubt the NCAA will ever read this, Stark's suggestion is in line with my recommendations. The NCAA should continually question fans, players, ex-players, and a cross-section of America. Stark is correct. It is not *their* game. The game belongs to *us*. And all the rules on celebration still hold for the NCAA.

Race and Expression

This final section reflects responses to two different questions. White athletes talked about race and expression in general. Then, once I put my pen down and began packing up to leave, *I unveiled my research agenda* of exploring attitudes about race, football, and expression. Nearly all of what Bevell, Monty, Stark, Nyquist, and Wunsch said about race was after I noted my research agenda, while all of Unverzagt's commentary was before I mentioned my additional purposes. The responses are not what I expected or asked for.

My hope was that the athletes would comment in detail about their understanding of White rules and norms for behavior and compare and contrast those to their particular observations of Black athletes they played with, against, or saw on television. What I got was a discussion of race and football centered around three themes. The first theme after the introduction is acknowledgement that "White athletes were raised with little exposure to Blacks," with a sub-theme that "Madison is a culture shock." This comes mainly from Nyquist, Stark, Wunsch, and Monty who all hail from virtually all-White environments. The second theme deals with how White athletes feel about socialization and behavioral—pattern differences they have noticed in the final section titled "racial impressions of behavioral and attitudinal formation."

Rural White Athletes Raised with Little Exposure to African Americans

Matt Nyquist grew up in a small Minnesota town that had no Black families. The three Blacks he knew in Cokato were all adopted and lived in White homes and so thus were not "Black" in a cultural sense, he realizes, because they were raised in "more of a White culture." Further, he had competed against only three or four Blacks in his entire football conference.

In a similar sense, Gerald Wunsch was raised in virtually all-White Wausau, which is located in northern Wisconsin and not far from the Minnesota border. There were African Americans and Asian Americans in Wausau, though few while he was growing up. He says more racial groups are moving there because of the good atmosphere, "because I think overall people up there aren't very racist at all." Steve Stark was raised on the Wisconsin-Illinois border, not far from Beloit—a city that has a small Black community. With the exception of Stark, the other White low-expressive athletes noted that the culture shock in coming to Madison was … well … shocking.

Wunsch says that though there were Blacks in his town, that "until you get to a bigger city like this, you really don't get the interaction." He sensed that Blacks in his hometown were friendlier but that there was more racial hostility in Madison, by both Blacks and Whites. He feels prejudice is a two-way street, that both groups are guilty, that "some people say, 'this person is Black, and this person is White' and because of that, I don't think racism is one way … I think they're both equally [race conscious]—it's both sides of the street."

Nyquist notes that it took him a couple of months to make the adjustment and to feel "comfortable." But his "total culture shock" was not only in dealing with the Black population in Madison, but also coming "from the middle of the bible belt" to a party school.[17] Add to this the unexpected shock of learning to deal with "White guys from different types of neighborhoods," that further confused matters of relating, having to deal with other "White people's culture—from New York!"

He says that he had to understand that people were raised a little different than he was and that once he figured this out, "it wasn't too bad." Thus, race, culture, and the rural-urban lifestyles come together in Madison and represent not only a shock to the urban athlete, but also a shock to the rural athlete. I had never considered that White people from rural areas would experience culture shock at meeting White urbanized people who had a bit of swagger. But it makes complete sense.

Monty notes that another program he considered, the University of Colorado, recruited some gang members out of Los Angeles who were great athletes but who found it hard to get along in Boulder, Colorado, because they come from "such a different background than everyone else." He readily admits, though, to getting some culture shock of his own when arriving in Madison. He didn't understand the speech patterns of Tony Simmons or Reggie Torian, two Black players who are both from Chicago: "The way that they grew up was so much different" from his own White, middle-class community.

Monty does note that Torian and Simmons "express themselves and they dance a lot and they are maybe more vocal than I am, louder—and that's just the way they grew up and that's the way they are, and they bring that to the game." This summarizes the way forward. Everybody is just a little bit different. Sometimes you have to learn about those differences in order to work as a team.

Impressions of Racial Behavior and Attitude Formation

In a continuation of his comments above, Monty notes that the game of football in the past has been dominated by "White middle-class people who set the rules," and that when White middle-class people play the game, they may not be "as vocal and going to dance as much because they don't have the rhythm, or whatever," ending by saying that dancing as expression is "good for the game." Eric Unverzagt aided Monty's adjustment to Black players at UW. Monty respects Unverzagt because he "accepts people for who they are, not if they are Black or White." Unverzagt, recall, is from predominantly Black Central Islip, NY.

Nyquist's ideas about appropriate behavior come via the culture of his father.[18] His father is first-generation Scandinavian, being the son of immigrants who were very "old school." That "old school" philosophy was transferred from grandparents to parents to Matt Nyquist, who learned that he should "hold in" emotion—or at least not display it. There were appropriate times to laugh, but crying, well, "It's the Scandinavian way of life. Never, ever cry. Never!" Another apparent way of life around the Nyquist household was to never take credit for work, but to always give praise to others. Thus, Nyquist sums up his father's approach to attention:

> He's always happy when he does something, never wants to take credit for it either. He's the kind of guy who likes to give everyone else all the credit all the time and never wants to take any of the credit for anything. He's always putting credit off. When his employees do stuff for him that's real good, and he probably does a good portion of the work, he'll never accept any credit. I think it's partially the Scandinavian, partially just the natural personality.[19]

The low expressiveness of Nyquist senior transferred to playing sport, also. Whether in college or in the driveway at home, Nyquist senior never physically expressed himself when he made a big play or when he beat his son in basketball. He also never talked after big plays or victory; he just won and let that be it. Nyquist concludes by commenting that his mother—part Scandinavian—is more expressive than his father, speaking more of what she feels, which is in his eyes the way more people acted, more "normal."

Gerald Wunsch, at the close of his interview, suggests why celebratory behavior might differ racially. He cites team socialization and individual motivation as reasons why behavior differs—why some Black athletes are more expressive that other athletes. White players are never told expressive behavior is allowable, and that separating oneself from the team or dancing was deeply frowned upon. "You waited for your teammates to celebrate." Contrast this to his thoughts of why Black athletes seek individual attention in football:

> I think the way the Black community is brought up, because of the fact that they had to fight to get out and to be an individual, you know … a lot of times you say, 'Well, all you can count on is you' and they have themselves. In football, it's an individual kind of thing that brings them to a scene, that allows them to succeed. Whereas I think in football, at least where I came from, was a situation where it was a team [concept].[20]

In all the statements thus far on race there seems to be agreement among White low-expressive athletes that racial differences do exist, and that at some level attempts have been made to understand those differences, which at first may be a "shock." Steve Stark makes a similar observation on racial differences in attitudes, specifically referees and how they call unsportsmanlike conduct penalties depending on their racial or geographical backgrounds. I thought his observation was insightful—that referees might differ in their calls on conduct penalties dependent upon their own backgrounds.

My reply question to Stark was whether or not a White referee from North Dakota would differ from a Black referee from Florida in how they might call unsportsmanlike conduct. His comment: "I think obviously those two people will probably have different opinions, but you know there could be two White referees from North Dakota that have very different opinions on it [celebrating]. You know there could be two Black referees that have a very different opinion on it also." Very well said, Mr. Stark.

Stark points up a very important distinction about diversity of opinions and attitudes (and subsequent behavior) both across and within racial groups. This is his lone comment on race, behavior, and attitudes, but it follows the pattern above from introspective low-expressive White athletes. These athletes were raised in virtually all-White surroundings and have begun, at least on some level, grappling not only with footballs and classes and university life, but also with the issues of racial difference.

What the chapter introduction and subsequent discussion points up is that coaches at the UW have intentionally developed a system of recruitment and retention that attempts to diffuse potential racial conflict. Unverzagt, in a note of caution, says that though there is a good mix of players, and that lockers in the dressing room are even divided to integrate the players, that he's "not going to say stuff doesn't exist." Indeed.

Racial understanding is a lifelong process. But the lack of racial strife and the intentionality of Alvarez's recruiting in the 1990s give us an idea for successfully moving forward with integrated teams. But I can equally caution about the lack of generalizability of my results to other Big Ten programs or other large university sports programs, given the uniqueness of Alvarez's approach.

Conclusion

White Americans, especially those from rural communities, most resemble my experiences with New Zealanders and their attitudes about community stability, low levels of expression, and deeply ingrained humility. These two groups would be at home together. Their similarities are striking. And both groups guard against arrogance and self-expression as if it were a disease that could kill the community fabric.

New Zealanders tend to feel far more at home around Canadians, but also might feel comfortable with rural Whites in the USA. They would still find rural Whites in the U.S. arrogant in ways Whites here would not understand. The next chapter points up why even the most reserved White Americans are considered arrogant by the standards of a nation that worships humility at every level of society.

Notes

1. The (White) acknowledged penalty is to be hit by the pitcher with the baseball. Being intentionally aggressed-upon by those in Black and Latino communities requires some sort of response, usually an in-kind physical response. Black and Latino players will often charge the mound. White players, when hit by a pitch have learned to "take it like a man" and to run to first base without rubbing the aching spot and vowing to do well in the next at-bat. The Black or Latino player charges the mound and gets called "unsportsmanlike" or violent for responding to "condoned" violence. There are of course White players who do charge the mound (sometimes called "feisty" or "competitive" and Black and Latino pitchers who hit or "brush-back" batters, including Bob Gibson of the St. Louis Cardinals (1960s) and Dave Stewart of the Oakland A's (1980s/90s). But there are two codes that exist, and despite occasional overlaps, different interpretations of on-field acts often lead to violence. There are also racialized ways of interpreting on-field acts depending on race of athlete and thus racialized articulations of those act.
2. Frey, 1994, p. 20.
3. If YouTube still exists in the future, you can peek at this bit of White connectivity with Black culture. Notice how approving his Black teammates are! https://www.youtube.com/watch?v=4Ul8fPnodlE.
4. Bevel, in Andrews, 1996b.
5. Unverzagt, in Andrews, 1996b.
6. Wunsch, in Andrews, 1996b.
7. Darrell Bevell cites in the University of Wisconsin 1995 football guide that one of the things he'd most like to do is to go "bass fishing with Steve Stark."
8. Nyquist's father was a very successful Division III football player.
9. Stark, in Andrews, 1996b.
10. Unverzagt, in Andrews, 1996.
11. Jeff Donaldson played for Houston, Kansas City and Atlanta during his professional football career.

12. Monty, in Andrews, 1996b.
13. Bevell, in Andrews, 1996b.
14. Ibid
15. Nyquist, in Andrews, 1996b.
16. Wunsch, in Andrews, 1996b.
17. His hometown of Cokato, MN, is a "dry" (no alcohol sales) town.
18. This discussion of Nyquist's father could easily fit in the section of fathers as mentors, but I choose to include it in the study of race to highlight White cultural socialization as passed to Nyquist by a first generation American. We get a rare peak at a distinctly cultural way of (non) expressing that serves as a window to the cultural norms of other Whites in the Midwest, especially Minnesota and Wisconsin, where many Scandinavians, Norwegians and Germans have immigrated.
19. Nyquist, in Andrews, 1996b.
20. Wunsch, in Andrews, 1996n.

9 Humility Abroad

New Zealand Sport, Women, and the Tall Poppy Syndrome

Craig Ferguson: "Do Australians give you a hard time for your success outside of Australia?"

Toni Collette: "No."

Craig Ferguson: "They never do that? The Australian Press are never snippy about people [succeeding] outside of Australia?"

Toni Collette: "Well, we have something called the Tall Poppy syndrome. Have you ever heard of that?"

Craig Ferguson: "Oh yes. I'm from Scotland and they hate me back home now."

Toni Collette: "If you are successful—'chop!'—they cut you down."

—The Late/Late Show with Craig Ferguson, July 2009

You think rural America has a tight-knit social fabric that adores humility and doesn't like change? You've met Fiona in Chapter 2, now meet her country in far more detail. Or should I say *our* country, as I've been a citizen of New Zealand since the year 2000. I've studied this country and its views on expression and celebration for many years, enjoying my time following rugby and cricket in person, on television, and as a member of the media.

This chapter is intricately tied to my project of interrogating behavioral norms and codes of conduct in the USA. Kiwi attitudes about the expression of athletes dwarf any ridicule we heap on ourselves in North America. Rarely do White

Americans get told they are arrogant, but it happens somewhere in the world every day. As a matter of fact, many New Zealanders told me as much whenever I gave my talks on sports.

That said, an in-depth review of Kiwi culture and customs gives us an amazing peek into a society steeped in the art of keeping all egos in check and expression uniform and tucked away. This is the direction many would like the USA to head toward. African Americans have been fighting against this wave since 1965. But there is little doubt that many in the USA would love this type of humility to rein supreme. You, too, may want this for America.

My review of the Tall Poppy Syndrome centers on successful female athletes in New Zealand. I also comment a bit more in detail about a former student of mine, and ex-Olympic athlete, Anna Simcic, and her battle with sports success and failure. Simcic is the most awarded female in New Zealand swimming history, having won silver and gold at the Commonwealth Games (a competition between nations like Canada, India, and Australia that formerly had an allegiance to England) and competed in the Barcelona Olympics (1992) and the Atlanta Olympics (1996).

She shares her story of victory, defeat, and coming home in 1996 to ridicule and name-calling, below. Her story is interwoven into the fabric of a society that has humility as a primary goal—whether you want it or not, and whether you are humble or not.

Background

People who speak negatively about the positive social outcomes or higher social standing of others are said to be "Tall Poppy choppers." The acts most negatively criticized are behaviors that draw social attention to the individual. Consider this statement: "Yahoo! I got an 'A' on my essay!" As simple as this sounds, this is a blatant example of a student separating herself from the group of Canterbury students around her. She is acting as if she is "better" than everybody else. She just did an end-zone dance.

This "interpretation" is akin to the football player who scores a goal and celebrates away from others. People might tolerate it at the moment, then, when to themselves say, "Did you see her gloating? I only got a B. She thinks she is a big shot! She's a real bitch! And her dress was crappy, too." The general idea is—never be the center of attention.

The Tall Poppy individual faces group sanctions for appearing to set themselves apart. The individual actor has breached the norms of appropriate conduct. Those norms center on humility and egalitarianism (more on egalitarianism and equality later). The individual involved may have no idea that her social actions are "standing out" from the group.

Indeed, the social actor may not be intending to separate herself from others at all. She might just be happy. "Study abroad" students who lived in New Zealand certainly had to confront this cultural difference when at Canterbury University. And no excuses such as "Mate, that's how we roll in the USA!" worked to persuade Kiwis that Americans weren't arrogant pricks. Fifteen-yard penalty and a loss of down, as they say in football.

When people accomplish some outstanding feat in New Zealand (launching a successful high-tech start-up, winning a music award, or earning an Olympic gold medal) they, by default, become somehow socially "taller" than everyone else around. Your job then, as a successful Kiwi, is to downplay your greatness so that others around you won't feel bad about their non-greatness. You are required to show public humility. Big time. If not, you, the *outstanding* individual, inadvertently *stand out* in the eyes of others. A big head is assumed. It is your job to show people your greatness is really "no big deal." Or else, you unwittingly become a "Tall Poppy" in the eyes of many—and ripe for chopping.

Tall Poppy chopping in a sporting context is the act of cutting the individual or team "down to size" after events where the team or individual stands out for some reason, typically a success event, which might seem odd. After all, in the USA we experience what is called "reflected glory" after our team wins a big game. Our chests are poked out for a few days—and we gloat.

Kiwis love a good All Black rugby test match win, too, but some wait for the team gloating with chopping knives at the ready, yet others downplay the victory or find minor faults to harp on. I've had my students tell me in the USA that they got all A grades in a semester, and one B+, and all their parents see is the awful-looking B+. It's kinda like that.

Kiwis want you to "back door" the win, as in, "We played awful today. Sure, we won, but we can't play this poorly and beat Australia next week. They've got a great team and we will have to practice harder." Perfect. New Zealand won, fifty-five to ten over Argentina, but no matter. Contextualizing a great win is an opportunity to showcase your ever-present humility via the coded talk New Zealand wants to hear. I would instruct my students to walk humbly up to their parents with their grades and say, "I really didn't do that well this semester. I can do much better. I worked hard in one class and all I got was a B+." Your parents will snatch the report card and scream with joy when they see all "A" grades in your other classes. That's perfect Kiwi contextualizing.

Self-presentation is everything in New Zealand. Athletes in social settings act according to strict codes of humility after victory lest they be accused of standing too tall above the norm. The social code warrants some "chopping" by others if you are perceived as too "up yourself" as they say in New Zealand. In essence, the Tall Poppy Syndrome in New Zealand is socially sanctioned verbal abuse directed at successful or unsuccessful teams or individuals.

The Tall Poppy Syndrome Globally

The origins of the phrase "Tall Poppy" go back to ancient times. The Roman historian, Livy, refers to the symbolic decapitation of the heads of the tallest poppies by the elder Tarquinius when walking in his garden. The message was conveyed to his son, Sextus Tarquinius, who then rid himself of the chief men of the state of Gabii and thus delivered the state unresisting to the Roman king.[1] The military idea, it seems, was to cut down the biggest and brightest in the opposing nation—Gabii in this case—thereby leaving the remaining nationals weakened and fearful of conquer.

The mythology behind Tall Poppies thus conveys two subterranean messages: (1) people will seek out those who are Tall Poppies for destruction, and (2) do not succeed, lest you be considered a Tall Poppy and thus ripe for being "chopped" by others. This extrapolated cultural theory of achievement has an intervening historical variable in the case of New Zealand, and that is the cultural ethic that promotes egalitarianism (equality) as a response to the class-based system prevalent in Great Britain that many fled in the 1800s. One of New Zealand's most endearing qualities is the concept of egalitarianism, much like the USA's concept of social equality, though both countries fall short of their altruistic social goals.

Verbal abuse of teams or individuals is not strictly a New Zealand trait. Indeed, a large majority of people who follow sport intensely have likely verbally chastised at some point in time either (1) players, (2) coaches, (3) owners, (4) teams, (5) referees, or (6) an entire nation because of their sporting failure. Part and parcel of being a fan is learning how to channel your negative emotions when your team or favorite player loses.

We love our teams or players, hate when our team or player loses, and quite often learn to "hate" the other team or individual. This sporting hatred (more akin to disdain) encompasses other teams, quite often if those teams are more successful than our own. While the New York Yankees, Dallas Cowboys, and Manchester United Red Devils might be the most popular teams in their respective sporting codes globally, they are also the most hated teams.

Part of the disdain people have for those teams is because of their historical domination and the appearance of blatant self-promotion and lack of humility. The Dallas Cowboys, after Superbowl success in the 1970s, fashioned themselves as "America's Team." The New York Yankees were so hated they were dubbed "The Evil Empire" by the Boston Red Sox, the other team comprising the duo that is said to be the best rivalry in U.S. sport.[2]

The Yankees are also the most successful sporting franchise in U.S. sports history. On the other hand, one reason the Chicago Cubs are so loved country-wide—besides being named after a cuddly animal—is that their *history of losing* has lasted well over eighty years. The Cubs were once the pillars of humility and futility in American sport. It was thought that if the Cubs were ever to win the World Series, this would be a sure sign of the approaching Apocalypse.[3]

To despise another for his or her success has broad social reach. People have exhibit jealousies and envy toward others all over the world, in many fashions, for various and sundry reasons throughout history. Pride in ourselves and our own and prejudice against other groups is sometimes envy and jealousy. Gunner Myrdal, in *An American Dilemma*, sees an ever-raging conflict and racial tension:

> … between the "American Creed," where the American thinks, talks, and acts under the influence of high national and Christian precepts, and, on the other hand, the … economic, social, and sexual jealousies; considerations of community prestige and conformity; group prejudice against particular persons or types of people …[4]

Psychologist Norman Feather, the most prominent researcher on the Tall Poppy Syndrome, though briefly mentioning North America, concentrates his research on Tall Poppy culture in Australia and Japan.[5] Feather notes that attitudes toward successful people are related to a person's own perceived competence and self-esteem.

For instance, the way that I react to others who have achieved success is often influenced by how I view myself. If I feel positive and competent, I am less likely to be a tall poppy cutter. By contrast, if I have low self-esteem and regard myself as incompetent, I am more likely to feel satisfied if a tall poppy falls from grace.[6] Feather may need to consult with the midwestern parents and athletes in the previous chapters as they might have a different view. Humility is the "grace" that they admire in their daily life and success, which promotes a strong sense of self and community. I would agree, though, that if someone comes back from "the big city" to his country town with gold chains, a Cadillac Escalade, and city slang and accent, he'd get the tall poppy treatment. Better to drive home in a Smart Car rocking a Packers hat.

Parenting is highly influential in shaping our view of others, and high achievers may well have been instructed early on in life by their parents to be humble and graceful after success, like both Reggie Torian and Darrell Bevell before his interview with the media. There might be many scenarios where people dislike the behavior of others (after success) not because of their own perceived low self-esteem or incompetence, but because of a parental (or ex-sporting coach) norm that screams: "That is inappropriate behavior!"

Microclimates and Microattitudes

Feather argues that people from Western societies (he includes Australia, New Zealand and the United States) typically *value* individual accomplishment and enterprise.[7] This is an "independent" view of the self, which he describes as "viewing self as separate from others, with a focus on the expression of one's unique internal attributes."[8] Feather cites American society as the epitome of this "independent" construction of self when he says that "individualism and achievement is commonly assumed to be a characteristic" in their culture.[9]

This idea of "independent" construction of self seems to contradict what happens in the Midwest with Badger athletes and socialization about "team" and behavior. It might be that each country, especially one as large as the USA, has microclimates of attitudes, just like there are weather microclimates in a region. As I type this, I am in the Bay Area, Northern California, an area of definite microclimates; cold and foggy in San Francisco, sunny and warm across the bridge in Oakland. Seven inches of rain north in Marin County, and one inch in the south here in San Jose over the past week.

Certainly, we can see how New Yorkers could be considered more independent and individual than people from Omaha. Micro-attitudes do indeed exist around the USA despite what the larger data on our behavioral norms are about "independence." Smaller communities appear far more interdependent.

Another theorist, Robert Whiting (1989), explores aspects of American and "eastern" culture in his book, *You Gotta Have Wa.*[10] Whiting explores the contrasting American and Japanese cultures in the context of baseball and seems to confirm Feather's ideas. Whiting sketches the different cultural values of Americans and Japanese by explaining that the traditional Japanese ideal is a humble, uncomplaining, obedient soul in life or in sport. The concept and practice of group harmony, or "Wa" is what most dramatically differentiates Japanese baseball from the American game.

While "Let It All Hang Out" and "Do Your Own Thing" are mottoes of American youth society, the Japanese have their own credo for behavior in the well-worn proverb, "The nail that sticks up shall be hammered down."[11] It is practically a national slogan and is the framework, it seems, from which many behavioral patterns flow.[12] This attitude comes close to what Black athletes experience when they express. Stick out—get hammered down.

The connectedness of human beings to each other is emphasized in Japan; individual autonomy "takes second place to the primary task of fitting in with the social context."[13] It is also worth noting that the Japanese value people being "humble" rather than overtly displaying their success. This sounds very close to how my White Midwestern interviewees constructed their local environment regarding fitting in.

The nail that sticks out in Japan will experience the same fate as the poppy that is tall in New Zealand and the African American or anyone who stands out with individual expression in the USA. Except in the microclimate of urban America or African American churches, or in the stands throughout the country where many different cultures have developed converging micro attitudes with Black style.

Humility and Egalitarianism

The Christchurch Press, in a story about Dr. Kelvin Duncan, co-inventor of New Zealand's highly touted antioxidant *ENZ*ogenol, described how the "Tall poppy knives [were] out to cut down a livewire academic," and how the "Persecuted venture capitalists flee NZ."[14] *The Press* reported on the favored personalities in New Zealand society—people who emphasized their "modesty" despite their success. In this vein, Sam Neill, a successful Kiwi (and Hollywood) actor, is depicted by *North & South* magazine as "not 'up himself'; he's the kind of star New Zealand can tolerate: Unassuming, low key, reticent."[15]

Neill explains that his "distaste for the showy" is definitely "part of his New Zealand conditioning," which includes this nation's "preference for knocking rather than praising."[16] "Knocking" is the Kiwi phrase for criticizing, or in Black speak, "dissing."

Another example of the special variety of the NZ Tall Poppy is provided by Finlay MacDonald in his article, "Poppy Culture: Off with our Heads." This deputy editor of *The Listener* magazine describes the "horribly familiar tune" that New Zealand is a "nation of knockers, a pathologically jealous race that cannot abide those who dare to be different, brilliant or successful."[17] Indeed, MacDonald argues that New Zealanders are so renowned for their chopping ability that they should "add a line [about the syndrome] to the national anthem."[18]

Conformity to normative humble and egalitarian behavior was evident in my interviews with White Midwestern United States athletes and with some Black athletes. The upshot of the interviews with White athletes was that successful athletes worked to maintain a consistency of behavior and did not want to unravel the deep social fabric that had been tightly woven in their communities over the past many years. There was a slowness of life in rural communities that was revered, and anything that appeared too different or too out of place was necessarily scrutinized.

Continuity over the years was a primary goal of athletes, and it appeared that, given the lack of extreme wealth or poverty in Wisconsin rural communities, egalitarianism thrived as a below-the-surface ideal. Even if one had come into wealth or fame, the behavior expected of the individual was supposed to be in close alignment with past social and behavioral demeanor. Maybe a couple of high-fives and a round of drinks at the pub, but nothing more.

The micro-attitude in poorer areas is that successful people need to come back and "shake things up," or point to the mountain and say, "You, too, can succeed!" Much like I do later in this chapter with a little boy. Acting the same old way after success will likely get you the same old results out of urban youth in need of some visual role-modeling. I think striking a good medium between outward success and joy—while closing the distance between you and your target audience—is key. You don't have to lose the gold chains, but drive a tiny Smart Car, Shaquille O'Neal.

British immigrants to New Zealand imported with them forward-thinking and smart ideals of egalitarianism in the hope that maybe, in a new country, they could reject the oppressive class structure of their homeland for something more democratic, more equal. This ideology of egalitarianism has survived in New Zealand over the past 150 or so years since first contact with the Maori native culture. Egalitarianism (and its less attractive first cousin, "sameness,") is thus the primary value climate within which the citizens of New Zealand work and play.

Do Maori sportspeople experience the Tall Poppy Syndrome differently because of unique cultural values, social history, and expressive micro attitudes? Merata Mita (*Patu*) comments about NZ society from a Maori perspective, which is even more distant from the United States and other Western models of individualism. She cringes about a NZ White society that "makes you individualistic and competitive" and that this conflicts with the Maori "cultural framework," which is "holistic" and values those who "share and nurture" and not those who "compete."[19]

One Maori proverb about the kumara (a sweet potato) is that "the kumara cannot say how sweet it is." This phrase is used in relationship to people talking positively about themselves and hints at the "collectivism rather than individual achievement" sentiment Maori culture might have toward Tall Poppies. The difference here is that while the Maori proverb suggests that speaking about your own value or worth is unbecoming, having value or worth granted to you by others, or "manna," is not such a bad thing.

Nelson Mandela had high manna around the world. He was held in high esteem. Mandela would never have said, "I have a great deal of manna—you should let me out of this jail." Manna is the phrase that at one and the same time grants high status while implying great humility.

What an amazing concept. In this regard, Martin Luther King would have similar manna to Nelson Mandela. Muhammad Ali's talk might not have garnered him much manna at the time, but his later years is where he earned his manna after decades of struggle. Manna is earned through deeds and through the sentiment of others toward the whole person. This conceptual framework would be a great way forward for young athletes looking to earn respect verses declaring it as a given.

Tall Poppy Sportswomen in NZ: A Survey of Experiences

Sport, and rugby in particular, holds a dominant position in New Zealand society and is linked to nearly everything. Culture and the Haka at one end, and dominant White (also called "Pakeha" by Maori) male culture at the other end. Many theorists of New Zealand society speak of the powerful position that men, especially Pakeha men, hold in this country.[20] Given that New Zealand is a highly gendered culture and sport is a gendered institution, do Kiwi sportswomen have any space to be Tall Poppies? If they do achieve at high levels, is their participation in poppy culture different from the sportsman?

An illustration of the effects of the Tall Poppy Syndrome on sportswomen is provided by Virginia Myers' depiction of Anne Audain in the book, *Head and Shoulders: Successful Aotearoa New Zealand Women Talk to Virginia Myers*. Audain, New Zealand's former leading middle-distance runner, appears to be described paradoxically; Myers describes her as "not afraid of the word success" and also as "unassuming."[21] Perhaps this is not a paradox, but rather the essential element of humility that enables successful people to be tolerated in New Zealand. You can be successful in New Zealand, just as long as you don't "skite"—or brag—about it.

This hypothesis is proven in Audain's case when she says that her sporting success was never attributed "any fuss" nor was she "ever pampered [or] told that [she] was wonderful."[22] She goes on to say that if people praised her, her father would add, "Anne's still got a long way to go." In addition, Audain describes her experience of people in New Zealand who would "begrudge" her winning in sport.

On the contrary, her experience in America was different because, she says, they "appreciate talent." For many athletes in America, the appreciation by fans can be overwhelming and suffocating. But for a foreign-born athlete competing in track and field and not used to receiving much praise, this change proved exhilarating.

Erin Baker, Christchurch resident and world-class runner for New Zealand in the 1980s and arguable the most outspoken athlete (male or female) in the past few decades, would make a good African American. She notes in *Guts, Tears and Glory* that:

> You have to be aggressive to succeed and people misinterpret that as arrogance. You get this bad image because you're positive about yourself, but you have to be. You can't do what most New Zealanders want you to do and say, 'Oh I hope I do well, because I'm not really very good.' You've got to stand out and say, 'I'm going to beat them, to take on the world', otherwise you never will … I think that's why every sportsperson in the world has a bad image because they have to be different and a little arrogant to succeed. After that year I matured, I knew I was going to be good, but not just because I was winning … it's a funny sense, knowing you can be ***good*** … It's not cockiness or bolshiness, it's a strength knowing your capabilities … I really believed I could win and I did.[23]

Baker's note on verbalizing belief in herself and her capabilities flies in the face of the norm in New Zealand—and many in America—which is to project the image to others that *you don't really believe in yourself or you aren't really that good*, even if *you do believe in yourself or think you are that good.*

African-Americans and other outspoken athletes in America have been questioned about their verbal esteem in media situations dating back to Muhammad Ali in the 1960s. As seen in Baker's comment, New Zealand audiences and media also misinterpret the positive attitude toward about oneself and winning. Baker's comment also criticizes the code-shifting humility framework that appears necessary to appease audiences.

On the one hand, highly trained international athletes must have a strong belief in their skills in order to succeed, and their host nations hope and pray they will. On the other hand, in order to not distance oneself too much from said audience, athletes must sing a different tune when reflecting on their own sporting chances. The difference between *actual sentiments* and *voiced sentiments* by athletes in media situations is a cause for what social psychologists call "cognitive dissonance," or the mental battle between two competing choices.

Recall, double-consciousness is the phrase coined by W.E.B. Dubois over one hundred years ago to describe the dissonance all African Americans have to tackle when they enter White institutions. Double-consciousness is the experience of having to appease (in voice and body) the White "out group" while maintaining a sense of Black self-respect and esteem. Some of New Zealand's top athletes experience a nation-based Kiwi double-consciousness as they negotiate the humility they must present to the public while maintaining an ego-driven high sporting self-esteem, which propels their competitive excellence.

Rachel Alexander, Christchurch resident, is another New Zealand elite athlete who experienced strong feelings of resentment of her success by people around her. Alexander excelled at the dangerous sport of hang-gliding. She was so good that she qualified to compete in international competition against the best males. In that competition she found herself resented by the men she competed against. No novelty there, as gender discrimination in Western societies is common. But she comments further, in my intensive interview with her, on the Tall Poppy Syndrome and on the alienation she felt within her own *family* after succeeding.

She noted that it is "not NZ culture to say that you're good at something. Someone else should say the things that you're good at. If you mention your own achievements, you're perceived as 'cocky.'"[24] Alexander's hard training and diligence led to financial and public success, which was the reason she and her mother grew apart … "She [Mom] could not 'relate' to a famous person." Alexander stood too high above the rest of the poppies.

It appears that the overriding social code, echoing New Zealand's own brand of enforced egalitarianism, is that no individual will be placed upon a pedestal, and further, there will be no "fuss" about any one person's achievements because everyone is, or should be, equal.

In the case of Christchurch native Anna Simcic, world-class swimmer, she found that sometimes when you fail in New Zealand society you are less than equal. Simcic was elevated to Tall Poppy status both by her accomplishments and by the propping-up of expectations by the media. She was, in the end, severely cut down to size after defeat.

Anna Simcic: A Study in Humility and Frustration

> I remember saying to my parents and my best friends ... If I ever get a big head please pull me back into my place. Because I don't like that ... I don't like to seem arrogant.[25]

The story of Olympic athlete Anna Simcic is probably not that much different, at first glance, from most athletes who compete in the Olympics in New Zealand, or for that matter, worldwide. Simcic achieved at a young age, made her way up the junior ranks, qualified for the Olympics, competed, did not win a medal (most do not), competed again (most never make it to a second Olympics), did not win a medal, returned home, and got on with her life. Nothing novel in that. But it is not the novelty of Anna's *path* into and out of sport that is worthy of note, but the commonality of her *experience*—how it converges with the public and private experience of other New Zealand athletes—that strikes a collective chord.

In total, Simcic was a world-class swimmer from the years 1987–1996. She ended her competitive career at the Atlanta Summer Olympics of 1996. In an intensive interview with Simcic, she uncovered problematic issues surrounding her career as a swimmer representing New Zealand. Our discussion centered around the omnipresent New Zealand media, the image of the "tough" Kiwi athlete, her return home after "failure" at the Olympics, and the Tall Poppy culture of New Zealand. Though the particulars of Simcic's career as a world-class athlete may differ from other New Zealand athletes, I suspect—given the testimony of Anne Audain and others—that there are strong overlaps in her experience with a female athlete who succeeds. Or fails.

Simcic achieved a high level of success at the Commonwealth games in 1990 and 1994, winning both gold and silver medals. She had a string of successes—as one might imagine of any world-class athlete—along the way leading up to competing at the Commonwealth games. Eventually, after just missing out on a place on the 1988 New Zealand Olympic squad that traveled to Seoul, she qualified for the 1992 Barcelona Olympics. She placed fifth in the finals of the 200-meter backstroke and immediately went to work preparing for the 1996 Atlanta Olympics, where she again made it to the finals (no small feat) and placed seventh in a field of eight.

We have discussed the Tall Poppy Syndrome in relation to success, but its more insidious twin in New Zealand rears its head when the populace pin their hopes on an individual/team to win on the world stage, in hopes of earning some globally "reflected glory," but the star athlete or team falls short of the goal. When Simcic lost, this thirst for esteem went unfulfilled and social anger/resentment was the residual. One incident of "chopping" Simcic had to bear on arrival home was a New Zealand man who yelled into her face, "You're a loser!"

Simcic on Media Hype & Pressure

Simcic notes that a friend of hers, Summer Saunders, an Olympic butterfly and medley swimmer for the United States in Barcelona in 1992, faced similar media scrutiny in the USA. She feels the media was quite nasty to Saunders for not winning gold in her first few races, even though she had won silver and bronze medals. After these events, Simcic learned to ease her expectations in the face of the media. When asked in most of her interviews, "Are you going for the gold?" her response would be a guarded statement: "I'd always point out that at the Olympics anything can happen … I was still behind a lot of the people in the world and I never publicly stated that I'm 'going for the gold,' even though a medal was well within my reach." The nation (via the media) had pinned their hopes on an arrogant goal, one might say, of "gold."

She stood there on the starting blocks with the media criticism stirring in the back of her mind, knowing that if she did not do well, the media—and others—would be saying that she should not have gone to the Olympics and represented New Zealand. She confessed after her admittedly less-than-average performance that she was too worried about a number of outside factors to concentrate on the race and perform on the day.

She admits that the measure of a good athlete is the ability to rise above all the hype and be your best when you need to be, and to that end she did not perform to her best. It is worth noting that the media and the intensity of the possible public scrutiny played into Simcic not performing on the day.

Simcic Returns Home to New Zealand

After her first Olympic "loss" in 1992, Simcic was afraid to return home. She did not know what people would think, or worse, what they might do. She apprehensively notes that she wondered whether people would spit on or throw rocks at her. Comments hurled at her, like "you're a loser!" were fine in her mind, by comparison. Her fears may have been unwarranted, but nonetheless, they were very real fears—and grounded in her perceptions of high New Zealand expectations and the repercussions for public failure. Rather than being a self-fulfilling prophecy or paranoia, which no doubt some will label Simcic's perceptions as, I feel her anticipation was based on a culturally normative reaction insight about her homeland.

That is, Simcic grew up absorbing the socially constructed value of winning and losing and, after losing, anticipated the public response based on past history.

The comments she initially brushed aside as "fine" began to wear on her. Expectations of Kiwis, she was finding, had been very high. "God, you're a loser" was a common reception she received when walking into Christchurch bars. She quickly found out that people's lips were a lot looser—and far more critical—once they started drinking.

She notes that Varsity—the University of Canterbury—was also an intimidating space, as were the streets of Christchurch, her hometown. As a student in a course of mine in the late 1990s, I noticed that no students sat near her. She'd catch people whispering about her just slightly within earshot in both campus and community spaces. She remained guarded in public, especially when people approached her. She became very self-conscious when performing as simple an act as walking down the street.

Simcic is aware that Kiwis become envious of others who receive attention, and Simcic had received an inordinate amount of attention the past few years. But she speaks to the contradictory nature of the chopping she received for her attention (and failure), which appears to be born of desire.

Simcic says that people in New Zealand culture "like to put you down and put you in your place. It's not good to stand up, not good to achieve. Yet, people want it themselves. Does that make sense? We're a small nation." Her endnote on small-nation status echoes earlier comments on the small, insular approach to public behavior by those in small, rural areas of the United States Midwest.

She concludes that she really does not know what New Zealanders want. Yet, she *does not* want to appear arrogant, perhaps at least aware of what New Zealanders *do not* want. In a telling anecdote, Simcic notes that she told family and friends, once she began to get media attention, to put her in her place if she ever got a "big head." She feels she has maintained an even-keeled personality, and more importantly, feels she has "not changed my personality, right through."[26]

She was never arrogant after winning a race, shouting "yeah!" or being otherwise conspicuous. She has a distaste for people who might yell, "I'm number one!" after a winning race, because it does not fit her personality. She would have yelled "yeah!" but only quietly, and only to herself, refraining from going ballistic at poolside in front of other athletes and fans.

Contrarily, she notes that it is great for some to show emotions, but not to go too far with it. There was a German friend at Berkeley who did, she feels, go too far, and she heard whispers in the crowd of "damned arrogant bastard!" She says New Zealand swimmers tend to be reserved and not "real showy." Simcic is the kind of person who will smile at success and celebrate "privately, because that is the kind of person I am … I've always downplayed [success] because I don't want to seem like a show-off … standing out" (Simcic).

Simcic may take the "not standing out" issue to extremes at times, possibly not wanting the public scrutiny of being a Tall Poppy.[27] On occasion when out on the town in Christchurch with long-time friend Amanda, they will reverse rolls. People will stare at them and inevitably approach them, asking, "Are you Anna Simcic?" Simcic will reply, "No, her name is Anna, my name is Poppy." Interesting choice of names, and fitting for the role she played in New Zealand sport in the 1990s.

Simcic on African Americans

While in the United States, and specifically during the Olympics, Anna had contact with African American students and athletes. One phenomenon she became aware of in classes at Berkeley was hostility toward her by Black students because she was White. Given the U.S. history of slavery, racial oppression, and discrimination by many Whites toward all but a few Blacks, part of the social paradigm of being an African American is to be suspicious of White Americans, especially those who smile and are friendly. Apologies, Anna. There is often a "guilty until proven innocent" approach toward Whites, the assumption being that Whites are racist until proven otherwise. This was likely more prevalent when I was a student in the 1970s and 1980s.

She admits to being naïve about Black-White historical relationships in U.S. history. The point here is that she became aware of subtle and not-so-subtle differences in how African Americans behaved toward her, Whites, and each other in public. One such difference she noticed was that African Americans were more vocal and outgoing. And more than anything else, Simcic especially found the African American emphasis on personal appearance intriguing.

Her most memorable recollection was an incident that happened in the 1992 Barcelona Olympics. The female athletes had to have a proof-of-femaleness test, which required that cells be taken from both tongue and cheek. The NZ athletes were tested along with the American track and field athletes. After the test, athletes were escorted to take photographs for their Olympic Village badges. Simcic was amazed at what she commented on as the "vanity of the African American woman athletes," who continually primped, applied make-up and lipstick, and demanded that photos be retaken if not perfect.

Simcic finally said to the African American woman, who was having her photo retaken once again and whom she felt was "drop-dead gorgeous ... what are you [going] on about?" Simcic, on the other hand, wore no make-up and took an awful photo, but refused to ask for another. One key phrase from this section that stood out was when Simcic noted that even though she wanted to have another photo taken, she would never have asked. As she noted about Kiwi culture, "We're very backward in coming forward."

Might this be another ramification of the Tall Poppy Syndrome, the idea that to ask for another photo—to ask for something out of the ordinary—would somehow single one out as different, and therefore, a much subtler Tall Poppy worthy of a little chopping?

There is no doubting that hair is a very important commodity for African American women. For that matter, Black men. Our hair needs to be just right. Simcic would have certainly seen this obsessive behavior we have with our hair had she known Florence Griffith-Joyner, who ran in the 1988 and 1992 Olympics with her long, painted fingernails, long braided hair, and bright red lipstick.

Kobena Mercer (1987) and Herman Gray (1995) both write extensively on Black male and female styles, but suffice it to say that what Anna Simcic experienced with the Olympic athletes was a far different norm from what she grew up with.[28] "You get what you get and you don't complain," was the social norm I experienced in everyday New Zealand situations at restaurants, supermarkets, and barbershops.

We can draw parallels with how Simcic was critiqued by New Zealanders to how she critiques appropriate and inappropriate behavior in public by African Americans. Her comments about African Americans serve as an opposite model by which to contrast New Zealand culture. Simcic also summarizes that the Black men were very expressive, and also wore "a lot of jewelry, gold, and stuff, and that is a stereotype you get over here" in New Zealand (Simcic).

In this example we see that she judges Black notions of nonverbal expression by the Kiwi standard of downplayed personal appearance and muted self-expression. She has monitored the "other"—in this case, African Americans—by Kiwi standards. Given her acknowledged lack of African American socio-cultural history, she might not have contextualized the behavior or judged it relative to the out-group's normative values.

New Zealand Culture is Evolving: So Should United States Culture

New Zealand succeeds at an incredible level in international sport. For its population size (4 million people in a country roughly the geographical size of California), New Zealand is among the most successful sports nations competing internationally. In a sporting context (and many other international contexts), New Zealand has much to be proud of. Quite possibly the success comes about because of a feeling of being not quite good enough as individuals within a national and international context.

"Cultural cringe" is one phrase New Zealanders often use when viewing their own international status, as I mentioned earlier (Chapter 2) about cricket and language at Lords. This attitude leads to humility about self, others, and sometimes the nation, though New Zealanders, it must be said, show a high level of pride when viewing the uniqueness of their nation in terms of natural beauty and global politics.

Socially enforced humility may very well be behind the national ethos to push hard "until the business is done." Whatever the cause of this high level of public humility, it comes at a cost to many individuals who have to negotiate newfound success on the home battlefield.

New Zealand culture is remarkable in that people, generally, do not let victory spoil them or get them "off track." There is a pervasive attitude among successful Kiwi athletes that one victory is but a step in some longer journey. This allows them to keep focus on the long-term goal. Also, the deep humility shown by even the most successful Kiwis athletes is, I believe, a very positive effect of the egalitarian ethic in New Zealand. Another positive is the "leave them alone—let them have their space" phenomenon, which is when New Zealanders do not crowd stars in their country and allow them (Simcic harassment notwithstanding) relatively hassle-free lives.[29]

Americans, by comparison, are often quick to crowd the personal space of those who are famous, leading to a claustrophobic environment for virtually anyone who has appeared in the media. This behavior, I believe, prevents many from ever achieving at all, fearing that they will lose their privacy and individuality.

The author has seen famous individuals eating in restaurants and walking the streets of Christchurch and people barely taking notice but to say, "There's so and so." The general attitude of the New Zealander toward the successful person in a public place is quite often nonchalant. Indeed, many Kiwi sports stars, because of relatively low professional salaries and short career life spans, still keep their "day jobs" (or work in the off-season) as farmers, shopkeepers, or university students.

It might be that as New Zealand enters the global community, she becomes more accepting of success and less closed-off to the achievement of individuals. Feather's hypothesis about individualistic societies verses interdependent societies is problematic when looking at nations like New Zealand, which appears high on both scales. New Zealanders, probably due to their great distance from other nations, appear very individualistic at times, especially unique/creative/working-from-nothing problem-solving with "#8 wire," as the saying goes.

The citations above about humility, though, show New Zealand to also be quite interdependent. American individualism, viewed in full when Americans come to live in New Zealand, sticks out in broad relief. The large Asian influx to New Zealand in the 1990s and 2000s may be a subtle commentary about both opportunity and a convergence with interdependent living styles.

If you have never experienced being severely cut down like Simcic, this critique may seem like an exercise in futility by the weak of spirit. But if you have experienced being harshly criticized after succeeding or feeling that your success was not acknowledged by parents or others, you know all-too-well that getting cut down is painful and can be a setback to self-confidence and the desire to achieve. This is likely what the Wisconsin basketball player Willie Sims experienced earlier in the book (Chapter 2) at the hands of his coach. While this level of self-policing in Kiwi society seems harsh, many still seem to wear their deputy badge as if guarding their culture against extreme individualism was their top priority.

On the global front, how does *Australia* cope with its newfound success embodied in sporting individuals? A common sociological notation in conversations with locals is that New Zealand draws its national psyche from a close association with England while Australia draws its behavior patterns from close ties with the United States. Might this lead to different responses to social success?

African American Arrogance: Afterthought

For years I've witnessed Kiwis struggle with compliments, rail against American egos, and chastise anyone who thinks they are a big shot. Not only did I slowly come to understand this side of New Zealand, I began doing the same thing. I stopped being arrogant. I actually gained a deep sense of humility. Fourteen years abroad can do that.

I recall coming home in 2001 for a sabbatical and enjoying my time at an Oakland Raider tailgate party at the coliseum. Kids ran around tossing footballs and eating tri-tip sandwiches and playing with their Pokémon cards. One little friend of my nephew came up and said, "Wow, Tony told me you are professor! How long have you been a professor?"

My answer was telling. I said, "Oh, it's no big deal. I'm just an everyday guy." I was showing my best New Zealand humility after five years. I was good.

He then said, "How long did it take you to become a professor?"

I told the 6th grader, "Just a few years. Now give me that football—I want you to go deep." I was a successful Kiwi, an official citizen, and I no longer held my Ph.D. as a big deal. I had grown my sense of humility and shrunk my ego. This is the way everybody should be, I thought. If we as a people could just not brag about any and everything, but instead keep working, we'd be fine. We'd be accepted. We'd truly be free. White people would like us.

Then it hit me. Hard.

I'm a Black man who grew up in a very tough city, attended a violent Jr. High and High school, and continually made serious adjustments in all-White environments where I was perceived as a 'Black threat' to everyday life.

Police? Yes, I've had my run-ins with police. Two police officers chased me on foot while another pursued me in a car—sure that I was the one who had committed a heinous crime. Luckily, a sista let me ride in her car to get away. I was an innocent boy simply returning to my sister's house after my job in Eastmont Mall selling Kinney Shoes. That was in the 1970s. In the 1980s, UC Davis police strip-searched my visiting Kappa brothers and me at gunpoint as we "looked just like six black guys who robbed the 7–11 last week." I was tossed in a patrol car in Cleveland for dealing drugs; in reality, I was selling family bibles and children's books for Southwestern Book Company during one of my college summers. I had police in Madison, Wisconsin, break into my apartment for fear I was a mass-murderer. Seems the chicken fat I left in the sink festered. Reminded the landlord of the smell from Jeffrey Dahmer's apartment in nearby Milwaukee when he had carved up bodies to later be eaten. I've had a personal relationship with being policed, like many other Black men. Who was I to pretend that my road to success was simple and ho-hum?

Then and there in that Oakland Coliseum parking lot it was not my burden to be humble and self-deprecating and pretend that what I had achieved by fighting for a Ph.D. was nothing short of an urban miracle.

It was my job as a Black man of somewhat dubious talent to let that young brotha know that I was "somebody," and that whatever adversity he might face, he's got "somebody" in him too, even though at the time he was just a little Pokémon boy eating Oreo cookies while ribs billowed smoke from a Weber behind him at a tailgate party.

I called him back after the long pass, leaned down, put my hand on his shoulder, and said, dead in his eyes, "Listen, Pokémon, it took me a long time to become a professor, but it was fun. Tough, but fun. And now it feels great when my students call me 'Professor Andrews' or 'Doctor Andrews', or better yet, 'Doctor V.' I attended Chico State not too far from here, then got a Ph.D. from a snowy school called Wisconsin, and I just flew in from my new home in a far-away place with a lot of White people and Hobbits, called New Zealand. And you know what? You can too." I continued.

"You can become a doctor or a lawyer or an entrepreneur. You can start your own business or become a great bus driver like your father. You can pretty much be anything you want—just like me. Because you are from Oakland, just like me. We're bad, young blood! So whatever it is you want to do, you can; because now you know somebody who looks just like you, and who used to hang out at the Oakland Coliseum at twelve years old just like you, who has made it."

That was it. That was my end-zone dance. I sent him deep again— accidentally towards the port-a-potties. My bad.

In most social situations a Black professor has to tread lightly regarding his or her background. But there are times when we have to be forceful and strong and an example for young women and men who might need a word of encouragement. Or vision. To not do so because of someone else's overarching custom of humility is to kick the ladder, so to speak, after we have climbed to the top. Nobody gets to the top of the academic or any other institutional mountain by himself or herself. If a young person asks about my status, who am I to hide? What kind of example is that? Why should I feel shame?

I caution students of race or culture or sport who might see the occasional bit of arrogance or ego or performance, that there are multiple meanings present—and multiple audiences. Most fans don't need to feel good about themselves by virtue of the play on the field or in the parking lot, but others, like the kid, do need a push in the right direction. In this sense, my time out of the USA in New Zealand over fourteen years gave me perspective.

My sojourn abroad helped me understand much better the White diaspora and their customs, practices, and attitudes. Not fully, but much more than I could ever learn roaming the countryside in the USA. A country steeped in the egalitarian ideal shows us how similar we are to each other here in the USA. We need to continually strive to be treated equally, but we are not all—nor should we be—the same. Further, whatever differences we have might pale in comparison to how different we are from our overseas neighbors. Kiwis have their own system, which is evolving, and works for them.

We can criticize them from our high horse, but we have no deep understanding of their cultural heritage and all the idiosyncrasies that have forged their way of life. In a similar sense, when Kiwis criticize the USA (mostly White people, thankfully. Black people got a "pass") they do so from a much more knowledgeable position, given they've watched our television shows, our movies and listened to our music and our global politicians since the 1960s. And still, they mostly know the U.S. from afar.

And that arrogance I used to have? I've got it back. But I see it now for what it is: A useful verbal tool of humor between Black men to joke about our fragile status (using ego ironically), a useful shield to deflect racism—and the occasional stink-eye—from those who disdain or fear us, and a dam to hold back the tears many of us want to cry but can't, as we are, after all, hyper-masculine. Pain of all sorts is what gives birth to our Black arrogance. And if used strategically, an occasional dose of positive self-worth can go a long way.

And, lest we forget, we live in an American society that is steeped in self-promotion. Athletes are encouraged to get Twitter accounts, as are journalists and Hollywood superstars. We talk about ourselves on Facebook and take "selfies" to show we are indeed having fun. We take pictures of our food, our babies, our pets and our loved ones. In the end, we have subconsciously done the dance of self-promotion of our distinct attitudes and our behaviors. It is no wonder, then, that athletes are moving with the flow of U.S. society.

Players want to separate themselves in some way from the guy in the helmet next to them. Athletes want to be individuals with distinct lives outside of the work they do, just like us. Self-promotion is hard for some of us, but for those of us with a three-to-four-year football career window, self-promotion might be vital for future survival outside of sport.

The White athletes in the previous two chapters may be a stark contrast to the lives of the Black athletes in earlier chapters—mostly to do with neighborhoods, parents, and coaches—but how we can mix on a team like Wisconsin (and many other teams) and work together in unison seems now to me not such a miracle at all.

I adore New Zealand culture and customs but adjusting was difficult at times. In Christchurch, I danced with two left feet.

Familiarity with American customs, however sharply White rural culture may contrast with my own Oakland background, is a challenge I welcome. The American dance of cultural difference is familiar to me. Dancing with Whiteness in the USA, though at times rocky and frustrating, is a dance I can do. Not always successfully, but at least I know many of the steps.

Notes

1. Feather, 1989, p. 265n; Feather, 1993, p. 67n.
2. For the record, the bitterest pro rivalry in U.S. sport is the Raiders vs. Forty-Niners, partially owing to the historical success of both teams. At one point in the rivalry, coach Bill Walsh instructed his wife to no longer attend Raider-Forty Niner games. There have been stabbings, brawls, and shootings at these occasions. Even in preseason games! Lord help us all if they ever meet in the Super Bowl.
3. I originally wrote this paragraph in 2015. Of course, the Cubs won the World Series in 2016. Apocalypse averted.
4. Myrdal, G. 1944, p. lxxi.
5. Please see Feather, 1989, 1991, 1993.
6. Feather, 1991, p. 121.
7. Feather, 1993, p. 67.
8. Ibid., p. 66.
9. Ibid., p. 73.
10. Whiting, 1989.
11. Ibid., p. 66.
12. These generalities should in no way imply an essentialized view of either Japanese or U.S. society. Many citizens in each country stray far from the norm—often out of spite for the norm. Whiting, in my view, is presenting a "gestalt" of the normative operating value system.
13. Feather, 1993, p. 66.
14. The Christchurch Press, 1999.
15. North & South magazine, 1998, p. 37.

16. Ibid, p. 33–37.
17. *The Listener*, 1997, p. 7.
18. MacDonald, 1997, p. 7.
19. Myers, V. 1986. *Head and Shoulders: Successful New Zealand Women Talk to Virginia Myers*. Auckland: Penguin Books, p. 38.
20. Please see Philips, 1980; Bunkle and Hughes, 1980; James and Saville-Smith, 1989.
21. Myers, 1986, p. 209.
22. Ibid., p. 210.
23. Baker, in Stratford, 1988, p. 16.
24. Alexander, personal conversation, 1998.
25. Anna Simcic, NZ Olympic Swimmer, personal conversation.
26. See Andrews (1997) for a discussion of the importance athletes put on consistency of behavior on and off the field and the desire to not appear "out of synch" with their "true" personalities by being too expressive during sport.
27. Simcic mentions two male tall poppy athletes who have, on occasion, been severely chopped down. One is fellow swimmer, Danyon Loader, the athlete Aotearoa New Zealanders love to hate. He is also the most successful athlete in ANZ Olympic history, winning two gold medals at Atlanta in 1996. Loader has a long ponytail and a goatee, which is cause for scorn and ridicule for some who say "what a girl, what ugly hair and goatee" (line 3937). Simcic knows him as a friend whom she understands as an individual with "his own sort of brand mark" (line 3938). The second athlete is Andrew Mehrtens, who wore the #10 jersey for the Canterbury provincial and Super 12 Rugby teams and was the perennial first five-eighths for the All Blacks in the 1990s.

    She noted at one game the contradictory nature of New Zealand fans during one of Mehrtens' less-than stellar performances at Jade Stadium (formerly Lancaster Park) in Christchurch. Fans yelled all over the stadium "you're such a loser, you're overrated" (line 3089). But had he converted the kicks, she feels fans would have yelled, "You're a God!" As she notes, "they just love you and hate you in the same breath" (line 3089).
28. Mercer, K. 1987. "Black hair/style politics." *New Formations*, 3. Gray, H. 1995. *Watching Race: Television and the Struggle for Blackness*. Minneapolis: University of Minnesota Press.
29. A top cricketer for Aotearoa New Zealand's international team (The Black Caps) says people will often bad-mouth him in public, often in bars. He says they won't come up to him, but rather will stand within earshot and bad-mouth him and the team. He says he believes "all they want to do is discuss cricket with me, but will not allow themselves to come over and speak." I had seen that same cricketer at a movie theater seated on a sofa after a movie and I was about to approach him when the young man I was with commented, "leave him alone. He's just like everybody else."

This case points up a phenomena long understood and discussed around Aotearoa New Zealand, the idea (and ideal) of the "egalitarian society," noted earlier in the paper. This concept stems from the historical notion that all Aotearoa New Zealanders are somehow equal—or should be. The notion is that no one person is necessarily better than another, regardless of accomplishment. And that one reason people "cut" each other down to size is because, well, the "tall poppy" was sticking out, and the natural order of things is to be equal. In the case of the cricketer in the theater, I believe the idea was to "treat him like everybody else," a variation of the egalitarian ethic and, I believe, a problematic but more positive response in this specific scenario.Kochman, T., 1981.

10 Fans, Celebrations, and NCAA Rules

What on earth do *fans* think about athlete expression and celebration? This was the starting point for a study of fans and their tolerance for sports celebration. The late Herb Simons and I decided in 2001 to survey fans in the San Francisco-Oakland Bay Area about their attitudes. We confined our study to (1) student athletes in revenue-generating sports, (2) athletes in non-revenue generating sports, and (3) people who were not students or athletes.

We surveyed over 300 people. Below is a review of their open-ended responses to one specific question:

> In college football, excessive celebration, spiking, end-zone dances, and inciting the crowd are acts that are penalized by the NCAA. Do you think race plays a factor in the making and enforcement of these rules? Yes, or no? Please explain.

The answers yielded seven general themes: (1) African American culture is expressive, (2) the NCAA rules are all about control, (3) the NCAA rules tolerate White behavior, (4) everybody is expressive, (5) respectful celebration is fine, (6) rules are color blind, and (7) rules promote good sportsmanship.

I've broken down the answers into gender and racial groups so as to get a general frame for the differences in attitudes across those groups. To be sure, there are no simple answers to who thinks what—all groups varied in their responses. But the themes shine through in each response, giving us a feeling for tolerance levels of individuals in gendered/cultural groups. More than anything else, we get a solid working idea of how fans process information about race and culture and rules.

My comment at the start is that people varied widely in their responses—and all groups showed variety. Likely, quite a few of the responses will resonate with how your grandparents, your parents, and how you feel. You might even find that you agree with comments that you would not have agreed with before reading the whole list. Some answers are short, some long, some ambiguous, and some very Black and White about the goodness or badness of rules, rule-makers, or us—the survey makers.

Some people thought we were racist for even asking the question. For the sake of clarity, it is not racist to question how you feel about race, just like it isn't sexist to ask about women's rights in the workplace or homophobic (or anti-Christian) to discuss opinions about gay and lesbian marriage issues. We do need to come out of the closet about race and not hold back our feelings when asked, hoping of course that with race—and all other touchy social issues—we can be respected for our opinions, even if disagreed with.

And make no doubt, I disagree with many statements below. I also understand the sentiment behind some of the comments I disagree with. I've decided to include these comments because if I am lobbying for fans to be included in the discussion of rules in sport—because it is indeed the fan's sport—then I also need to include their comments in the larger argument I present in the book.

That said, you'll notice how different we are from each other. We might have a long way to go before we get some agreement on acceptable behavior on the sporting field. I thank each respondent for their willingness to put their true thoughts on paper. My hope is that you, the reader, appreciate the diversity of thought within and across groups.

I include the gender, race, and athletic affiliation of the respondents. This sample was collected in and around the Oakland-San Francisco Bay Area in 2001 and, though respondents come from all over the country, should not be taken as an accurate sample of U.S. thought on the matter. But you will get a strong idea across race, gender, and sport what people in the local area think and feel about celebratory expression, rules, and race—from Filipino to Middle Eastern to Pacific Islander to Korean—a huge cross-section. And sports as varied as lacrosse, rugby, football, and crew. This was fun.

> In college football, excessive celebration, spiking, end-zone dances, and inciting the crowd are acts that are penalized by the NCAA. Do you think race plays a factor in the making and enforcement of these rules? Yes, or no? Please explain.

Black Female Non Student-Athletes

#54. Yes. Race has something to do with celebration rules. These dances and forms of celebration were made famous by popular African American players. The large majority of people who do these dances are Black. I think the NCAA just make these rules to control, restrict, and make these athletes more "civilized" in their White minds. I know that race is a factor because for the most part dancing, which is mostly done by Blacks, is being ridiculed. But when a White quarterback, like Brett Favre, points to the opposing fans, he is simply "acknowledging success."

This is one of the longest answers—and from someone who has obviously thought about this issue. She has noticed, first, that African American male athletes do dance in the end-zone (or on the field of play) more than White athletes, and that these dances are "popular." She echoes what I've said in the text about the "civilizing" process of rules. She is careful to note that these acts are also ridiculed by, I am assuming, non-Blacks. Which means she is likely aware of the subtle ways in which announcers put down players. What I find most interesting about her statement is that she notices the contradiction of announcers who imply that White athlete expression is normal. She says, cynically, that White expressive athletes are let off the hook and not ridiculed. Her implication is that White athletes are part of the "norm" and that announcers have the power to determine who is civilized and who is not. She might suggest we listen more carefully to the words announcers use to describe both Black and White athlete behaviors.

#182. No. Race has nothing to do with celebration rules. It's just someone's way of showing excitement. If they were doing something disrespectful then they could get in trouble. People dance every day and don't get in trouble for it.

Subject #182 might be answering two questions. Her first answer says directly that race has nothing to do with celebration rules. She goes on to answer the question, "Why do people celebrate?" And finally, she comments that it is the disrespectful dancing—not dancing in and of itself—that is the cause of the trouble. And the rules. But yes, people do dance every day, and do not get into trouble. Especially in Black churches.

#377. No. Race has nothing to do with celebration rules. It is unsportsmanlike. The NCAA is still trying to teach these young men. This is an important part of being respectful of your opponents.

Who gets to teach? What are their qualifications to teach? Are they teaching us based upon some knowledge they have gained from education? Of course not. They were raised by their parents in their neighborhoods with their coaches telling them the way it should be done in the 1940s and 1950s (no disrespect to those decades. I was born then, too). Respect is a cultural concept that varies by individual. I don't respect people who talk during movies. I don't respect burger joints that serve me a sandwich that looks nothing like the photo on the billboard in the lobby. Most people would say these social crimes are insignificant. Respect is personal. So, while I am conscious that something is being taught by the league patriarchy, I think what most concerns rule-makers is that athletes behave like rule-makers want them to behave.

#217. Yes. Because I'm not racist. I am also Black. But it's often Blacks that dance around like that. We got "soul power"!

James Brown talked and sang about soul power. And while I can't quite define it, I know what #217 is talking about. There is a desire to express one's joy in the moment with an individual flourish that emanates from deep within. When the emotion is genuine. But sometimes, people just want to show off.

#353. Unsure. I'm unsure but it's definitely possible since African Americans are known for being rowdy. Perhaps they relate it to a street-gang mentality.

Say *what*? Let me clear my throat. As a Black female you are definitely aware of the stereotype of Black men as being rowdy and gang-inclined. But we have to confront two social realities alongside that awful stereotype. Gang life is confined to primarily urban pockets and represents a slither of African American male life. I'd guess that there were as many members of the Ku Klux Klan (KKK), neo-Nazi party, skinheads, and extreme gun-toting survivalists in the U.S. as there are members of Black gangs (I am guessing). And lest we forget the many bully police in U.S. history and crooked court systems. I'd classify all of the above as "rowdy," also. Your "unsure" comment speaks to the dilemma that referees have as they have to ask, "What the hell is that expression? Will this get out of hand?"

#61. Yes. African American culture encourages open expression and recognition of accomplishments. This follows many Black players onto the field, which can be negative to the sport.

You are right, #61, that African American culture does encourage open expression and recognition of accomplishments. But we both know that Whites generally don't understand—or accept—why we bring it to the field. And I do agree that this can sometimes be a negative to the sport. Most of the negative association comes from a misinterpretation of the actions as personally targeted, and as intended to demean an opponent. I recall selling books door-to-door during my college summers for Southwestern Book Company.

Once, in Cleveland, a woman slammed her door in my face. Hard. So hard the wind swept my hair back. I told my sad tale to my sales manager, hoping for sympathy. He said, "Vernon, here's the deal. Mrs. Jones [that's what we called all customers] doesn't dislike you. She dislikes the guy trying to sell her fifty-dollar family bibles at 9:30 in the morning while she is going through a divorce. It's not personal. She doesn't even know you." Wise words to get my butt back out into the sales field. In the NFL, receivers and cornerbacks know each other very well. But many players direct their joy to local fans or to the cameras. Sometimes, it isn't personal. It's a show for the fans.

#189. No. Everybody does it to get attention. I understand exactly what you mean. Everybody likes attention. Well, most of us. The lyrics from one of my favorite Pretenders song, *Brass in Pocket*, says it best about athletes who want to be noticed:

Got brass in pocket
Got bottle I'm gonna use it
Intention I feel inventive
Gonna make you, make you, make you notice

Got motion restrained emotion
Been driving Detroit leaning
No reason just seems so pleasing
Gonna make you, make you, make you notice

Gonna use my arms
Gonna use my legs
Gonna use my style
Gonna use my sidestep
Gonna use my fingers
Gonna use my, my, my imagination

'Cause I gonna make you see
There's nobody else here
No one like me
I'm special, so special
I gotta have some of your attention give it to me
Got rhythm I can't miss a beat
Got new skank it's so reet
Got something I'm winking at you
Gonna make you, make you, make you notice

Gonna use my arms
Gonna use my legs

Gonna use my style
Gonna use my sidestep
Gonna use ...

Thank you, Chrissie Hynde and the Pretenders, 1979. They understood the situation perfectly. I've listened to this song for many years not grasping the significance of the lyrics. Yes, this song is supposed to be about a waitress after a boy, but for me, it means much more. Attention. Expression. Individuality. Thank you, #189, for reminding me. (Songwriters: Christine Hynde and James Honeyman-Scott.)

#292. Yes. Black athletes tend to be the more flamboyant celebrators and those players tend to be the worst penalized.

Flamboyant celebrators. I think I like that. Rules committees don't like that.

#206. Yes. I don't know why but most of the team owners are White and most of the people dancing in the end-zone and other things like that are Black.

Let me see. Hmmm. Why are the team owners White and the players dancing, Black? I'll spare you the lecture on U.S. history, power, and control. But wouldn't it be fun to see the owner's pad-up and play a game where the players made up the rules? I'd pay for that. First rule: After scoring a touchdown, the old player must do the moonwalk. And then twerk. And then slam-dunk over the goal post. And do the Lambeau Leap into the crowded end-zone beer-soaked seats. Failure to comply with the rules will result in a fifteen-yard penalty and a fine of $10,000.

#208. Yes. Because they are happy they scored a touchdown and they show their joy by dancing.

When I am happy over anything in life, I am embarrassed to show my joy in public. That is from years of being around White people who shut me down. But recently, I've been less shy about my body and movement. But if I ever truly get my mojo back, I would likely shout like James Brown and (attempt to) dance like Michael Jackson. Just go buck-wild and get happy. Joy is whatever comes out of me at that moment—like an exclamation mark.

#207. Yes. I think it does. Because a long time ago Blacks couldn't even play sports. That all changed with Jackie Robinson. Blacks started playing on sports teams.

Before baseball allowed Blacks to play, the Negro leagues were venues where athletes put on a show to gain crowds. They'd have fun and acknowledge the crowd as part of the fun. Not quite as much as the Harlem Globetrotters, but you get the general idea. Just like amateur athletes organizing and playing baseball for the fun and enjoyment of it all. Which sometimes makes me wonder aloud about our style in White contexts, and if sport in America would be more fun for White fans if Black players were suddenly not allowed to play. I sometimes get the feeling many people prefer we would have never set foot on the field of dreams. And that's about the time I hear a White person say something crazy like, I prefer cities with more diversity—this town is too White. How crazy-beautiful is that?

#46. Yes. Race plays a factor in making and reinforcing all rules, in my opinion.

I think #46 is on to something. Race decides how rules are made and how rules are reinforced. That allows for some flexibility by those who make the rules to sometimes show lenience for players (or anyone in society) who break the rules. If race is a factor, like #46 believes, then race plays a role in who is penalized. While I do not completely agree that Whites get off the hook most of the time by rule-makers, we are forced to ask, "Is the entire process of making rules and enforcing rules fair and equitable?"

#323. Yes. In society race is still an issue and will be forever, but the minorities are more looked down upon for showing excitement during sporting events.

Okay. Got it, #323. But don't you think "forever" is a long time? If you are right, and race will be with us for many years, there might be a time in the future when *Blacks* get to make the rules. These rules would be far beyond what I hinted at above with the owners in the end-zone after touchdowns. I mean *all* the rules in society. Whites can understand their total racial domination more vividly by way of example. For ten years, allow Black folks to be in charge of all street naming. And road designs. And airport parking lots. And the faces on money. And allowable gashouse emissions from U.S. industrial companies. Just like White people are now. (Note to self: Make sure that if this dream is ever a part of a reparations package that we have token Whites on boards and commissions [who agree with us] so as not to appear too self-serving. Just like NCAA and NFL committees often do.)

White Female Student-Athlete

#263. Yes. Lacrosse. Arguably race is a factor in the rules governing college football. The NCAA is an organization headed up predominantly by White individuals while those football players who have the opportunity or play the position to show excessive celebration are of different races (Black). Perhaps the rules are not enforced/made due to race, but it just happens to work out that way. Conversely, though quarterbacks who are predominately White seem to get penalized less for exciting the crowd.

I want to thank the parents and teachers of #263 for making her conscious of the many subtleties of race, sport, and social power-relations. I want to encourage students on both sides of the cultural divide to use words like "arguably," "perhaps," and "seems." Though I sometimes get a bit fired-up, I too believe in a balanced approach when it comes to race issues. Well, not always.

#124. No. Volleyball. Race? Who said anything about race? I think they are pretty fair. It is for sure not a racial issue.

I said something about race, #124. My bad. As they say in America, if you smelt it—you dealt it. This never would have been a race issue but for me bringing it up. This is not about race, right? Many note that the rules are really about sportsmanship. Or politeness. Or team. Or respect. Race has nothing to do with it. Like sitting at a Woolworth's counter and eating lunch in the pre-1964 South. It's wasn't a matter of race. It was only a matter of decency. And respect. And separation. And social norms. No harm or racism intended, but people should just have known their place. Things were separate and equal, but otherwise pretty fair. Amen.

#71. No. White. Tennis. I think it goes along with what your coach allows. If you have a coach who will not tolerate that behavior, then it will not happen. But they must respect the coach.

For many athletes, coaches are God-like father figures—respected at all costs. For others of us who suffered with alcoholic coaches who didn't know squat about the game, we tolerated our coach but had little respect for him. Coaches, when good, consider their athletes and work in unison with players to create a team culture. One of my students at San Jose State had a father who coached for many years at a school with a proud heritage and great team culture: De La Salle. They just made a movie about Coach Bob Ladouceur, titled, *When the Game Stands Tall.*

#77. No. White. Tennis. I think this rule is enforced to keep the players' heads in the game and to always stay focused and humble.

I certainly agree with part of this statement. I think the reason for the rules are different from the goals of teams to keep players' heads in the game, to keep them focused on their assignments, and to keep them humble. These are all rules I abide by when I play sport or write an academic article for publication. I separate these rules from how I later celebrate once the task is complete. But as we all know, a touchdown in the first quarter does not a victory make. There is still much game left to play and players do fall prey to early-success syndrome—thinking the game is over when they do something great early in a contest. I respect athletes who make the next catch like it means the Super Bowl championship.

Stay focused. Keep your head in the game. Humility is a personal choice and an internal state that does not always coincide with what one displays publicly.

#81. Yes. Pacific Islander. Cross-country & Track. Yes, I think race plays a factor in making and enforcement of these rules. The majority that dances (and practically every time I see an athlete dance in football) are African Americans. Race plays a factor because African American are stereotyped to know how to dance well, perform in front of crowds, etc. This stereotype is followed by most African American athletes to show that they are "manly."

Let's skip ahead to the "manly" part of #81's discussion. I have to agree, when growing up in Oakland, knowing how to dance well was considered manly. Like being good at comedy, dressing well, achieving in sport, or wearing the perfect "afro" hairstyle. I'll own that one. So maybe this is akin to being in control of one's local environment. Lord knows we had control over little else. So maybe Black men search for shows of powerful masculinity in ways we are barely aware of. Not everybody, but maybe those who do express flamboyantly might be seeking to externalize manliness. Or maybe, like #217 said above, it's soul power.

#79. No. White. Track & Field. Anyone who breaks the rules, no matter who they are, should be penalized.

The rules are, after all, objective. Which means no race of men or women should have any affirmative action "pass" card that allows them to behave like disrespectful citizens only out to showboat and make fools of themselves. We are all equal, and the rules are all equally enforced. And anyone who thinks these rules were not made with complete objectivity—and with no racial influence—must be racist himself. America would never make a rule that advantaged one group and disadvantaged another. Now shut up and play. And quit whining—or I'll give you something to whine about.

#111. Yes. Hispanic. Track & Field. Because majority of NCAA administrators are White, and the rules are based on the "White" ways that have been set.

Let's hope that, on occasion, rules can be "re-set."

#298. No. Mexican American. Soccer. If a player scores a touchdown or makes a good play they should be allowed to celebrate for a minute and not be penalized.

Okay. Here's a change. An athlete who thinks celebrations are okay as long as we set some parameters on the process. This might be the way forward. Not that anyone has ever done a one-minute dance, but I get the point. Set some parameters, some agreed-up boundaries, and see where that takes us.

#293. No. Caucasian. Soccer. Maybe Whites in authority see this celebration as more of instigation and aggression when Black people do it and they wish to control it … then again maybe not.

Yes! Good, #293! Instigation and aggression is one consistently occurring interpretation of Black expression. May not be what the penalized athlete had in mind, but I can see this clearly. Throwing at a batter following the player who hit the home run can be considered instigation and aggression by a pitcher. Which obviously should be banned, also. Right? Then again, maybe not. Maybe aggression is condoned as more of the American way. Except when aggression involves Black men. I think that's why pro hockey allows fighting and pro basketball doesn't.

#275. No. Caucasian. Soccer. No response. I can't check either of them. It seems like the only people ever being shown for these acts are of color but that is the media's fault. White people do it as much as Blacks, it just seems Blacks get the credit more.

"Get the credit more ..." and get the penalties more. Ever think the media might be giving us what we want ... or reinforcing what we already believe to be true?

#342. Yes. White. Crew. It would appear from watching TV the majority of players that do end-zone celebrations are Black and they are trying to stop them from expressing individuality.

Expressing individuality is the key. I like when players celebrate with their teammates. On occasion, I like when teammates egg a player on to do his individual expression. Individuality in a team context should not appear like a foreign language.

#104. Yes. White/Caucasian. Crew. I don't think the decision is directly based on race but I think race is involved unconsciously.

Brilliant. I am fine with cutting rule-makers some slack here. They may not be consciously making rules that target Black athletes at all. I looked back on my own dating life and noticed I was not consciously targeting lighter-skinned Black women to date, but that was the result. I was unconsciously choosing women who looked like my sisters, my mother, and my aunts and cousins. Once conscious of this strange habit, I was able to choose—with knowledge of my own biases—*who* I wanted to be with rather than *who my history* was choosing for me. Informed and history-conscious decision-making is the way forward for committees of all types, African American committees, included.

#120. No Response. White. Crew. Depends on the player and referee. Race might play a role in it. Black people usually show off more, so maybe refs say, "Oh, that is okay," because he is Black. But if a White person does it, it's wrong.

Nice twist, #120. I agree that referees might cut some slack for Black athletes but monitor White athletes even more and penalize based on some idea of their "natural" parameters. Very novel. And at the micro-level, a Black referee equally could penalize a Black player out of cultural cringe much more so than a White athlete who "barely scratches the surface" with his butt shaking. As much as my analysis is group-level and at times overarching, I am aware that each decision must be made with the game context in mind. And each referee calls upon a different interpretation of the rules and possibly his own background when deciding.

White/Other Female Non-Collegiate

#24. Yes. Filipino. Most displays of emotions by African Americans are viewed as bragging, etc. When White athletes do it, it is them "just having fun," for example, Brett Favre trash talks, dances, fights, etc., and announcers always just say—he is "having fun" or "loves the game." When Black athletes celebrated you always hear the announcer say, "there's no place for this in the game."

Brett Favre was a top quarterback when this survey was administered in 2001. We loved Favre, so this is not intended as a knock on him. Black athletes loved Favre, also. He was a bit of a southern hillbilly from Mississippi whose emotions ran high into the Green Bay Packer sky. Announcers raved about his enthusiasm and passion for the game. He was the ultimate team player who, as the scholar notes above, "loved the game." I wish announcers said that about other non-Favre athletes who get the "no place for this in the game" backlash. They deserve better.

#15. Yes. Asian. I think it's considered "black" to do these things, but I think everyone should. Ultimately, sports are mock battles. Historically, celebrations, taunting ... have been a part of most battles between people and people (not machines and people).

Know your history, people. She's right. Sport has been used as a way to train the military since Rome and Sparta. Further, "taunting" before a battle is as old as Homer's legendary Achilles circling Troy, yelling, "Hector!" (Heckling, as it were). Lest we forget, the Aotearoa New Zealand Maori used to perform the Haka before war—and still perform the Haka before contemporary All Black international rugby matches. War and sport—interlocked. Baseball and football players still put on "eye-black" to intimidate the opposition by appearing a bit more menacing.

#137. Yes. Lithuanian-Irish/Jewish-Catholic/White. In a grossly stereotypical sense, Black athletes are more exteriorly emotional, less stoic. These penalties are biased on racial/social values of stoic White people who seem as though they don't feel human emotion.

Given this book's topic, I'll have to own the grossly stereotypical emotional exteriors you speak of, #137. I do attempt to moderate those stereotypes by showing various backgrounds and players who see expression in very different ways. But yes, our strong suit is not stoicism. But your commentary on your own culture is fascinating—that stoic White people seem as though they don't feel human emotion. Maybe emotion has been trained out of White athletes, Brett Favre and friends being the exception. Or maybe they channel it into aggression on the field or find some other way to express. Or maybe they follow the dictum: "There is a time and a place for everything."

#87. No. Mexican. I don't think so. I feel they implement these rules in order to maintain order. Otherwise it could get out of hand.

I'm glad someone finally said it: Things could "get out of hand." I can recall numerous scenes in supermarkets, department stores, and coffee shops where I watched White parents let their kids run roughshod and throw tantrums while we all watched in horror at the casual attitude of the parents who seemed to be saying, "So what, my kid is just being a kid, get over it." I always thought, "If I ever tried anything like that, my mother would slap me into next Thursday." Blacks parents maintain order in kids' lives early on, and once grown, young adults express as they see fit. Whites seem to have zero control over kids socially at a young age but enforce strict norms once young adults hit society. So, it would seem, that Whites don't mind a little social expression. And that Blacks, at an early age, learn that social expression is punished. I don't know quite what to make of all this, but I've wanted to point out this irony. This does not represent any sociology on my part whatsoever, and you can take me to task by reminding me that your White parents did have strict control over your behavior in public and that your Black parents let you yell and run loose through Sears and J.C. Penny. My only take-away from these observations is my feeling that Whites "own" society, so they get to determine when, and where, and for how long kids and adults can socially express themselves.

#91. Yes. Asian American. Simple, discrimination, and there's nothing else to it.

Simple discrimination by the NCAA and NFL rule-makers, I'll assume, and not the referees. I understand that referees are merely attempting to enforce the rules, though they, too, can fall prey to personal bias. Oh, I forgot—referees and umpires are balanced and fair. Thank you, New Zealand.

#95. No. Chinese. Race alone doesn't. However, those who grow up in cultures that praise this kind of showing off are more likely to do this.

Simply said, simply understood. "Praise" is an interesting word choice, suggesting not only religious devotion, but also Black social agreement.

#177. Yes and no. Australian. Yes, since the NCAA is discriminatory. No, since these days anything can be interpreted as racist to some race.

All right, I accept the challenge. While it is true that "anything is racist" is a stretch, I do think that "nothing is racist" is also a stretch. We are left to interrogate each individual act, each law, each police incident, and each court case on its own merits. I have attempted to make a case about discriminatory practices by the NCAA and NFL regarding celebration rules. And I've also pointed out that there are times when Blacks get it wrong about discrimination. I certainly have in my own life. It thus begs the question, when Whites say, "This isn't racist at all—it applies to everyone," can they be wrong? Of course they can. If critics want to, they can forever say, "Just because a flesh-colored Band-Aid doesn't fit your skin-color, that doesn't make it discriminatory or racist." Right. Sometimes a Band-Aid is just a Band-Aid. I'm suggesting that we be more inclusive, such that the committee to determine "flesh-colored" is a little more varied in its flesh representation. The flesh-color of football players has changed since the 1940s.

#179. Yes. Asian. I think most of the excessive celebration and spiking and end-zone dances come from mostly Blacks; however, they are also some White players also doing this kind of acts. I think it is more a celebration than showing off.

Celebration vs. showing-off? Good call on the differences, #179. These are distinctions that need further debate on flesh-colored committees.

Black Male College Football Student-Athletes

#332. No. I don't think race has anything to do with this. Any race would break a rule, but I don't think they should have a certain rule for dancing in the end-zone. I think they should have younger guys make the rules now days.

Are we ready to turn the reins of society over to youth? Are we ready to reduce the rule-making committee's average age from (I'm guessing) eighty-five to, say, fifty? Forty years old? Of course not. You are a crazed young man, #332, for thinking power wants to be inclusive and democratic. (But I love your idea.)

#334. Maybe. Only because all the players are Black, and the Man is White.

Well, it is obvious that #334 was sitting close to #332 at the local Black Panther meeting. I haven't heard mention of "The Man" in many years. Maybe because I'm a part of the system and not in touch with everyday Black life. But you are right. The players are Black. And The Man is flesh-colored. Here's hoping "The Man" is a bit more in touch with society than he was in the 1960s.

#341. Yes. Blacks dance, Whites don't.

Insert your own fun experience with White males dancing here __________. In my experience, I'd say Blacks dance more than Whites, but that Whites do give it a try. And some, many, succeed at dancing with a sense of rhythm and conviction. While I, on the other hand, am convinced that my recycled dance styles from the 1970s and 1980s are as Black as ever. In truth, I dance with conviction, which is the only move I've got left on the dance floor. Bust a move, White guy.

#252. Yes. More African American males are prone to excessive celebration. By nature, us African Americans enjoy boasting and showing our greatness when we do something well.

This brotha owns it. He's not backing down. He's calling it what it is. His experience and brashness is what we might be trying to squash in sport. Lord knows, we've squashed #252's positive attitude about any achievement down through history and in nearly every sector of institutionalized society. Maybe we own him one place to boast about his greatness: Sport.

Black Male Non Student-Athlete

#265. Yes. I think they want to control emotion and outbursts, which are what African American athletes do. It is to control them and their emotions. It is said that it is about discipline, but it is about control.

This is a political statement. The young brotha thinks Black bodies are a site for control. "Discipline" is the overall catchword he feels is used to justify the social/sporting control, but he doesn't waiver about what he feels is the true heart of the matter. To take back some middle ground, I'd say the issue might center on both discipline and control. And in addition, punishment.

#50. Yes. Race always plays a factor in America: School, sport, higher education, and entertainment. Whites have slowly made fun of or tried to stop the expressions of Black people.

Well, not always. Many Whites have fought the good fight over the years, whether promoting Black entertainers or bringing African Americans into sport. And many White professors and public figures, especially, teach in a way that breaks down the barriers of privilege and power dynamics in society, whether focusing on race or gender, sexuality, the differently abled, or economic barriers to social success. I've noted two of my favorites, Joe Feagin and Tim Wise. But many, many other Whites lead us forward and deserve "props" for going against the grain of their own privilege. Oh, I'm sorry, you were probably talking about The Man, not the ninety-nine percent of those Whites who lack power and ultimate authority. My bad. Keep representing, White and non-White professors of change.

#36. No. Just old men trying to keep the focus on the game, but I think celebrations help motivate the crowd. The crowd comes to be entertained, so let the athletes give them a show.

We have been presented, above, with a key distinction that separates how many of us view sport: Is it a job, or is it entertainment? Is it work, or is it a childhood game played by grown-ups? Is it a path for your family out of poverty, or a way to show your deep humility in the face of your family's historical success? How we view the purpose of amateur and professional determines much of how we feel about people's behavior in sport. For #36, sport represents entertainment. We all notice pregame television commercials exploiting expressive athletes to hype up sporting contests. Our #36 simply says, give the crowd what they want—entertainment. Give 'em a show!

#53. Yes. It depends. I am going to go on limb and say that most of the people (showboating) in football [are black]. I know its sensationalism, but still. I think the NCAA football wants football to go back to how it used to be, which was predominately White.

I am inclined to agree and disagree with your last line, #53. I think the NCAA has no issue with Black athletes, per se, but you are right in thinking they want to go back to a day when White behavioral norms ruled the day. I think if Black players behaved exactly like Whites, we might not have a problem. This might seem to contradict much of what I have said in this book. But I believe much of what ills U.S. society is the crush of people who say, "Things should be the way *we* want them to be." So it is no small statement to say that the NCAA wants things to be just like they used to be—in terms of expression. The NCAA likely enjoys the diversity they now exploit. The shame is in saying, "We love you as athletes, but we don't respect you as people. Keep running and catching, but your *culture* has no place in our sport. Learn *our* cultural ways and behave like we say, and everything will be just fine." Just like it used to be.

White/Other Male Non-Revenue Athletes

#70. Yes/No. Baseball. Because rules are enforced on everyone. But I'm sure people of different races like to show other races their success.

Some of us do and some of us don't like to show others our success. We need rules, #70. And we need a few funkier seats at the buffet table when we sit down to decide the range of ways we can show success in sports. What if James Brown were on the committee? What if Nelson Mandela were to join James—and Beyoncé—on the celebration rules committee? To keep it real, let's add a generational twist to the committee by adding Honey Boo Boo Child. I think she'd add some flavor. She has no problem showing other races her success.

#287. Yes. Crew. I think race does play a factor in these decisions, because the majority of athletes who play football are Black. Because of this, Black athletes can be stereotyped as selfish and individualistic. So this can have an influence on decisions made regarding excessive celebration.

When you frame it that way, celebration rules make sense. Nobody wants to look at selfish and individualistic athletes on Saturday and Sunday, right? Especially Black people, who should be reveling in the chance to show they are ready to be full U.S. citizens by acting right and showing some humility. Maybe this line of thinking influences the decisions you speak of, #287. I've said elsewhere in this book that I think over the past 300 years you'd be hard-pressed to find a more humble, hardworking, unselfish, patient, peaceful group of people in the Western World than African Americans. Think of the amount of slavery deaths, sun-up-to-sun-down working in cotton fields, the rampant rape of Black women by slave owners, social abuse and humiliation pre- and post- Civil War, Jim Crow lynching's, police brutality, backwoods court decisions, no voting rights, and failed social plans for full integration, and we see how African American culture could easily be reframed as "unselfish" and working harder (no wages) for America than any other group.

Starting the clock at 1965 and judging Black people from then onward is a historical flaw that taints Black contributions and denies our uniqueness in the social arena. Call us other names, but not selfish—unless you remember we helped make this country great—at a huge wage discount. And don't call us individualistic—unless you include the couple hundred years when we weren't allowed to be individuals in this society. Nice work, #287.

#276. Yes. American. Crew. I think race always plays a factor when people make any set of rules. Unfortunately, people aren't always forward and honest about it.

They can't be honest about it. Companies, universities, the federal government, and sports teams must always appear to be "encouraging diversity." They don't have to actually *do* anything. The *appearance* of equality and valuing difference is what we look for and respect. Ever hear of a company saying, "We don't honor diversity and equality"? Of course not. That's like not brushing your teeth before a big date. But just because you brush your teeth doesn't mean your teeth are healthy. There are certain things we have to do to keep up appearances. And if there is anything Americans do well, it is pretend that all is well. It was easier to be honest about matters of race and culture and behavior pre-1965, when there was no social harm in being frank about hatred or dislike or movement away from "the way things should be." My Black friends tell me it is easier to live in the South in 2014 because at least you know where you stand with Whites. In the North (as within many institutions), you never know. Good point, #276, about the lack of honesty inherent in how we discuss our social rules.

#83. Yes. Korean. Golf. With governing body in sports which is predominately White, the board members or committee persons who establish the rules and regulations of the game have a cultural background that caters toward White society. On the other hand, Black athletes share their culture via their behaviors during sporting events, such as football and basketball.

Even Korean golfers know what time it is. He even highlights the sports where most Black expression is evident—in football and basketball.

#114. No. Mexican. Swimming. The players are penalized regardless of race. It is to keep the game under control and moving smoothly.

I think the game would move more smoothly with a few less beer, truck, and mobile phone commercials.

#291. Yes. Tennis. The White power structure represses the darker in sports through rules and regulations.

I think #291 is just playing with me. Why don't I give a different take on the matter. I think Whites *want* to express themselves more and want to be more expansive with their rules. But their history—forefathers, parents, and White social norms—just won't allow them to loosen up. Slowly but surely, they are, though. Even elderly White gentlemen are now "fist-bumping" and high-fiving each other. Put on a Michael Jackson hit song and they move about in their chairs, ready to break loose. Physical movement and the power to express our emotions with dance and gestures and noise of all sorts has been siphoned out of many Whites (and Blacks like me) to the point where any movement and show of emotion seems foreign, like the language of children. But deep inside we all want the freedom to bust loose like nobody's business. Let Black folks (or South Americans) teach you. Ask somebody. Give up the repression, uptight rules, and celebration regulations, and gain your emotional and expressive freedom. Let us lead the way.

#297. No. Track & field. Everyone has emotions and shows them in sports. Definitely not.

I agree that everyone has emotions—but many don't show them in sport. What we tend to condone as "acceptable" is the emotion of anger and aggression.

America is obsessed with anger and aggression in many arenas, but especially sport. The extremes of anger and aggression are a subtext to contemporary discussions of MMA fighting, boxing, professional football and concussions, race-car drivers and fighting, and the aggressive use of vehicles as weapons. Just ask Tony Stewart.

#86. Yes. Track and field. I think that the small powers of the NCAA enforce rules. Old White, tradition men won't change or compromise with any new trend because they think it is corrupting the game. I think that players can't corrupt a game, because a game is always going to be a game.

I want to side with NFL and NCAA managers and committee members. Most, if not all members see themselves as stewards of the games they oversee. They consider themselves in charge of ensuring the continuity over the years, and that the games they represent stay healthy and vibrant. There is a natural, conservative wall they put up when change appears too radical. They don't know how to justify rules that go against their upbringing and socialization. It is my hope they read this book with an open mind toward the future generations who might admire a game endowed to them that is full of inclusion, diversity, and flexibility. After all, in the neighborhood games we play in America, we all have a say.

Conclusion

"White Noise: A constant background noise; especially one that drowns out other sounds." Merriam Webster dictionary.

I have become a victim of my own socialization. I was raised on a steady diet of James Brown, Muhammad Ali, and Richard Pryor. Because these figures were bigger than life, they became the buffet table I ate from for nourishment. There were always enough African American legends to metaphorically dine out with, including Maya Angelou, Marvin Gaye, Willie Mays, Aretha Franklin, Michael Jackson, Michael Jordon, and Magic Johnson. In my later years I've had brunch with Jackie Joyner-Kersey, and Venus and Serena Williams, wondering how they win with grace, and poise, and style.

I am a victim of being raised to revere these individuals as larger than life—as transcendent—as far better than I was, or ever would be. But I always knew there was a kinship through blood that united us, somehow, someway, back to the same slave ship sea-of-bones trail from Africa to the USA. These superstars were mine. My main goal was to try, on occasion, to mimic them and their dancing, singing, joke telling, or sports playing. I was struggling to be bigger than life, like them. If I could just bust that James Brown move, I could touch a bit of their glory. What a wonderful fantasy. When your neighborhood isn't teaming with role models and mentors, you have to make up your own fantasies about behavior that will get you to the top.

My older siblings, cousins, and neighborhood kids in the 1960s and 1970s always learned the latest moves way before I did and were cooler at everything, including sport. They, too, wanted to be cool—that was our highest possible achievement—being called cool. That protected us from bullies, got us in good favor with girls (and boys, for the girls), and got us chosen for sports teams. "Pick him—he's cool." That's how it worked. If you were cool and talented, then you had nearly everything. If you were cool, talented, and good-looking, well, you were nearly home with the trophy. But if you had all seven tools—coolness, talent, good looks, dancing ability, could play the dozens and keep people laughing, could fight, and, finally, had individual flair, a signature move, or whatever gesture that made you unique—then you had it all—the Ph.D. of the ghetto.

Now you have to understand that most of us didn't have *any* of the first six tools. But we could all make a heartfelt attempt at number seven—individual flair. That's the only one not predetermined by God, or so we thought. That's the one thing we practice and do. Not only in sport, but individuality in clothing, or how we walked, the slang we used, or how stylish we wore our hair. We did anything we could to *stand out* or be noticed as unique—since we weren't moving on up anywhere, like the Jefferson's, anytime soon. I never dreamed of a future. It was live for the day in Oakland—hope to *last* for a future.

So, I do apologize for my upbringing that likely has little in common with other African Americans, save for those around me. But if I look closely at the NFL and squint my eyes, I can imagine that a few NFL athletes who perform and entertain and celebrate and express individuality know the taste of local flavor, of chocolate Sundays in neighborhoods or churches.

There is a resonance I feel when great Black athletes perform well, male or female. I had a great resonance for the African American women who performed the luge at the winter Olympics in 2014 in Russia. When they excel—and look good doing it—I experience the same reflected glory Whites feel when Team USA wins a winter Olympic gold medal.

I am attached to a cultural history that is bigger than the game or me. It is kinship. And kinship is what motivates this research. Too many African Americans fail to see the kinship we share with each other. And I don't mean all the good kinship that might make us feel proud, but also the bad kinship—the kind that produces crack addiction or alcoholism in my family, and the families of many others. When we disown those who embarrass us or make us cringe, we lose a sense of kinship.

The right to freely express our individuality resides, for African Americans, somewhere high or low on the scale of positive or negative behaviors. We don't all agree on social behaviors—some of us think that learning how to make it up the social food chain with education and near-perfect diction is "selling out," while others of us think sagging pants and tattoos and end-zone dancing is "the end of our culture." That's what kinship is all about. We've been taught to think that we have to all agree on anything—or we are not "unified." And of course, if we are not unified, we really don't deserve what we are asking for because, well, we don't *all* agree on desegregation, or reparations.

Find me one major social issue all-White people agree to. While the crickets chirp as you search for that impossibility, just resolve that it's okay not to have to agree to everything for us to still be kinfolks bound by a history and unbound in our individual glory.

This book was never just about sport, even though I've talked about sport endlessly for 260 pages. As noted early on, sport represents a microcosm of society. The ills you see in society you will see in a nation's sport, and vice versa. I experienced the vice versa. That is, the criticism leveled at athletes is what I'd felt though my years as an undergraduate and later as a Black corporate employee in a nearly all-White environment, the legendary fly in the glass of milk. Which is why, in the 1980s, I had a gnawing in my stomach as I read a newspaper excerpt of Thomas Kochman's book, *Black and White Styles in Conflict*. I discovered a hidden treasure buried deep—years of repressed emotions.

Kochman pointed out vividly how Black and White students in college classrooms, and indeed Blacks and Whites in general, had little idea of how the other communicated and understood body language. We put each other down when often we completely misread social cues. I was thought greedy or ill-mannered by my White peers if I accepted the last slice of pizza offered to me. I never knew you were not supposed to accept the last slice. I never knew you were to defer to the person asking because they obviously wanted the last slice, which is why they asked me if I wanted it.

White people's logic was very different from Black people's logic, which in this case was, "If you don't eat this, Vernon, it will go to waste. And there are starving people in Africa ..." So, I grabbed the slice and ate it. This was a small social transgression, but many other, much larger incidents colored how people saw me in a negative light. I might have deserved the criticism. But we were speaking a different language, as Kochman notes, which ultimately led to mass confusion and misinterpretation.

My racial repression ran so deep and hurt so much that before long I needed to quit my corporate job, sell my new BMW and Silicon Valley house, and focus my attention on fighting my "White whale" head-on: Black cultural shame.

It would be easy enough, though self-indulgent, to chart my own experience at feeling dismal and cheap and disrespected in society or institutions. Blackness has its downsides. At the same time, I do know that as African Americans go, I've had it good—especially with the institutions and White people I have been associated with. Not so for some friends, who still mistrust Whites. Many still feel demeaned.

So, rather than write a chronology of my simple life, I set out to study a much broader social canvas: How do people learn what they learn about culture and the behavior of members of out-groups? I further wanted to know: What institutional structures were in place that prohibited the freedom of various forms of cultural expression, such as the use of clothing, cultural hairstyles, and body language? How are Black bodies policed in society and in sports, and further, are we connecting—more than we are disconnecting—in our social institutions?

It struck me as obvious that the institution of sport offered a visual laboratory for recording and documenting not only the *problems* between groups, but likely some of the *solutions*. Sport would thus be my laboratory for the next 30 years. And after 30 years viewing one tiny aspect of U.S. society, I can say that there are valuable lessons other social institutions can learn from sport, and lessons sport can learn from progressive institutions. Combined, these are the five biggest lessons I've gleaned from the intersection of culture, institutions, sport, and diversity inclusion. Those who want to succeed at cultivating productive work and play environments will:

1. Learn to more fully integrate committees that influence codes of conduct in language, clothing and other artifacts, or behaviors of any kind. If your company has a growing amount of, say, Vietnamese employees, make sure as you move forward more than a few Vietnamese are involved in codes-of-conduct committees—and hiring committees. As your numbers grow, you need to realize others might be better at sorting out talent you might miss.
2. Make sure any grievance committee has teeth—teeth to change the status quo and to undo any wrongs. If people are to feel respected, then having channels to dispute rulings—and to make their cultural case—goes a long way toward establishing self-efficacy.
3. Learn the history of social groups other than your own. Just for the hell of it, and also because you might be working for one of them. Pick up

a book or movie about trans or other LGBTQIA+ individuals and learn how they prefer to be addressed. Learn about Muslim family life. Read up on Native Americans and health issues. Learn about Irish subjugation by the English. Learn about the troubled past between Japan and Korea and why the World Cup was the Korea/Japan World Cup—and not the other way around. I lived in New Zealand for fourteen years and became a passport-carrying citizen. My view of the world is much better informed given my sojourn. Follow your friends when they travel overseas or discuss other cultures on Facebook. Question and learn. Which leads me to #4.

4. Listen. Shut up and listen. Then ask questions. Then ask forgiveness if you have crossed a line. As I questioned my feminist friends about women, I crossed the line many times and had to quickly master the "forgiveness" aspect. But you don't learn unless you actively listen, and you don't truly grow unless you ask questions fearlessly. Ask Black people about their experiences, both good and bad, with police. I've been chased by cops, searched at rifle-point, accused of dealing drugs and tossed in a cop car, and I can still manage to wave at nearby cops when passing. But I am fearful. I have a reason to be. Many Blacks can't breathe—and are eternally holding their passive hands up asking for patience. Black Lives Matter.
5. Accept that you don't know. You can't know everything. And even when you study for years—like as long as I've studied White people—you realize you are only knowing the group as a person would sitting on a cave floor viewing the outline of a culture as it walks past. Always think, "Am I merely sitting on the floor of Plato's imaginary cave looking up at shadows?"—when you think about how you've learned about other groups. That includes what you have learned from parents, relatives, neighbors, or your local radio host or nightly news. The more you accept that you truly don't know a cultural group, the more you will be willing to listen. And as any outsider will tell you, the most wonderful feeling we feel is when someone says, "Wow, I didn't know that. Say more ..."

There are other, minor, lessons in understanding diversity that have proven useful in classrooms, institutions like Hewlett-Packard, governmental agencies like the department of defense, countries like New Zealand, and environments as foreign and familiar as the streets of Oakland, California. These lessons have been gleaned from my mother, father, sisters and my brother, in addition to many other sources long since forgotten. They may work for you, also, as you make your own private journey towards understanding people not like yourself (which means everybody).

1. Work hard to see each person as an individual, not part of a group.
   (a) This is not as easy as it might seem. But each one of us has hundreds of thousands of bits of data that inform who we are and make us distinct even from our twin brother or sister. If you can fight all the noise in your head to entertain each person as an individual, you will be surprised how many people you tell, "I had no idea you were like that. I thought ..." which will allow you to point up your stereotype of red headed women, college students in Texas, football players, or ex-Black Panthers. We are so given to framing people that sometimes we forget to allow our minds to color outside the lines ...
2. Remember, people are a part of larger social groups and have distinct histories, so respect that.
   (a) This may seem to *contradict* #1 but consider another angle on people when talking about social issues or history. That is, don't assume that because you were raised in a great middle-class home and had high-caliber teachers, a college scholarship and great job offers, that the person who doesn't has brought things upon themselves. Or that simply because your teacher is White, that they can't possibly relate to the African American experience. Our group affiliations educate us in the ways of our in-group while at the same time possibly constricting our views of racial out-groups. There seems to be limited space for processing difference. But do it anyway.
   (b) Acknowledge that Whites may not have had as much emphasis on the body and movement and style as someone in your Black neighborhood. Hell, not everyone in my Black neighborhood had rhythm and soul. But that same neighborhood can inform me that our experience with the police is very different from many of my fellow White students or professors. And not all White experiences with police are wonderful and rosy. Interrogating how in-group dynamics inform our personal perceptions and frame our social norms helps people be mindful that not everyone was raised the same way.
   (c) We are all members of many social groups (student, family, sports team, exercise club, veteran, work) and though each member is unique, those members still share many traits in common. While we should refrain from stereotyping people in groups, we certainly are free to generalize

about "trout fishermen and women" or "skateboard culture," always remember rule #1—everybody is just a little bit different.

3. Remember, we all enjoy social privileges—some more than others.
   (a) Yes, not only Whites enjoy social privileges in U.S. society. Men have many privileges women don't enjoy; attractive women and men have many privileges unattractive women and men don't have, especially when seeking jobs; tall people enjoy more privileges generally than short people, especially when choosing for pick-up basketball games; rich men enjoy more privileges that poor men, especially in the dating game; engineering and computer science graduates with 3.5 GPA's often can experience more privilege on the job market that, say, art majors with the same grade point average.
   (b) On the micro-social level, many of us enjoy privileges often unknown to others—and sometimes known. When Whites enjoy White privileges, they often cannot see the privilege because everyone they know experiences the same privilege. This is what is called, "everyday life." There are a series of interactions which lead one to fall into what we social scientists call the "false consensus hypothesis," which simply states, "everybody experiences the world the way I do." Truth is, many don't. "But they must," you think, "because everyone I know sees things the same way." By way of a major failure in capitalism, I can explain.

During the 1970s, it was explained that executives at a major U.S. car manufacturer in Detroit tried in vain to explain to the CEO that they needed to move car development to more economical models so as to save fuel and compete with new, fuel-saving Japanese models rolling into the USA. Big cars, they reasoned, "are on the way out." The CEO rode home that day from his Detroit office and said, "What the hell are they talking about! All I see on the road here in Detroit is big, beautiful, American cars. Who cares about smaller fuel-efficient cars! We are doing just fine!"

Of course, he'd see large American cars on the road in Detroit. Everyone either worked for the American car machinery in and around Detroit—or knew someone who did. Support was strong for the CEO's feelings. But he didn't bother to drive around California. If he had, he would have noticed that Toyota, Datsun, and Honda were taking over.

Before this study, I didn't know that the first end-zone dance in U.S. history was by a White man—and didn't even happen in an end-zone. Forever we will know the man who signed his signature in a way that stated, "Check me out," by how he danced his pen across a page and did a back flip when he finished his pen dance. His name was John Hancock. *Of course*, John Hancock is the originator. He was *The Man*, but in a good way.

We have all been looking for an individual signature since then. Before you blame Muhammad Ali, just know that one of our whitest forefathers signed the declaration of independence and inspired Ali. Without that mighty John Hancock, we might only have Cassius Clay, and not Muhammad Ali. And without Ali, we would not have so varied and vast an amount of celebratory expression in profession and collegiate sporting history.

This begs the ultimate question for this work, a question I've gotten when overseas in New Zealand: Why do Black people celebrate? In the face of our kinship's horrific history, why the heck are we smiling and dancing anyway?

This is the major question—and a curious point of contention with academics who scold me for over-studying sport and wasting my talents (such as they are) on trivial matters. "Arrogant, over-paid, and untrained Black athletes don't need to be studied—they need to be trained," is the sentiment. But people in New Zealand are forced to learn about the Civil Rights Movement as their bit of U.S. history, and they are horrified when they learn how we have been historically treated. And yet we smile and dance and go on as if the past is a distant memory. Which in some ways might not be a bad way of going about life. But it is a nagging question.

And as to why we smile, dance, and wave our hands in the air like we just don't care—when we should otherwise be pissed-off about our history and current state of affairs, rioting at every chance after some awful cop shooting of yet another Black youth. Well, we each go about reflecting on this in our own way. The way I see it, we have many ways to move forward in this society. We are tired of being at the bottom. We see ourselves as American. We'd like to still think the American dream is something we can achieve. We want people who make the rules to respect us as Black and as Americans, too. We want the benefit of the doubt: Connection.

And we moonwalk in the end-zone or elongate the national anthem with soul or dress sharp and shout loudly in church because, somehow, some way, emotion always finds a way to express itself. It can express in antagonistic ways, if provoked. But we most often choose the joyous route since given the freedom to express in 1964. Accept that radical self-expression is how we will sometimes roll. We are test-driving our new freedoms. Go ahead. Express yourself. Lose control. Make some *real* White noise.

The End

Bibliography

Abe, I. 1988. "A Study of the Chronology of the Modern Usage of 'Sportsmanship' in English, American and Japanese Dictionaries." *The International Journal of the History of Sport*, 5(1), 3–28 (p. 3).

Abrahams, R. 1992. *Singing the Master: The Emergence of African American Culture in the Plantation South*. New York: Pantheon.

Adell, S. 1994. *Double-Consciousness/Double Bind. Theoretical Issues in Twentieth Century Black Literature*. Urbana and Chicago: University of Illinois Press.

Alexander, R. 1998. Personal conversation.

Allport, G. 1968. "The Historical Background of Modern Social Psychology." In G. Lindzey & E. Aronson (Eds.), *The Handbook of Social Psychology* (pp. 1–80). Reading, MA: Addison-Wesley.

Anderson, B. 1991. *Imagined Communities: Reflections on the Origins and Spread of Nationalism*. London: Verso.

Andrews, V. L. 1991. *Race, Culture, Situation and the Touchdown Dance*. University of Wisconsin-Madison Sociology Department. Master's Thesis. University of Wisconsin, Madison.

Andrews, V. L. 1996a. "Black Bodies—White Control: Race, Celebratory Expression and the Contested Terrain of Sportsmanlike Conduct." *Journal of African American Males*, 3, 2.

Andrews, V. L. 1996b. *Race, Celebratory Expression and the Contested Terrain of Sportsmanlike Conduct: A Case Study of a Big Ten Football Program*. Dissertation. University of Wisconsin-Madison.

Andrews, V. L. 1997. "African American Player Codes on Celebration, Taunting and Sportsmanlike Conduct in College Football." *Journal of African American Males*, 4, 1.

Andrews, V. L. 2000. "Black Fields of Dreams. The Transference of the New Zealand Sports Club System to the African American Community." Special issue on Race, Sport and Professionalism. Irving Horowitz, editor. *Society*, 37(3), 40–44.

Andrews, V. L. 2004. "Self-Reflection and the Reflected Self: African American Double-Consciousness & the Social (Psychological) Mirror." *Journal of African American Society*, 10, 4.

Andrews, V. L. & R. G. Majors. 2004. "African American Nonverbal Culture." In Reginald Jones (Ed.), *Black Psychology*, 3rd edition. Hampton, VA: Cobb and Henry.

Ashe, A. 1988. *A Hard Road to Glory: A History of the African-American Athlete*. New York: Warner Books, Inc.

Atkinson, P. & D. Silverman. 1997. "Kundera's Immortality: The Interview Society and the Invention of Self." *Qualitative Inquiry*, 3, 304–325.

Awatere-Huata, D. 1993. "Rugby, Racism and Riot Gear: New Zealand in the Winter of 1981." In W. Ihimaera, H. Williams, & D. S. Long (Eds.), *Te Ao Marama: Regaining Aotearoa: Maori Writers Speak Out* (pp. 94–97). Auckland: Reed Books.

Ball, M. 1995. *Footrot Flats*. Auckland: Hodder Moa Beckett.

Banaji, M. R. & D. A. Prentice. 1994. "The Self in Social Contexts." *Annual Review of Psychology*, 45, 297–332.

Battle, M. 2006. *The Black Church in America: African American Christian Spirituality*. Hoboken, NJ: Wiley.

Bayard, D. 1995. *Kiwitalk: Sociolinguistics and New Zealand Society*. Palmerston North: Dunmore Press.

Bell, C. 1996. *Inventing New Zealand: Everyday Myths of Pakeha Identity*. Auckland: Penguin.

Bell, C. 1997a. *Ritual: Perspectives and Dimensions*. New York: Oxford University Press.

Bell, C. 1997b. "Ritual Reification." In Graham Harvey (Ed.), *Ritual and Religious Belief: A Reader* (pp. 265–285). New York: Routledge.

Bevell, D. 1996. Personal Conversation.

Bradburn, N. M. 1983. "Response Effects." In P. H. Rossi, J. D. Wright, & A. B. Anderson (Eds.), *Handbook of Survey Research* (pp. 289–328). New York: Academic Press.

Braxton, E. K. 1998. "The View from the Barbershop: The Church and African-American Culture." *America Magazine*, February 14, 18–22.

Bryson, B. 1989. *The Babe Didn't Point: And Other Stories about Iowans and Sports*. Compiled and edited by Michael G. Bryson, Sr., and Michael G. Bryson, Jr. Ames: Iowa State University Press.

Bunkle, P. & B. Hughes. 1980. *Women in New Zealand Society*. Auckland: George Allen & Unwin Australia Pty Ltd.

Burnim, M. 1985. "The Black Gospel Music Tradition: A Complex of Ideology, Aesthetic, and Behavior." In Irene V. Jackson (Ed.), *More than Dancing*. Westport, CT: Greenwood Press.

Byers, W. c1995. *Unsportsmanlike Conduct: Exploiting College Athletes*. With Charles H. Hammer. Ann Arbor: University of Michigan Press.

Cameron, J. 1993. "Fair Play and Playing Fair: The Context of Good Manners." Paper presented at the International Olympic Academy Session for Educators." Olympia, Greece, p. 4.

Camp, W. 1893. "Walter Camp's Book on College Sports." In *The Rise of American Sport*. New York: Century.

Camp, W. ND. "The History of Walter Camp: 1859–1925." Walter Camp Foundation, Inc. Website: https://waltercamp.org/pages/about/walter-camp/ (accessed August 31, 2020). p. 1.

Capital Times, Wisconsin, Fall, 1989.

Capone, S. 2007. "Transatlantic Dialogue: Roger Bastide and the African American Religions." *Journal of Religion in Africa*, 37, 336–370.

Caponi, G. D. 1999. "The Case for an African American Aesthetic." In G. Caponi (Ed.), *Signifyin(g), Sanctifyin', & Slam Dunking: A Reader in African American Expressive Culture* (pp. 1–44). Amherst: University of Massachusetts Press.

Carter, D. 1996. Personal conversation.

Cashmore, E. 1990. *Making Sense of Sport*. New York: Routledge.

Charmichael, S. & C. V. Hamilton. 1967. *Black Power*. New York: Vintage Books.

Clarke, G. & B. Humberstone. 1997. *Researching Women and Sport*. London: Macmillan.

Clemmitt, M. 2007. "Black Churches Cater to Suburban Middle Class: Poor, Inner-City Blacks Are Being Left Behind." *CQ Researcher*, 17(43), 122–123.

Cooley, C. H. 1902. *Human Nature and the Social Order*. New York: Scribners.

Crump, B. 1960. *A Good Keen Man*. Wellington: Reed.

Culler, J. 1986. "Jacques Derrida." In H. Adams & L. Searle (Eds.), *Critical Theory Since 1965* (pp. 154–179). Tallahassee: Florida State University Press.

Cummings, P. 1949. *The Dictionary of Sports* (p. 420). New York: Ronald Press Company.

Curtis, J. & J. Loy. 1978. "Race/Ethnicity and the Relative Centrality of Playing Positions in Team Sports." *Exercise and Sports Sciences Review*, 6, 285–313.

Denzin, N. K. 1989a. *Interpretive Interactionism*. Newbury Park, CA: Sage.

Deutsch F. M., D. N. Ruble, A. Fleming, J. Brooks-Gunn, & C. Stangor. 1988. "Information-Seeking and Maternal Self-Definition during the Transition to Motherhood." *Journal of Personality and Social Psychology*, 55(3), 420–431.

Dinerstein, J. 1998. "Lester Young and the Birth of Cool." In G. D. Caponi (Ed.), *Signifyin(g), Sanctifyin', & Slam Dunking: A Reader in African American Expressive Culture* (pp. 239–276). Amherst: University of Massachusetts Press.

DuBois, W. E. B. 1903. *The Souls of Black Folk*. Greenwich, CT: Fawcett [1961].

DuBois, W. E. B. 1920. "The Souls of White Folks." In *Darkwater: Voices from Within the Veil*. New York: Harcourt, Brace and Company.

Duneier, M. 1992. *Slim's Table: Race, Respectability and Masculinity*. Chicago, IL: University of Chicago Press.

Durie, M. H. 1997. "Identity, Access and Maori Advancement." *New Zealand Journal of Educational Administration*, 12, 41–46.

Dyer, R. 1997. *White*. New York: Routledge.

Dyson, M. E. 1993. *Reflecting Black: African-American Cultural Criticism*. Minneapolis: University of Minnesota Press.

Dyson, M. E. 1994. "Be Like Mike? Michael Jordan and the Pedagogy of Desire." In H. Giroux & P. McLaren (Eds.), *Between Borders*. New York: Routledge.

Edwards, H. 1972. *The Sociology of Sport*. Homewood, IL: Dorsey Press.

Elias, N. 1978. *The History of Manners*. Oxford: Blackwell.

Elias, N. 1982. *Power and Civility*. Oxford: Blackwell.

Ellis, C. & A. P. Bochner. 2000. "Autoethnography, Personal Narrative, Reflexivity: Researcher as Subject." In N. K. Denzin & Y. S. Lincoln (Eds.), *Handbook of Qualitative Research*, 2nd Ed.. Thousand Oaks, CA: Sage Publications.

Emery, D. 2009. "The Seventh-Inning Stretch: Origin (or not) of a Baseball Tradition." About. Com.

Esposito, B. 2007. "Hobey Baker: The Legend Lives On." *Hobey Baker: Character Builds Excellence*. 15 January. https://www.hobeybaker.com/about.

Ethier, K. A. & K. Deaux 1990. "Hispanics in Ivy: Assessing Identity and Perceived Threat." *Sex Roles*, 22, 427–440.

Falla, J. c1981. *NCAA, The Voice of College Sports: A Diamond Anniversary History, 1906–1981*, 1st ed. Mission, KS: NCAA, p. 53.

Feagin, J. 2001. *Racist America: Roots, Current Realities, & Future Reparations*. New York: Routledge.

Feagin, J. & M. P. Sikes. 1994. *Living with Racism: The Black Middle-Class Experience*. Boston, MA: Beacon Press.

Feather, N. T. 1989. "Attitudes Towards the High Achiever: The Fall of the Tall Poppy." *Australian Journal of Psychology*, 41(3), 239–267.

Feather, N. T. 1991. "Attitudes Towards the High Achiever: Effects of Perceiver's Own Level of Competence." *Australian Journal of Psychology*, 43(3), 121–124.

Feather, N. T. & I. R. McKee 1993. "Global Self-Esteem and Attitudes Toward the High Achiever for Australian and Japanese Students." *Social Psychology Quarterly*, 56(1), 65–76.

Fimrite, R. 1991. "A Flame that Burned too Brightly." *Sports Illustrated*, March 18, p. 79.

Fiske, J. 1993. *Power Plays Power Works*. New York: Verso.

Fiske, J. 1996. *Media Matters*. Minneapolis: University of Minnesota Press.

Fiske, S. T. & S. E. Taylor. 1991. *Social Cognition*, 2nd ed. New York: McGraw-Hill.

Floyd, S. A., Jr. 1995. *The Power of Black Music: Interpreting Its History from Africa to the United States*. New York: Oxford University Press.

Fordham, S. 1993. "Those Loud Black Girls: (Black) Women, Silence, and Gender 'Passing' in the Academy." *Anthropology and Education Quarterly*, 24(1), 3–32.

Fougere, G. 1981. "Shattered Mirror." *Comment: A New Zealand Quarterly Review*, 14, 12–14.

Frey, D. 1994. *The Last Shot: City Streets, Basketball Dreams*. New York: Houghton Mifflin Company.

Gecas, V. 1990. "Contexts of Socialization." In M. Rosenberg & R. Turner (Eds.), *Social Psychology: Sociological Perspectives*. New Brunswick, NJ: Transaction Publishers.

George, N. 1992. *Elevating the Game: Black Men and Basketball*. New York: Harper Collins Publishers, Inc.

Gibson, H. 2004. Personal letter.

Gilroy, P. 1993. *The Black Atlantic: Modernity and Double-Consciousness*. New York: Verso.

Giroux, H. A. 1998. "Youth, Memory Work, and the Racial Politics of Whiteness." In J. L. Kincheloe, S. R. Steinberg, M. R. Nelson, & R. Chennault (Eds.), *White Rein: Deploying Whiteness in America*. New York: St. Martin's Press.

Glazier, S. D. 2001. *Encyclopedia of African and African-American Reli*gions. New York: Routledge.

Goffman, E. 1959. *The Presentation of Self in Everyday Life*. New York: Doubleday Anchor Books.

Gordon, M. 1964. *Assimilation in American Life*. New York: Oxford University Press.

Gray, H. 1995. *Watching Race: Television and the Struggle for Blackness.* Minneapolis: University of Minnesota Press.

Greene, R. 2008. "Twenty Years Later Ickey Shuffle Still Lives." *Las Vegas Sun.com.* September 10. https://m.lasvegassun.com/blogs/sports-unlv/2008/sep/10/20-years-later-ickey-shuffle-still-lives-contest-f/

Greenfield, J. 1975. "The Black and White Truth about Basketball." *Esquire,* 170–171. October, 1975.

Grimes, R. L. 1982. *Beginnings in Ritual Studies.* Washington, DC: University Press of America.

Guttmann, A. 2004. *Sports: The First Five Millennia.* Amherst and Boston: University of Massachusetts Press, p. 1.

Haar, Gerrie ter. 1995. "Ritual as Communication: A Study of African Christian Communities in the Bijlmer District of Amsterdam." In Jan. Platvoet & Karel van der Toorn (Eds.), Pluralism and Identity: *Pluralism and Identity: Studies in Ritual Behavior* (pp. 115–142). Leiden: Brill Academic Publishers.

Hacker, A. 1992. *Two Nations: Black and White, Separate, Hostile, Unequal.* New York: Scribners.

Hanna, J. L. 1997. "Black/White Nonverbal Differences, Dance and Dissonance: Implications for Desegregation." In A. Wolfgang (Ed.), *Nonverbal Behavior: Perspectives, Applications, Intercultural Insight.* Seattle, Washington: Hogrefe & Huber Publishers.

Haraway, D. 1991. "Situated Knowledges: The Science Question in Feminism and the Privilege of Partial Perspective." In *Simians, Cyborgs, and Women: The Reinvention of Nature* (pp. 183–202). New York: Routledge.

Hart, J. 1983. "A Princeton Lament." *National Review,* September 30, p. 1194.

Henderson, T. & P. Knobler. 1987. *Out of Control.* New York: Simon and Schuster, p. 243.

Herskovits, M. J. 1941. *The Myth of the Negro Past.* New York: Harper and Brothers; Boston: Beacon, 1958.

Hewitt, J. P. 1991. *Self and Society: A Symbolic Interactionist Social Psychology.* Needham Heights, MA: Allyn and Bacon.

Holloway, J. E. & W. K. Vass. 1993. *The African Heritage of American English.* Bloomington: Indiana University Press.

hooks, b. 1992. "Representing Whiteness in the Black Imagination." In L. Grossberg, C. Nelson, & P. Treichler (Eds.), *Cultural Studies.* New York: Routledge.

Holt, G. S. 1972. "Stylin' Outta the Black Pulpit." In Gena Caponi (Ed.), *Signifyin(g), Sanctifyin' and Slam Dunking: A Reader in African American Expressive Culture* (pp. 331–347). Amherst: University of Massachusetts Press.

Horrocks, R. 1984. "No Theory Permitted on These Premises." *AND,* 2, 119–137.

Hraba, J. 1994. *American Ethnicity.* Itasca, IL: F. E. Peacock Publishers, Inc.

Hunt, L. & M. O. Hunt. 2001. "Race, Region and Religious Involvement: A Comparative Study of Whites and African Americans." *Social Forces,* 80(2), 605–631.

Hunt, M., P. B. Jackson, B. Powell, & L. C. Steelman. 2000. "Color-Blind: The Treatment of Race and Ethnicity in Social Psychology." *Social Psychology Quarterly,* 63, 352–364.

Huntley, K. 1996. Personal conversation.

James, B. & K. Saville-Smith. 1989. *Gender, Culture and Power: Challenging New Zealand's Gendered Culture.* Auckland: Oxford University Press.

James, C. L. R. 1993. *American Civilization.* Grimshaw, A. & K. Hart (Eds.). Cambridge, MA: Blackwell.

Jones, Homer. ND. http://en.wikipedia.org/wiki/Homer_Jones_(American_football).

Jones, J. M. 1986. "Racism: A Cultural Analysis of the Problem." In J. F. Dovidio & S. L. Gaertner (Eds.), *Prejudice, Discrimination and Racism.* San Diego, CA: Academic Press.

Kochman, T. 1981. *Black and White Styles in Conflict.* Chicago, IL: University of Chicago Press.

Kyle, D. G. 2007. *Sport and Spectacle in the Ancient World.* Maine: Blackwell Publishing.

Lapchick, R. 2003. *Racial and Gender Report Card.* Orlando: University of Central Florida.

Lavoie, M. (1989). "The Economic Hypothesis of Positional Segregation: Some Further Comments." *Sociology of Sport Journal*, 6, 163–166.

Leonard, W. M. II. 1978. "Stacking in Collegiate Basketball: A Neglected Analysis." *Sociology of Sport Journal*, 7, 294–301.

Lipsyte, R. 1975. *SportsWorld: An American Dreamland.* New York: Quadrangle/New York Times Book Company.

Lipsyte, R. 1994. "Pro Basketball; The Art of Trash Talk Not Limited to a Court." *Sunday*, Late Edition—Final. Page 8, June 5.

London, M. 1996. Personal conversation.

Loy, J. & J. McElvogue. 1970. "Racial Segregation in American Sport." *International Review of Sport Sociology*, 5, 5–24.

Majors, R. G. & J. M. Billson. 1992. *Cool Pose: The Dilemmas of Black Manhood in America.* New York: Lexington Books (MacMillan).

Margolis, B. & J. A. Piliavin. 1999. "'Stacking' in Major League Baseball: A Multivariate Analysis." *Sociology of Sport Journal*, 16, 16–34.

Marqusee, M. 2000. *Redemption Song: Muhammad Ali and the Spirit of the Sixties.* New York: Verso, p. 297.

Maslow, A. 1943. "A Theory of Human Motivation." *Psychological Review*, 50(4), 370–396.

McCullough, C. 1996. Personal conversation.

McKay, B. & K. McKay. 2009. "Boxing: A Manly History of the Sweet Science of Bruising." *Health Sports*, May 30. https://www.artofmanliness.com/articles/boxing-a-manly-history-of-the-sweet-science-of-bruising/

Mead, G. H. 1934. *Mind, Self and Society.* Chicago, IL: University of Chicago Press.

Mercer, K. 1987. "Black Hair/Style Politics." *New Formations*, 3, 33–54, Winter.

Merton, Robert K. 1957. *Social Theory and Social Structure.* New York: The Free Press.

Miller, Brian. 2008. "D. Jackson is Why the NFL Banned Celebrations." Fansided (Online). http://phinphanatic.com/2008/09/18/d-jackson-is-why-the-nfl-banned-celebrations/.

Minh-ha, T. T. 1995. "No Master Territories." In B. Ashcroft, G. Griffiths, & H. Tiffin (Eds.), *The Post-Colonial Studies Reader* (pp. 215–218). London and New York: Routledge.

Moghaddam, F. M., D. M. Taylor, & S. C. Wright. 1993. "Culture and Social Psychology." In *Social Psychology in Cross-cultural Perspective.* New York: W.H. Freeman and Company.

Monty, P. 1996. Personal conversation.

Muldoon, R. 1977. *The Rise and Fall of a Young Turk.* Wellington: A. H. & A. W. Reed.

Muldoon, R. 1981. *My Way.* Wellington: Reed.

Myers, V. 1986. *Head and Shoulders: Successful New Zealand Women Talk to Virginia Myers. Auckland.* New Zealand: Penguin Books.

Myrdal, G. 1944. An American Dilemma. New York: Harper & Brothers.

National Football League. 1990. "History of NFL Rule Changes." *National Football League's Digest of Rules*, p. 39.

National Football League Digest of Rules. 1990. "History of NFL Rule Changes," p. 39.

National Review. 1983. "A Princeton Lament." September 30, p. 1194.

NCAA Rules. 1995. Section 2, Non-contact Fouls: Unsportsmanlike acts.

Nicholson, L. 1995. "Interpreting Gender." In L. Nicholson & S. Seidman (Eds.), *Social Postmodernism: Beyond Identity Politics* (pp. 39–63). Cambridge: Cambridge University Press.

Nyquist, M. 1996. Personal conversation.

Olson, E. 2001. "Signs of Conversion, Spirit of Commitment: The Pentecostal Church in the Kingdom of Tonga." *Journal of Ritual Studies*, 15(2), 13–37. (p. 14)

Orsi, R. A. 1985. *The Madonna of 115th Street: Faith and Community in Italian Harlem, 1880–1950.* New Haven, CT: Yale University Press.

Otis, J. 1993. *Upside Your Head! Rhythm and Blues on Central Avenue.* Hanover, NH: Wesleyan University Press.

Oxford English Dictionary, The. 1971. Oxford: Oxford University Press.

Patillo-McCoy, M. 1999. "Church Culture as a Strategy of Action in the Black Community." *American Sociological Review*, 63: 767–784.

Patterson, M. B. d. 1998. "America's Racial Unconsciousness." In J. L. Kincheloe, S. R. Steinberg, M. R. Nelson, & R. Chennault (Eds.), *White Rein: Deploying Whiteness in America* (pp. 104–121). New York: St. Martin's Press.

Perkins, H. & G. Cushman. 1993. *Leisure, Recreation and Tourism.* Auckland: Longman Paul.

Philips, J. 1980. "Mummy's Boys: Pakeha Men and Male Culture in New Zealand." In P. Bunkle & B. Hughes (Eds.), *Women in New Zealand Society* (pp. 217–241). Auckland: George Allen and Unwin Australia Pty Ltd.

Pierson, D. 1991. "Icky Rule Is Proving to Be Sticky for NFL." *Chicago Tribune*, March 24, p. 8.

Raboteau, A. J. 1994. "Fire in the Bones: African-American Christianity and Autobiographical Reflection." *America*, 170(18), 4–9.

Raboteau, A. J. 1995. *A Fire in the Bones: Reflections on African-American Religious History.* Boston, MA: Beacon Press.

Ramirez, M. & M. A. Brachear. 2006. "Struggling to Fill Needs, Pews." *Chicago Tribune*, February 12, B1.

Richards, T. 1999. *Dancing on Our Bones: New Zealand South Africa Rugby and Racism.* Wellington: Bridget Williams Books.

Rickford, J. F. & A. E. Rickford. 1976. "Cut-Eye and Suck-Teeth: African Words and Gestures in New World Guise." *Journal of American Folklore*, 89, 294–309.

Rigauer, B. 1981. *Sport and Work.* (Translated by Allen Guttmann). New York: Columbia University Press.

Riggs, M. 1986. *Ethnic Notions.* Documentary.

Rose, T. 1994. *Black Noise: Rap Music and Black Culture in Contemporary America.* Connecticut. Wesleyan University Press.

Rugby Football History.Com. ND. "William Webb Ellis." http://www.rugbyfootballhistory.com/webb-ellis.html

Ryan, J. 1997. "Sportsmanship not Just Lacking in Sports; Winning Is Clearly the Priority in Nearly all Aspects of Life. But that We Recognize Sports' Shortcoming Is Promising." *The Sporting News*, November 17, p. 8.

Said, E. 1979. *Orientalism.* London: Routledge & Kegan Paul.

Sailes, G. 1998. "An Examination of Basketball Performance Orientations among African Americans." In G. Sailes (Ed.), *African Americans in Sport.* Piscataway, NJ: Transaction Publishers.

Scheier, M. F. & C. S. Carver 1980. "Individual Differences in Self-Concept and Self-Process." In D. M. Wegner & R. R. Vallacher (Eds.), *The Self in Social Psychology.* New York: Oxford University Press.

Schwartz, B. 1999. "Memory and the Practice of Commitment." In B Glassner & R. Hertz (Eds.), *Qualitative Sociology as Everyday Life.* Thousand Oaks, CA: Sage.

Scott, J. C. 1990. *Domination and the Arts of Resistance: Hidden Transcripts.* New Haven, CT: Yale University Press.

Sered, S. S. 1996. "Ritual Expertise in the Modern World." In *Women as Ritual Experts: The Religious Lives of Elderly Jewish Women in Jerusalem.* Oxford: Oxford University Press.

Silverman, D. 1993. *Interpreting Qualitative Data: Strategies for Analyzing Talk, Text and Interaction.* London: Sage.

Simcic, A. 1998. Personal conversation.

Simmons, T. 1996. Personal conversation.

Simons, H. 2003. "Race and Penalized Sports Behaviors." *International Review for the Sociology of Sport*, 38/1, 5–22.

Sinclair, K. 1990. *The Oxford Illustrated History of New Zealand.* Oxford: Oxford University Press.

Smith, E. & K. Harrison. 1997. "Stacking in Major League Baseball." *Journal of African American Men*, 2(2/3), 113–130.

Smith, E. & W. M. Leonard. 1997. "Twenty-Five Years of Stacking Research in Major League Baseball: An Attempt at Explaining This Re-Occurring Phenomenon." *Sociological Focus*, 30, 321–331.

Smith, E. & M. Seff 1990. "Race, Position Segregation and Salary Equity in Professional Baseball." *Journal of Sport and Social Issues*, 13, 92–110.

Smith, J. Z. 1987. "To Take Place." In Graham Harvey (Ed.), *Ritual and Religious Belief: A Reader* (pp. 26–50). New York: Routledge.

Smith, Y. 1996. Personal Conversation.

Stallybrass, P. & A. White. 1986. "Introduction." In Graham Harvey (Ed.), *Ritual and Religious Belief: A Reader* (pp. 139–162). New York: Routledge.

Stark, S. 1996. Personal conversation.

Steinberg, Stephen. 1989. *The Ethnic Myth: Race, Ethnicity and Class in America.* Boston, MA: Beacon Press.

Stephenson, Barry. 2003. "Ritual Criticism of a Contemporary Rite of Passage." *Journal of Ritual Studies*, 17(1), 32–41.

Stevens, M. 2004. "De La Salle Coach is on the Mend." WWW.SFGate.com, p. 2.

Stratford, T. 1988. *Guts, Tears and Glory: Champion New Zealand Sportswomen Talk to Trish Stratford.* Auckland: New Women's Press.

Stravinsky, John. 1997. "The Long Reach of Muhammad Ali." *Biography*, 10927891, Dec 97, 1, issue 12.

Takahashi, M. & T. Olaveson. 2003. "Music, Dance and Raving Bodies: Raving as Spirituality in the Central Canadian Rave Scene." *Journal of Ritual Studies*, 17(2), 72–96.

Telander, R. 1994. *From Red Ink to Roses: The Turbulent Transformation of a Big Ten Program.* New York: Simon and Schuster.

Thompson, R. F. 1983. *Flash of the Spirit: African and Afro-American Art and Philosophy*. New York: Random House.

Thompson, R. F. 1966. "An Aesthetic of the Cool: West African Dance." In Gena Caponi (Ed.), *Signifyin(g), Sanctifyin' and Slam Dunking: A Reader in African American Expressive Culture* (pp. 72–86). Amherst: University of Massachusetts Press.

Toon, A. 1996. Personal conversation.

Torian, R. 1996. Personal conversation.

Trenberth, L. & C. Collins. 1999. *Sport Business Management in New Zealand.* Palmerston North: Dunmore Press.

Turner, K. B., D. Giacopassi, & M. Vandiver. 2006. "Ignoring the Past: Coverage of Slavery and Slave Patrols in Criminal Justice Texts." *Journal of Criminal Justice Education*, 17(1), 181–195 (p. 186).

Unverzagt, E. 1996. Personal conversation.

Urban Dictionary, entry by Sean, January 19, 2004: "He Hate Me" http://www.urbandictionary.com/define.php?term=he+hate+me.

Waldorf, J. 1975. *NCAA Rules Committee Chronology of 100 Years, 1876–1976.* Shawnee Mission, KS: The National Collegiate Athletic Association, p. 26.

Wandzilak, T., T. Carroll, & C. J. Ansorge. 1988. "Values Development Through Physical Activity: Promoting Sportsmanlike Behaviors, Perceptions, and Moral Reasoning." *Journal of Teaching in Physical Education* 8(1): 13–22.

Weisenfeld, J. 2007. *Hollywood Be Thy Name: African American Religion in American Film, 1929–1949.* Berkeley: University of California Press.

White, S. & G. White. 1998. *Stylin': African-American Expressive Culture from Its Beginnings to the Zoot Suit.* Ithaca, New York: Cornell University Press.

Whiting, R. 1989. *You Gotta Have Wa: When Two Cultures Collide on the Baseball Diamond.* New York: Macmillan Publishing Company.

Wideman, J. E. 1990a. "Michael Jordan Leaps the Great Divide." *Esquire*, November 1990.

Wideman, J. E. 1990b. "Michael Jordan Leaps the Great Divide." In Gena Caponi (Ed.), *Signifyin(g), Sanctifyin' and Slam Dunking: A Reader in African American Expressive Culture* (pp. 388–406). Amherst: University of Massachusetts Press.

Wiggins, D. K. 1997. *Glory Bound: Black Athletes in a White America.* Syracuse, NY: Syracuse University Press.

Wilson, O. 1992. "The Heterogeneous Sound Ideal in African-American Music." In Gena Caponi (Ed.), *Signifyin(g), Sanctifyin' and Slam Dunking: A Reader in African American Expressive Culture* (pp. 156–171). Amherst: University of Massachusetts Press.

Wise, T. 2003. "Whites Swim in Racial Preference." *AlterNet.*

Wunsch, G. 1996. Personal conversation.

Zirin, D. 2005. *What's My Name, Fool?* Chicago, IL: Haymarket Books.

Index

GLOBAL INTERSECTIONALITY OF EDUCATION, SPORTS, RACE, AND GENDER

Billy Hawkins, *General Editor*

The Global Intersectionality of Education, Sports, Race, and Gender series responds to the interesting dialogue and unique social phenomena in the global context produced by the intersections of race, sport, gender, and culture. Global Intersectionality explores these intersections and expands the literature on how each inform our thinking around certain dominant ideologies. This series examines how sporting practices in the United States are becoming the global norm in defining what is sport, thus our understanding of race, gender, and culture.

The purpose of this series is to inform sport enthusiasts, college students, educators, researchers, policy makers, and other stakeholders—who are social justice oriented—about the role sport has in contributing to informing cultural ideology, reproducing and reinforcing race and gender ideologies. It also seeks to foster an understanding of how this social phenomenon, that is often situated as merely entertainment or a recreational activity for leisure, has shifted into a cultural practice that can engender global socio-political relations. The topics will include critical moments in sport, as well as broader social movements in sporting context. In addition, this series will discuss topics ranging from youth to professional sporting experiences with attention given to the socialization and educational processes inherent in these experiences as it relates to race, gender, and culture.

Titles in this series will employ a variety of methodologies, including, but not limited to, qualitative, quantitative, mixed methods methodological approaches, non-empirical and socio-historical approaches that incorporate primary and secondary data sources. For additional information about this series or for the submission of manuscripts, please contact:

Peter Lang Publishing. Inc.
Acquisitions Department
80 Broad Street, 5th Floor
New York, NY 10004

To order other books in this series, please contact our Customer Service Department:

peterlang@presswarehouse.com (within the U.S.)
order@peterlang.com (outside the U.S.)

Or browse online by series: www.peterlang.com